ORGANIZATIONAL DEVELOPMENT

Organizational Development gives readers an understanding of organizational structures and presents a new and easy-to-understand framework which describes the three dimensions of organizational interventions.

Interventions in organization often fail. This has been widely acknowledged: many books exist about the topic, and many approaches are proposed to guide organizational interventions – but to no avail – so it remains difficult to design and guide them. This is the first book to (1) provide readers with an understanding of organizational structures and why it is both relevant and difficult to change them, and (2) present a model consisting of three underlying dimensions of interventions. The authors describe how this model can be used to design interventions in organizational structures.

Containing practical guidelines to show how interventions can be designed and controlled, this book should be considered essential reading for postgraduate students of organizational development, design, and change, and practitioners carrying out organizational development projects.

Jan Achterbergh (MSc Philosophy; PhD Policy Sciences) is Assistant Professor of Organizational Design and Development at the Nijmegen School of Management of the Radboud University Nijmegen, the Netherlands, since 1999. His research interests include organizational structures and business ethics, interventions in organizations, and the design of organizational networks.

Dirk Vriens (MSc Psychology; PhD Policy Sciences) is Associate Professor of Organizational Design and Development at the Nijmegen School of Management of the Radboud University Nijmegen, the Netherlands. His current research interests include organizational cybernetics, designing organizational structures, and moral behaviour in organizations.

ORGANIZATIONAL DEVELOPMENT

Designing Episodic Interventions

Jan Achterbergh and Dirk Vriens

LONDON AND NEW YORK

First published 2019
by Routledge
2 Park Square, Milton Park, Abingdon, Oxon OX14 4RN

and by Routledge
52 Vanderbilt Avenue, New York, NY 10017

Routledge is an imprint of the Taylor & Francis Group, an informa business

© 2019 Jan Achterbergh and Dirk Vriens

The right of Jan Achterbergh and Dirk Vriens to be identified as authors of this work has been asserted by them in accordance with sections 77 and 78 of the Copyright, Designs and Patents Act 1988.

All rights reserved. No part of this book may be reprinted or reproduced or utilized in any form or by any electronic, mechanical, or other means, now known or hereafter invented, including photocopying and recording, or in any information storage or retrieval system, without permission in writing from the publishers.

Trademark notice: Product or corporate names may be trademarks or registered trademarks, and are used only for identification and explanation without intent to infringe.

British Library Cataloguing in Publication Data
A catalogue record for this book is available from the British Library

Library of Congress Cataloging-in-Publication Data
Names: Achterbergh, Jan, author. | Vriens, Dirk Jaap, 1963-
Title: Organizational development / Jan Achterbergh and Dirk Vriens.
Description: Abingdon, Oxon ; New York, NY : Routledge, 2019. | Includes bibliographical references and index.
Identifiers: LCCN 2019005178| ISBN 9781138907027 (hardback) | ISBN 9781138907034 (pbk.) | ISBN 9781315695228 (ebook)
Subjects: LCSH: Organizational change. | Organizational sociology.
Classification: LCC HD58.8 .A288 2019 | DDC 302.3/5—dc23
LC record available at https://lccn.loc.gov/2019005178

ISBN: 978-1-138-90702-7 (hbk)
ISBN: 978-1-138-90703-4 (pbk)
ISBN: 978-1-315-69522-8 (ebk)

Typeset in Bembo
by Swales & Willis Ltd, Exeter, Devon, UK

CONTENTS

List of illustrations vi
Acknowledgements ix

1 Introduction 1

PART I
Interventions in organizational structures: theoretical underpinnings **21**

2 Understanding organizations as social systems 23

3 Organizational structures 46

4 Episodic interventions in organizational structures 102

PART II
Designing interventions in organizational structures **137**

5 The 3-D model in overview 139

6 The functional dimension 151

7 The social dimension 209

8 The infrastructural dimension 256

References 346
Index 351

ILLUSTRATIONS

Figures

1.1	Interactions, interaction premises, and the organization's societal contribution	3
1.2	The functional and social dimensions of the 3-D model	9
1.3	The 3-D model in outline	9
1.4	Roadmap of the book	19
2.0	Roadmap of the book	23
2.1	Four organizational activities and the organizational infrastructure	28
2.2	The relation between interactions and interaction premises	38
2.3	Relation between formal and informal premises and interaction	38
2.4	Summary of organizations as social systems experimenting with their meaningful survival	44
2.5	Episodic change is required if interaction premises can no longer be changed for the better by means of the interaction they condition	45
3.0	Roadmap of the book	46
3.1	The contribution of the organizational structure	47
3.2	The main activity of an organization making furniture	49
3.3	Decomposition with respect to parts of an activity into two sub-activities	49
3.4	Example of two aspectual sub-activities	50
3.5	Two examples of a structure	53
3.6	High (a), low (b) and intermediate (c) functional concentration	56
3.7	Description of one particular structure in terms of the values of the design parameters	62
3.8	The contribution of the organizational structure (as described by design parameters)	62
3.9	Adequate structures support the four basic activities if they have a low probability of disturbances and enough regulatory potential	68
3.10	An organizational structure with high values on all design parameters	70
3.11	The effect of high values on design parameters on the four basic activities	72

3.12	HPVSs have difficulty realizing variables related to quality or organization and quality of work and enabling reflection on and adaptation of interaction premises	79
3.13	An organizational structure with low values on design parameters	85
3.14	Low value parameter structures	95
4.0	Roadmap of the book	102
4.1	Basic model for understanding interventions	106
4.2	Iteration and recurrence (example implementation)	110
4.3	Extended model for understanding interventions	111
4.4	Modes of organizational change	116
4.5a	Organizational interventions	118
4.5b	Interventions in organizational infrastructures	123
4.5c	Continuous intervention in organizational structures	124
4.5d	Modes of organizational change	127
4.5e	Episodic interventions triggered by recurrent structure-driven problems	133
5.0	Roadmap of the book	139
5.1	The 3-D model, its functional, social, and infrastructural dimensions in relation to the goal and the object of the intervention	141
5.2	The 3-D model and its logic of use	148
6.0	Roadmap of the book	151
6.1	Order characteristics	185
6.2	Segmentation option I: product groups	188
6.3	Segmentation option II: module groups	189
6.4	Segmentation option III: component groups	190
6.5	Segmentation option V: phase groups	191
6.6	Regulation between segments	195
6.7	Regulation between flows	196
6.8	Segmentation at W (shared overall planner, parallel project segments including 'external' sub-contractor segments)	199
6.9	The relation between design, implementation, and evaluation	204
7.0	Roadmap of the book	209
7.1	Interpenetration and overlap between social goals	246
8.0	Roadmap of the book	256
8.1	The required proximate intervention effort	271
8.2	High parameter values, knowledge, skills, and motivation and the intervention's progress	285
8.3	Skilled incompetence in high parameter value structures	291
8.4	Example of a dynamic intervention structure	309

Tables

1.1	Episodic and continuous change	13
2.1	Formal and informal interaction premises: some examples	35
3.1	Operationalization of the organizational societal contribution into quality of organization and quality of work	64
4.1	Functional goals in the intervention	108

4.2	Differences between continuous and episodic interventions in organizational structures	128
6.1	General variables expressing quality of organization and quality of work	157
6.2	Examples of variables related to flexibility	159
6.3	The set of variables selected for explanation (second column)	161
6.4	Result of the gap analysis (the list of Vi[e] – last column)	165
6.5	Design parameters used in a structural diagnosis	167
6.6	Connecting the actual values of parameters to problems	170
6.7	Relation of parameters to the concerning the variable production time	180
6.8	Design heuristics per design step	198
7.1	Social goals in the intervention: motivation, adoption, integration	213
7.2	Schein's conception of a three-stage model of the change process	213
7.3	Examples of types of drivers of organizational change	217
7.4	Overview of motivation	222
7.5	Cumulative overview of motivation and adoption	228
7.6	Cumulative overview of the goals on the social dimension	237
8.1	Current status of the intervention	267
8.2	Desired status	269
8.3	Required proximate intervention effort	273
8.4	Examples of simple and programme designs	312
8.5	High and low parameter intervention structures and the three conditions	323
8.6	Goals and activities that may be served by intervention technology	326
8.7	Job-based criteria for the selection of facilitators	337
8.8	Checking the intervention's infrastructure for robustness	342

ACKNOWLEDGEMENTS

Many students, practitioners, colleagues, and friends helped to develop the ideas that are contained in this book. We would like to thank you all for your support, discussions, and comments. We hope that we have managed to convey in the book all that we have learned from you.

Some persons, however, should be mentioned in particular. To begin, we would like to thank Bart van Kasteren, who developed the first ideas underlying the 3-D model as a part of his research project. Bart, your input and that from Pierre van Amelsvoort were vital to the development of the main model discussed in this book. Moreover, we would like to thank Jac Christis, Liesbeth Gulpers, Hans Lekkerkerk, Matthijs Moorkamp, Berber Pas, Harrie Regtering, KlaasJan Renema, Armand Smits, Herma van Laar, and Patrick Vermeulen, who took the trouble of reading and commenting on chapters of the book.

1
INTRODUCTION

1.1 Organizational development: designing episodic interventions

In a nutshell, this book is about a specific type of organizational development: so-called *episodic interventions*. In particular, the book is about episodic interventions in the *structure* of organizations, and the goal of the book is to present a '3-D' model that helps to understand and flexibly design episodic interventions in organizational structures.

To appreciate the above topic and goal of the book, we want to start this introduction with a brief, preliminary explanation of our perspective on organizations, structures, and (episodic) interventions. Explaining our ideas about these concepts is for a large part what we set out to do in this book, so a full appreciation can only be arrived at at the end of the book. Here, we just want to provide a rough sketch of these concepts to be able to gain an understanding of the book's topic and goal.

1.1.1 Organizations

To start with, organizations are described as *social systems delivering a societal contribution*. The contribution refers to the role of organizations in society. Inspired by Aristotle's ethics and politics, we'll say that in modern society, organizations can positively contribute to the well-being of societal members. They can do so: (1) by means of the societally valuable products or services they provide, (2) by means of providing non-product or non-service-related positive side effects such as employment or the well-being of employees, and (3) by making sure that negative side effects (e.g. pollution, inequality) are avoided as much as possible. Of course, not all organizations define their own contribution in this way, and in fact, many 'contribute' to society in a negative way – e.g. by providing value-less products or services, by not caring about positive side effects, or by creating negative side effects. Even though many of these latter organizations exist, and even though much of what we have to say about episodic interventions will also help such organizations – we have organizations in mind striving to deliver a 'positive' societal contribution – we'll refer to this positive contribution as 'rich meaningful survival' (see Chapter 2, or Achterbergh and Vriens, 2010, for an elaboration of the societal contribution of organizations).

Organizations deliver their societal contribution as a *social system*, i.e. as *a system of interlocking interactions*. Although it takes some time and effort to really understand organizations as systems of interactions (cf. Giddens, 1979; Luhmann, 1984; Chapter 2 in this volume) the basic idea is simple: it means that organization members interact with each other and thereby realize the organization's contribution. It also means that an organization is seen as the (evolving) set of these interactions. So, for instance, it is by means of such joint interactions of organization members over time that organizational goals (which express the organization's contribution to society) are set, and that primary processes realizing these goals are performed. All the interactions relevant for realizing the organization's contribution are part of the organization as a system of interactions, as a social system.

The interactions of organization members, by means of which the organization's contribution is set and realized, are influenced by several factors. For instance, the interactions of organization members depend on the *tasks* these members are assigned. For example, the organizationally relevant interactions an employee of the 'painting' department in a furniture factory engages in have to do with realizing her job as a 'furniture painter', so such interactions may be about the type of paint, the available equipment, the number of chairs that need to be painted, etc. She will not likely be involved in interactions about setting the long-term goals of the factory. In fact, the type of task one is assigned to defines the topics about which one interacts and also with whom one is supposed to interact. As we will argue, the way tasks are defined and related – the organization's *structure* – has an important influence on organizational interaction.

Organizational interaction is also influenced by organizational goals (as interaction is always directly or indirectly related to these goals) or by organizational culture (which, for instance, provides 'informal rules' about how organization members should interact).

Structures, goals, and culture are examples of factors that influence organizational interaction. Following scholars on organizations as social systems, we call such factors 'interaction premises' – and we discuss more of these interaction premises throughout the book. Now, what is interesting here is that there is a 'circular' relation between interactions and interaction premises (cf. Giddens, 1979; Luhmann, 1984; Chapter 2 in this volume). That is, interactions are influenced by interaction premises, as we have just explained, but these interaction premises are themselves also partly shaped by means of interaction. For instance, the structure of an organization co-determines interaction, but the structure itself is made by organization members who interacted about what an appropriate structure might be. And as a result of that interaction, these members decide to define and relate tasks in a particular way, thus shaping the structure, i.e. shaping an interaction premise. The same holds for goals – they are decided upon in interaction, and once 'in place', they act as anchors for further interaction.

So, as shown in Figure 1.1, the organization's contribution is delivered in interaction (A), and this interaction is influenced by interaction premises (such as structure, goals, or culture – B). Moreover, these premises themselves are shaped by interaction (C).

Besides the view that the relation between interactions and interaction premises is a circular one, one of mutual dependence, we also want to stress that it is necessarily a 'continuous' relation. That is, once particular interaction premises are 'in place', it is not certain that these premises will continue to condition the interactions in such a way that they smoothly realize the organization's societal contribution. In fact, due to all kinds of unforeseen circumstances or developments, it may turn out that certain goals should change – e.g. because of a change in demand – or that the way in which certain tasks are defined and related turns out to be inefficient and should be altered. As we will argue, this uncertainty

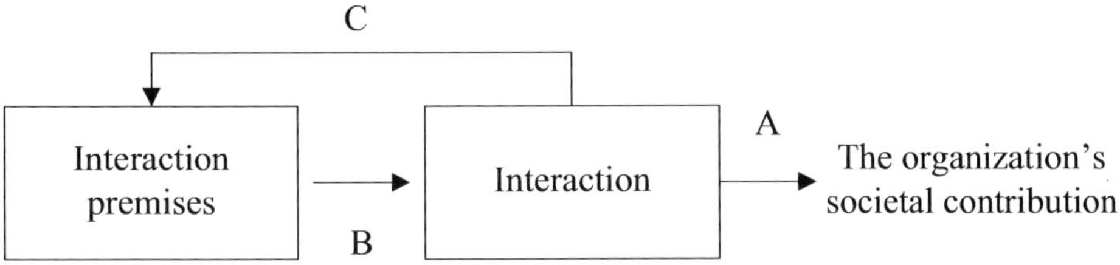

```
                    C
         ┌──────────────────┐
         ▼                  │
  ┌─────────────┐    ┌─────────────┐    A    The organization's
  │ Interaction │───▶│ Interaction │────────▶ societal contribution
  │  premises   │    │             │
  └─────────────┘    └─────────────┘
                 B
```

FIGURE 1.1 Interactions, interaction premises, and the organization's societal contribution

is fundamental for organizations, and the best one can do is to *experiment* with interaction premises. That is, one can decide to choose some set of goals *per hypothesis*, realize them by means of interaction, and hope that the organization's contribution is viably secured by this set of goals. One should monitor the appropriateness of the chosen goals and alter them if necessary. The same holds for the way tasks are defined and related. One may select a particular structure (because one thinks it is an appropriate one), implement it, monitor it, and change it if it turns out to harbour inefficiencies. That organizations can never be certain about the goals or structures they select, and hence need to experiment, seems to be managerial common sense. Here, we just want to stress that interaction premises are subject to continuous experimentation – and that this experimental change takes effect in interaction.

1.1.2 Organizational structures and their development

Based on these ideas, we can introduce the notion of *development* as the intended improvement of interaction premises – as changing interaction premises in such a way that they better support organizational interaction in realizing the organization's societal contribution. In particular, the development of the *structure* of organizations (as a form of organizational development) is the intended improvement of the way tasks are defined and related. Organizational (and structural) development usually comes about in experimentation (as described previously), and can hence be regarded as inherent to the continuous relation between interaction and interaction premises.

Structural development can sometimes become problematic in organizations. In fact, it can become so problematic that what we call 'episodic interventions' are needed. However, before we can understand what these interventions are and why they are required, we first need to gain some idea of why structural development may be problematic.

To this end, consider someone – let's call him Josef – working in some organization (for the moment, it does not matter whether this organization is a bank, a hospital, or some factory) who has been assigned to a job which has the following characteristics:

- The job is coupled to many or all of the organization's products or services (e.g. Josef, as a nurse, treats all types of patients – e.g. having different kinds of illnesses; or Josef, as a worker in a factory producing furniture, performs production activities for all different classes of furniture).
- The job comprises only a tiny fraction of all the activities needed to produce these products or services (e.g. Josef the nurse is only allowed to help with washing patients, Josef the furniture factory employee's job is just to drill holes in pieces of wood).

- The input that is needed to perform the job depends on different other workers that have equally small jobs (e.g. Josef the nurse awaits a sign from some other nurse if a patient is ready to be washed, the job of Josef the driller depends on the arrival of pieces of wood from some other worker).
- For the preparation (planning, tooling) of the activities, the job depends on other persons working in equally small jobs in other units of the organization (e.g. the nurse receives a plan of all patients who need to be washed during a particular day; the driller receives a similar plan and is dependent on the machine maintenance carried out by others).
- If something goes wrong in the production process that Josef can fix himself, he is not allowed to deal with this problem. For regulatory purposes, the job depends on other 'managers' who fix the problem for Josef (e.g. if a patient is being seen by a doctor when Josef arrives, the washing activities should be rescheduled or left to someone else; the need to replace worn-out drilling equipment should reported to a regulator, who instructs others to replace it).
- Josef's job is supervised by managers who only monitor a fraction of the tasks involved in the primary process and who themselves are monitored by yet other managers. In Josef's organization, a hierarchy of managers is in place.
- Josef is required to produce a particular output of a particular quality per time unit (e.g. the nurse should wash 50 patients a day, which should take no more than 5 minutes per patient).

Now, the structures consisting of jobs like Josef's are complex networks of highly dependent small jobs with a large hierarchy of managers (cf. Mintzberg, 1983; de Sitter, 1994). Typical examples are bureaucratic organizations, like many general hospitals, large governmental organizations, or functionally concentrated factories.

In general, such structures tend to have several negative effects. They negatively affect employee well-being and production effectiveness and efficiency. Although it takes some theoretical effort to explain these effects in detail, we can already intuitively understand that these structures cause such problems. Without being thorough and complete, it can already be appreciated that a complex network of many highly dependent jobs and a hierarchy of managers is error-prone, as every dependency relation is a possible source of errors. And, as jobs lack the regulatory potential to deal with these errors, these errors tend to affect many other jobs in the network. Second, if disturbances need to be dealt with by means of separate managers, it takes time to repair problems. And the more removed these managers are from the jobs in which the disturbances occur, the more difficult it becomes to think of regulatory measures that do justice to the specific circumstances in which the error occurred. Similarly, the less overview such managers have of the complex network of production jobs, the more difficult it becomes to think of measures that are not just local sub-optimizations – i.e. measures that may fix a local problem, but that lead to a disturbance in another part of the organization. Being error-prone and lacking regulatory potential, then, is problematic for production time and product quality.

Structures with the jobs described previously not only have a negative effect on production time and product quality, they also affect the well-being of employees. For instance, as employees are involved in only a tiny part of the complete process and perform small activities for many products or clients, it is difficult for them to have an overview of the whole production process and to have an idea of the end products and services they contribute to.

This may lead to alienation. As a nurse, for instance, Josef sees many patients with respect to only a very tiny aspect of the care they receive. In this case, he can neither picture the whole process of providing care nor connect to a patient and appreciate the effect of the care that is delivered. In such cases, care professionals tend to lose touch with patients and the care they once hoped to provide.

Being involved in small jobs with virtually no regulatory potential also makes it difficult for Josef to develop himself as a professional. There simply is not much to learn about or to develop in. Moreover, a job that is dependent on many other jobs and in which you cannot deal with disturbances yourself the moment they occur is likely to cause stress. Reaching job targets in the face of many disturbances and in the absence of regulatory potential leaves one with the feeling of being utterly out of control.

In the end, this kind of professional alienation, lack of development, and lack of control may lead to a loss of professional identity, and indeed, may come at the cost of the "soul of professionalism", as Freidson (2001) put it. And of course, these problems with employee well-being are not only existent in bureaucracies housing professionals – they can be found in many organizations with similar structures.

In fact, many of us have encountered, in one way or another, the problems caused by large bureaucratic organizations and their inadequacy to deal with them. Here, we want to stress that these problems mainly exist because these organizations have structures that are error-prone and lack regulatory potential.

1.1.3 Episodic interventions

Stating that bureaucratic organizations, because of their structure, find it difficult to realize their goals efficiently and effectively, and that employee well-being in these organizations is under severe pressure is – to say the least – almost a truism. We have known this for a long time. However, here, we want to use this knowledge as a starting point for stressing the relevance of episodic interventions. That is, we argue that these organizations *have often lost their capacity for 'normal' structural development, because of their structure. In such a case, an episodic intervention may be required to regain the capacity for structural development.*

As we argued, bureaucratic organizations have problems realizing goals and employee well-being because of their structure. And hence, they need to improve their structure. But improving this structure has become problematic *because* of the state the structure is in. The current structure disables its own improvement – we say that the structure has become self-inhibiting.

In 'healthy' organizations, structural deficits can be solved by 'normal' continuous structural development. That is, in this case, organization members continuously monitor the way their job is structured and whether this causes the experienced work-related problems. Based on their assessment, they change the structure of their work in order to deal with the experienced problems. Even though such changes are local changes, they may still contribute to the structural development of the whole organization if tasks are sufficiently connected, if communication about changes is sufficiently embedded in tasks, and if employees have a sufficient overview of the whole process.

However such 'normal' continuous structural development is problematic in bureaucratic organizations employing Josefs and their managers. In these organizations, monitoring and changing the structure is no formal part of the small operational jobs. Instead, it is the formal responsibility of the hierarchy of managers. But, as these managers are distant from the primary process, it is difficult for them to appreciate the connection between problems in the primary process and the organizational structure. Moreover, as the structure of these organizations is quite error-prone, the hierarchy of managers is often caught up in dealing with all these disturbances – leaving them with little time to change the structure. And, as managers themselves have only a limited management scope (being responsible for only a part or aspect of the complete process – e.g. they only manage a set of activities of the primary process or are responsible for human resources (HR), logistics, marketing, or whatever aspect), they have difficulty in developing an overview of the complete process; indeed, they often only have a narrow perspective. So, in these organizations, normal continuous structural development is no longer part of operational jobs. Moreover, the managers who should change the structure may come up with solutions too late, with irrelevant solutions, or with solutions that make things even worse – e.g. by making jobs even smaller.

In such organizations, operational employees may feel the need to change the structure informally – i.e. despite the formal 'efforts' of the hierarchy of managers, and implement informal 'workarounds'. But, given the lack of overview of these employees and the lack of communication about these changes, such informal structural changes tend to be only local sub-optimizations.

Normal structural development, then, seems to be undermined by the structure itself. However, to survive, the organization needs to alter its structure. Since this is problematic because of the structure itself and since this structure cannot be altered by 'normal' structural development, another type of structural development is needed: *episodic interventions*.

For now, we will define episodic interventions in the structure of organizations as 'intentional, deliberate, comprehensive changes to the organization's structure that have their own separate temporary intervention organization' (see also Chapter 4, in which we will go into this definition in detail).

Episodic interventions are *deliberate* and *intentional*, as they have the explicit goal to change the structure and do so by means of explicit deliberation (which involves, for instance, explicitly devising alternative structures and deliberating about the choice between them). They are also *comprehensive*, as they set out to change the structure of a large part or even the whole organization – not just a local change. Finally, episodic interventions have their own *separate, temporary intervention organization* on top of the standing organization, with a clear beginning and end. In this intervention organization, different individuals participate (e.g. organization members and/or consultants) who have tasks and use tools dedicated to the intervention itself. And once the structure has been changed, the intervention organization ceases to exist.

Compared to the 'normal' continuous interventions, episodic interventions are comprehensive (instead of local) and have their own dedicated intervention organization. If normal continuous structural development, which is part of the daily activities of organization members, is inhibited by the structure, an episodic intervention which is *not* a part of these daily activities is required. In this case, a separate dedicated organization intervenes in the structure of the standing organization. As we will argue, such changes often lead to a considerable structural change – to a new structure in which normal continuous development is again possible. In this way, an old 'episode' in the (structural) history of organizations finishes and a new one begins.

Although we will have much more to say about the need and nature of episodic interventions in later chapters, we hope that the reader has some gained some idea of them and that their function is to comprehensively redesign the structure to free the organizations from the impasse of detrimental, self-inhibiting continuous structural development.

1.2 The 3-D model: its outlines and use

In the book, we want to present a model that can help to understand and flexibly design episodic interventions in organizational structures. This model has three dimensions: the functional, social, and infrastructural. These three dimensions directly relate to three basic challenges faced by the episodic interventions in organizational structures. These challenges are:

1. ensuring that a *well-designed structure* is implemented in the organization – the functional dimension;
2. ensuring that the new structure is *integrated in the interaction premises and interactions* of organization members – the social dimension;
3. *designing the infrastructure of the intervention organization* in such a way that it helps to meet challenges 1 and 2 – the infrastructural dimension.

Let us explain these challenges and dimensions in some more detail.

1.2.1 The functional dimension of the 3-D model

The first dimension is the *functional dimension*. On the functional dimension, goals are specified that should be realized in order to increase the probability that a 'well-designed' structure is implemented in the organization. By a well-designed structure, we understand a structure that 'functions well', that is, a structure that can realize the goal of the intervention. This goal, for instance, can be 'restoring the organization's capacity for continuous adaptation', 'increasing the performance of the organization', 'increasing the quality of work in the organization', or a combination of these or other goals. A well designed structure, then, is a structure that has the characteristics that are needed to enable the realization of the goal of the intervention.

The goals on the functional dimension that should be realized in the intervention in order to increase the probability that a well-designed structure is implemented are:

1. *diagnosis* – finding problems and their structural causes and formulating a solution space;
2. *design* – finding a structure that allows to deal with the problems and/or their causes;
3. *implementation* – making the designed structure into an organizational reality;
4. *evaluation* – assessing whether the problems are solved by means of the implemented structure.

Here, we simply list these functional goals; they will be further explained in Chapter 6.

1.2.2 The social dimension of the 3-D model

The second dimension is the *social dimension*. As indicated in the previous section, organizational structures are social phenomena; they function as interaction premises, i.e. as points of orientation for the production of interactions, and they are reproduced and changed by means of interaction. An episodic intervention in the structure of an organization therefore also entails intervening in a social system. Because of this, such an episodic intervention not only has a functional, but also a social dimension. By means of the intervention, both the structure-related interaction premises and the interactions based on these premises should be changed in such a way that the new structure is 'integrated' into the interaction premises and interactions of organization members and thereby becomes the new social reality.

The social dimension of the 3-D model specifies the goals that should be realized in the intervention in order to change the interaction premises and interactions of organization members. These goals are:

1. *motivation* – organization members develop the motivation to let go of current and move to new interaction premises and interactions and adopt the episodic intervention as a means to do this;
2. *adoption* – based on justifiable confidence, organization members willingly commit to new helping interaction premises and interactions that can (re)produce an improved organizational structure that allows for the realization of the goal of the intervention;
3. *integration* – organization members have irreversibly integrated new interactions and interaction premises into their repertoires that both (re)produce the organization's new and improved structure and allow for the realization of the goal of the intervention.

In Chapter 7, these social goals will be discussed in more detail.

Please note that in order to make an episodic intervention in the structure of an organization a success, the goals on *both* the functional and the social dimensions should be realized.

Successfully realizing *only* functional goals would mean that the new structure is well-designed; a design is made of a structure that can realize the goal of the intervention. However, because this new structure is not socially integrated into the interaction premises and interactions of organization members, the well-designed structure only remains a plan; the structure does not become a new organizational reality.

Successfully realizing *only* social goals would mean that a new structure is integrated into the interaction premises and interactions of organization members, i.e. the structure becomes a new organizational reality. However, in this case, the structure may be badly designed, undermining instead of enabling the realization of the goal of the intervention.

So, in order to realize the goal of the intervention, *both* the functional and social goals in the intervention should be realized (see Figure 1.2). This is where the third dimension of the 3-D model comes in.

1.2.3 The infrastructural dimension of the 3-D model

We have already explained that episodic interventions in self-inhibiting organizational structures need a temporary and separate intervention organization in order to support the intervention. In this intervention organization, organization members (and possibly clients, suppliers, or other stakeholders) participate in intervention activities (e.g. participate in the redesign of their own work), possibly using tools and techniques that support these intervention activities.

Now, if the episodic intervention is to be a success, i.e. if the goal of the intervention is to be realized, the intervention organization needs to be designed in such a way that: (1) the 'right' human resources, with the 'right' knowledge, skills, and motivation (human

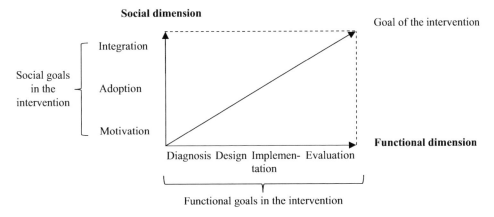

FIGURE 1.2 The functional and social dimensions of the 3-D model

resources), (2) using the 'right' tools and techniques (intervention technology), (3) work together in a network of intervention tasks (intervention structure) that can realize functional and social goals in the intervention.

Together, these three factors: (1) the intervention structure, (2) the intervention technology, and (3) the knowledge, skills, and motivation of the human resources involved in the intervention constitute the *intervention infrastructure*. So, in order to realize the functional and social goals in the intervention, and thereby the goal of the intervention, a well-designed intervention infrastructure is needed.

The third dimension of the 3-D model, the infrastructural dimension, lists the three factors that constitute the intervention infrastructure: the intervention structure, intervention technology, and human resources involved in the intervention (see Figure 1.3).

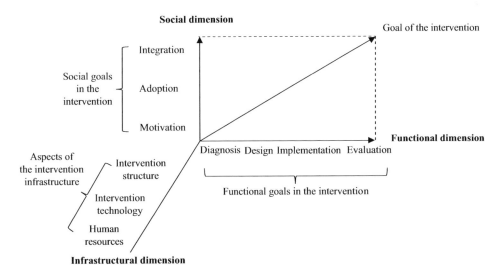

FIGURE 1.3 The 3-D model in outline

1.2.4 How the 3-D model can be used

Given this rough outline of the 3-D model, its use can be summarily described. It is the purpose of the 3-D model to help understand and flexibly design episodic interventions in organizational structures. Given our understanding of episodic interventions based on the outline provided, flexibly designing an episodic intervention means designing the infrastructure of its intervention organization in such a way that it enables the realization of functional and social goals in the intervention.

Therefore, in order to design the infrastructure of the intervention organization, one starts by setting so-called 'proximate' functional and social goals in the intervention. These proximate functional and social goals are functional and social goals that are 'next in line' to be realized. For instance, at the start of the intervention, 'diagnosis' and 'motivation' may be set as proximate functional and social goals. Given these proximate functional and social goals:

1. intervention activities – in this case, activities related to 'diagnosis' and 'motivation' – are grouped into intervention tasks that can be performed by human resources that should be involved in the intervention (intervention structure);
2. intervention techniques and tools are selected that are needed in order to perform these intervention tasks (intervention technology);
3. human resources are selected and/or trained in order to perform the intervention tasks using the selected intervention technology (human resources).

In this way, an intervention infrastructure is designed that is geared to the realization of the selected proximate functional and social goals. Once these selected proximate functional and social goals are realized, or if unexpected problems or opportunities present themselves, new proximate functional and social goals may be set and/or a new design of the intervention infrastructure may be made.

This procedure of selecting new proximate functional and social goals and (re)designing the intervention infrastructure that can help realizing these goals, in principle, goes on until the final proximate functional and social goals in the intervention – 'evaluation' and 'integration' – have been realized. By realizing these final functional and social goals in the intervention, a well-designed organizational structure (functional dimension) is integrated into the interaction premises and interactions of the relevant organization members (social dimension), thus realizing the goal of the intervention.

It is in this way that the 3-D model can help to understand and flexibly design episodic interventions in organizational structures. Chapter 8 will further elaborate these ideas about the flexible design of the intervention infrastructures of episodic interventions.

1.3 And now for something different

In a number of ways, this book is different from other literature on or presuppositions about organizational change in general, and episodic interventions in particular. Reading about episodic interventions and talking with students, colleagues, and practitioners, we encountered a number of interpretations of these interventions that differ from the way we understand them in this book. By collecting and assembling these interpretations, we constructed a kind of 'straw man interpretation' of episodic interventions that we use here to highlight features of our approach that, in our view, differ from conceptions assembled in the straw man. Please note that we do not use our straw man interpretation in order to argue that other conceptions are wrong and we are right. We just use it to highlight features of our approach towards episodic interventions that are worth highlighting because, as we see them, they are somehow different.

1.3.1 Zooming in, instead of zooming out

To begin, this book differs from textbooks that zoom out and address 'organizational change' as a general phenomenon (e.g. Beer and Nohria, 2000; Burnes, 2000). In our book, we decided to zoom in because we think that 'organizational change' is a topic that is too variegated to be treated in a general way. We think that, when talking about organizational change, it is relevant to take at least the *kind*, *object*, and *context* of change into account.

First, different *kinds* of organizational change should be distinguished, ranging from the continuous self-production of the organization as a social system to episodic interventions in particular parts or aspects of organizations. Because these different kinds of change introduce different theoretical and practical issues (e.g. theoretically explaining the dynamics of the self-production of organizations as social systems versus practically designing an intervention organization), it is not unlikely that addressing these different issues requires a variety of specialized theoretical approaches, concepts, methods, and tools (e.g. social systems theory versus cybernetic principles supporting design).

Second, different *objects* of change should be distinguished. For instance, as an object of change, the culture of an organization differs from its technology. Although changing some part of an organization's technology (e.g. introducing a new machine or information and communications technology [ICT] system) may be tightly coupled to cultural change (and vice versa), it is still relevant to pay attention to differences between these objects and requirements these differences set for attempts to change these objects.

Third, different *contexts* of change should be distinguished. As indicated previously (and as will be argued in later chapters), changing an organization with a complex and hierarchical organizational structure is a different and more challenging enterprise than changing an organization with a simple structure that allows for semi-autonomous teams. Such different contexts of change set different requirements for the concepts, models, and tools needed to realize change either in or of these contexts.

Now, if the 'kind', 'object', and 'context' of change are used to zoom in on the topic of this book, it can be said that it deals not with organizational change in general, but with episodic interventions (kind) in organizational structures (object) of organizations that currently have complex and hierarchical structures (context). It is in this way that our book differs from general text books on organizational change.

1.3.2 Episodic interventions: combining their functional and social dimensions

Unlike literature that specializes in either the functional dimension of episodic interventions in organizational structures (e.g. literature on organizational design) or their social dimension (e.g. literature on organizational learning and social transformation), this book is an attempt to pay attention to *both* the functional and the social dimensions of episodic interventions. Moreover, in the book, we want to *relate* these dimensions in a way that supports the flexible design of the infrastructure of intervention organizations.

As indicated, paying attention to only the *functional* dimension – that is, to activities such as the diagnosis, design, implementation, and evaluation – comes at the risk of forgetting the social and experimental character of episodic interventions. Although, in concept, a well-designed structure may result from a one-sided functional approach, almost no attention is paid to the social goals that should be realized if organization members are to transform their own behaviour in order to integrate the new organizational structure into their organizational behaviour.

Paying attention to only the *social* dimension of episodic interventions means that complex processes by means of which organization members transform their own behaviour receive careful attention and support. This focus on changing practices of organization members, however, may come at the expense of the functional aspects of the intervention. As a result, the quality of the redesign may be poor. If this happens, the new structure undermines instead of supports the organization's meaningful survival.

Because one-sided attention to either the functional or the social dimension of episodic interventions in organizational structures can be hazardous, the 3-D model pays attention to both dimensions. And what is more, it uses functional and social goals that should be set on these dimensions as points of departure for the flexible design of intervention infrastructures that can support the realization and adaptation of these functional and social goals.

1.3.3 Episodic interventions as a mode of organizational change

In an influential paper on organizational change, Weick and Quinn (1999) discuss episodic and continuous change as opposites. They argue that dependent on how you see change, as episodic or continuous, you bring in different: (1) metaphors of organization, (2) analytical frameworks, (3) intervention theories, and (4) ideas about the role of the change agent. For brevity's sake, we summarize Weick and Quinn's comparative overview of episodic and continuous change in Table 1.1.

Although we agree with a lot of the things that are argued by Weick and Quinn, there is one seemingly small difference (with big consequences) between how we approach change in our book and how Weick and Quinn approach it in their paper. This difference is that we do not oppose episodic change to continuous change, but episodic *interventions* to continuous *interventions*, and that we regard both types of interventions as *modes* of organizational change. Let us explain what this means and why it is relevant.

In this book, we conceptualize organizations as social systems. As such, organizations are involved in continuous processes of self-production (or *autopoiesis*, as Luhmann, 1984, calls it). In these processes of self-production, interactions are produced against a changing background of interaction premises that function as points of orientation for the production of new interactions. Both the continuous production of new interactions and the change of interaction premises can, metaphorically, be described as a continuous process of 'birth', as a 'flow', or as a 'flux'. Given this perspective on organizations as social systems, we would argue that being an organization and being in flux are one and the same thing. Moreover, we would argue that everything that happens in organizations as social systems happens in this flux.

Because everything that happens in the organization as a social system happens in the organizational flux, we consider episodic and continuous interventions as two types of interventions that are a part of the organizational flux. They are two of the many *modes*

TABLE 1.1 Episodic and continuous change

	Episodic change	*Continuous change*
Metaphor of organization	Organizations are 'inert'; change is infrequent, discontinuous, and, if it happens, intentional	Organizations are emergent and self-organizing; change is constant, evolving, and cumulative
Analytic framework	Change is an occasional interruption, a divergence of equilibrium, involving a dramatic (macro, distant, and global) intervention in the deep structure of the organization that aims for short-run adaptation	Change is a "pattern of endless modifications in work processes and social practices", involving close, local, micro accommodations that enable long-run adaptability
Intervention theory	Change involves: 'unfreezing' the inert organization, 'transition' changing the organization, and 'refreezing' the organization	Change involves: 'freezing' the flux, 'rebalancing' patterns that block the flux, 'unfreezing' resumes the flux
Role of change agent	The change agent is a prime mover who creates change	The change agent is a sense maker who redirects change

Source: Abbreviated and adapted from Weick and Quinn (1999, p. 366).

of that flux. So, besides modes of organizational change that are not intentional and do not involve deliberation, episodic and continuous interventions are modes of organizational change that do involve intentions and deliberation (of course, this does not foreclose that episodic and continuous interventions have unintended effects and involve interactions that are not the result of deliberation).

Now, how is this perspective on organizational change and episodic and continuous interventions different from the one introduced by Weick and Quinn, and why does this difference matter?

To begin, let us take a look at what Weick and Quinn call the 'metaphor of organization'. In our book, this metaphor is that of the organization as 'emergent' and 'self-organizing'. Or, to be more precise and less metaphorical, in the book we consider organizations as a particular type of self-producing social systems. This, in turn, implies that we interpret organizations as a continuous flux of interactions that are produced against a background of changing interaction premises. So we would argue that there is no episodic change as opposed to continuous change (of course, we do argue that there are episodic interventions as opposed to continuous interventions). Being a social system called 'organization' means being a flux. Outside this flux, there is no organization. And because organizations as social systems are a flux, they cannot be 'inert', cannot be 'frozen', and therefore do not need to be 'unfrozen'.

This social systems perspective on organizations also means that our 'analytic framework' is that of change as a "pattern of endless modifications in work processes and social practices" (Weick and Quinn, 1999, p. 366). Both episodic and continuous interventions are particular modes of change within this 'pattern of endless modifications'.

As particular modes of change, episodic and continuous interventions have in common that they are intentional and involve deliberation. However, because they are a part of the continuous self-production of the organization as a social system, of the pattern of endless modifications in work processes and social practices, the intentional and deliberative character of episodic and continuous interventions does not imply that these interventions can or should evolve according to some 'blue-print' project plan, be approached in a 'top-down' fashion, or be a considered as a feat of 'industrial engineering'. As will be argued, episodic and continuous interventions are processes of continuous trial and error, of muddling through. They are a kind of experiments that require continuous situational adjustments of functional and social goals as well as of the means (e.g. the intervention organization, in the case of episodic interventions) that are needed to realize these goals. This means that in our book we do not see episodic interventions as 'projects' that can be planned in advance by a small group of managers, consultants, or engineers. We see them as experiments that require situational and flexible design and may involve many parties in different roles.

1.3.4 Flexible design of the infrastructure of intervention organizations

In order to perform an episodic intervention in the structure of an organization, an intervention organization is required. Simplifying matters a bit, it can be said that this intervention organization is a temporary organization, 'on top of' or 'parallel to' the organization that is being changed. This intervention organization has its own intervention infrastructure: i.e. its own intervention structure, technology, and human resources. As mentioned at the start of this section, in the process of writing this book, we noticed that there are presuppositions about episodic interventions, intervention organizations, and intervention infrastructures that differ from the ideas presented in this book. In order to highlight these differences, it is useful to discuss five of these presuppositions.

Presupposition 1

The intervention infrastructure consists of only a relatively small group of organization members who participate in the intervention, representing their colleagues: the presupposition of representation and exclusion.

In his contribution to the first special issue of the *Journal of Applied Behavioral Science* on large group interventions, Axelrod (1992) points at a number of problems related to what he calls the 'parallel organization' approach towards implementing sociotechnical change.

In his contribution, Axelrod, following Kanter and Stein (1982), defines a 'parallel organization' as a "temporary organization set up alongside the regular organization". This parallel organization, then, is "composed of committees or task forces that are multilevel and multifunctional in nature". One of the features of a parallel organization is that it "involves relatively few people in the actual design of the new organization". This low degree of involvement, in turn, leads to the problem that "the members of the parallel organization typically are extremely excited and passionate about the change, whereas the rest of the organization feels left out in the cold". Moreover, because, "management and employees are not involved in the process except through their representatives in the parallel organization, they frequently feel outside the process, do not feel that they can adequately influence change, and are often labelled as resistant" (Axelrod, 1992, p. 500).

The presupposition here seems to be that the parallel organization includes a selection of representatives of the total workforce in the parallel organization, excluding all other members of that workforce. Hence the presupposition of representation and exclusion.

In one sense, the parallel intervention organization as portrayed by Axelrod is similar to the intervention organization as we understand it in this book. It is a temporary organization, with its own intervention structure, technology, and human resources that are organized parallel to or on top of the organization in order to realize the goal of the episodic intervention.

However, there also is an important difference between the parallel organization as portrayed by Axelrod and our conception of the intervention organization. In the intervention organization as we conceive it, in principle, *all* organization members can perform intervention activities. In principle, no one is excluded from participation. Dependent on functional and social goals that are set in the intervention, all, most, or some organization members can participate. And what is more, dependent on these goals, clients, suppliers, or other parties that have a stake in the intervention can participate as well. In this sense, our view of the intervention organization differs from the one discussed by Axelrod. In 'our' intervention organization, in principle, all organization members and other relevant parties can participate. Participation, therefore, is not necessarily representative participation, including some organization members and excluding others.

Presupposition 2

The infrastructure of the intervention organization is designed at the start of the intervention and then exists unaltered until its end: presupposition of permanence.

Reading or talking about intervention organizations, one might get the impression that their infrastructures consist of 'units', e.g. a steering committee, a number of intervention teams, and a project administration, that are designed at the start of the intervention and continue to exist until the intervention's end. Thus, intervention organizations are portrayed as consisting of more or less permanent 'entities' that exist unaltered throughout the intervention. Hence the presupposition of permanence.

This is not how we conceive of intervention organizations in this book. In our view, intervention organizations and their infrastructures are dynamic. And we think they need to be, for two reasons.

The first reason is that as the intervention progresses, new functional and social goals will be set. For instance, at the start of the intervention, 'diagnosis' and 'motivation' may be the functional and social goals in the intervention. Later on, these goals may be replaced by 'design' and 'adoption'. In order to realize these new functional or social goals, new intervention activities should be performed that may be grouped into new intervention tasks. This means that the structure of the intervention organization changes as the intervention progresses. Moreover, the performance of these new intervention tasks may require new intervention tools. Thus, the intervention technology may change during the intervention. Finally, as new functional or social goals are set, new participants may need be involved in the intervention, so human resources involved in the intervention organization may change as the intervention progresses. Therefore, because of the dynamics of functional and social goals in the intervention, the intervention infrastructure that is needed in order to realize these goals probably will be dynamic too.

The second reason for the dynamics of intervention infrastructures has to do with the experimental character of episodic interventions. It is inherent in these experiments that things can go wrong (problems) or better than expected (opportunities). In order to either address these problems or grasp opportunities, it may be required to 'situationally' alter aspects or parts of the intervention infrastructure by changing its structure, technology, or human resources. So, because of the experimental character of episodic interventions, their infrastructure may be dynamic too.

So our conception of intervention organizations highlights their dynamic character. As such, this conception differs from those conceptions that portray intervention organizations as permanent, unchanging entities.

Presupposition 3

The design of the intervention infrastructure can be more or less standardly 'copied' from 'blueprints' that, for instance, are described in the literature: presupposition of blue-print design.

The dynamic character of intervention infrastructures – i.e. their relation to changing functional and social goals as well as to problems or opportunities that present themselves during the intervention – implies that their design is 'situational'. By 'situational', we mean that given selected functional and social goals and given assessments of the current status of the intervention (including its problems and opportunities), parts or aspects of the intervention infrastructure are designed or redesigned. The aim of this situational (re)design is to construct an intervention infrastructure that, for the time being, best fits the realization of the selected functional and social goals in the intervention and enables parties involved in the intervention to both deal with problems and exploit opportunities that present themselves. Because situational (re)design is always related to the particulars, i.e. to salient features of the actual status of an intervention, it is almost impossible to (re)design the infrastructure of the intervention organization by copying blue-print designs that, for instance, can be found in text books. That is why in this book we do not present such a general blue-print design. Instead, we develop a conceptual model (the 3-D model), a procedure, and heuristic principles that support the situational (re)design of the intervention organization as the intervention progresses.

Presupposition 4

The intervention organization is designed by managers or consultants that manage the intervention: presupposition of managerial design.

Another presupposition about intervention organizations and their infrastructures is that they are designed by managers or consultants. Although workers, professionals, clients, suppliers, or other parties can 'participate' in the intervention – for instance, by diagnosing or redesigning their own department – and thus become a part of the intervention organization, the intervention organization itself is presupposed to be set up and managed by managers or consultants.

Although we do not deny that this presupposition of 'managerial design' of intervention infrastructures holds true in a lot of cases, we explicitly include the possibility that participants in the intervention (workers, professionals, clients, etc.) are involved in the management of their own intervention activities. This management, in the first place, can refer to dealing with problems that present themselves in the intervention. Second, it can refer to redesigning parts or aspects of the intervention infrastructure. Third, it can refer to setting new functional and social goals in the intervention. So, in this book we explicitly include the possibility of participants in the intervention organization (other than managers or consultants), designing and redesigning the intervention infrastructure they are a part of.

Presupposition 5

The intervention organization is there to manage the intervention: presupposition of focus on regulation and control.

In literature on episodic interventions, these interventions are sometimes portrayed as 'projects' that should be 'managed'. 'Project management', then, becomes a separate and specialized topic within management literature that deals with the regulation and control of (intervention) projects. Given its focus on the regulation and control of projects, concepts such as 'deliverables' (in terms of 'functionality', 'costs', and 'time'), 'milestones', 'steering groups', and 'project administrations' come to dominate this particular strand of management literature. It is almost as if managing an intervention project is more important than actually performing it. And as a result of this, it seems as if the intervention organization is there to manage the intervention.

In our book, we want to turn this focus on regulation and control around by paying most of the attention to the actual *performance* of episodic interventions – that is, to the operational intervention activities that should be performed in order to realize the goal of the intervention. So the main question is not "How to design an intervention organization by means of which the intervention can be best regulated and controlled?" It is rather "How to design an intervention organization that enables the performance of the actual operational intervention activities that should realize the goal of the intervention?" In this sense, our book differs from literature on project management: the regulation and control of an episodic intervention are not central, but rather enabling the operational intervention activities that should realize the goal of the episodic intervention.

1.4 Layout of the book

In this book, we aim to introduce a model, the 3-D model, that can support organizational development by means of episodic interventions in the design of organizational structures.

In order to introduce this model, the book is organized into two parts. Part I discusses the theoretical framework that underpins the model. Part II introduces the 3-D model itself.

The theoretical framework discussed in Part I addresses three main topics: organizations as social systems conducting experiments, organizational structure, and characteristic features of episodic interventions that aim to change the structure of organizations.

Chapter 2 introduces our perspective on organizations as social systems conducting experiments with meaningful survival. In this chapter, we explain: (1) what we understand by meaningful survival, (2) what activities and conditions are needed for meaningful survival, (3) that performing these activities and selecting these conditions always have an experimental character, involving unpredictability, risk, and error, and (4) that organizations are social systems, which means that experimentation in organizations is a thoroughly social activity. The concepts presented in Chapter 2 set the stage for all the following chapters.

Chapter 3 discusses organizational structures. It explains what organizational structures are and why the design of organizational structures is important for the meaningful survival of organizations. Moreover, Chapter 3 introduces criteria that can help distinguish organizational structures that support meaningful survival from organizational structures that undermine it. Because this book is about episodic interventions in organizational structures, understanding what these structures are, what their relevance is, and what their design should look like in order to support meaningful survival is crucial for an understanding of the rest of the book.

Chapter 4 is about episodic interventions. In this chapter, relevant characteristics of episodic interventions in organizational structures are discussed that should be taken into account when constructing a model that should support these interventions. It will be argued that episodic interventions have a functional, social, and infrastructural dimension. Moreover, it will be argued that these interventions have a deliberate and intentional character and that they too are a kind of experiments. Finally, it will be argued that episodic interventions are 'agonistic', involving power and politics, and always involve moral issues that should be taken into account.

Together, Chapters 2, 3, and 4 provide the 'building blocks' that allow for the construction of the 3-D model that is the topic of the second part of the book.

In order to facilitate the discussion of the 'parts' of the 3-D model, Chapter 5 provides an overview of the model as a whole. It summarily discusses the model's three dimensions – the functional, social, and infrastructural – the 'logic of use' of the model, and the power and moral issues that are an intrinsic part of its application.

Chapter 6 is devoted to the functional dimension of episodic interventions in organizational structures. It discusses the activities – diagnosis, design, implementation, evaluation – that should be performed in order to increase the probability that a structure is designed and implemented that 'functions well' – that is, that can realize the goal of the intervention.

Chapter 7 deals with the social dimension of episodic interventions in organization structures. This is relevant because an organizational structure may be well designed functionally, but if the behaviour – interactions and interaction premises – of organization members does not change in such a way that this well designed structure becomes an organizational reality, then the episodic intervention would still be a failure. The social dimension of the 3-D model is about social goals that should be realized during the intervention in order to durably change the interactions and interaction premises of organization members in the intervention. These social goals are: motivation, adoption, and integration.

In order to realize functional and social goals in the intervention, a temporary intervention organization is required. This intervention organization has its own (dynamic) intervention infrastructure. This intervention infrastructure consists of the intervention structure, the intervention technology, and human resources that perform/support the intervention. Given the need for an intervention infrastructure, the question of its flexible design presents itself. This is the topic of Chapter 8. In Chapter 8, first a procedure is introduced that can support the flexible design of intervention infrastructures. Second, factors that can affect the progress of episodic interventions in organizational structures are discussed. These factors are relevant because they should be taken into account when designing intervention infrastructures. Third, the design of the three aspects of the intervention infrastructure is discussed: the intervention structure, intervention technology, and human resources involved in the intervention.

Figure 1.4 shows an overview of the parts and chapters of this book; it provides a roadmap that will reappear at the beginnings of each of the following chapters.

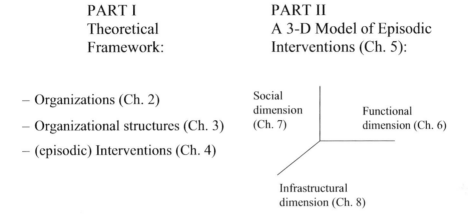

FIGURE 1.4 Roadmap of the book

PART I
Interventions in organizational structures
Theoretical underpinnings

2

UNDERSTANDING ORGANIZATIONS AS SOCIAL SYSTEMS

Episodic Interventions in the Structure of Organization

PART I
Theoretical Framework:

– Organizations

– Organizational structures

– (episodic) Interventions

PART II
A 3-D Model of Episodic Interventions:

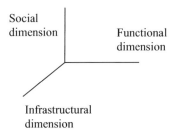

FIGURE 2.0 Roadmap of the book

2.1 Introduction

In this chapter, we present our perspective on organizations. Discussing this perspective in a book on episodic interventions is relevant because these interventions imply an understanding of organizations. In the previous chapter it was argued that episodic interventions are related to organizations in a least three ways. First, they aim to fix (actual or projected) problems of or in organizations. The nature of these problems is immaterial; it could relate to problems with the learning capacity of organizations, with shareholder value, with internal or external cooperation, etc. By fixing these organizational problems, interventions, in the end, set out to secure organizational survival. In this sense, it could be said that interventions are realized *for* organizations. Second, episodic interventions aim at solving problems by altering something in the organization. In particular, they set out to change (parts of) the infrastructure of organizations (in this book, we focus on the organizational *structure* as a specific part of the infrastructure). In this way, one could say that episodic interventions are realized *in* an organization. And third, episodic interventions evolve by means of organizational interaction, against the background of organizational 'interaction premises' conditioning these interactions. In fact, episodic interventions are defined as projects having their own separate, dedicated (temporary) infrastructure, which refers to a group of individuals having specifically assigned tasks, interacting with each other, using particular tools and techniques, to realize the intervention. In this way, an intervention project can be regarded as a kind of 'organization' of its own – often a temporary sub-system of the organization it sets out to improve. So episodic interventions can be said to be realized *by* organizations.

Episodic interventions, then, are realized for, in, and by organizations. Given this intricate relation with organizations, it is, in our view, helpful to understand what organizations are. This knowledge may help to understand the organizational problems interventions are aimed at, what the organizational infrastructure is, what interventions set out to change, and how to set up and regulate the organization of the intervention project itself. In this chapter, we therefore unfold a perspective on organizations, and discuss how this perspective helps to make sense of episodic interventions.

Our perspective (which is discussed extensively in Achterbergh and Vriens, 2010) highlights that organizations: (1) are 'social systems', (2) have a particular purpose, 'meaningful survival', and (3) continuously need to experiment to attain this purpose. The goal of this chapter, then, is to provide a description of organizations by explaining these three characteristics. We explain social systems in section 2.2, meaningful survival in section 2.3, and conclude in section 2.4 with a discussion of organizational experimentation.

2.2 Organizations as social systems: interaction and interaction premises

The proposed perspective of organizations as social systems entails that: (1) in organizations, continuous social interaction between organization members is central, and (2) this interaction is conditioned by so-called 'interaction premises'. In this section, we will elaborate on what these interactions refer to and the types of interaction premises, and we will go into the relation between interaction and interaction premises.

2.2.1 Social systems: interaction

Organizations are inherently social. Everything that happens in them is 'socially embedded' – they are social systems. This links up with many definitions that can be found in literature on organizations, describing them as "a group of people interacting with each other" (e.g. Morgan, 1986). Such definitions highlight the *interaction* between people as an important organizational characteristic, and thus refer to their 'social' nature. Meaningful interaction, which may refer to communication (Luhmann, 1984) or joint (communicative) behaviour (e.g. Feldman and Orlikowski, 2011), is required to ensure that organization members connect to each other and become more than a mere aggregate of individuals. Indeed, this is what makes a group of people a social entity – and the same holds for organizations.

Of course, in organizations, the interaction between individuals is not just any interaction. To count as meaningful *organizational* interaction, it should have a particular focus. Following scholars from organizational theory and design (e.g. de Sitter, 1994; Nadler and Tushman, 1997; Achterbergh and Vriens, 2010), this focus can be derived from four basic activities which every organization – be it not-for-profit organizations like governments, municipalities, and non-governmental organizations (NGOs), or for-profit organizations ranging from small and medium-sized enterprises (SMEs) to large multinationals – needs to perform. That is, all organizations have to:

1. realize transformation process leading up to the organization's products and services; this activity is called 'performing primary processes';
2. deal with disturbances in these transformation processes (to make sure that they can continue to deliver their contribution); this activity is called 'operational regulation';
3. set goals related to their primary processes (e.g. in terms of type of products, number of products; quality of products, and/or a contribution to society); this activity is called 'strategic regulation'.

In addition, organizations have to:

4. make sure that 'organizational conditions' are installed so that all activities (including this fourth one) can be performed; this activity is called 'regulation by design'.

In our view, meaningful organizational interaction relates to these four basic activities.

To explain these four activities, let's consider a simple organization – a child psychology practice, employing three psychologists and an assistant.

Activity 1: performing primary processes

In order to survive as a practice, it provides psychological care to children. Providing this care is the primary process of the practice – and by realizing this process, the practice delivers a contribution to its environment and thus 'maintains its existence'. This primary process can be described at different levels of detail. 'Providing psychological care' might be the lowest level of detail. Descriptions like 'contact with patient', 'referral to one of the three psychologists', 'intake of patient', 'diagnostic sessions', 'treatment sessions', 'billing', and 'final evaluation' are descriptions at a higher level of detail. At an even higher level of detail, one may find descriptions of the diagnostic and treatment sessions for several types of psychological problems. So the first organizational activity this practice has to perform in order to survive is to realize the primary processes that deliver a particular set of services to the environment.

Activity 2: operational regulation

While performing these primary processes, many disturbances may threaten to (or actually) influence these processes. A patient may not show up, two patients may show up at the same time, a psychologist may fall ill, a psychological test may no longer be available online, etc. Something needs to be done to make sure that the primary process of providing psychological care can continue despite such disturbances. 'Damage' to the primary process should prevented or repaired. This kind of 'dealing with disturbances in order to continue the primary process' is called operational regulation. Examples include rescheduling patients, distributing the patients of a sick colleague among the remaining psychologists, using a paper version of a psychological test, etc. Because disturbances are bound to occur, it should be clear that without operational regulation, primary processes cannot be carried out properly and will eventually come to a standstill. Every organization, then, needs to be able to perform operational regulation *vis-à-vis* its primary processes.

Activity 3: strategic regulation

Primary processes realize particular goals, and these goals need to be set. For instance, the practice may strive to see a certain number of patients in order to secure its income. As another goal, the practice may choose to deliver a particular type of psychological care (e.g. a focus on children with psycho-somatic disorders), and the practice may state that delivering the services should never come at the cost of the psychologists' quality of work. Setting goals is called strategic regulation. Moreover, in the course of time, it may turn out that certain goals need to be reformulated. This also belongs to strategic regulation. For instance, suppose that the demand for treatment of psycho-somatic psychological care decreases because the government has decided that such care should be delivered by psychiatrists. In this case, a new focus needs to be found, or the practice may decide to stop its activities. Finding a new focus (or stopping its activities) entails that goals should be reset to adapt to changes in the environment.

Based on the discussion of these three activities, it can be appreciated that by means of primary processes and their operational regulation in the first two activities, goals are *realized*, whereas by means of strategic regulation, goals are *set* and *adapted*.

Activity 4: regulation by design

In order to perform primary processes, to deal with disturbances, and to set goals, certain organizational 'conditions' need to be put in place. At least three types of conditions can be discerned: 'human resources', 'technology', and an 'organizational structure'.

Organizations need knowledgeable, skilful, and motivated human resources. Without them, activities cannot be performed properly. In the current example, human resources as a condition refers to the four members of the practice (and their level of motivation, professional knowledge, and skill). A second condition for performing organizational activities refers to 'technology' – a broad set of means referring to all but the human resources in organizations. It consists, for instance, of buildings, machines, furniture, tools, or ICT. In the example, technology includes the building housing the practice, the ICT used, the psychological tests, the toys used in sessions with children, tables and chairs, etc. It should be clear that without such technological means, organizational activities cannot be performed.

A third condition for performing organizational activities is the 'organizational (or task) structure' – i.e. the way tasks are defined, allocated and related. A task, in essence, describes what an organizational unit (a department, a team, a person) needs to do and realize. This implies that a unit performs certain actions and uses certain technology in order to obtain a particular goal set for that unit. Ideally, the tasks of all units are defined and related in such a way that if all units perform their task adequately, the four organizational activities are performed and the overall goals of the organization are realized. So, at the level of individuals, tasks describe what these individuals are supposed to do in terms of performing certain actions and/or in terms of reaching certain targets. In order to perform their task-related actions, the application of their skills and knowledge and the use of certain technological means are implied. An organizational structure defines tasks, and thus relates human resources and technology to organizational activities and goals. Of course, without some sort of task structure, human resources wouldn't know what to do and nothing would happen in organizations.

To see how tasks may be defined and related in the example, one may imagine that the task of the assistant comprises primary process actions like making contact with patients, assigning patients to a psychologist, sending bills, and evaluation. It may also comprise operational regulation with respect to these actions.

The task of a psychologist may comprise primary process actions like diagnosis and treatment of patients. It may also comprise operational regulation concerning these primary process activities. Moreover, the task of psychologists may include monitoring and adjusting the infrastructure and goals of the psychological practice.

In order to perform the organizational activities, then, three types of conditions should be in place: human resources, technology, and an organizational structure. We call the particular set of conditions at some moment in time the 'organizational infrastructure' (cf. Achterbergh and Vriens, 2010). So the organizational infrastructure of the psychological practice at some moment in time consists of:

1. the particular members (human resources) of the practice (with their skills, knowledge, and motivation), as well as the particular efforts to develop these skills, knowledge, and motivation;
2. the available technology at this moment;
3. the particular way tasks are defined and related.

We previously discussed three organizational activities: performing primary processes, operational regulation, and strategic regulation. Moreover, we argued that three types of conditions are required to perform these organizational activities. We defined the organizational infrastructure as the particular actual realization of these conditions. An important fourth organizational activity can now be introduced: 'designing an adequate infrastructure' – i.e. making sure that the proper conditions for the activities are installed. This fourth activity is called 'regulation by design'.

In the example, this would entail:

1. ensuring that the members of the organization have and keep on having the proper skills and knowledge, e.g. by means of installing a system of peer review and training – these are examples of providing an adequate infrastructure with respect to human resources;
2. renting a particular building, making it suitable for psychological care activities, buying and installing ICT, buying certain diagnostic tests – these are examples of making sure that the technological aspects of the infrastructure are adequate;
3. Defining and allocating specific tasks to the assistant and the psychologists (see earlier text for examples) – this refers to designing the 'structure' part of the infrastructure.

Regulation by design aims at providing an adequate infrastructure – human resources, technology, and structure. This infrastructure is adequate if, based on it, the organizational activities can be performed efficiently and effectively. This means that the infrastructure should enable primary processes, operational regulation, and strategic regulation. All these activities require human resources, technology, and the definition and assignment of tasks. Now, if a particular infrastructure is no longer suited for performing primary processes, operational regulation, or strategic regulation, it needs to be changed. Such a change belongs to the activity 'regulation by design'. So, by means of regulation by design, an infrastructure is changed.

The activity 'regulation by design' is itself also performed by human resources as part of their task, employing particular technology. That is, performing the activity 'regulation by design' itself requires an infrastructure. In fact, one could say that there exists a circular relation between the activity 'regulation by design' and the infrastructure it produces regulation by design produces a particular infrastructure, and based on that infrastructure, the activity 'regulation by design' can be performed.

If we consider our example, the present infrastructure (the psychologists and assistant, their tasks, and the available technology) may at some point become problematic. This may be the case, for instance, because some tests are outdated, computers have become too slow, or because the available psychologists can't handle the increase in the number of patients. In this case, the members of the organization may decide to buy new tests, to buy a new computer, and to hire a new psychologist. To do so properly, they may first search the Internet for suitable tests and computers, and use it to attract a new psychologist. Moreover, in the process of selecting a new member, they may administer a personality test to applicants, and they may hold job interviews in their practice. Finally, they may actually buy a new test and computer, and they may actually hire a new psychologist. In this example, the present infrastructure – the members of the psychology practice (human resources), ICT, building, testing (technology), and structure (as the members consider it their task to do something about the problems in the current infrastructure) – is employed to redesign the infrastructure. So, based on the infrastructure, the activity 'regulation by design' is performed – which results in a changed infrastructure.

In Figure 2.1, we summarize our argumentation with respect to the organizational activities each organization needs to perform.

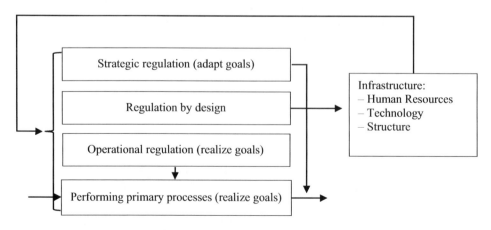

FIGURE 2.1 Four organizational activities and the organizational infrastructure

The figure depicts the four basic organizational activities. Moreover, as can be seen in the figure, the four organizational activities are based on a particular infrastructure, and this infrastructure can itself be re-designed by means of the activity 'regulation by design'. In addition, the figure also makes apparent that strategic regulation is about adapting goals, whereas performing primary processes and their operational regulation are about realizing goals.

In this section, interaction between individuals has been introduced as central to the idea of organizations as social systems, and we indicated that this interaction realizes four basic organizational activities, and is conditioned by the infrastructure.

2.2.2 Social systems: interaction premises

As we discussed, interaction between organization members is conditioned by the organizational infrastructure. However, organizational interaction is also conditioned by the goals set in organizations, and by so-called 'basic assumptions' about "external adaptation and internal integration" (Schein, 1992, p. 12). Following Luhmann (1984, 2000) on social systems and organizations, it can be said that infrastructures, goals, and 'basic assumptions' act as *premises* conditioning interactions. In this section, we briefly explain the function of interaction premises in general, and we discuss 'basic assumptions', goals, and infrastructures as particular types of interaction premises.

The function of interaction premises

Describing organizations the way we did in the previous sections introduces interactions as key elements of organizations, and it implies that somehow, interactions link up with each other to form a system of interconnected interactions. Interactions, however, are ephemeral phenomena. Interactions like communication between individuals or just handing over material only exist for a short period of time. In fact, they often start to disappear the moment they appear. Moreover, after interactions have finished, individuals may engage in new interactions. They may, for instance, react to previous interactions, e.g. continue a previously started conversation. It is also possible that they engage in a new interaction which is not so much a reaction to direct previous interaction, but which nevertheless is appropriate in the context of the four basic organizational activities. For instance, one may start a discussion on the effectiveness of the current way of operating a machine. However, even though this discussion is not a direct reaction to previous interaction, it can be regarded as a reference to more remote previous interactions, e.g. the interactions resulting in the decision to implement the current way of operating the machine. In this way, this discussion can be said to follow up previous interaction in a more 'indirect' way. So interactions can be said to lead to follow-up interactions – either directly or indirectly (see also Luhmann, 1984, who discusses the 'production of communications by communications' in social systems in a comparable way).

Organizations, then, are systems of impermanent interactions which lead to new impermanent interactions. To make sure that the emerging system of interactions is a coherent system, i.e. a system consisting of interactions 'belonging' to a particular organization, interaction premises are required. These premises structure the production of organizational interactions in several ways. First, they act as so-called "normative points of reference" giving direction to further interaction (Achterbergh and Vriens, 2010, pp. 147ff). For instance, once a goal is set, future interactions may take this goal into account. If the psychologists decide to start administering IQ tests (a new goal), interactions about the type of test that needs to be used, about how to communicate this new service, about making someone responsible for this service, about how to evaluate the results of tests, etc. all refer to this goal. One could say that this goal ensures that these interactions make organizational sense; they 'belong' to this organization because of their reference to this goal.

Being a normative point of reference entails that interactions are 'in line' with interaction premises: they should somehow fit the set of goals or the infrastructural conditions (e.g. the tasks) that have been defined. As such, these premises open up a set of 'expectable' interactions which, at the same time, also functions as a background for marking non-fitting interactions. After, for instance, a decision is made to launch all future marketing campaigns via social media, a meeting about contracting a call-centre to approach clients by phone can be seen as a deviating interaction. As organization members know (or are supposed to know) the set of expectable interactions, they (know that they) can be held accountable for deviations – and hence they may think twice before engaging in such interactions. And, although it may sometimes be a good thing to deviate from what is expected (and even to argue that there might be a reason to change our expectations), interaction premises do have this 'normalizing' function.

Although more can be said about the function of interaction premises, here it suffices to say that interaction premises condition interactions in organizations: they serve as a more or less stabilized (but still changeable – see below) background against which continued organizational interaction emerges and makes sense *as* organizational interaction.

'Basic assumptions' as interaction premises

To explain so-called basic assumptions as interaction premises, it is helpful to remember that interaction in organizations is geared to four main activities, which, in turn, are focused on issues of adaptation and realization. Interaction is, as Schein (1992, p. 11) formulates it, related to: "(1) survival, growth and adaptation in their environment, and (2) internal integration that permits daily functioning and the ability to adapt". Schein further describes how organization members engage in a process of learning with respect to adaptation and realization. When confronted with adaptation and realization problems, solutions are proposed. If these solutions are new, they only have the status of hypotheses. They only reflect values and beliefs about what *should or may* work. So, for instance, if the psychologists face a decline in number of clients, and hence of profit, they may think of increasing advertising, because they believe that that may work (the advertising example is Schein's). If acting on this belief (performing interactions realizing an increase in advertising) actually works out, Schein discusses that not only will the group learn about the suitability of particular actions (increasing advertising), but also about the 'validity' of the assumptions that served as a background for generating these actions (in the example: the belief that in times of declining sales, increasing advertising is a way out). In general, if a solution based on a set of basic assumptions (beliefs and values) is successful repeatedly, it will occur to the group that "what once was a hypothesis, supported only by a hunch or a value [. . .] is in some larger sense 'correct' and must reflect an accurate picture of reality" (Schein, 1992, pp. 19–20). By means of such learning processes, Schein argues, the beliefs and values serving as a background for generating solutions gradually become taken for granted, unconscious, even non-discussable basic assumptions that guide organization members in 'perceiving, thinking and feeling' about organizational matters (cf. Schein, 1992, Chapter 2).

So, in line with Schein, we argue that the set of taken-for-granted basic assumptions about what the world is like, and how things ought to be – i.e. a shared, taken-for-granted, and deeply embedded cognitive and moral frame – acts as a premise for interaction as these assumptions guide organization members in perceiving, thinking, and feeling about organizational matters.

As a moral frame, taken-for-granted basic assumptions refer to 'values that ought to be valued' – to deeply embedded beliefs of organization members about what is worth pursuing (for its own sake). More or less collectively held values about, for instance, the desired quality of services and products, the relevance of working life, indeed, about "the nature of human nature" (Schein, 1992, Chapter 6), or about what it means to live a fulfilled life as a human being serve as anchors for organizational interaction. In the example of the psychology practice, beliefs about the relevance of the societal value (mental health) a psychologist is supposed to contribute to and beliefs about the reasons why a professional should pursue this societal value (e.g. for its own sake, and not for the sake of economic gain) guide interaction. They can, for instance, guide interaction about the goals set for the practice: e.g. whether it should focus on doing more (easy to administer and profitable) IQ tests at the expense of (time-consuming and less profitable) psychological treatments. A shared, taken-for-granted moral frame also guides the design of the infrastructure, as it may, for instance, help to determine the way professionals are monitored and rewarded/sanctioned. If professionals are trusted to pursue a particular societal value for its own sake, different monitoring and control systems are put in place than when professionals are seen as self-centred land-grabbers (for a description of such different moral frames describing the "nature of professionalism" and their effect on systems of professional accountability, see Evetts, 2013; Freidson, 2001; O'Neill, 2002).

As a cognitive frame, taken-for-granted basic assumptions refer to deeply rooted and uncontested (1) representations of relevant entities in the world, and (2) ideas about causes and effects. They refer to shared, taken-for-granted knowledge about what the world looks like and how it works. This knowledge helps organization members to jointly understand the world – it provides meaning, and leads, as Schein (1992) and Scott (2008) have it, to shared 'patterns' of understanding. It may include rather abstract shared assumptions about "reality, truth, time and space" (cf. Schein, 1992, pp. 94ff), and assumptions that are more directly tied to organizational life, e.g. about the function of marketing, or about the relation between the organization and its clients or competitors. Such cognitive frames co-determine the selection of goals and infrastructures. If the function of marketing is seen as providing clients with information about products or services, different marketing tools and techniques will be employed than if marketing is primarily seen as persuading clients to buy certain products or services. Similarly, shared cognitive representations can also guide the development of certain routines in, for instance, the way organization members interact with clients. In the case of the psychologists' practice, it may be that in the course of time, a collectively held representation of different types of patients emerges, and along with it, ideas about how these types usually react to therapists and treatments. Such knowledge guides interaction with patients as it may, for instance, lead to assigning patients to certain therapists, or selecting certain types of treatment.

In general, then, it can be said that taken-for-granted, basic assumptions serve as interaction premises. They condition organizational interaction, in that they serve as a moral and cognitive background for *generating* and *evaluating* solutions to organizational problems of adaptation and realization (e.g. goals and infrastructures). They have a 'generative' moment, as they open up a space of possible goals and infrastructures. They also have an 'evaluative' moment, as the success of proposed solutions (goals and infrastructures) is always assessed against the background of the held basic assumptions. This may be problematic, as it can lead to a confirmation bias. In fact, given their embeddedness and the fact that they are taken for granted, it may be very hard to avoid this bias (and even to avoid self-fulfilling prophecies). For instance, based on a shared implicit idea that human beings basically act out of egocentric motives and will take advantage of others if given the opportunity (see Schein, 1992, pp. 23–24, for a similar example) it won't come as a surprise that some organizations decide that professionals working for them shouldn't be given too much autonomy. Instead, jobs should be designed in such a way that they grant professionals a minimum of discretionary freedom, and professionals should be monitored and controlled tightly. Given the resulting jobs and systems of accountability, professionals may, in turn, find that they can no longer do their jobs as professionals (as their discretionary freedom has been curtailed too much) and may drop out or start to behave in an unprofessional way – they may engage in box-ticking behaviour or in 'only' trying to reach the targets set for their work, targets which may have little to do with professional work, such as the infamous target of increasing 'patient satisfaction' (effects along these lines are vividly described by O'Neill, 2002; Schwartz and Sharpe, 2010). Based on the same basic assumptions that guided the design of the professional jobs and control systems in the first place, one may now evaluate the resulting unprofessional behaviour (box-ticking, only reaching pre-defined targets) as a proof of the untrustworthiness of professionals, and decide that jobs with even less autonomy and more control may be needed. Although this is a particularly gloomy picture of the role of basic assumptions, the fact that it is very difficult to escape them in generating and evaluating solutions to organizational questions remains. In fact, this may be one of the reasons why episodic interventions are sometimes needed, as they can help to break free from the deeply rooted beliefs about what is "right and good" (see also Schein, 1992, pp. 22ff, for the difficulty about moving beyond basic assumptions). We will pick up on this issue in Chapter 4.

Before we turn our attention to goals and infrastructures as interaction premises, we want to devote a final word to basic assumptions. From what we have discussed, it may appear that these assumptions only develop within an organization. Although a set of idiosyncratic assumptions can indeed emerge in an organization, or even in organizational sub-groups, it should be noted that values and cognitive schemes may have their origins beyond the 'confines of the organization'. If, in a certain community, child labour is disapproved of, up to the point that this disapproval is firmly embedded and taken for granted, this value will probably also be a part of the basic assumptions of organization members stemming from this community. It may thus condition interaction about, for instance, selecting suppliers. Similarly, societally acceptable ideas about human nature and accepted values regarding living a fulfilled human life may also act as organizational assumptions about dealing with clients and colleagues. In this way, "societal values are woven into the fabric of the organization" (Achterbergh and Vriens, 2010, p. 154). Something similar holds for the shared descriptive representations and frames that help to make sense of the world. This knowledge partly rests on previous extra-organizational experience and education, and is further refined and changed in the interactive practices of organization members. That basic assumptions extend organizational borders and can have their origins outside organizations is also a basic premise of institutional theory. As Suddaby and Viale (2011), for instance, write: "organizational actors are viewed as being embedded in institutionalized world views and taken-for-granted assumptions" (p. 425), and they explain that actors do not only attend to organization internal assumptions, but also to those stemming "from their institutional environments" (p. 425). And, given the embeddedness of actors in institutional environments, Suddaby and Viale also discuss that these world views and assumptions act as social institutional pressures, making it very difficult for actors to "conceive of alternate arrangements" (p. 425) – thus expressing an institutional theory version of the confirmation bias.

Goals and infrastructures as interaction premises

As we have discussed, shared basic assumptions serve as a background for generating and evaluating 'solutions' for the organizational issues concerning adaptation and realization. Based on them, organizational goals and infrastructural parts develop, which in turn affect organizational interaction. In the previous section, we discussed basic assumptions as interaction premises; in this section, we will discuss how organizational goals and infrastructural parts which develop against the background of basic assumptions also function as interaction premises.

That *goals* condition interaction means that organizational interaction should always relate to the formal or informal goals governing organizational activities. Similarly, the three *infrastructural parts* (human resources, technology, and structure) each condition interaction. For instance, human resources may condition interaction, which means, basically, that the particular individual organization members will refer to their individually held and shared knowledge, experience, values, and capacities as a background to engage in interaction. Technology can also condition interaction, as interaction can, for instance, be mediated by technology (e.g. ICT-based interaction), and technology can facilitate or frustrate interaction (e.g. the particular layout of workspaces can make it more or less easy to communicate with others). Finally, interaction can also be conditioned by the organizational structure, because the way tasks are defined and related to each other influences, for instance, which members interact with each other about which topics.

Formal and informal interaction premises

To further explain the conditioning nature of goals and the infrastructure, a distinction can be made between those goals and parts of the infrastructure which are formally decided upon and those which are not.

We'll say that goals and parts of the infrastructure are *formally* decided upon if they have been explicitly selected according to accepted organizational rules which were installed for making such selections. Premises which are selected according to such rules have a binding character, meaning that organization members are generally supposed to take these premises into account and can be held responsible for (not) doing so. Often, the rules governing the formal selection of an interaction premise as well as the formally selected premises themselves are made explicit in some medium (in a contract, a policy document, a code of conduct, a set of procedures, a description of tasks, etc.).

Take as an example hiring a new organizational employee. In this case, an individual is added as 'a part of the human resource part of the infrastructure' and as a member of the organization, given the specific knowledge, skills, and motivation, he or she will act as a premise, conditioning interactions. Hiring a new employee is a formal decision because it explicitly follows rules set for it, and once the decision is made, it has binding consequences. The rules set for selecting an employee may, for instance, be that the selection can only be made if a description of the position was made public, if internal and external candidates were able to react, if a selection committee was installed, if this committee agreed upon the relevant criteria for selection, if written applications and interviewed candidates were selected according to these criteria, if the selection was motivated, and if the selection was agreed upon by the senior human resources officer. Once the decision is made according to these rules, it has a binding character, granting the employee organizational rights and duties. In the case of hiring personnel, the set of rules which are followed are often written down in some document explaining how such decisions should be made. Similarly, the decision itself is also made explicit in, for instance, a contract. In this example, both the rules governing the decision and the decision itself have an explicit counterpart, but this need not always be the case for formal decisions, as we define them.

In general, the rules governing the decision to select an interaction premise (a goal or some part of the infrastructure) refer to the context in which a particular type of decision should be made, who should be involved in such decision, who has the authority to make the final decision, and under which conditions the decision is seen as a valid decision. These rules themselves also belong to the infrastructure – they are part of the structure. As a result, such rules can themselves be changed (most often only as a result of formal decision making). Once a decision about a goal or infrastructural part is made according to the accepted and agreed upon rules, it leads to a goal or infrastructural part (an interaction premise) which has a binding character. This means that members who do not take this (new) premise into account may formally be sanctioned for not doing so. If the task description of a doctor which has been formally decided upon indicates that some standard procedure should be followed when treating particular patients, disciplinary measures are possible if the doctor decides not to follow the procedure.

By contrast, *informal* interaction premises are not the result of an explicit decision following a set of explicit and accepted rules for them. As a simple example, suppose that one member of the psychology practice once started to check the amount of paper in the printer and refilled it when necessary. In due time, this may have developed into a habit, resulting in the fact that the paper only gets refilled by this person. Developing habits in this way may lead to an 'informal' task which has never been formally decided upon (following some explicit and accepted set of rules) and which is therefore not formally a part of one's job description. Nevertheless, the habit becomes an informal part of the structure and leads to expectations on the part of all involved. As such, it also conditions interaction.

Formal and informal goals and infrastructures as interaction premises

Given the distinction between formal and informal interaction premises, we can divide goals and infrastructures into two subclasses (see Table 2.1 for examples in each of these classes), which we will discuss briefly.

As Table 2.1 indicates, a distinction between formal and informal goals is possible (first row in the table). Formal goals are goals that result from explicit organizational (strategic) decision making and are guiding organizational interaction. For instance, decisions to produce

TABLE 2.1 Formal and informal interaction premises: some examples

	Formal	Informal
Goals	Formal goals (e.g. type of products; number of products)	Emergent, enacted goals
Infrastructural parts:		
Human resources	Membership Systems of accountability	Informal social norms about how organization members interact with each other
Structure	Formally defined task structure	Workarounds Side-stepping the hierarchy 'Informal' tasks
Technology	Acquired machinery, ICT, tools Formally defined architecture	Idiosyncratic/'performative' use of tools and space

2000 cars this month, to stop producing cars of type X, or to produce according to sustainable guidelines are *formal* interaction premises if they were decided according to the organizationally accepted rules governing those decisions (e.g. the rule that they have been made by those having the authority to make such decisions). Often such goals are made explicit in documents. Examples of informal goals are those that emerge from interaction and which need not be the same as the those that are formally decided upon. These are the 'lived' or 'enacted' goals (cf. Argyris and Schön, 1978). A formally stated goal may be 'sustainable production in every way conceivable', but the enacted goal may very well be a sub-standard version of this sustainability (e.g. because the current infrastructure doesn't allow for sustainability 'in every way conceivable').

Table 2.1 also gives examples of formal and informal infrastructural interaction premises. Applying this distinction to 'human resources and their characteristics' (second row) highlights as formal examples the decisions with respect to organizational membership of employees (see earlier text), or the formally installed systems of accountability by means of which employees are monitored, evaluated, and rewarded/sanctioned (e.g. Ferreira and Otley, 2009). An example of informal HR premises may refer to the set of informal social norms about how organization members are supposed to behave (cf. Scott, 2008, p. 55) towards each other or towards those outside the organization. Norms governing the interaction among organization members may, for instance, include ideas about whether or not it is acceptable to approach senior management by email, internal dress codes, the rituals and habits that emerge during meetings, whether or not one can expect to help or be helped, or that doing overtime is normal. In our example, norms regarding the interaction with those outside the organization may include the expectation that a patient is not sent away after a 45-minute consultation if he or she is showing strong emotions, or it may include the expectation about the types of clothes one wears when seeing a patient. Even though these expectations have not been formally selected as interaction premises, they do guide interactions. As sets of expectations, they define implicit boundaries for interaction. And, if violated, they may become an explicit subject of communication between organization members.

As can be seen in Table 2.1, a difference can also be made between a formally decided *structure* and the informal tasks emerging in interaction (third row in the table). The formally defined task structure refers to the tasks or job descriptions (in terms of explicitly defined targets, goals, and procedures) at several organizational levels (e.g. individual, team, departments), and to the formal linkages between these tasks (e.g. a plan indicating the routing of an order – including several different workstations) which were formally decided upon – e.g. selected by designers who had the explicit mandate and authority to define such a structure, or by managers who had the explicit authority to change parts of a previously designed structure. The paper-filling task discussed earlier is an example of an informal task – it emerged as a habit, and not as an explicitly selected task according to a set of rules governing the selection of a task. Other examples of informal tasks may include all kinds of ad hoc workarounds to fix problems emerging in the formal structure. For instance, a psychologist may find out that a general practitioner (GP) made a mistake in referring a patient. The formally decided structure prescribes that the patient should see the GP again, get a new referral, and have a new intake. A workaround may be to call the GP, ask to alter the referral, and to skip the intake. If this works out, it may develop into a practice which is employed every time mistakes are made. Side-stepping the hierarchy – e.g. directly asking a colleague to help solve a problem instead of first asking permission from a boss (if that is the formal way) – may be another example belonging to the informal structure. In some organizations, the inclusion of managers in case of problems emerging in primary processes may have become nothing more than a ritual – in such cases hierarchical relations may only exist on paper, and side-stepping the hierarchy may have become an informal practice. It should be clear that in all these cases, both formal and informal structures condition interaction: I may engage in interaction because it fits my formal job description, or because it has become an informal habit.

With respect to technology as a part of the infrastructure (last row in Table 2.1), a similar distinction between formal and informal may be applied. 'Formal' may refer to technology that has been acquired, installed, and used as a result of an explicit organizational decision following the rules set for it – for instance, the installation of a conveyer belt or a particular software application. Similarly, the layout of workstations or offices may have been designed in line with some accepted set of rules governing such decisions. However, the installed technology or a designed layout should be affirmed as relevant for carrying out work by those who use the technology. This affirmation is a social process of trial and error which may lead to context-specific, idiosyncratic applications (or 'non-applications') of technology. Given the actual practice of work, formally introduced technological artefacts may thus be understood and employed in ways that may not fit its formal intention. In fact, as Nicolini (2012) describes, the practice of our work determines how we understand, accept, and use technology. Informal technology, then, may refer to the specific, unintended use of the available decided technology. As with formal and informal structures, both types of technology may function as a background for organizational interaction.

'Culture' and interaction premises

In this section, we have discussed basic assumptions as well as (formal/informal) goals and infrastructures as interaction premises. In this discussion, basic assumptions appeared as a more or less shared moral and cognitive frame serving as a background for generating and assessing both formal and informal goals and infrastructures.

Until now, we haven't used the term 'culture', although (as used by authors such as Schein, 1992; Scott, 2008) it is closely related to the notions developed here. Of course, the 'basic assumptions' we discussed are the same as those of Schein, who describes them as the "essence of culture" (1992, p. 10). Moreover, the informal goals and infrastructures also often feature in descriptions of culture (e.g. as the informal norms and routines governing our behaviour). When we use the word 'culture' in this book, we refer to both the basic assumptions and to the informal/undecided goals and infrastructures. Of course, the formal goals and infrastructures also reflect basic assumptions (they can, in fact, be treated as Schein's artefacts) and hence always have a 'cultural' moment – but we will not refer to them as culture.

2.2.3 Social systems: the reciprocal relation between interaction and interaction premises

What is special about the relation between interactions and the interaction premises is that these premises not only condition interaction, they are also (partly) shaped, produced, and reproduced by the interactions they condition.

This reciprocal relation holds for goals and for the parts of the infrastructure. Goals, for instance, are set in interactions realizing the basic activity 'strategic regulation' and, as we discussed previously, once they are set, they function as interaction premises. Moreover, goals can also be reset by means of interaction, and hence it can be said that a set of goals is both a result and a condition for organizational interaction.

A similar reasoning holds for the (formal and informal) parts of the infrastructure: as set of interaction premises, they function as a condition for interaction (related to the four basic organizational activities), but as these infrastructural parts are either formally decided upon in interaction, or (as informal parts) gradually emerge and stabilize in interaction, they are also the result of these interactions.

Finally, the reciprocal relation also holds for the basic assumptions acting as a background for generating and assessing goals and infrastructures. As such, they condition interaction. And, as we discussed, these basic assumptions stabilize as a result of organizational learning processes with respect to implementing solutions to questions of adaptation and realization – learning processes that are realized in interaction.

Basic assumptions, goals, and infrastructural parts, then, condition organizational interaction, and this interaction, in turn, further shapes the basic assumptions, goals, and organizational infrastructures. In short, their relation is one of mutual dependence and co-constitution (see Figure 2.2).

With respect to the relation between interaction and interaction premises, some important remarks should be made.

The first remark has to do with the transient character of interactions and interaction premises. With other authors (e.g. Giddens, 1979; Luhmann, 1984) we regard both as changing phenomena, yet there is a difference with respect to their 'fluidity'. Interactions constitute a continuous flux. In this respect, Giddens (1979, pp. 8 and 27) describes how the 'durée of social life' consists of a continuous flow of action, and Luhmann (1984) describes organizational social systems as a continuous production of decisions by decisions. Interaction premises, although they also change as a result of the flow of interactions (either actions, communications, or decisions), have a more stable character. If they changed as quickly as interactions, they would lose their conditioning character.

A second remark relates to what we mean by 'conditioning'. Conditioning doesn't mean (a strict causal) determination of interactions. Although interaction premises differ in the way and degree to which they constrain or enable interactions, they do not strictly determine them.

38 Interventions in organizational structures

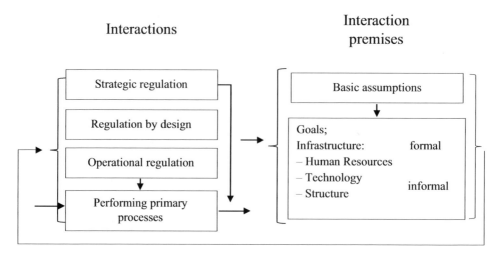

FIGURE 2.2 The relation between interactions and interaction premises

They act as (normative) points of reference for interactions (cf. Achterbergh and Vriens, 2010), and as a "social order" (cf. Schatzki, 2002) continuously opening up directions for the flux of interactions. In this way, interaction premises leave open the possibility of variations in interactions. As Luhmann (1984) would have it, interaction premises 'structure' the flow of interactions (communications in Luhmann's theory) by pointing at a set of possible, contingent 'follow-up' interactions from which one is 'selected'. It is important, then, that interaction premises do not causally determine the flow of interactions; they do, however (as Giddens, 1979, p. 25, would have it), "constrain and enable" this flow.

A third remark has to do with the relation between formal and informal interaction premises and how they condition interaction (see Figure 2.3).

In general, formal interaction premises (goals and parts of the infrastructure) have been formally selected to guide organizational interaction. As such, these premises are intended to have a binding character – i.e. interaction should take these premises into account (see earlier). And, as long as they do, interactions reinforce the formally selected premises.

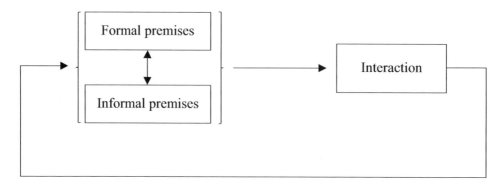

FIGURE 2.3 Relation between formal and informal premises and interaction

Moreover, as we have discussed, in interaction, goals and habits may evolve that do condition interaction, but that have never been formally decided upon. Such informal premises can exist alongside formal premises (one can imagine that the paper-filling task discussed previously can become a habit in some formally decided structure without harming this formal structure). But informal premises may also come into being instead of formal premises. In such a case, it may be that the formal premises are changed (because the emerging informal premises are taken as a sign that the formal ones have become obsolete), or it may be that the informal premises are called to a halt. As it is rather impossible to foresee and install *the* best possible formal premises (see later in the text), one should, as we will argue, design formal premises that allow for change. To explain: suppose, for instance, that a particular task has been defined formally. Organizational task-related interactions should be carried out given this formally defined task. However, it may by that while carrying out these interactions, it is discovered that there is a slightly better way to perform the task than formally defined. In interaction, one may go on experimenting and find even better ways without formally redefining the task. In such a case, an 'informal drift' occurs, resulting in an emerging practice which no longer fits the original formal structure. Based on the effectiveness of the resulting practice, it may be decided to redefine the formal structure. And this new structure may give rise to a new cycle of experimentation and 'informal drift'. As we will discuss below, formal premises should allow for such experimentation: they should always allow for their own change! Now, as will become apparent in Chapter 4, some arrangements of formal premises (for instance, formal structures like bureaucracies) have lost this capacity – they have become 'self-locking organizations' which call for episodic interventions.

A last remark about explaining organizations in terms of a mutually dependent relation between interactions and interaction premises is that this line of thought is discussed by other authors as well. It can, for instance, be found in Giddens' (1979) structuration theory when he discusses its main thesis, which he calls the 'duality of structure' (e.g. pp. 25ff). For Giddens, social systems "comprise the situated activities, reproduced across time and space" (p. 25), and the structures of social systems are "structural properties, [i.e.] the rules, and resources, or sets of transformation relations [. . .] constraining and enabling" the activities of a social system (p. 25). Given these descriptions, the central idea of duality of structure entails that "the structure, the structural properties of social systems are both medium and outcome or the practices they recursively organize" (p. 25). So the model can be related to structuration theory, in that Giddens' social system relates to the continuous flow of interactions, structure relates to Giddens' rules, resources and sets of transformation relations and the recursive relation between social systems, and structure is related to the mutually constitutive relation between interaction premises and interactions.

A similar comparison can be made with Luhmann's (1984) social systems theory. He describes organizations as a continuous process of 'self-production' – i.e. a process in which decisions produce follow-up decisions. This production process is structured by what he calls "decision premises". These decision premises select a set of possible follow-up decisions, from which one becomes the actual follow-up decision (for a detailed description, see Achterbergh and Vriens, 2010). In this way, the continuous flux of decisions is directed by decision premises. Moreover, decision premises can be altered by decisions, and if it they are, they will direct the production of decisions differently. Without going into the details of the production of decisions by decisions and the precise function of Luhmann's decision premises, it may be clear that decisions, decision premises, and their mutually dependent relation is closely related to our model of organizations. In fact, elsewhere (Achterbergh and Vriens, 2010) we stay closer to Luhmann and discuss organizations in terms of decisions and decision premises instead of interactions and interaction premises.

The basic reciprocal relation appearing in our model can also be found in both institutional and practice theory. Scott (2008), for instance, describes the relation between institutions and human interactions. He describes institutions as consisting of "rules, norms and cultural cognitive elements [...] that guide behavior" (p. 49). And he adds that "rules, norms and meanings arise in interaction, and [...] are preserved and modified by human behavior" (p. 49). So again, the distinction between interactions and interaction premises (for Scott: institutions) can be discerned, as can the recursive relation between them. This is not completely surprising, as Scott's description of institutional theory relies partly on the work of Giddens.

In practice theory, we can observe similar ideas (cf. Nicolini, 2012; Feldman and Orlikowski, 2011). Feldman and Orlikowski (2011, p. 1242) argue that a cornerstone of practice theory is the mutual constitutive relation between "social orders" and human agency. As they put it: "social orders (structures, institutions, routines, etc.) cannot be understood without understanding the role of agency in producing them, and, similarly, agency [...] must always be understood as already be configured by structural conditions". So again we recognize the central theme of interactions, interaction premises and their mutual constitutive relation. Many other authors have come up with similar thoughts (e.g. Bourdieu, 1977, 1990; Schatzki, 2002; Gherardi, 2000) – but here it suffices to say that our way of conceptualizing organizations has much in common with contemporary organizational theory.

2.3 Organizations aim at 'meaningful survival'

In the previous sections, we discussed the first characteristic of organizations as we conceptualize them. That is, we discussed organizations as social systems, consisting of interactions and interaction premises. In this section, we want to highlight a second characteristic of organizations, which is about their purpose. As discussed earlier, interactions in organizations are tied to four basic activities. By means of these activities, organizations set and realize goals. If goals can be realized in a better way, a change in the infrastructure is required. And if goals set by the organization are no longer seen as relevant, these goals should be reformulated, or the organization may decide to stop its activities – which also entails a reformulation of its goals. Formulating (and reformulating) goals and trying to realize these goals in an adequate way can be said to serve an overall organizational purpose: the organization's 'survival'. But, one may ask, what does survival mean?

As Beer (1979), for instance, describes it, organizational (or any system's) survival should be seen as "maintaining a separate existence in its environment". In this view, an organization should be able 'to continue to exist' in its environment. However, this description seems to be incomplete. Suppose, for instance, that an organization formulated the goal of eradicating malaria and that it succeeded in realizing that goal. By formulating this goal, the organization seems to aim for its own abolishment. Once it has reached its goal, there is no need for the organization to 'continue to exist' (cf. Achterbergh and Vriens, 2010, p. 10). Its existence has become pointless. 'Maintaining a separate existence' in its environment, then, is only relevant if it serves the provision of a meaningful contribution to the organization's environment. Otherwise, the separate existence is pointless. In line with this argument, we describe survival as 'maintaining a separate *and meaningful* existence'. We will refer to this description of survival as 'meaningful survival'.

The 'meaning' which is related to survival should be conceived as the intra-organizational conception of the contribution of the organization to society, and should be regarded as an answer to the question 'What is the point of the organization's survival?' Of course, there are many possible conceptions of this 'point' (e.g. increasing shareholder value, or contributing to creating conditions for societal members to live a fulfilled life – to mention but two possibilities). Our argument here is that survival without this 'meaning' doesn't make much sense.

Meaningful survival is in danger if an organization's contribution is (or threatens to be) no longer valued by the environment. In this case, goals expressing this contribution may be reformulated. Suppose, for instance, that the practice's contribution of 'delivering psychological care for psycho-somatic disorders' may no longer be valued by the environment because the government decided that such care should no longer be delivered by psychologists, but by psychiatrists. In this case, goals expressing a new contribution should be formulated, or the psychologists may decide to dissolve their practice.

Meaningful survival is also threatened if a contribution is not adequately realized. Suppose that the psychology practice sets out to deliver the contribution of providing psychological care to abused children – a contribution that *is* valued by the environment. However, unfortunately, the practice performs poorly, e.g. because it has to treat too many children, or because one of the psychologists turns out to lack the required experience. In that case, the infrastructure might be redesigned (e.g. by hiring extra personnel and/or introducing a system of training and supervision to deal with the inexperienced psychologist). Another possibility might be to set different targets (e.g. to limit the number of children the practice will treat). This latter solution belongs to strategic regulation.

So meaningful survival entails that organizations formulate goals that express a meaningful contribution to their environment and that this contribution is adequately realized. Therefore, meaningful survival depends on strategic regulation – i.e. the ability to formulate (and reformulate) goals expressing a meaningful contribution to its environment – and on the ability to realize this contribution by means of its primary processes (and their operational regulation). And as we have discussed previously, strategic regulation, primary processes, and operational regulation, in turn, require an adequate organizational infrastructure.

Meaningful survival, then, is what the four activities, and hence organizational interactions, aim at: by means of (re)formulating goals and realizing goals, organizations hope to maintain a separate, meaningful existence in their environment. At the same time, meaningful survival thoroughly depends on these four activities; if they fail, it may mean that goals become obsolete and/or that goals are no longer realized adequately. And, as these four activities depend on the organization's infrastructure, meaningful survival, in a sense, depends on the adequacy of this infrastructure.

2.4 Meaningful survival requires experimentation

Meaningful survival requires that organizations formulate goals expressing a meaningful societal contribution. In order to realize these goals, organizations should perform primary processes and operationally regulate them. Moreover, in order to formulate goals and realize them, organizations should design and implement adequate infrastructural conditions. However, all these organizational activities are inherently risky and uncertain.

To explain why these activities are risky and uncertain, it should first be stressed that there are always many possible goals, operational regulatory actions, and infrastructural configurations to choose from. So performing strategic regulation, regulation by design and operational regulation always involves selection. At the same time, because of the fundamental environmental and organizational complexity and uncertainty, there is no a priori or even a posteriori (experience-based) rule one can use to determine *with certainty* that one particular choice (with respect to goals, operational regulation, and infrastructural conditions) is the best alternative. And, as meaningful survival depends on goals, operational regulation, and infrastructures, this means that there is no way to determine with certainty how meaningful survival can be secured.

So, while carrying out the four organizational activities, we are always faced with uncertainty because we don't know beforehand the effect of a particular option (goals, infrastructural conditions, and operational regulatory actions) from which we have to choose. The activities are risky because even without this certainty, we need to select goals, operational actions, and infrastructural configurations. Securing meaningful survival, as it depends on uncertain activities and as selection is required, then becomes a risky endeavour.

This is common managerial knowledge, of course. Every manager knows that it is impossible to determine beforehand, with certainty, which set of goals will (continue to) express a meaningful contribution to the environment. Although we can gather information and make an educated guess about the (continued) appropriateness of goals, we cannot be certain. The best we can do is to formulate the 'hypothesis' that a particular set of goals will help us to survive meaningfully. After formulating these goals, we may try to realize them in the hope that they will indeed be appreciated as meaningful. In that case, we 'test' the hypothesis that these goals will help us to survive. However, it may turn out, at some point after their implementation, that these goals are not or are no longer valued and should be reformulated, e.g. because our assumptions were wrong, or because of changed circumstances. The moment that happens, a new hypothesis is formulated – the hypothesis that the *changed* set of goals will secure meaningful survival.

This process of (1) formulating a set of goals (per hypothesis), (2) testing (implementing and assessing) these goals (realizing them and finding out if they are indeed valued), (3) keeping them if it turns out that they are valued, and (4) reformulating them if it turns out that survival is threatened by keeping them is fundamental to strategic regulation. As we have no (and cannot have) complete knowledge about the environment and the future, this process is inescapable. So the child psychologists may formulate the goal 'providing psychological care for psycho-somatic disorders' in the hope that it expresses a meaningful and valued contribution. They may 'test' this hypothesis by actually providing this kind of care to find out just how meaningful it is. If they provide this care adequately and patients are and remain satisfied, the psychologists may stick to the hypothesis that this kind of care is indeed valued. However, the moment a change in governmental regulations makes this care no longer a relevant goal for the child psychology practice, a new hypothesis should be formulated – i.e. a new type of care should be provided. However, this new hypothesis is uncertain in the same way as the old one was, and so the process of experimenting with goals repeats itself.

We describe the process of 'formulating hypotheses, testing (implementing and evaluating) them, and reformulating them if needed' as a process of 'experimentation'. Previously, we described strategic regulation as an experimental process. Similarly, operational regulation and regulation by design are experimental processes. For instance, to deal with a disturbance, several options may be available – e.g. if one psychologist falls ill, the patients may be redistributed among the remaining psychologists, or they may have to wait until the psychologist returns. Now, if one chooses to redistribute the patients, one assumes that this will help to continue the primary process and in the end secure the meaningful survival of the practice. This assumption is a hypothesis about the effect of the regulatory measure, and is put to the test by actually redistributing the patients. However, it may turn out that patients don't want to be assigned to another therapist and would rather wait. In this case, the hypothesis 'redistributing patients is a good way to deal with the illness of a psychologist' is tested and evaluated to be wrong. Operational regulation is an experimental process. We cannot foresee all possible consequences of our actions and/or predict all changes in circumstances, so we necessarily have to act *ex hypothesi*. Of course, our accumulated knowledge about what did and didn't work in similar circumstances may guide us, but it cannot help us to gain certainty.

Similarly, choices with respect to infrastructural conditions (enabling the interaction realizing the four basic organizational activities) are uncertain, and hence regulation by design is also an experimental process. In this activity, the main hypothesis is: 'this particular set of infrastructural conditions will adequately enable the organization to perform the four organizational processes'. For each part of the infrastructure, this hypothesis can be refined (e.g. into 'This particular way of defining and allocating tasks . . .' or 'This particular physical layout of production facilities . . .' or 'This particular reward system to motivate personnel . . . will adequately condition the performance of the four activities') For the same reasons presented earlier, it is also impossible to know with certainty that a particular infrastructural configuration will be adequate, so regulation by design is also a risky affair.

In sum, strategic regulation, regulation by design, and operational regulation are 'experimental activities' – they necessarily have to rely on a continuous process of formulating, testing, and reformulating hypotheses. They are therefore inherently ongoing, risky activities. And, as meaningful survival depends on these activities, securing meaningful survival itself is an organizational experiment. As we describe in Achterbergh and Vriens (2010, p. 17), even though the choices made in the activities described are fundamentally uncertain, choices *have* to be made, otherwise meaningfulness is certainly threatened. Therefore, organizations necessarily and continuously conduct experiments.

2.5 Our perspective on organizations and episodic interventions

To summarize, our perspective on organizations entails that organizations are regarded as social systems in which organization members interact to realize four basic activities which are geared to experimenting with 'meaningful survival'. This interaction is conditioned by interaction premises, i.e. basic assumptions, and (formal and informal) goals and infrastructural parts. Moreover, we discussed that interaction and interaction premises are reciprocally related: interaction premises condition interaction, and by means of interaction, interaction premises change.

So what is at stake in organizations is meaningful survival. This entails (1) the continuous (re)production of the organization as a social system (i.e. the reproduction of the interaction premises enabling interaction, and the continuation of the interactions based on these premises), and (2) the adaptation and realization of the societal contribution of the organization – which occurs in interaction. The top of Figure 2.4 summarizes the idea of meaningful survival: the continuation of interactions (conditioned by interaction premises) realizing a particular societal contribution.

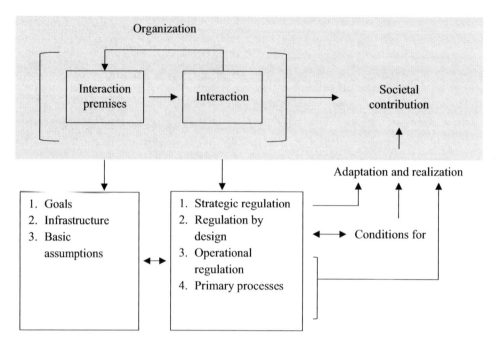

FIGURE 2.4 Summary of organizations as social systems experimenting with their meaningful survival

The experiment with meaningful survival entails that in interaction, four basic activities are realized. That is, by means of interactions related to the activity 'strategic regulation', meaningful survival is translated into relevant organizational goals defining the organization's societal contribution, and these goals are monitored and changed. In short, by means of strategic regulation, the societal contribution is 'adapted'. In addition, in interaction, primary processes are performed and regulated operationally, and in this way, the societal contribution translating meaningful survival is 'realized'. And lastly, interactions in organizations are also related to making sure that a (formal and informal) infrastructure is in place, which acts as a condition for the basic activities, and hence as a condition for adaptation and realization of the societal contribution. Moreover, we indicated that adaptation, realization, and selecting conditions are always risky and uncertain – and require continuous experimentation. The relation between the four basic activities and adaptation and realization of the organization's societal contribution is depicted at the right-hand bottom side of Figure 2.4.

As we discussed, interaction (by means of the four basic activities) is conditioned by interaction premises (basic assumptions, and both formal and informal goals and infrastructures), which, in turn, come about by means of interaction. Goals can be reset formally, or they can gradually shift emergently (informally) – which are both instantiations of strategic regulation. Similarly, infrastructures can change in a formal or informal way (formal or informal regulation by design). And, lastly, as a by-product of all four basic activities, basic assumptions can gradually change. So the relation between interaction premises and interactions is one of mutual dependence and constitution (see left-hand bottom side of Figure 2.4).

In all, experimenting with meaningful survival comes about in interaction (realizing the four basic activities), by means of which the societal contribution of the organization is adapted and realized. Moreover, interaction and interaction premises are reciprocally related: interaction is conditioned by interaction premises, and interaction co-constitutes the interaction premises.

What emerges from our perspective is that organizations are continuously changing: there is a continuous flux of interactions which is not only realizing and adapting meaningful survival, but which also results in change in the interaction premises conditioning them. Given this continuous change, one may ask whether episodic interventions are still relevant. Although this question will be answered in full in Chapter 4, we want to briefly present a preliminary answer.

As we discussed in this chapter, formal interaction premises – in particular the formally defined infrastructure – may sometimes cease to facilitate interactions in a proper way. They may hinder the ongoing experiment, and thus frustrate (1) the effective and efficient realization and adaptation of meaningful survival, and (2) the required change of the (formal) interaction premises. If interaction premises have been selected that no longer allow for their own change (or make such change very difficult), then, as we will argue, episodic interventions are needed. The aim of such interventions is to redefine the formal infrastructure in such a way that it can again condition interactions to effectively and efficiently realize the four basic activities and (as a part of it) change the interaction premises, if necessary (see Figure 2.5).

So, for instance, as many authors point out, machine bureaucracies have often lost the capacity to change the formal structure if the environment requires it. It is difficult to change the structure because the structure itself has been designed in such a way that tasks no longer have the overview nor the regulatory capacity to bring about the required change. In such cases, the change cannot come about given the current interaction premises; instead, these premises should first be changed themselves. And this change often requires an episodic intervention (for a similar line of argumentation, cf. van Amelsvoort, 1998; de Sitter, 1994).

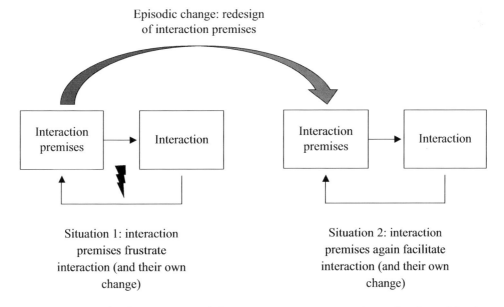

FIGURE 2.5 Episodic change is required if interaction premises can no longer be changed for the better by means of the interaction they condition

3

ORGANIZATIONAL STRUCTURES

Episodic Interventions in the Structure of Organization

PART I

Theoretical Framework:

– Organizations

– Organizational Structures

– (episodic) Interventions

PART II

A 3-D Model of Episodic Interventions:

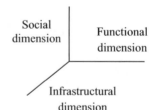

FIGURE 3.0 Roadmap of the book

3.1 Introduction

In this book, we discuss episodic interventions aiming at changing the *structure* of organizations. Therefore, it makes sense to devote some space to explaining these structures – the topic of this chapter. In previous chapters, we introduced the organizational structure as "the way tasks are defined and related into a network of tasks", and we discussed the relevance of the organizational structure as an interaction premise (i.e. as part of the infrastructure) conditioning organizational interaction.

As we will argue, the structure is a particularly relevant condition because it may take on a form which can severely frustrate the organization's continued meaningful survival. In such cases, the structure should be changed, but it can be that the structure has taken on a form which disables the required redesign of the (infra)structure itself (for similar reasoning, see Galbraith, 2000; de Sitter, 1994)! In these cases, the required change of the structure cannot be left to emergent or continuous change; it needs an episodic intervention.

Given this background, it is relevant to understand what adequate structures, i.e. structures enabling the continued experiment with meaningful survival, look like. Explaining these structures is the topic of this chapter. Unfortunately, this is a difficult and rather technical subject, and to help the reader digest it, we would like to start with an outline of the structure of our explanation (see Figure 3.1).

As we discussed in Chapter 2, organizational interaction refers to four basic activities: performing primary processes, operational regulation, regulation by design, and strategic regulation. In addition, we discussed that these interactions are conditioned by interaction premises, including goals, infrastructure, and basic assumptions. The organizational structure is part of the infrastructure, and hence co-conditions the basic activities (see left-hand side of Figure 3.1). Finally, we discussed that the basic activities aim to secure the organizational contribution to society (arrow A in Figure 3.1). These activities should also enable reflection on and adaptation of the interaction premises (arrow B in Figure 3.1). Based on these ideas, the desired contribution of an organizational structure can be stated: the overall function of the organizational structure is to contribute to enabling organizational interactions – the four basic activities – in such a way that (A) the organization's societal contribution is secured and (B) that the interaction premises may be altered (both formally and informally). In this chapter, we set out to explain this contribution of organizational structures.

Even though our argumentation is, at times, quite technical, the basic idea of 'adequate structures' is something that everyone who has ever worked in an organization can relate to. A structure is the way tasks are defined and related, so a job and its place in the network of jobs depend on the structure. And the way jobs are defined and related influences their efficiency and effectiveness and the quality of our working life. In fact, it is not difficult to see that some

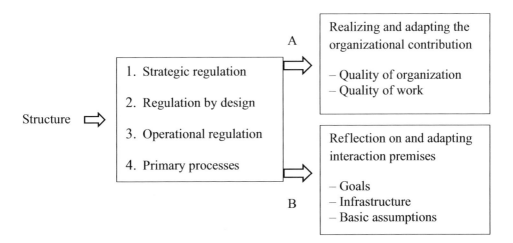

FIGURE 3.1 The contribution of the organizational structure

structures have a more positive influence than others. For instance, structures in which jobs contain only a few simple activities, in which jobs depend on many other jobs in the network, in which jobs face many disturbances, and in which jobs lack the potential to deal with these disturbances are often problematic structures. Such structures result in uninteresting, stressful work in which one may have a hard time realizing job targets. In this chapter, we will argue that structures with simple jobs which are related to and dependent on many other jobs (e.g. prototypical 'bureaucratic' structures) are often problematic structures, and that structures with more complex jobs which are less dependent on other jobs may be seen as better structures (cf. de Sitter, 1994; de Sitter and den Hertog, 1997; Nadler and Tushman, 1997).

We organize our argumentation as follows. We start by discussing the notion of organizational structures in Section 3.2, where we describe structures in a general way, and we introduce so-called design parameters to describe structures in more detail. Next, in Section 3.3 we turn our attention to *adequate* structures. As it will turn out, we derive requirements for adequacy from our model of organizations (as put forward in Chapter 2) and from organizational cybernetics. These requirements relate to effects A and B, as discussed previously. In Section 3.4 we discuss the *form* of adequate structures. Here, we apply the structural design parameters discussed in Section 3.2 and show that the requirements set for structures in Section 3.3 are met if these design parameters have particular (i.e. 'low') values. In Section 3.5 we conclude and relate our idea of adequate structures to our model of organizations and to episodic interventions.

3.2 Organizational structures

Quite generally, an organizational structure can be described as "a network of related tasks" (cf. Achterbergh and Vriens, 2010, p. 231). To understand what this network amounts to, we start off from Mintzberg's (1983) discussion of designing structures. As he describes it, designing a structure entails that one should first decompose the main organizational activity into various smaller sub-activities, assemble these sub-activities into tasks, and next, coordinate the resulting tasks. In this section, we will follow a similar logic: we argue that a task is a set of sub-activities allocated to some 'operational unit' (an individual, team, department, or other organizational unit), and we describe structures as networks of related tasks.

To discuss structures as a network of related tasks, we devote Sections 3.2.1–3.2.3 to introducing structures in a more general, intuitive way. We will first describe two general ways by means of which the main organizational activity can be decomposed into sub-activities, then we will describe how these sub-activities can be assembled into tasks, and how tasks are related into a network of tasks. In Section 3.2.4 we introduce so-called structural design parameters to be able to describe structures in a more detailed way.

3.2.1 A general approach to defining organizational structures (1): two ways of decomposing organizational activities

We define a task as a set of sub-activities which comes into existence by decomposing the main organizational activity. In order to understand this definition, it should first be clear what an activity is and how it can be decomposed into sub-activities.

Following Ashby's (1958) ideas on transformations, an activity can be said to consist of three parts: a begin state, a process, and an end state (see Figure 3.2). An activity refers to the unity of these three parts, and highlights that there is some process causing the begin state to change into the end state. The main activity describing, for instance, an organization making wooden furniture consists of a begin state – consumers who want to be provided with furniture (an order) and material input (e.g. wood) – and a desired end state – consumers who received the requested furniture. The process should make sure that this end state is realized (see Figure 3.2)

All activities, thus conceived, can be decomposed into sub-activities in at least two basic ways: with respect to 'parts', and with respect to 'aspects' (cf. de Sitter, 1994; Achterbergh and Vriens, 2010).

A decomposition of an activity A with respect to its 'parts' defines two or more activities, which, in sequence, realize the end state of A. In this way, the main activity A is split up into several sub-activities which realize a part of the total activity A. Figure 3.3 depicts how two new sub-activities can be defined by decomposition with respect to parts. This is done as follows: the begin state of the first sub-activity (A1 in Figure 3.3) is also the begin state of the original activity A, and the end state of the first sub-activity is the begin state of the second sub-activity, etc. The end state of the last sub-activity (A2 in Figure 3.3) is also the end state of the original decomposed activity A. So, for instance, the activity A, 'providing customers with wooden furniture', can be decomposed 'partially' into several sub-activities: 'sawing', 'drilling', 'painting', 'assembling', 'storing', and 'transporting'. These sub-activities are sequentially related to providing wooden furniture. They all have their own partial desired end state, of which the last end state coincides with the end state of the

FIGURE 3.2 The main activity of an organization making furniture

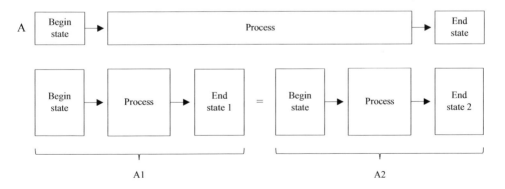

FIGURE 3.3 Decomposition with respect to parts of an activity into two sub-activities

Note: End state 1 is the inserted end state. End state 2 is the same as the original end state.

50 Interventions in organizational structures

original activity. Decomposition with respect to parts always involves 'inserting' desired end states between the original begin state and end state, and defining processes of sub-activities that, in sequence, realize all the resulting end states (both the inserted ones and the original end state).

Activities can also be decomposed into 'aspect-related' sub-activities. In this case, a characteristic (an aspect) of the *whole* activity is identified, which is then used to define two (or more) sub-activities. These 'aspectual' sub-activities do not insert end states between the original begin state and end state. Rather, they still cover the complete original activity (from begin state to end state), but only with respect to the selected characteristic. For instance, suppose the organization producing furniture makes tables and chairs. In this case, one can select the characteristic (aspect) 'type of furniture' to distinguish two sub-activities: one sub-activity providing chairs, and one providing tables. These sub-activities only relate to one aspect of the begin state and the end state: i.e. to one type of furniture (see also Figure 3.4). So each of the two sub-activities is only tied to one ('its own') type of furniture. Beside 'type of product', other aspects can also be selected for identifying sub-activities, like:

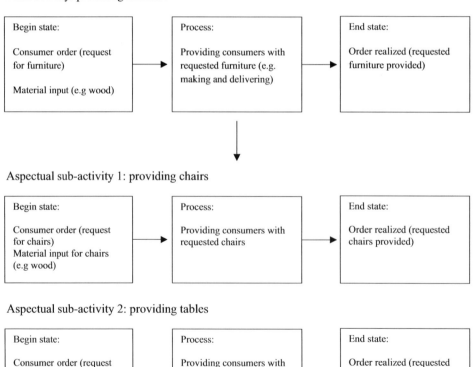

FIGURE 3.4 Example of two aspectual sub-activities

Note: The aspect chosen is type of output.

'type of clients' (e.g. resulting in sub-activities providing furniture for industrial and non-industrial clients) or 'geographical region' (with sub-activities servicing their own region) (for such aspects, see Mintzberg, 1983; de Sitter, 1994).

There is one case of aspectual decomposition that merits special attention: the difference between a so-called 'operational' and 'regulatory' aspect of an activity can be used for identifying specific sub-activities. As de Sitter (1994) argues, every activity has an *operational* aspect which refers to the activities actually realizing the end state. For making furniture, it may consist of the activities sawing, drilling, assembling, and painting. The *regulatory* aspect refers to all activities enabling the smooth performance of these operational activities – i.e. activities that make sure that one knows what to make (goals have been set), that the means for making the furniture are available (the infrastructure is in place), and that disturbances are dealt with (operational regulation).

The regulatory aspect of an activity, then, refers to strategic regulation, regulation by design, and operational regulation. The operational aspect refers to the activities realizing the output. If these aspects are used to define tasks, regulatory and operational sub-activities are identified and assembled into regulatory and operational tasks.

In all, activities can be decomposed in two basic ways. Moreover, decomposed activities can themselves be decomposed. It is possible to repeatedly apply the two forms of decomposition and end up with a large set of sub-activities.

3.2.2 A general approach to defining organizational structures (2): defining and relating tasks

Given a set of sub-activities – resulting from repeatedly applying the two basic forms of decomposition to the organization's main activity – a task can be defined by assigning a sub-set of these sub-activities to some 'operational unit', i.e. someone or some group of individuals responsible for realizing this sub-set of activities. A task, then, describes which operational unit should perform which set of sub-activities. Note that a task implies that the operational unit has the tools/equipment to carry out the assigned sub-activities. Tasks can be defined at several organizational levels (business units, department, team, or individual members).

If tasks are defined by assigning sub-activities in this way, dependency relations between tasks also come into being. That is, the two forms of decomposition of an activity immediately imply a relation between the resulting sub-activities. A decomposition of an activity with respect to parts results in at least two sub-activities which are sequentially related. Similarly, a decomposition with respect to aspects stresses the dependence of a set of tasks dedicated to one aspect (e.g. one type of client or product) and the independence of tasks which are dedicated to different aspects (i.e. other types of clients or products), or it stresses the relation between regulatory tasks and operational tasks. So, by defining tasks, their position in a network of tasks also becomes apparent.

The configuration of tasks, i.e. the grouping of sub-activities into tasks and the relations between tasks in a network, is what we call the 'organizational structure' (here, we follow de Sitter, 1994). In addition, de Sitter (1994, p. 91) identifies two sub-structures:

1. the production structure – the grouping and coupling of operational tasks;
2. the control structure – the grouping and coupling of regulatory tasks.

With respect to our model of organizations, the production structure has to do with realizing the primary processes, while the control structure relates to tasks that realize the three forms of regulation.

To summarize, a structure has been introduced as a network of related tasks, and designing a structure involves: (1) decomposing the main activity into sub-activities, and (2) defining tasks, i.e. selecting sub-activities and assigning them to operational units. Moreover, by defining tasks, relations between them are also introduced, thus resulting in network of tasks.

Given a set of sub-activities resulting from repeatedly decomposing the main activity, quite a large number of structures (networks of related tasks) is possible, and a relevant question for designing structures is how to arrive at an *adequate* one. This question will be the topic of Sections 3.3 and 3.4.

At this point, we need to say a few words about the difference between formal and informal structures, as introduced in Chapter 2. As we discussed, a structure is formally decided upon if it has been explicitly selected according to accepted organizational rules which were installed for making structural selections. By contrast, an informal structure is not the result of a decision following a set of explicit and accepted rules for them. Formal structures are always the result of explicit intentional deliberation. Informal structures may be arrived at explicitly or implicitly. As an example of an implicit structural change, we discussed a case in which a sub-activity (refilling paper for a printer) was implicitly assigned to one of the members of the organization. Now, the 'procedure' or logic for arriving at a structure (decomposition into sub-activities, selection of sub-activities into tasks, relating tasks into a network) may seem to have been introduced as a deliberative, discursive, and intentional set of activities. And, indeed, sometimes it is, and may be employed to arrive at a formal or informal structure explicitly. However, as informal structures can also change less deliberatively and intentionally, the procedure needn't always be followed explicitly and intentionally. However, in the remaining sections we will discuss designing structures as an intentional, deliberate activity, resulting in a formal structure, without denying informal change and the fact that formal structures, once designed, may immediately start to change informally.

3.2.3 A general approach to defining organizational structures (3): a simple example

To appreciate the definition and relation of tasks into an organizational structure, based on the previous two forms of decomposition, let's consider a simple example of a butcher who wants to design a structure (i.e. defining and relating tasks) involving four persons: three apprentices and the butcher himself. In order to design a structure, he first decomposes the main activity realizing the raison d'être of the butcher's business: providing clients with meat. Possible decompositions are:

1. A decomposition into an operational and regulatory sub-activity – in this case, the operational sub-activity refers to activities like preparing meat, displaying meat, and selling meat. The regulatory sub-activity includes strategic, design, and operational regulation.
2. The operational sub-activity can be decomposed into parts, using the activities mentioned previously as a point of departure. This results in three new sub-activities: preparing meat, displaying meat, and selling meat.
3. The regulatory sub-activity can be further decomposed into three new sub-activities: strategic regulation, regulation by design, and operational regulation.

These three decomposition steps result in six sub-activities, which now have to be assigned to the four persons and related into a structure (please note that this is just a simple example – more sub-activities can be thought of).

One way of doing this is depicted in Figure 3.5a. In this structure, the butcher himself performs the regulatory sub-activities and the apprentices each perform one of the operational sub-activities. So, out of the set of resulting sub-activities, the three regulatory sub-activities are all assigned to the butcher – thus defining his task. Similarly, the apprentices have as their task only one operational sub-activity. This resembles a rather standard sequential structure with operational job specialization (cf. Mintzberg, 1983; Thompson, 1967). Another structure is depicted in Figure 3.5b. Here, the apprentices all have a similar task – i.e. all three of them prepare, display and sell meat. This resembles a more 'horizontal' or 'parallel' structure (cf. Daft, 2009; de Sitter, 1994).

Notice that, as we just said, both ways of assigning tasks already implies particular relations between the tasks. Regulation, for instance, implies an activity that is regulated. Similarly, decomposition into parts implies that tasks are sequentially related. So, in relating tasks into a structure, these implied relations should be taken into account. In the structure

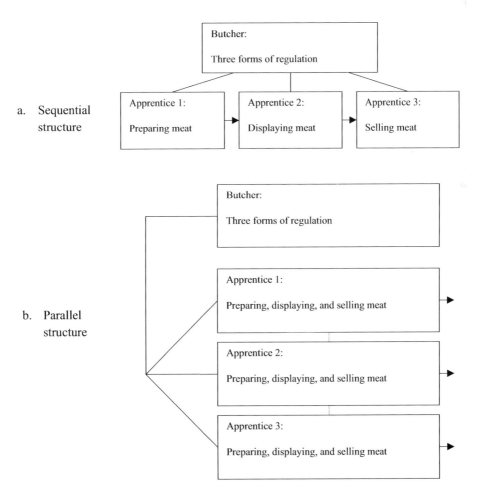

FIGURE 3.5 Two examples of a structure

in Figure 3.5a, for example, the sequential relations between the operational tasks and the relation between regulatory and operational tasks are depicted. In Figure 3.5b there is no sequential relation, but operational tasks are related in the sense that apprentices should not hinder each other in performing their tasks, or should take care of shared resources, although, strictly speaking, this is a form of operational regulation, which might be assigned to the apprentices as well. In fact, in both structures, normally, some form of operational regulation may be assigned to operational capacities, i.e. to deal with small disturbances, but this need not distract us here.

3.2.4 A more detailed approach to defining organizational structures: structural design parameters

Previously, we used two basic types of decomposition to describe organizational structures. However, describing structures can be done in a much more detailed way, using so-called 'design-parameters', which are, in fact, specific instantiations of decomposition in parts and aspect. Design parameters have been developed and discussed by several authors in organization theory (e.g. Pugh et al., 1968; Donaldson, 2001; Mintzberg, 1983; Nadler and Tushman, 1997; Galbraith, 1977; de Sitter, 1994; de Sitter and den Hertog, 1997). Although different authors discuss different parameters, we will use the set of seven parameters proposed by de Sitter (1994), as it seems to be a complete set and effectively encompasses most of the parameters put forward by others. We will argue that every organizational structure can be described by means of these parameters. That is, each of these parameters can have different 'values', and, dependent on these values, the organization's structural layout has particular characteristics, enabling or disabling organization members to act in particular ways. For instance, if the value of the design parameter 'separation' (see later text) is 'high', organization members in the operating core of the organization have little decision authority regarding the regulation of their own work (cf. Pierce and Delbecq, 1977). This may not help them to learn to solve job-related problems by themselves. By contrast, if the value of this parameter is 'low', organization members in the operating core do have regulating capacity to deal with job-related problems themselves. In this way, design parameters can be used to *describe* structures. Moreover, design parameters can also be used in a *normative* way. That is, given (context-dependent) desired values of the design parameters, one can design or redesign an organizational structure and make sure that the parameters reach these values. In this book, this normative use of design parameters is relevant, as it is our main thesis that *episodic interventions in organizational structures should be geared to changing the structure into one which has low parameter values.*

In this section we discuss the seven design parameters proposed by de Sitter (1994) and explain what it means to have 'high' and 'low' values. As will become apparent, three types of design parameters can be distinguished:

1. those related to the production structure; in particular, we distinguish three parameters of this type:
    a. the degree of functional concentration;
    b. the degree of differentiation of operational activities;
    c. the degree of specialization of operational activities;

2. those related to the control structure, in particular:
   a. the degree of differentiation of regulatory activities into parts;
   b. the degree of differentiation of regulatory activities into aspects;
   c. the degree of specialization of regulatory activities;
3. one design parameter describing the relation between operational and regulatory activities, and hence the relation between the production and control structure – the degree of separation.

In the text that follows, we'll go into to these three classes of design parameters.

Design parameters describing the production structure

Degree of functional concentration

The first parameter describing the production structure refers to the relation between operational tasks and order types. In particular, we define the degree of functional concentration as the degree to which operational tasks are (potentially) related to all order types (cf. the parameter 'functional concentration' as discussed by de Sitter, 1994, and Achterbergh and Vriens, 2010).

In this definition, an order is a specific, individual demand for a product or service, e.g. a client demanding a particular chair or some form of care. An order type is a particular sub-set of all orders, e.g. all demands for a particular type of chair, or all furniture made for the south region. Now, given several order types (and such sub-sets can always be identified – see later text), a maximum (i.e. high) degree of functional concentration means that all operational activities are potentially related to all order types. Typically, organizations with high functional concentration have operational units (e.g. functional departments) in which tasks are clustered based on the similarity of activities, or knowledge and skill (cf. the idea of functional grouping in Mintzberg, 1983). As an example of a high degree of functional concentration, consider a factory producing two types of chairs and three types of tables (so, based on this output, one may identify five sub-sets of specific orders – five order types). In this factory, all operational activities are grouped into operational departments: all sawing activities are grouped into a 'sawing department', all drilling activities into a 'drilling department', all painting activities into a 'painting department', and all assembly activities into an 'assembly department'. Each operational department processes all five types of furniture, hence all operational activities are potentially coupled to each of the order types (see Figure 3.6a). So, in this factory, someone who is assigned to a 'sawing' task may be sawing pieces of wood for all types of furniture. In fact, all operational employees are potentially coupled to all order types.

Lower degrees of functional concentration entail that operational tasks are *not* coupled to all order types – but only to one or a few of them. Given several order types, one way to decrease functional concentration is to make sure that each of the defined order types has its own dedicated set of operational activities. In this case, organizational units are formed which have their own personnel and equipment dedicated to their 'own' order type. For instance, with respect to the factory producing the five types of chairs and tables (i.e. five order types), a decreased level of functional concentration might be attained by making sure

56 Interventions in organizational structures

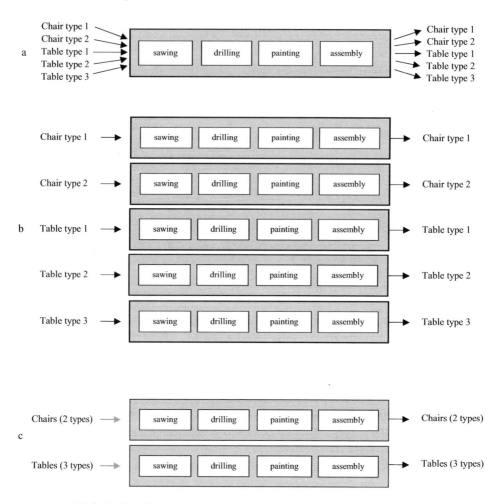

FIGURE 3.6 High (a), low (b) and intermediate (c) functional concentration

that each type of chair and table has its own dedicated set of activities (see Figure 3.6b). In this case, five dedicated sets of activities (relatively independent 'parallel production flows') can be recognized.

In Figure 3.6c an intermediate level of functional concentration is given, with two relatively independent sets of activities, one dedicated to two order types (the two types of chairs) and one dedicated to three order types (the three types of tables).

For both cases, it should be noted that the operational tasks in the 'parallel units' are only coupled to the order type(s) this unit is dedicated to. So, in Figure 3.6b an employee with a 'sawing' task working in the unit related to chair type 2 only performs this task for this type of chair – not for tables. This task is therefore only coupled to orders for chair type 2 – it is not coupled to the other order types. Something similar holds for the situation in Figure 3.6c, only now employees are coupled to more order types. Hence, the degree of functional concentration in Figure 3.6b is lower than that of Figure 3.6c because, as the number of order types with their own dedicated sets of operational tasks is higher in Figure 3.6b, an (average) operational task is potentially coupled to fewer order types.[1] So, given the proviso stated in note 1, the greater the number of (groups of) order types with their own dedicated set of operational activities, the lower the functional concentration.

Sometimes, it may not be possible or feasible to further decrease the level of functional concentration. For instance, if all order types in some factory have an operational activity in common which requires expensive and complex technology, it may be impossible to organize independent flows for each order type and equip them with this technology. In such a case, this resource should be shared and the activity employing this resource might be coupled to all order types. Such resources limit the degree to which functional concentration can be decreased. However, flows can still be built which are as independent as possible, i.e. flows which are dedicated to a sub-set of orders as far as possible, but share the undividable capacities. Another example of a situation in which there is a limit to the number of independent flows has to do with the degree of capacity utilization per flow. If flows emerge that produce a sub-set of orders for which there is limited demand, these flows may be inefficient. De Sitter (1994, p. 155) introduces a minimum capacity utilization percentage of 80 as a heuristic. Whether this number is correct in all situations is immaterial; what is relevant here is that inefficient flows (in terms of underutilization) should be avoided.

In the previous explanation, we used product types to identify order types. However, the total set of orders may be split up into different sub-sets (order types) in a number of ways. Order types for the furniture factory may, for instance, be (1) tables and chairs (here, there are only two order types) or (2) large tables, large chairs, small tables, and small chairs (four order types) or (3) oak, pine, and plastic furniture (three order types). Several authors discuss a number of bases for identifying order types. Mintzberg (1983, pp. 48–49), for instance, mentions:

- place – referring to where a segment of the market demanding orders resides, resulting in geographical order-categories, such as orders for region north, orders for region south;
- client – classifying orders in terms of the types of clients demanding them, such as large industrial clients or small business clients, public or private clients;
- output – classifying orders based on the products or services provided, such as types of furniture, types of healthcare.

More criteria for defining sub-sets of orders have been discussed (e.g. de Sitter, 1994), but the above suffice for our purposes.

The degree of functional concentration is relative to the number of order types that are defined. But of course, the more order types that can be defined and serve as a suitable base for independent parallel production flows, the lower functional concentration can get. So, if one is to look for low functional concentration, one option is to define as many suitable order types (with their own dedicated set of operational activities) as possible. We'll go into defining and designing flows in much more detail in Chapter 6.

A final remark about functional concentration has to do with the difference between so-called 'internal' and 'external' order types. Previously, the orders are demands placed by external customers which could be clustered into several types, serving as a base for identifying units with their own dedicated production flows dedicated to these order types. However, as de Sitter (1994), explains, 'orders' can also be seen as *internal* requests for particular output. For instance, an assembly department which assembles 20 different product modules (which come from the production department) into six different products, can be said to place 20 'orders' with the production department (every time they are assembled). These are internal, rather than external orders. Now, the same logic of determining functional concentration as explained previously can be applied based on internal orders. Suppose that these product modules (just like the type of furniture previously) are treated as order types. In that case, the functional concentration of the production department is high if all tasks of that department are potentially coupled to all product modules. It is lower if these modules are produced in, say, four parallel production flows (each making five modules) to which tasks in that flow are dedicated. This leads to decreased functional concentration in only part of the organization (the production department). And so, even though the modules are part of all external orders (and hence, functional concentration based on external order types is high), functional concentration based on internal orders can be decreased.

If we consider the difference between external and internal orders, the parameter 'degree of functional concentration' should also be adapted to include both types of orders. It should be noted that identifying external order types mostly has a higher impact on the degree of functional concentration than internal order types, as identifying flows based on external order types affects all operational tasks, while internal order types only affect tasks in a part of the operational process (e.g. in the previous example, it only affects tasks in the production department). In the remainder of this chapter, we will refer to functional concentration based on external order types. The difference between 'internal' and 'external' order types (and their associated flows) will be picked up when designing organizations at a 'macro' and 'meso' level (see Chapter 6).

Degree of differentiation of operational tasks

The second design parameter related to the production structure takes de Sitter's (1994) notion of differentiation of operational activities into 'production', 'preparation', and 'support' activities as a point of departure. Operational activities (e.g. those related to producing chairs – see the earlier example) may refer to (1) activities that actually produce a chair ('production' activities, like sawing, drilling, painting and assembling) or to (2) 'preparation' activities, i.e. activities required to make all the necessary material, tools and information available for the production activities (e.g. planning, providing raw-material, or installing machines). Both production and preparation activities are directly order-related. That is, for each specific set of orders, preparation and production activities are required to make sure that this specific set of orders is realized. For instance, a specific set of orders requires specific planning and a specific amount of raw material (preparation). It also requires the performance of a specific set of production activities producing this specific set of orders.

The third set of operational activities is called support activities. These are not directly tied to orders, but help to realize and connect the two other operational activities which *are* directly tied to producing output. This third set of operational activities includes, for instance, maintenance, technical services, or internal logistics.

Now, the design parameter 'degree of differentiation of operational tasks' has a maximum (high) value if operational activities are grouped into separate 'production', 'preparation', and 'support' tasks. It has a minimum (low) value if operational tasks include production, preparation, and support activities. So an organization with a high value on this design parameter has separate planners, salespeople, material handlers, maintenance employees, and workers responsible for production activities. In an organization with lower values on this design parameter, employees may, for instance, have a task in which they have to perform production activities, co-decide on the planning, and take care of the daily maintenance of the equipment they use themselves.

Degree of specialization of operational tasks

The third design parameter, the degree of specialization of operational tasks, refers to the degree to which operational tasks contain only a small part of the complete operational process. The degree of specialization has a minimal (low) value if operational tasks cover the complete operational process – e.g. like a traditional carpenter in his own studio responsible for all operational activities necessary for making a table. The degree of specialization increases if the complete operational process is split up into sub-activities and if these sub-activities are allocated to separate tasks. In this way, employees only perform a small part of the complete operational process. In a factory producing tables, one employee may, for instance, only perform the drilling activity. Two prototypical organizations with a high value on this parameter are 'functional organizations' and 'line organizations' (cf. de Sitter, 1994). In functional organizations, departments exist in which employees perform similar specific sub-activities of the complete process of realizing an order (e.g. a factory producing furniture with separate sawing, drilling, painting, and assembling departments). Line organizations are organizations with conveyer belt-like sequential production processes. In these organizations, employees typically only perform a very small part of the total production process.

Of all the design parameters, this is the one on which almost all authors agree. It is often referred to as division of labour (as described by Adam Smith in 1776; see Smith, 1977), specialization (Pugh et al., 1968), or (horizontal) job specialization (Mintzberg, 1983).

Design parameters describing the control structure

Degree of differentiation of regulatory activities into 'parts'

To explain this design parameter, it should first be acknowledged that the activity of regulation necessarily includes three sub-activities ('parts'): 'monitoring', 'assessing', and 'acting' (cf. de Sitter, 1994) Suppose that someone is performing an operational activity – say, making a chair – and that this activity is being regulated. This regulation, which was defined as dealing with disturbances, includes monitoring of 'what is going on' with respect to the operational activity. Typically, monitoring requires a set of indicators which define what should be monitored, such as quality indicators (e.g. whether a chair passes some durability test) or quantity indicators (e.g. the number of chairs produced in a week). Basically, monitoring refers to gathering information with respect to these indicators. Regulation also requires assessing whether 'what is going on' is desired or not. Typically, assessment includes a comparison of the indicator values with norm values and a judgement with respect to their difference (e.g. this week we will produce ten chairs less than agreed upon, but this is due to the fact that one employee is ill, so the difference should not be seen as a serious structural problem). And, finally, regulation requires 'acting', i.e. taking some measures to make sure that a problematic difference between actual and desired values on the indicators regarding the operational activities is dealt with. This can refer to all forms of regulation (i.e. operational regulation, regulation by design, and strategic regulation – see later text). Now, the degree of differentiation of regulatory activities into parts has a maximal (high) value if the monitoring, assessment, and acting sub-activities are assigned to different tasks. It has a low value if these sub-activities are integrated into one task.

Degree of differentiation of regulatory activities into 'aspects'

To understand this design parameter, we refer back to Chapter 2, in which we explained that in organizations, three forms of regulation exist: strategic regulation (setting and resetting goals), regulation by design (designing and redesigning the infrastructure), and operational regulation (dealing with day-to-day disturbances in operational processes given the existing goals and infrastructure) – see also the previous section. The degree of differentiation of regulatory activities into aspects has to do with whether these three forms ('aspects') of regulation are assigned to separate tasks or whether tasks exist containing all three forms of regulation. A high value of such differentiation means that different forms of regulation are assigned to different tasks – e.g. an organization in which the board makes strategic decisions, the 'technostructure' (cf. Mintzberg, 1983), is responsible for designing and redesigning the infrastructure, and operational managers take care of operational regulation. Low values of this type of differentiation entail that tasks contain all three forms of regulation. This can be found in a small enterprise in which the owner makes her own strategic decisions, designs her own shop, and regulates operational activities herself. Intermediate levels refer to organizations in which, for instance, teams of operational employees also perform operational regulation, and co-decide on and co-implement the infrastructure (e.g. with respect to the type of tools and equipment they use), and are involved in setting goals for their work. Several professional organizations in healthcare have transformed their structure to include tasks with a low level of this form of differentiation (see later text).

Degree of specialization of regulatory activities

Just like operational activities, regulatory activities can also be broken down into small sub-activities, irrespective of parts and aspects. So, instead of monitoring a complete operational process, one can also design two, three, or more tasks responsible for monitoring one half, one third, or even a smaller proportion of the complete operational process. Or one can design operational regulation only focusing on product quality or on efficiency. In a hierarchical setting, regulatory tasks can also focus on other regulators. In that case, specialization of regulation means that the number of regulatory tasks under supervision decreases. Instead of one task in which 20 sales managers are monitored, two new tasks may emerge, each monitoring ten sales managers. A high degree of specialization of regulatory activities means that the regulatory scope (e.g. part of the production process, or scope of control) becomes smaller. A low degree of specialization of regulatory activities means that regulatory tasks have a broader scope in terms of a larger part of the operational process or a larger number of regulators under supervision.

Design parameter describing the relation between operational and regulatory activities (and hence the relation between the production and control structure)

Degree of separation

This design parameter refers to the degree to which regulatory and operational activities are assigned to different tasks. As we discussed previously, de Sitter (1994) points out that every activity has a regulatory and an operational aspect. Separation refers to the degree to which these two aspects are assigned to different tasks. A maximal (high) value of this design parameter leads to structures in which operational tasks contain as few regulatory activities as possible. Organizations with a minimal (low) value on this parameter consist of tasks in which operational and regulatory activities are integrated as much as possible. Organizations with a high value on this parameter have one set of tasks dedicated to the production structure and a separate set of tasks dedicated to the control structure. By contrast, in organizations with a low value, tasks contain activities relating to both structures.

Separation entails assigning the regulatory and operational aspects to different tasks. This holds for every activity, and therefore also for regulatory activities such as operational regulation, regulation by design, or strategic regulation. These activities, too, have an operational and a regulatory aspect. For instance, the operational part of 'operational regulation' is performing all the sub-activities required to carry out a particular way of dealing with a disturbance. It includes, for instance, monitoring, assessment and implementation activities. These operational activities themselves require goals (norms used in the assessment step) which are provided by strategic regulation, infrastructural conditions (which are the result of regulation by design), and as sub-activities, may themselves be subject to disturbances (e.g. something goes wrong during assessment): operational regulation itself requires 'operational regulation'. As separation is about assigning regulatory and operational aspects of activities to different tasks, and as this may refer to all type of activities, including regulatory activities, it may lead to a hierarchy of regulatory activities.

3.2.5 Describing organizational structures: a brief summary

The aim of Section 3.2 was to introduce the notion of organizational structure. After a general introduction, we argued that every structure can be described in terms of seven structural design parameters. Each structure has particular values on these parameters. To illustrate, Figure 3.7 shows a description of a structure in terms of its values on the design parameters.

In all, the design parameters are our way of operationalizing organizational structures (see Figure 3.8). This way of describing structures will also help us to delineate adequate structures. That is, as will become apparent in the rest of this chapter, we argue that inadequate structures have high values on all/most design parameters and that adequate structures have low values. However, before we can understand why 'low parameter value structures' are the better ones, we first need to explain what we mean by 'adequate' structures – the topic of the next section.

3.3 Adequate organizational structures: requirements

As we discussed in Chapter 2 and in Section 3.1, the main function of an organizational structure (as part of the infrastructure) is to enable the continuous meaningful survival of the organization. This, in turn, entails that a structure should contribute to enabling organizational interactions (i.e. the four basic activities) in such a way that (A) the societal contribution is secured, and that (B) interaction premises can be reflected upon and altered (see arrows A and B in Figure 3.8). Therefore, the overall description of adequate structures can already be

62 Interventions in organizational structures

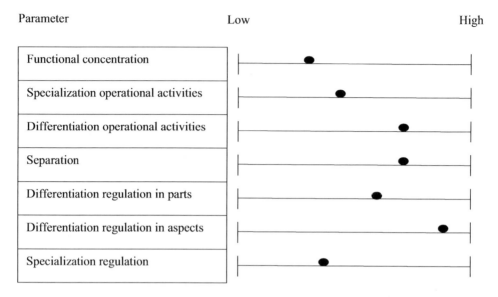

FIGURE 3.7 Description of one particular structure in terms of the values of the design parameters
Note: Values are the dots on the parameter 'scales', ranging from a low to a high value.

given – they should enable the four basic activities in order to realize effects A and B. In order to further specify this idea of structural adequacy, one needs to understand (1) the idea of interaction premises, (2) what the societal contribution entails, (3) how basic activities relate to reflecting on and changing interaction premises, and to realizing and adapting the societal contribution, (4) what organizational structures are, and finally, (5) what adequate structures are, i.e. how structures enable the basic activities in the required way.

Fortunately, several of these questions have already been answered. Let's briefly examine what we have and haven't discussed with respect to the five issues:

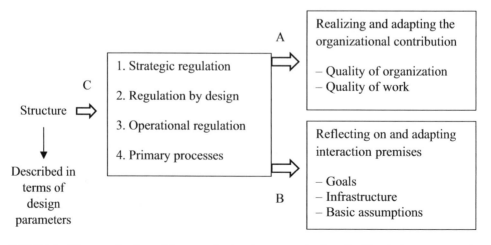

FIGURE 3.8 The contribution of the organizational structure (as described by design parameters)

1. We already discussed issue #1 in Chapter 2. We discussed the nature of interaction premises: they comprise goals, infrastructures and basic assumptions.
2. We discussed issue #2 in Chapter 2 in a general way, but we haven't yet specified the operationalization of this contribution into quality of organization and quality of work (arrow A in Figure 3.8; here, we follow de Sitter, 1994). We will go into this operationalization in Section 3.3.1.
3. We also discussed that basic activities are related to interaction premises and to realizing and adapting the societal contribution of organizations in a general way. In Section 3.4 we will further specify this relation.
4. We discussed the concept of organizational structures (issue #4) in the previous section.
5. As yet, we haven't specified the desired characteristics of structures which make them enable the four basic activities (arrow C in Figure 3.8). We derive these characteristics from cybernetics (cf. Ashby, 1958; Achterbergh and Vriens, 2010). We introduce these characteristics in Section 3.3.2 and argue in Section 3.4 that structures having these characteristics are indeed the structures we're looking for.

So in this section we discuss how the societal contribution of organizations can be operationalized (Section 3.3.1), and we will go into the cybernetic requirements of adequate organizational structures (Section 3.3.2). In Section 3.4 we will discuss the form of adequate structures – i.e. we argue that adequate structures should have low values on the design parameters.

3.3.1 Operationalizing the societal contribution into quality of organization and quality of work

De Sitter (1994) argues that whatever *specific* societal contribution an organization selects to pursue, this contribution can always be described by two general classes of 'organizational criteria' that should be met. That is, he proposes that every organization should meet (1) criteria belonging to what he calls the category 'quality of organization' and (2) criteria that belong to the category 'quality of work'.

The class of criteria labelled 'quality of organization' expresses the organization's potential to realize and adapt the societal contribution in an efficient and effective way. It refers to criteria pertaining to flexibility (the ability to react to fluctuations in demand by realizing short production cycle times, and by having sufficient product variations and a variable product mix), control over order realization (the ability to provide products and services at the expected quality standards, in a reliable and timely way), and innovativeness (the ability to define and improve relevant products and services; or to put it more in terms of our model, the ability to define and improve the organization's contribution to society). This class of criteria pertains to the realization and adaptation of the specific organizational societal contribution.

The criteria belonging to the class 'quality of work' express the degree of meaningfulness of organizational jobs. These criteria have to do with being a 'good employer', and describe the effective 'mobilization of human resources' (cf. de Sitter, 1994). At the same time, these criteria reflect whether organizational opportunities are created for employees to 'live a fulfilled life' in the context of doing their jobs (cf. Achterbergh and Vriens, 2010; Vriens et al., 2018a). De Sitter argues that there are two general indicators for quality of work: the degree of absenteeism and the degree of personnel turnover. These reach adequate levels if jobs

TABLE 3.1 Operationalization of the organizational societal contribution into quality of organization and quality of work

First level		Second level
Quality of organization	Flexibility	Short production cycle times
		Sufficient product variations
		Sufficient product mix
	Control over order realization	Reliable production time
		Reliable production
		Effective quality control
	Potential for innovation	Strategic product development
		Short innovation time
Quality of work	Low level of absenteeism and personnel turnover	Opportunities to (1) be involved, (2) learn, and (3) develop
		Controllable stress conditions

Source: Adapted from de Sitter (1994, p. 42).

enable organization members to learn and develop themselves, to feel involved with their work, and if organization members can deal with work-related stress.

In Table 3.1 we list the quality of organization and quality of work criteria (adapted from de Sitter, 1994, p. 42). As can be seen, two 'levels' can be distinguished: one indicating a general variable (e.g. 'flexibility' or 'level of absenteeism') and a second level indicating the organizational variables that help realizing adequate levels of the general variable (e.g. the opportunity to feel involved, to learn, and to develop is an organizational variable that needs to be realized in order to realize low levels of absenteeism and personnel turnover).

The two classes of criteria are quite general, and hold for every organization. For specific organizations with a specific societal contribution, these criteria should, however, be translated to fit their specific societal contribution. That is, given the specific societal contribution of an organization (e.g., producing high-quality durable furniture in a sustainable way), the two classes of general criteria should be translated into criteria operationalizing this specific contribution. For instance, flexibility should be translated into criteria covering the specifics of this organization in this specific environment. This reasoning is quite comparable to the logic of the Balanced Scorecard (cf. Kaplan and Norton, 1996), which identifies four classes of general organizational variables that should be translated into specific indicators for success for every individual organization.

So the specific societal contribution of an organization can be made explicit by means of the two classes of organizational criteria – quality of organization and quality of work. Moreover, these criteria describing the organizational contribution are realized by means of the four basic activities. And, based on this logic, we want organizational structures to enable these four basic activities in such a way that they can realize the organization's contribution.

3.3.2 A cybernetic perspective on structural adequacy

Achterbergh and Vriens (2010) and de Sitter (1994) use cybernetics to clarify the adequacy of organizational structures enabling the four basic activities, which, in turn, set out to realize the two classes of organizational criteria, and by means of which interaction premises are changed (arrow C in Figure 3.8). Based on cybernetics, it can be said that these four activities are supported by a structure if:

1. a structure itself is not a source of disturbances; and
2. a structure comprises the means to deal with disturbances.

The second criterion means that structures should have the regulatory potential to either remove disturbing events (attenuation, cf. Achterbergh and Vriens, 2010), or to deal with the *effect* of disturbing events (in an active or passive way – cf. Ashby, 1958).

We will now briefly discuss these cybernetic desiderata of structures.

Structures should themselves not be a source of disturbances

To elaborate these two general desiderata for organizational structures, it should first be clear that a disturbance is some event or state of the world that has the potential to negatively influence the relevant organizational criteria (i.e. they negatively affect the realization of 'quality of organization' and 'quality of work' variables, or they impair reflecting on and changing basic assumptions). De Sitter (1994, pp. 23–26) explains that structures, i.e. the network of related tasks, may themselves be a source of disturbances in at least two ways. That is, he argues that the probability of disturbances in a structure is affected by (1) the number of relations in the network and (2) the 'variability' of these relations.

As de Sitter sees it, the higher the number of relations in the network of relations, the higher the probability of disturbances, as every relation introduces a possible source of disturbances. Typically, an operational task in a factory (say, 'sawing' in a factory producing furniture) has many relations with other tasks – e.g. with planning, monitoring, maintenance, material handling, internal logistics, etc. Each relation is a possible source of something going wrong – planning too late, wrong planning, monitoring too strict, maintenance takes too long, etc. The more relations a task has, the higher the probability of disturbances for the task. This logic also applies to the whole network of tasks: the more relations in the network, the higher the probability of a disturbance.

The probability of disturbances in a network of tasks also depends on what de Sitter calls the 'variability' of the relations in the network. This refers to the variety of content of these relations. This content may be either physical, e.g. semi-finished products, material or tools, or non-physical, e.g. instructions, requests, messages, or other information. De Sitter argues that the more varied this content is (i.e. high variability), the higher the probability of disturbances. Achterbergh and Vriens (2010) give an example illustrating why this is the case. The example describes a simple structure in a restaurant with only two tasks: a waiter task and a chef task. Between these tasks, there is only one relation. This relation has to do with the waiter passing on orders for meals to the chef and the chef handing over prepared meals to the waiter. Clearly, the number of relations in this network of tasks is low, but the variability of this one relation may be quite high. This refers to the number of different orders a waiter passes on to the chef and to the number of prepared meals the chef finishes and that have to be served by the waiter. This variability depends on the number of items on the menu. Now, high variability may not only lead to disturbances as it may increase the number of mistakes (e.g. if there are ten different types of salad with ten different types of dressing, it is easier to make a mistake compared to a case where there is only one salad with a standard dressing). High variability also leads to disturbances in another, more important way. In this example, high variability means that the chef may have to prepare many different meals – all having their own specific recipe, required ingredients, cooking activities, and tools. This involves a large number of different activities that all need to be coordinated by the chef – which clearly increases the probability of something going wrong. In general, if tasks in a network are coupled to all types of orders (as in organizations with functional departments), the variability of the relations is higher than in organizations in which tasks are coupled to only a sub-set of order types (e.g. organizations with business units dedicated to only a few order types). So, as de Sitter has it, structures may vary with respect to the variability of the relations in the network.

Of course, there is a large array of possible disturbances influencing the relevant organizational criteria, but the two types we just discussed have in common that they directly relate to the way a structure is designed. In fact, de Sitter's advice for designing structures is to make sure that they have as few relations as possible, and as low variability as possible. In this way, the degree to which structures are themselves sources of disturbances decreases.

Structures should comprise the means to deal with disturbances

As has become apparent, structures should be designed in such a way that they are not a source of disturbances. However, this does not, of course, mean that all disturbances affecting the organization can be designed away. Many disturbances are not caused by the (infra)structure of the organization and still need to be dealt with. Moreover, even ideal structures may still be a source of disturbances (as structures will always include relations and a certain level of variability). And last, given the fundamental environmental and organizational complexity and uncertainty (and our limited cognitive capacities), as a rule, unforeseen disturbances are bound to emerge. So organizations should have the regulatory potential to deal with disturbances. For structures, this means that tasks should be designed in such a way that they comprise enough regulatory potential. That is, in structures, operational regulation, regulation by design, and strategic regulation should be built into tasks.

Operational regulation deals with disturbances *given* the existing organizational infrastructure and goals. Its aim is to apply regulatory potential to make sure that actual disturbances are dealt with and the primary processes can continue (see Chapter 2 and Achterbergh and Vriens, 2010) without changing the infrastructure or goals. In practice, operational regulation takes care of the day-to-day disturbances impinging on operational processes. Some design theorists and practitioners hold that operational regulation should be included in a task separated from operational work (to create an overview, or to avoid burdening operational workers with regulatory tasks). Others argue that it makes sense to build operational regulation into operational tasks (to decrease the distance between the location where problems emerge and the instance dealing with them). In any case, operational regulation should be included in organizational tasks.

Regulation by design deals with disturbances by changing the infrastructure of organizations. Its aim is twofold. First, by means of a change to the infrastructure, the probability of disturbances may be decreased – even down to zero, in which case the disturbance is completely removed. For instance, if a lack of knowledge among organization members is a source of disturbances, hiring new knowledgeable personnel or launching a training programme are two examples of changing the infrastructure (its human resources part) to the effect that the disturbances no longer occur. In a similar way, ineffective structures may be redesigned in order to become structures that themselves generate fewer disturbances, and hence become more effective. For instance, bureaucratic structures with a large hierarchy and many short-cycled, small operational tasks have been found to be notoriously weak at responding swiftly to changes in demand. Such structures may therefore themselves be said to be sources of disturbances. Redesigning bureaucracies into more 'organic organizations', as proposed by, for instance, Nadler and Tushman (1997), results in structures that generate fewer disturbances. Changing the (infra)structure with the aim of removing disturbances (or decreasing their probability) is called attenuation (cf. Beer, 1979; Achterbergh and Vriens, 2010).

Second, the infrastructure may be changed with the aim of building more operational regulation into the organization. For instance, it may be found that new suppliers deliver goods faster but slightly less reliably (e.g. shipments may contain flawed material). To deal with this new disturbance, the task of the operator receiving the shipment may be changed so that the shipment is checked and the supplier is called right away if it turns out to be problematic. Building in this new type of operational regulation into the infrastructure is called amplification (cf. Ashby, 1958; Beer, 1979; Achterbergh and Vriens, 2010). Now, the capacity for regulation by design (both by means of amplification and attenuation) should be built into the structure of the organization – it should be part of the organization's tasks.

By means of redefining goals (strategic regulation), disturbances can also be dealt with. Consider, for example, that disturbances make it impossible to deliver goods within the time agreed upon. In such a case, it may be possible to renegotiate the delivery time (and price). Or, if some type of wood is particularly difficult to process, it may be possible to no longer make furniture consisting of that type of wood, so the organizational output changes. In both cases, resetting organizational goals is a means to deal with disturbances. In the end, strategic regulation redefines the organization's contribution to society (see Chapter 2). Now, as with operational regulation and regulation by design, strategic regulation should be built into the organization's structure.

Wrapping it up: requirements set for organizational structures

As a brief summary of the requirements set for organizational structures developed in this section, consider Figure 3.9. The most general description of the desired contribution of a structure is that it (as interaction premise) should enable interactions and thus help realize the organization's meaningful survival.

In this section, we further detailed this description and stated that an organizational structure should support the four basic organizational activities in such a way that they (A) contribute to the adaptation and realization of the organization's societal contribution (arrow A in Figure 3.9). We discussed that this contribution can be described in terms of two sets of criteria, one pertaining to what has been called the quality of organization, and one to the quality of work. In particular, it should enable setting and resetting of goals (adaptation), the smooth operation of primary processes, and their operational regulation (realization). Moreover, a structure should also enable (B) the continuous reflection on and improvement of interaction premises (arrow B in Figure 3.9). Here, it should support the basic activity of design in order to (re)create an infrastructure that helps to realize and adapt the societal

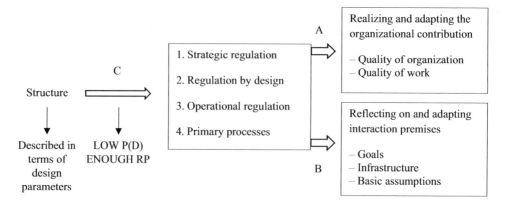

FIGURE 3.9 Adequate structures support the four basic activities if they have a low probability of disturbances and enough regulatory potential

contribution. By supporting the basic activity of strategic regulation, reflection on and improving goals as interaction premises are enabled. And, last, a structure may help to create possibilities for reflection on and adaptation of basic assumptions – even though the nature of these basic assumptions makes such reflection difficult.

To realize the contribution of structures as described, it was further proposed to follow several authors on (organizational) cybernetics, and suggest that adequate structures support the basic activities (so that they deliver the desired contribution) if they are themselves not a source of disturbances, and if they comprise of the required regulatory potential. In Figure 3.9, we use this logic to specify arrow C as indicating the cybernetic requirements of organizational structures: structures should have a low probability of disturbances, LOW P(D), and sufficient regulatory potential (ENOUGH RP). In the next section, we will discuss what these structures may look like.

3.4 Adequate organizational structures: form

After describing the adequacy of organizational structures in terms of the above requirements, one may ask which *form* structures should take so that these requirements can be met. Here, we follow de Sitter (1994), who provides a general answer to this question. As he argues, the requirements for adequacy are met by structures of which the values on the design parameters are as low as possible. As we will argue, structures with high values on the design parameters (high parameter value structures, or HPVSs) are themselves a source of disturbances and don't have the required regulatory potential to deal with disturbances. Therefore, they face problems in realizing the four basic activities and hence will fail to meet the main criteria A and B (see Figure 3.9). As we will argue, low parameter value structures (LPVSs) will stand a better chance of realizing these criteria. In the next two sub-sections, we set out to show the effect of both types of structures on the two main criteria. To structure our argumentation, we first discuss why structures with high values on the design parameters are structures that cannot meet the requirements set (Section 3.4.1). In Section 3.4.2 we turn our attention to structures with low values on design parameters and argue that they are in a better position to meet the criteria set.

3.4.1 Why high parameter value structures don't meet the criteria set for structural adequacy

In this section, we set out to argue that HPVSs are problematic. The main idea is that HPVSs have a high probability of disturbances, and lack the required regulatory potential to deal with disturbances. Because of that, they have problems realizing the four basic activities, and hence fail to meet the two main criteria for structural adequacy.

To structure our reasoning, we will first give an example of an HPVS. Next, we discuss why high parameter values (HPVs) impair the adequate realization of the four basic activities. And, after we have discussed the effect of HPVSs on the four basic activities, we discuss why they fail to meet the two main criteria.

An example of a high parameter value structure

As we stated earlier, every organization has a particular value on the design parameters. And as de Sitter (1994) holds, the higher these values, the more structures become sources of disturbances and the less they have the required regulatory potential. To understand why this is the case, we describe in this section an example of an 'ideal typical' organizational structure with high values on all design parameters.

Figure 3.10 shows a structure with high values on all design parameters. It has a high level of functional concentration, meaning that all operational tasks are coupled to potentially all order types ($X_1 \ldots X_k, Y_1, \ldots Y_m, Z_1 \ldots Z_n$).

If, for example, X stand for chairs, of which there are k=4 types, Y stands for tables, of which there are m=3 types, and Z stands for cupboards, of which there are n=3 types, this structure should be prepared to process $2^{4+3+3} -1$ (1023) different order combinations, which may all require different materials, preparation activities, and production activities, etc. (compare to the example of the waiter and chef given earlier). A high level of differentiation of operational tasks entails that preparation, production, and support activities are assigned to different tasks (often in different functional departments). Moreover, specialization of operational activities leads to a large number of small jobs with a short cycle time. As Figure 3.10 indicates, operational activities are separated from a hierarchy of regulators (parameter: separation). These regulatory jobs have been differentiated into jobs dedicated to strategic regulation, regulation by design, and operational regulation; and into jobs tied to monitoring, assessment, and adjustment activities (this differentiation isn't made explicit in the figure). What is depicted is the specialization of regulatory tasks into small tasks with only a limited regulatory range.

What emerges is what de Sitter calls a complex network of simple jobs. Jobs are simple as most of them have a small scope – i.e. operational tasks with a short cycle time, covering only a small part of the total production process, or regulatory tasks with only a small regulatory coverage. These jobs also have little regulatory potential to deal with their 'own' disturbances, as this potential has been separated and differentiated away to other jobs. The structure is complex because it contains a large number of interfaces relating a large number of simple jobs. These types of structures have been treated by other authors as bureaucratic or Tayloristic organizations (cf. Mintzberg, 1983; Donaldson, 2001).

As an example of an organization with high values on the design parameters, consider one of the many hierarchical, functionally concentrated, and bureaucratic home care organizations. The goal of many of such organizations is to provide home care to elderly people,

70 Interventions in organizational structures

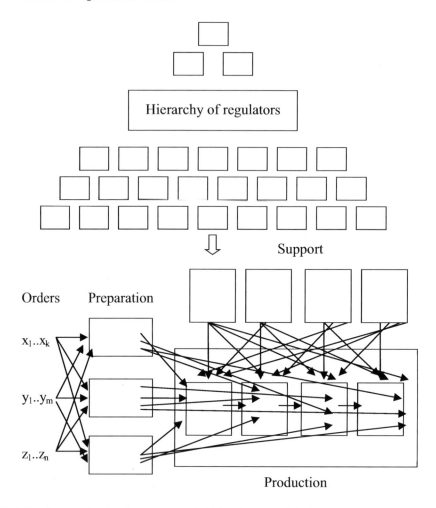

FIGURE 3.10 An organizational structure with high values on all design parameters

ranging from paramedical care (e.g. putting on compression stockings, preparing medication, or monitoring basic bodily functions like blood pressure) to assistance with daily activities like washing, cleaning, or cooking. Often, monitoring and, if possible, securing socio-psychological well-being and the promotion of independence are mentioned as goals in such organizations. The production structure of many of these home care organizations is organized in such a way that:

1. Caregivers perform only a small task (e.g. 'putting on compression stockings' or 'washing') having a short cycle time. That is, these tasks should be performed within a limited amount time. In these organizations, then, the degree of operational specialization is high.
2. Caregivers are potentially coupled to all types of clients (high degree of functional concentration).

3. Care, preparatory, and support activities are assigned to different tasks. For instance, the preparation (e.g. planning, routing, and availability of material needed for care activities) may not be a part of the task of caregivers. Similarly, caregivers may not perform support activities like maintaining their means of transportation, or installing and maintaining the proper software on their cell phones. So the degree of operational differentiation is high.

The control structure also has high values on the design parameters. That is:

1. Most regulation is separated from the operational jobs of caregivers.
2. In regulatory tasks, monitoring of disturbances is often separated from assessing their impact and from dealing with them. Often, caregivers should report a direct disturbance to a regulator (e.g. forwarding the fact that they won't be on time for their next appointment, that they have been given the wrong pair of stockings, that some client has fallen downstairs, etc.). Dealing with these disturbances is in most cases not part of the job of a caregiver, but is handled by a regulator who, for instance, provides the caregiver with a new plan. Monitoring of overall disturbances (e.g. reasons for a decrease in client satisfaction), assessing them, and coming up with actions countering them is not part of the caregiver's job. In all, these structures have a considerable degree of differentiation of regulation into parts.
3. Strategic regulation, regulation by design, and operational regulation are assigned to different regulators. Strategic regulation is the responsibility of CEOs, while often specific staff are assigned for optimizing parts of the infrastructure (e.g. providing caregivers with the necessary ICT). Operational regulation is often the responsibility of direct supervisors.
4. Different types of regulation related to parts of the operational process are also put in place. For instance, regulation of planning and routing problems is handled by different regulators than problems with required material. In some cases, supervisors are only tied to a particular type of care (overseeing, for instance, only activities related to house cleaning or personal hygiene or personal health). So these organizations also have a considerable degree of regulatory specialization

In all, in the 'high value' home care organizations caregivers perform small operational tasks and see many different clients for a short amount of time. They also have little regulatory potential themselves – setting goals, providing infrastructural arrangements, and dealing with disturbances are taken care of by regulators who don't participate in the operational process.

High parameter value structures impair the realization of the four basic activities

In this section, we want to show that HPVSs have a negative effect on realizing the four basic activities (arrow C in Figure 3.11). In order to do that, we first discuss the part of the structure that is related to the organization's primary processes: the production structure. After this, we turn our attention to the part of the structure which realizes the three types of regulation (operational regulation, regulation by design, and strategic regulation), also called the control structure.

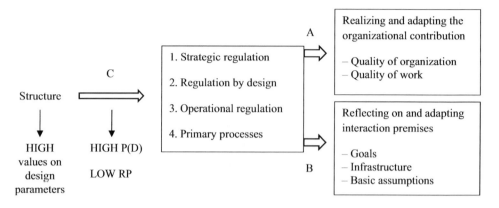

FIGURE 3.11 The effect of high values on design parameters on the four basic activities

The effect of high values on design parameters on primary processes

Before we start explaining the effect of high values on design parameters of the production structure by means of which the primary processes are carried out, it is helpful to remember that the relevant design parameters in this respect are (1) the level of specialization, (2) the level of differentiation into production, support, and preparation tasks, and (3) the level of functional concentration.

A high level of specialization of operational activities and a high level of differentiation of operational activities into production, preparation, and support tasks result in an increase of relations in the network of operational tasks. Specialization entails that the total operational process is split up into small tasks which, in sequence, should realize the complete process. The more specialization, the more sub-tasks in the sequence of tasks. As these tasks are all related into this sequence, more specialization also means more relations between sequentially related tasks. In the factory producing furniture, each task contributes in a small way to the end result, and the output of one task is taken up by a next task which, in turn, delivers its own small contribution. In the high parameter value home care organization described previously, each operational care task consists of a small part of the total care process. After this contribution is delivered, a next task 'processes' the client. In this case, there exists a relation between the tasks in the sense that tasks are performed sequentially (one task needs to be finished before the next one can start). The more specialization, the more operational tasks performing the operational process, and hence, the more relations in the operational network of tasks.

Differentiation into production, preparation, and support activities also increases the number of tasks and relations in the operational network. In the home care organization, planning (preparation) was assigned to a separate task and was not part of the care (i.e. production) tasks themselves. This introduced a relation between those carrying out the planning task and those performing the care task. The more differentiation, the higher the number of relations in the operational network.

A high level of functional concentration entails that an operational task is potentially coupled to all order types – increasing the variability of the relations in the network of tasks.

In the home care organization, each caregiver is potentially coupled to all clients. This may lead to variability in many ways, depending on the different relevant order types one identifies. For instance, if the clients differ with respect to their mental and physical health, it can be problematic that caregivers see all types of patients (especially if specialization is high and tasks have a short cycle time). One may imagine that putting on compression stockings in the case of a mentally and physically disabled elderly person takes more time than in the case of someone who is not disabled. If you, as a caregiver, are potentially coupled to all patients, and the cycle time for putting on stockings is an average (short) time, keeping to the plan may be problematic. Moreover, as other caregivers also deliver their type of care to patients and are scheduled to do so just before you arrive, below-average performance may not help you, because you may have to wait until the other caregiver is finished. Or, if you are coupled to potentially all patients, but they live scattered throughout the city, transportation to all of them may become problematic (especially if the allowed transportation time is an average). In both cases, problems may be resolved by means of complex planning and regulation, taking into account the individual characteristics of different clients. Things may get even worse if the different characteristics of orders also entail the use of different tools, equipment, or materials (e.g. different types of compression stockings), or if they entail different ways of performing the task (e.g., in the case of a mentally disabled person, putting on stockings may require a different approach). In fact, as de Sitter argues, every order combination has a specific set of demands qua planning, materials, tools, sequence of activities, etc. Therefore, as we said earlier, if a network of tasks is coupled to many different order types, they need to exchange information and material related to all these different order types (and order combinations related to these order types), and hence the variability of the relations in the network increases. In line with the above reasoning (see de Sitter, 1994), the higher the variability, the higher the probability of disturbances. The furniture factory described earlier, with seven different order types, needs to be able to exchange information and material through its network of tasks related to $2^7 -1$ (=127) different order combinations. As can be appreciated from this calculation, the addition of one order type dramatically increases the variability, and with it the probability of disturbances. So the more orders (and the more they differ), the more difficult it becomes to realize individual task targets, and hence the output of the network as a whole.

In general, high levels of specialization and differentiation increase the number of relations in the production structure. And, as every relation is a potential source of disturbances, high levels of these parameters increase the probability of a disturbance in the network. Functional concentration increases the number of orders (and order combinations) a task is related to, and as every order (combination) has different demands, the variability of relations (which is needed to take these different demands into account) increases, meaning that realizing individual and aggregated task targets gets more problematic.

Besides the increase in the number of relations (specialization and differentiation) and variability (functional concentration), high levels of these parameters also lead to problems in other ways. High values on these parameters result in an operational network with many small, repetitive jobs with a short cycle time which are potentially coupled to many orders. As a result, employees may easily lose track of what they are contributing to – they only see the small activity they are performing, which is only a small part of the complete process. In such organizations, employees have difficulty in picturing the whole process; in fact, they often receive batches of semi-finished products and instructions on how to process these batches.

They often don't know who or what workstation was involved in the process before them, and they don't know where their own output will be going. This situation greatly impairs regulation – see the later text.

In addition, producing in batches, which is common in functionally concentrated structures (e.g. to reduce workstation waiting time, which occurs if different orders require operations of a different duration) also means that semi-finished products tend to get 'stuck in stock'. De Sitter (1994) holds that, on average, products are processed only 5% of the total time they spend in functionally concentrated factories –so they are waiting to be processed for 95% of this time (p. 47). Similar figures are put forward by authors discussing lean production (e.g. Womack et al., 1990; Womack and Jones, 1996). Moreover, as different products often have different routings along different functional departments, it requires a lot of effort to plan these routings and to keep track of them. In fact, Christensen et al. (2010) argue that dealing with the effects of these routings comes at the cost of a large number of overhead activities. They call the costs associated with such overheads the "cost of complexity" (pp. 92–93). Christensen et al. (2010) calculated that in an average tertiary hospital the 'overhead burden rate' (i.e. the overhead costs (in dollars) for every dollar spent on direct labour) is about eight (p. 90). As these authors argue, in such hospitals, much time and effort is "required to manage the number of pathways that patients might traverse between admission and discharge [. . .] activities like scheduling, expediting, repair, and rework, record-keeping; and moving storing and retrieving things and people" (p. 95). So, in order to plan and keep track of orders in high parameter value organizations, a lot of extra effort is required.

The effect of high values on design parameters on the three forms of regulation

As the reader may recall, the parameters describing the control structure (which realizes the three basic regulatory activities) are differentiation of regulatory tasks into aspects and parts, and regulatory specialization. Here, we will also include the degree of separation as a parameter relevant to the control structure. Now, high values on these parameters result in a complex network of small regulatory tasks with a small regulatory scope. A small scope means that these regulatory tasks only deal with a small regulatory object, be it a small part of the operational process or a small set of other regulatory activities. Separation sets the regulatory network apart from operational tasks and introduces a hierarchy of regulators (and hence increases the number of relations in the network). Differentiation of regulatory activities in parts and aspects results in an increase of regulatory tasks (and relations among them), and specialization of regulatory tasks results in many regulatory tasks with a small scope. Now, the increase of values on all of these parameters leads to an increase in the number of relations of the regulatory network. And, as we discussed earlier, the higher the number of relations in the network, the higher the probability of disturbances.

However, an increase in the probability of disturbances due to an increase in the number of relations is not the only problem caused by high values on the parameters related to the control structure. The second main problem is that in these structures, regulatory potential diminishes. Impoverished regulatory potential comes about in several ways. First, as de Sitter (1994) argues, separation results in a network of regulators who are themselves not directly involved in the (operational) work they regulate. This introduces a delay because operational disturbances are not dealt with immediately. They are, instead, 'processed' by a hierarchy of operationally detached regulators. In the home care example, disturbances were not dealt with by caregivers themselves; they were communicated to regulators who were external to the primary process. Besides a delay, these regulators also have an "informational disadvantage". As these regulators are detached from the process in which disturbances occur, they "lack first-hand information about the nature and context of the disturbance" (Vriens and Achterbergh, 2011, p. 419), and as they lack this information as well as context-specific operational know-how, it may be difficult to come up with fitting regulatory actions. Delayed and irrelevant responses to problems in primary processes have, of course, always been the hallmark of centralized bureaucratic hierarchies (cf. Donaldson, 2001). In such organizations, a high degree of separation means a loss in the potential to react to operational disturbances promptly and adequately. In such organizations, then, product cycle times tend to increase, and control over the production process tends to decrease.

In the home care case, many examples of such delayed and detached regulation can be given. Caregivers were deprived of regulatory potential and were not allowed to deal with disturbances themselves. Instead, they were to report disturbances (e.g. a patient who fell ill) and await further instructions, which always took time (e.g. after a while, the caregiver was asked to wash the patient anyway and wait until a doctor arrived) and might not be relevant (the visit of the doctor turned out to be unnecessary; the patient had fallen ill because she forgot to take certain medication, which she often did – just checking the medication could have been sufficient). In fact, the regulatory action itself caused additional waiting time and distress.

High levels of regulatory differentiation and specialization make matters even worse, as they entail that regulatory potential is dispersed among many regulators with small regulatory tasks having a small scope. Such regulators only see a small part of the operational process (e.g. a regulator responsible for the sawing department) or they are only responsible for a small aspect of it (e.g. a regulator responsible for maintenance of the stamping machine). As a result, they may lose track of the whole process, and as regulators, lack of a grasp of the whole process, control of quality, or production time becomes problematic.

A high level of operational specialization, separation, and regulatory specialization also entails the loss of the potential to communicate about and jointly deal with problems. As regulators (and operational employees) cannot really have an idea of what the complete process looks like, it becomes problematic to discuss with others down the line how to jointly solve a problem. If during my task as a caregiver (say, washing a client) I experience a severe delay, it might be relevant to contact the caregivers who will visit the client after me (e.g. the caregiver who puts on stockings and the one who helps the client to dress) to inform them and maybe to discuss a solution. But this isn't possible because I don't have any idea of who will visit the client after me and because I don't have the regulatory potential to discuss and implement solutions. Instead, I should contact a regulator, and, given the problems mentioned earlier, solutions may thus come late, or not at all, or they may be irrelevant. In the example of the patient falling ill because she forgot to take her medication, the caregiver might have checked the intake of the medication and discussed with the caregiver responsible for medication what to do. This requires knowledge about the whole care process, and the regulatory potential (and time) to check some possible causes of problems, and communicate with others about solutions. And, again, this knowledge, regulatory potential, and time have been organized away in HPVSs.

In high parameter structures, separation and both operational and regulatory specialization may also come at the expense of a loss of the number of possible regulatory actions (de Sitter, 1994). To explain, suppose that a caregiver performs six different care activities and has the regulatory potential to deal with disturbances affecting any of these six activities. Now, if something goes wrong during, say, the first activity, the caregiver might try to solve this problem and decide to perform the other activities more quickly – or even decide to skip one of the other activities. This way of dealing with disturbances is only possible because of the broad scope of operational regulation – covering all six activities. The moment regulation is specialized and the caregiver no longer regulates activities two to six, the suggested overall solution can no longer be selected by the caregiver.

In high parameter value structures, the potential for regulation by design is also threatened. As an understanding of what the complete process looks like is lacking, and as the scope of regulatory tasks is small, relevant integral improvements to the infrastructure are difficult to obtain. In fact, process improvements initiated by operational employees are necessarily confined to the small sub-process they are tied to. Given their lack of knowledge about and overview of the whole process, such improvements are often only sub-optimizations. This may be repaired by making the process or infrastructural improvements the duty of regulators detached from the process. But the regulators' lack of understanding of the complete process, their detachment, and lack of connection with other (regulatory) tasks also make such improvements difficult for these regulators. So the lack of overview, time, and regulatory potential make experimentation with infrastructural conditions in operational tasks rather problematic, if not impossible. And at the same time, lack of overview and involvement in operational processes also make changes to the infrastructure made by detached regulators problematic. In all, the natural "positive infrastructural drift" which comes about when organization members – in communication – gradually learn how to improve their jobs becomes problematic, if not impossible, in HPVSs.

Besides a lack of infrastructural experimentation, high parameter value organizations also impair strategic regulation – i.e. (re)setting goals. As regulators have tasks with only a small scope, they have no idea what the complete operational process looks like and are not in touch with the overall goals and output of the organization, therefore appreciating the effect of a change in the goal of their sub-part of the process on the rest of the process, or on organizational goals and output, is difficult. Regulation by control in the sense of defining new products is also difficult. Product innovation is problematic, as it typically requires an integrated perspective on organizational competencies and environment. But as regulators lack an insight in these competencies (they are only tied to a small part or aspect of them) and are only in touch with the market from their own differentiated perspective (e.g. operations, marketing, logistics, etc.), such an integrated perspective is hard to obtain. In the home care example, for instance, organizational competencies had become rather invisible, as care was split up into small sub tasks, and as regulators lost touch with clients who they no longer saw, it became very hard to think of new relevant types of care.

High parameter value structures don't meet the two main criteria for organizational adequacy

Previously, we discussed that HPVSs have a high probability of disturbances, and lack the required regulatory potential to deal with them. Because of that, the four basic activities are difficult to realize. In this section, we want to show that this means that these structures fail to meet the two main criteria for structural adequacy – i.e. they have trouble supporting the realization and adaptation of the organization's contribution to society, and they have trouble reflecting on and adjusting interaction premises.

Problems with realizing and adapting the organization's contribution to society

The first main criterion has to do with realizing and adapting the organization's contribution to society – which has been operationalized in terms of quality of organization variables (variables referring to flexibility, control over order realization, and innovation) and quality of work variables (variables related to the well-being of human resources).

Quality of organization High values on the design parameters affect the quality of organization variables. They lead, for instance, to long waiting times – e.g. because of the many disturbances that may occur and the inability to promptly and adequately deal with them, and because of the inevitable batch-and-queue production in functionally concentrated structures. Long waiting times make it difficult to realize short 'product cycle times' – which, in turn, are required to be able to react swiftly to changes in demand, i.e. to show flexibility, which was introduced as a quality or organization variable.

HPVSs also have a hard time realizing 'control over order realization', another quality of organization variable. As we discussed, high levels of parameter values make it very difficult to keep track of orders throughout the system. Moreover, because they result in structures with a high probability of disturbances, the planning of orders also becomes very difficult. On top of that, detached regulation makes a swift and relevant reaction to disturbances problematic. And not being able to deal with disturbances in one part of the process causes delays and hence affects other parts of process. In such structures, disturbances have the tendency to get dispersed throughout the network of tasks. This, in turn, makes keeping track of orders, and planning, even more problematic. It also makes control over the production process in terms of being able to realize reliable production time difficult. The same holds for the control of quality of the output. Product quality during the production process (including anticipating possible failures of the end product) is extremely difficult as operational activities and regulatory activities are confined to a small contribution to the end product. Even though the output of these small contributions may be rigidly specified, the effect of small variations which do occur is hard to predict, and given the small task and short cycle time, also difficult to repair.

As we discussed previously, both process and product innovation is also hard to realize in HPVSs. Because of the small scope of regulatory tasks and a lack of overview of the production process, process innovations which are not just sub-optimizations are difficult to obtain. Similarly, because of the regulatory differentiation and specialization, an integrated perspective on product or goal improvements is hard to realize. In all, the realization of the quality of organization variables in HPVSs is difficult.

Quality of work Besides a negative effect on quality of organization, HPVSs also have trouble realizing quality of work variables. As de Sitter (1994) sees it, quality of work relates to levels of absenteeism and personnel turnover. And these variables are in turn affected by (1) the degree to which employees can develop and learn while doing their job, (2) the degree to which they feel involved, both socially and intrinsically, and (3) the degree to which they experience job-related stress. Unfortunately, as de Sitter argues, HPVSs don't do a good job with respect to all these variables (see also Achterbergh and Vriens, 2010).

Achterbergh and Vriens (2010) describe how HPVSs impair learning and development. Functional concentration, separation, specialization, and differentiation result in uninteresting, repetitive operational work with a short cycle time, deprived of regulatory potential. It also results in uninteresting regulatory tasks with a small scope. In such tasks, there is not much to learn. They don't challenge employees to experiment with new ways of doing things and learning, nor do they "mobilize them to the best of their abilities to contribute to the organization's viability" (p. 264). Learning is limited to the few activities a job consists of. Learning about how to contribute to the goals and output of the organization is virtually impossible – because of the small tasks, and because of the lack of overview of the process and connection to the output and goals of the organization. Living a fulfilled life in the context of doing one's job in the sense of developing skills, practical wisdom, and moral virtues – which is one way of describing the development of what it means to be a human being (cf. Vriens et al., 2018) – is just impossible in HPVSs. If we look at the example of the home care organization, it is easy to see that learning is confined to small activities – e.g. improving the way compression stockings can be put on. And, although this may lead to some efficiency, it hardly appeals to development as a care professional.

Similar problems hold for the degree to which employees experience job-related involvement. In explaining this kind of involvement, we follow Achterbergh and Vriens (2010), who distinguish 'social' and 'intrinsic' job-related involvement. Feeling 'socially involved' while doing a job has to do with being "actively engaged in a network of social relations associated with the job" (p. 264). Feeling intrinsically involved comes about if "one is able to see and appreciate the point of the task – i.e. its contribution to the process of producing something as well as to the product itself" (p. 264). Such involvement may be more or less active. It can be more active if one can actually co-contribute to setting goals with respect to the output or to designing the infrastructure required to realize the output. The least active form is if one is only aware of the contribution of one's job. Now, as many psychologists and sociologists have established, a lack of social and intrinsic involvement leads to feelings of isolation (a sense of job-related loneliness) and alienation (a sense of job-related meaninglessness), which may turn a job into a dreadful experience. Regrettably, HPVSs have small, repetitive jobs with a short cycle time and a lack of regulatory potential. Carrying out these small, repetitive activities does not require the active participation in a social, job-related network. At best, you see other people as their repetitive job touches yours. Seeing what one is contributing to, both in terms of the process or of the end product, is virtually impossible because of the lack of overview of the process. Moreover, active intrinsic involvement is also problematic, as most jobs lack the regulatory potential to do so (and they lack an idea of the complete process and goals the organization realizes anyway). Isolation and alienation have been the topic of many papers on current HPVS health care organizations. For instance, Banks (2004) discusses how nurses stop feeling involved because of the way organizations are structured. And indeed, if we look at the home care example, it is easy to see that care professionals feel completely alienated from the goal of really taking care of someone and cannot feel connected to the patient any more if all they do is put on compression stockings all day for a great many patients. In the Netherlands, this was a reason for many home care nurses to quit (Monsen and de Blok, 2013).[2]

A third way in which HPVSs are problematic for the quality of work is that in these structures the probability of job-related stress is quite high. Realizing the targets set for a job in an HPVS may be problematic because, as we have discussed, such jobs may face many disturbances (the probability of disturbances is high in such organizations) and, at the same time, these jobs lack the regulatory potential to deal with these disturbances. So employees working in such jobs need to realize targets, face many possible problems in doing so, and can't do much about them. Now, as many authors point out, this job situation – facing problems and being unable to solve them – induces job-related stress (cf. Karasek, 1979; de Sitter, 1994; Christis, 1998). In fact, in HPVSs this lack of control is structurally built into a task, hence feelings of stress are unavoidable.

To summarize, HPVSs are not good at realizing quality of work variables. Employees in HPVSs may well find themselves doing meaningless, stressful jobs sapping away their energy and joy. Indeed, not only may seeing the point of doing these jobs become hard, the gloomy prospect of living a pointless working life beckons. As several authors point out, this is anything but an exaggeration for the caregivers in HPVS home care organizations (cf. Monsen and de Blok, 2013; Banks, 2004). Being trapped in simple, repetitive jobs, seeing many patients for a very short amount of time, finding themselves unable to really connect with patients and deliver the care they had hoped to deliver and had been trained to deliver, feeling utterly frustrated about being unable to perform up to their own professional standards, caregivers became disengaged from their work, or even left these organizations. In these organizations, the possibility for professional work as a caregiver is organized away, or, to paraphrase Freidson (2001), such organizational structures drive out the "soul of professionalism".

In all, HPVSs don't do a good job at realizing and adapting the organization's contribution to society (see Figure 3.12). They lead to an increase in the probability of disturbances – high P(D) – in the network, and to a decrease in regulatory potential –low RP (left part of Figure 3.12). This results in a problematic realization of the four basic activities, which, in turn, impairs realizing the variables related to quality of organization and quality of work (arrow A in Figure 3.12). And as the organization's contribution is

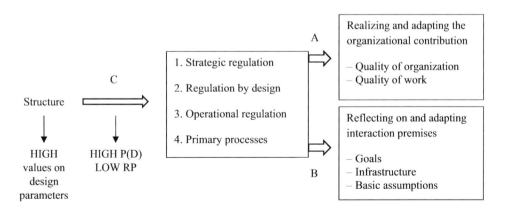

FIGURE 3.12 HPVSs have difficulty realizing variables related to quality or organization and quality of work and enabling reflection on and adaptation of interaction premises

operationalized in terms of these variables, both realizing this contribution (performing primary processes and their operational regulation) and adaptation (redefining the goals instantiating it) are problematic.

Problems with reflecting on and adapting organizational interaction premises

The second main criterion for organizational structures is that they enable the reflection on and change of interaction premises – i.e. the organizational goals, the infrastructure, and basic assumptions (see arrow B in Figure 3.12). We will first deal with goals and infrastructure. After that, we will turn to the prospect of changing basic assumptions in HPVSs.

Reflecting on and changing organizational goals and infrastructure   Based on the previous discussion, it can already be appreciated that HPVSs do not really help us to think about and change goals and infrastructures. We have already discussed the fact that HPVSs have a hard time realizing the basic activities 'regulation by design' (which results in an infrastructure) and 'strategic regulation' (which results in a set of goals). Therefore, we have, in fact, already established that reflecting on and changing goals and infrastructures is difficult in HPVSs. Even so, we want to briefly note the effect of problematic goals and infrastructures as interaction premises in HPVSs.

As we discussed in Chapter 2, goals act as an interaction premise, in that the basic activities should reflect them. Ideally, they realize them, adapt them if necessary, and provide the infrastructural conditions for this realization and adaptation. Ideally, in organizational interactions, goals are continuously acted upon; they are a basis for realizing the four basic activities, and during their realization they can be adapted if necessary. However, in HPVSs this ongoing reflection on and change of goals as part of the basic activities may be seriously impaired. Being out of touch with goals and organizational output, truly reflecting on how operational jobs relate to these goals and output can, of course, no longer be a part of these jobs. Moreover, being out of touch with the primary processes and their infrastructural conditions, detached regulators may change goals in a way that the connection with these processes and conditions is lost. Both situations break the (ideal) natural chain of setting goals, adjusting conditions, realizing goals, resetting goals, etc.

Reflecting on and changing the infrastructure is what the basic activity regulation by design is about. And, as this activity is impaired in HPVSs, relevant changes to the infrastructure may be problematic. So, as some authors note (e.g. Fruytier, 1994), the structure has become its own enemy: it has lost its capacity to change itself. Or, to borrow a term from Ashby: the system shows self-locking properties. Ideally, the structure should support a 'natural infrastructural drift' (cf. Chapter 2). That is, it should be able to continually reflect on and, if necessary, change itself to make sure that it promotes supportive conditions for continuous experimentation. As Galbraith (2000) puts it, it should be able to continuously "regenerate" itself. But unfortunately, in HPVSs, this continuous regeneration has become problematic.

In Chapter 2, a distinction between formal and informal goals and infrastructural parts was made. One of the ideas was that formal goals and infrastructures, once defined, set the scene for their own change, which was based on the 'enactment' of goals and infrastructural parts in organizational practices. Thus, informal goals and infrastructures emerged – which could be a source for changing their formal counterparts, which, in turn, gives rise to a new informal 'drift'. However, as can be derived from what has been said in this chapter, HPVSs are formal structures that curtail the informal infrastructural and goal-related drift. In such cases, episodic interventions may be needed.

Reflecting on and changing organizational basic assumptions   That HPVSs are bad at changing goals and infrastructures can already be derived from the previous sections. However, to see that these structures may also have a negative effect on reflecting on and changing basic assumptions – the third interaction premise – requires some additional explanation.

As the reader may recall from Chapter 2, basic assumptions refer to a more or less shared, implicit and taken-for-granted cognitive and moral background for generating and evaluating solutions to organizational problems of adaptation and realization. Their 'generative' moment referred to the space of possible solutions they open up. Their 'evaluative' moment referred to the fact that the success of proposed solutions (goals and infrastructures) is always assessed against the background of the basic assumptions. We also noted that, once these assumptions have established themselves, it may be very hard to change them – given their taken-for-grantedness.

In this section, we discuss the prospect of reflecting on and changing basic assumptions in HPVSs – even though this is hard anyway, given their nature. We approach this issue in two ways. First, we argue that the nature of at least some of the basic assumptions that arise in such structures makes change difficult. Second, we will briefly look at the structural conditions in HPVSs for becoming aware of basic assumptions and for changing them.

Types of basic assumptions

In HPVSs, it may be difficult to establish a shared set of basic assumptions with respect to dealing with organizational problems of adaptation and realization, as most employees lack an idea of the nature of these problems, let alone of their system-wide solutions. Basic assumptions related to job content tend to be restricted to functional departments (cf. the idea of differentiation found in Lawrence and Lorsch, 1967). What is possible, though, is that in HPVSs shared assumptions emerge about *why* jobs are organized in a particular HPV way – about *what is needed* to perform them in these structures, or about the *consequences for the working self* in such structures. And these assumptions further shape how we think of ourselves and our jobs. In fact, as we will argue, the basic assumptions arising in HPVSs may have a self-preserving nature, obstructing their own change.

Basic assumptions about why jobs are organized in an HPV way   As Morgan (1986) describes, many of us think of organizations as machines that can be broken down into many specialized parts, and whose functioning, i.e. the efficient realization of predetermined goals, depends on the functioning of these parts. Based on this metaphor, one may come to believe that high parameter value designs are quite 'natural' – in HPVSs, each part has its own designated function in a complex network of parts. The HPV structure, by means of which specialized parts are defined and connected, is deeply ingrained in the machine metaphor. As a result, the necessity of building structures along these lines seems to remain an uncontested issue. A related shared assumption may be the idea of inertia (cf. Weick, 2000), which indicates that organizations, because of their nature, have difficulty changing with the same pace as their environment, and are themselves difficult to change. Once an organization, as a complex network of intricate parts, a complex machine, has been set in motion, it is difficult to change. And, as Weick discusses, implied in this way of perceiving organizations is that continuous experimentation is difficult to realize. Also implied is that change initiated by individual (operational) parts is rather impossible. A third set of basic assumptions underlying the design of HPVSs is about why employees are motivated to do their work at all. If, as in agency theory (cf. Jensen and Meckling, 1976; Wruck, 2000), egocentric motives are stressed, structures should be designed in such a way that decision authority should be separated from operational work, securing job-external control. All of these basic assumptions may leave employees of HPVSs with the idea that their job is inevitably defined the way it is, and that there is no point in changing it. It may also make that designers favour a particular way of building structures (isomorphism and mimicry seem to be institutional variations on this theme; cf. Scott, 2008).

Basic assumptions about what HPVS jobs require   Other assumptions that may develop in the context of HPVSs have to do with what is required of employees to do their jobs. In production organizations, one may gradually learn and accept that efficiency is what matters, and that it comes about by job specialization and external control. And as a result, we may expect of ourselves that we contribute to efficiency by our own specialization and lack of decision authority. Similarly, in (machine) bureaucracies, one may come to see that following rules – or as Jos (1988) puts it, "develop[ing] a habit of painstaking obedience" – is required to perform "the tasks that are entrusted [. . .] by those above them in the hierarchy" (pp. 329–330). Working in HPVSs (and lacking knowledge of or experience in non-HPVSs), we may gradually come to believe that realizing bureaucratic goals of efficiency and uniformity (cf. Freidson, 2001) is served by specialized, separated structures, requiring a specific dedication and mind-set.

Basic assumptions about the working self in HPVSs   As a result of being immersed in HPVSs, we may also develop assumptions about our working self. In line with Foucault's (1977) discussion of the disciplines (see Achterbergh and Vriens, 2010), employees in HPVSs are subjected to 'regimes of trivialization', as employees are supposed to react with the same activities to the same external cues (some command, or material arriving at a workstation). This tends "to shape us into something we neither are nor want to be: [. . .] indifferent cogs in a larger production process producing us as indifferent cogs" (Achterbergh and Vriens, 2010, p. 310). Moreover, as we are subjected to hierarchical monitoring and control systems with their categories and norms used for evaluation, and as our working life depends on meeting these criteria, we gradually come to see ourselves 'with the eyes of our guards', i.e. in terms of the criteria set for us. If these criteria become more and more abstract proxies of what we really do, or if they are reduced to only a very few indicators of our work (e.g. if in our care example, caregivers are only evaluated in terms of 'patient satisfaction scores'), then we may lose track of what we *could* contribute; we only have a crippled image of what we are or can be. Caregivers, for instance, may come to see themselves as producing patient satisfaction scores instead of as professionals providing care (cf. Tsoukas, 1997). Both trivialization and seeing ourselves 'with the eyes of our guards' leave employees with a rather degraded view of the working self. If our basic assumptions about the 'working self' develop along these lines, we may come to see that such degradation is inevitable and, in the end, even accept our organizational misery.

The basic assumptions described previously (and these are just some examples) have an effect on setting goals, designing infrastructures, and on how we perform our work in HPVSs. Given the assumptions described previously, quality of organization goals will receive more emphasis than quality of work. Moreover, quality of work goals will have a specific focus (e.g. development and learning relates to specialization). Moreover, the basic assumptions affect design choices, in that they favour structures along HPVS lines. Finally, our idea of how to perform our job and what is required for it is shaped by basic assumptions, as described previously. Once these basic assumptions have emerged, they will serve as a background for all kinds of problems which we may encounter while performing the four basic activities. In HPVSs, this may lead to even more specialization, separation, and detached monitoring and control. These assumptions may thus result in a seemingly inescapable reinforcement of HPVSs. Hence, the basic assumptions arising in HPVSs seem to undermine the prospect of their own change.

Structural conditions for reflecting on and changing basic assumptions

Basic assumptions form an uncontested, taken-for-granted cognitive and moral background for dealing with organizational problems. Their taken-for-grantedness and uncontestedness make them hard to change in any organization. A first step in changing basic assumptions is that we should become aware of them, which means that organizational problems and the solutions we come up with become subject of reflection. If we systematically ask ourselves what the causes of particular problems are, why we think that particular solutions will work, and try to come up with alternative explanations or solutions, we may uncover certain basic assumptions. However, such reflection takes time, and requires knowledge and a deep understanding of the problems organizations face and of the proposed solutions. Moreover, this reflection is served by a social embeddedness which may help us engage in a critical dialogue and jointly discuss the shared background and come up with solutions (cf. Moore, 2005, and MacIntyre, 1999, who argue along similar lines in the context of uncovering our moral values). Ideally, the social context should extend organizational boundaries to increase the prospect of incorporating different perspectives.

Besides awareness, changing basic assumptions assumes experimenting with different ways of approaching organizational problems and discovering that other ways of perceiving them may also work. And, again, this requires time, room for experimental manoeuvring, and critical (social) evaluation of and reflection on the outcome of these experiments.

Unfortunately, the conditions mentioned previously for changing basic assumptions are hardly available in HPVSs. In such structures, tasks with a short cycle time lack the time for reflection and experimentation. Moreover, given the small scope of most tasks, reflection on basic assumptions in the sense of gaining a deep understanding of organizational problems, their causes, and of alternative ways of perceiving problems to uncover the basic assumptions is hardly possible. These problems and their causes remain invisible as one's job is only related to a small aspect of them. This lack of overview also makes experimentation and reflection on alternative solutions rather unfeasible. And as a result, not only is it difficult to become aware of basic assumptions, but their change also seems difficult. In addition, as we have discussed, tasks in HPVSs have been defined in such a way that organization members are not an active part of a social network. In isolated jobs, jointly discussing and reflecting on any subject is problematic. And, given their lack of overview, interaction cannot really be about subjects that transcend their small jobs.

84 Interventions in organizational structures

So, in all, HPVSs don't do a good job of realizing and adapting the organization's contribution to society (see arrow A in Figure 3.12), as discussed previously. And, as we discussed in this section, they also have trouble in supporting the reflection on and adaptation of interaction premises (see arrow B in Figure 3.12). In such structures, goals and infrastructures are difficult to change and particularly problematic basic assumptions may arise. In fact, such structures may well lose the ability to alter themselves and may require episodic interventions.

3.4.2 Why low parameter structures stand a better chance of meeting the criteria set for structural adequacy

Having discussed the low likelihood of HPVSs meeting the criteria for structural adequacy, we will now argue that structures with low parameter values (LPVSs) stand a better chance of meeting these criteria. The main line of reasoning basically mirrors the one given in the previous section on HPVSs: LPVSs have a reduced probability of disturbances, and an increased regulatory potential. And, because of that, they have, compared to HPVSs, fewer problems realizing the four basic activities, and hence a better prospect of meeting the two main criteria for structural adequacy – realizing and adapting the organization's contribution to society and reflecting on and changing the organization's interaction premises.

As in the previous section, we will start with an example of an ideal typical LPV structure. Next, we will discuss why low parameter values support the adequate realization of the four basic activities. And finally, we will argue that they have a better chance of meeting the two main criteria set for organizations.

Structures with low values on the design parameters

Figure 3.13 shows an ideal typical organizational structure with low values on the design parameters. In these structures, a low value of functional concentration results in several semi-autonomous 'parallel production flows' dedicated to a sub-set of orders. In Figure 3.13, three such flows are given – one dedicated to the orders belonging to product type X, one dedicated to Y, and one to Z. If X, Y, and Z stand for the same categories of order types as in the high parameter example (chairs, tables, and cupboards, with the same number of order types in each category; i.e. three, three and four respectively) the number of different order combinations per production flow decreases dramatically. In the chair and table flows, this number of combinations is now $2^3 - 1 = 7$, and in the cupboard flow it is $2^4 - 1 = 15$.[3]

In each order flow, low levels of differentiation of operational activities make sure that production, support, and preparation activities are integrated into tasks as much as possible. Similarly, a low level of operational specialization results in tasks covering the whole production process – at least as large as possible. Employees having tasks with low levels of operational differentiation and specialization have broad and coherent jobs which, ideally, cover operational activities relevant for the production of the complete job to be done (cf. Nadler and Tushman, 1997). In such structures, employees no longer perform small jobs with a short cycle time in functional departments, but they are part of so-called semi-autonomous teams (cf. Galbraith, 1973; de Sitter, 1994) which perform production, support, and preparation activities themselves and are responsible for the production of a complete product or service.

Organizational structures 85

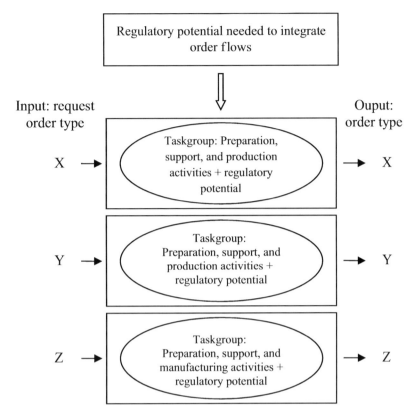

FIGURE 3.13 An organizational structure with low values on design parameters

Additionally, these teams have the required regulatory potential to produce their own flow-related output (low level of separation). Moreover, due to low levels of differentiation of regulation into parts and aspects, teams can perform the complete regulatory cycle of monitoring, assessment, and adjustment with respect to their own operational activities. They can take care of operational regulation themselves; they are allowed some form of regulation by design, related to providing and improving infrastructural means relevant for realizing the required output; and they are allowed some form of strategic regulation, enabling them to adjust goals related to the required flow output (e.g. renegotiating product specifications with clients). The jobs of team members in structures with low parameter values resemble the jobs of members of the self-contained task groups that Galbraith (1973) and de Sitter (1994) have in mind, or the jobs in so-called 'organic' structures (Burns and Stalker, 1961; Donaldson, 2001) or 'horizontal' and 'agile' structures (cf. Anand and Daft, 2007). As Nadler and Tushman (1997) observe, such structures "center around interdependent business groups that have back-to-front responsibility [. . .] [and are organized] around complete business processes" (p. 141).

Low parameter structures result, ideally, in relatively autonomous order flows in which output is realized by self-contained teams having the operational and regulatory potential to completely produce the output. However, in such structures, not all regulation is found within the flows; some form of regulation with respect to the total set of flows is still needed.

For instance, a form of overarching strategic formulation, or some regulation by design by means of which certain economies of scale can be realized, or some form of operational regulation dealing with interferences between flows (cf. the coordination function of Beer, 1979) is still required. So, in low parameter structures, some form of regulation securing the integration of flows is still needed. Note, however, that this type of regulation does not necessarily mean that it should be the job of someone or some group that is not (also) working in the flow. It may be the joint responsibility of employees representing flow teams.

At this point, we should make an important note about the low parameter value structures as described here. It should be noted that the description is a rather extreme case of low values on design parameters, and that in practice there is a limit to how low these values can get. For instance, in principle, one may design autonomous flows for each separate product type. However, this may result in the underutilization of some flows if the demand for 'their' product is low. Capacity utilization in flows, then, poses limits to the degree of functional de-concentration. Similarly, sometimes a production process may simply be too complex to be carried out by one team. In such cases, teams should be assigned to segments of the production process. The complexity of the production process therefore also sets boundaries to lowering the values of design parameters. However, de Sitter's overall recommendation is *to build structures with parameter values that are as low as possible, given the specific organizational and market conditions.*

In all, while high parameter value structures are described as complex networks with simple jobs, low parameter value structures can be described as simple networks with complex jobs (see de Sitter, 1994; de Sitter and den Hertog, 1997).

As an example of an LPV structure, consider Buurtzorg (Dutch for 'neighbourhood care'), a Dutch home care organization with the same goals as the home care organization presented earlier, but which organizes its work quite differently (cf. Monsen and de Blok, 2013; Nandram, 2015a, 2015b; Verloop and Hillen, 2014). This home care organization consists of teams of up to 12 nurses who perform all relevant care activities. Moreover, these teams are coupled to a sub-set of clients (who live in the same neighbourhood) and the teams have the regulatory potential to deal with disturbances they come across themselves. In particular, in Buurtzorg:

1. There is a low level of specialization, as team members are able to perform and actually do perform all care activities.
2. Functional concentration is low, as caregivers are only tied to the clients of one neighbourhood.
3. The teams of caregivers also perform relevant preparation (like planning and routing) and support activities themselves.

In all, the production structure of Buurtzorg entails that caregivers only see a few clients each day for whom they perform all care tasks. Moreover, they are all involved in preparation and support activities.

The control structure of Buurtzorg is also different from the traditional home care organization discussed earlier. In particular:

1. There is little separation. Much of the regulatory potential is part of the tasks of team members. As a sign of the integration of operational and regulatory tasks, Monsen and

de Blok (2013) report that each team can "develop its own 'personality' functioning as a unified whole [...]. The nurses decide together what to do, and each team is recognized for its collective wisdom and knowledge of what is best for its patients and community" (p. 57).
2. Regulatory tasks like monitoring, assessing, and intervening are carried out by team members themselves as they encounter problems in their work. These tasks are also a joint team responsibility, as team members discuss operational problems and assist each other in finding solutions.
3. Team members also have a considerable say in setting goals for their own team, given the overall goal of Buurtzorg and given the particulars of their own neighbourhood. Moreover, they are also allowed considerable freedom in designing infrastructural conditions. One exception is the ICT system used for sharing experience (relating to care or care management) among teams. Operational regulation is the responsibility of team members themselves.
4. Team members have regulatory responsibility for the complete care process. Operational regulation is not split up into small sub-tasks.

The Buurtzorg organization, then, consists of teams that are largely self-sufficient, in the sense that they are enabled to perform a complete process and are given the regulatory potential to do so (cf. Galbraith, 1973; de Sitter, 1994).

Low parameter value structures support the realization of the four basic activities

To show that LPVSs have a positive effect on realizing the four basic activities, we will first discuss, as we did with HPVSs, the part of the structure related to realizing primary processes (the production structure). Please recall that the relevant design parameters in this respect are the degree of operational specialization, the degree of operational differentiation, the degree of functional concentration, and the degree of operational specialization. After that, we will go into the control structure (the network of tasks realizing the three basic regulatory activities). The relevant design parameters with respect to the control structure are the degree of regulatory differentiation into parts and aspects, the degree of regulatory specialization, and the degree of separation.

The effect of low values of design parameters on realizing the primary processes

A low level of specialization of operational activities and a low level of differentiation of operational activities into production, preparation, and support tasks result in 'integrated' operational tasks with a broad scope. Low differentiation means, ideally, that a task includes all preparation, support, and production activities needed to realize a complete product or service. A low level of specialization means that a task is not split up into jobs with a short cycle time, but that, ideally, a task covers the complete production process. In the case of Buurtzorg, the home care organization presented earlier, this is realized in 'neighbourhood teams' of caregivers who do their own weekly and daily planning, perform care activities themselves, and who perform some support activities. Moreover, these teams consist of caregivers who perform all the necessary care activities for one client, and hence see these clients for a longer time. Because of low levels of specialization and differentiation, there are fewer, more complex tasks in LPVSs than in HPVSs. And, as a result, the number of relations in the LPVSs network is greatly reduced.

A low level of functional concentration results in tasks that are only coupled to a sub-set of the total amount of order types (and hence orders). As we stated earlier, in structures with a low level of functional concentration, the variability of the relations between tasks decreases. In a furniture factory with seven different types of furniture, and in which tasks are related to all orders (i.e. high functional concentration), the network of operational tasks should be prepared to handle 127 (2^7-1) different order combinations. As discussed before, each order combination requires (1) a different set and sequence and of operational activities (e.g. planning, drilling, sawing, planing, etc.) and (2) different interactions between operational tasks (information or required material). And, as a consequence, the variability (the variety of the relations in the network) should reflect these 127 order combinations. Reducing functional concentration, e.g. making three parallel flows (dealing with two, two, and three types of furniture respectively) greatly reduces the number of order combinations in each flow (this number is now, per flow: (2^2-1 (=3), 3, and 7). As the variability reduces dramatically, the probability of disturbances also drops. As tasks are now coupled to only a few order types, and therefore fewer order combinations, performing these tasks becomes simpler and they require less time (e.g. to change material or to adjust machines). And, as there are fewer routings per flow, planning and keeping track of products also becomes easier. In the case of the home care organization, low functional concentration is realized by tying teams of caregivers to only a few clients (only those who live in the same neighbourhood). This reduces problems with transportation which arise in the situation in which a caregiver is coupled to potentially all patients. Moreover, within the teams, the same caregiver was often tied to the same client – reducing the functional concentration even more.

In LPVSs, then, low levels of specialization, differentiation, and functional concentration reduce the number of relations and the variability of these relations. This, in turn, reduces the probability of disturbances.

Besides this decrease of the number of relations in the network of tasks and the reduction of variability, low levels of specialization, differentiation, and functional concentration also have a positive effect on the production structure in other ways, which essentially mirror the effects of high levels of these parameters (see earlier).

First, as tasks are now 'integrated' tasks in which employees perform all necessary activities related to the production process from front to end, i.e. who are able to deliver a complete product or service, and as these tasks are only coupled to a sub-set of products, employees can gain an overview and understanding of the complete process. Having this overview greatly enhances regulation (see the discussion on the control structure later in the text). In addition, it enables employees to be in touch with the end products, and hence the output and goals of the organization.

Second, in LPVSs waiting time can be reduced. In structures with high functional concentration, producing in batches is common, as we discussed earlier. In structures with low functional concentration, batches can become smaller – even as low as batches of one (which is called single piece production – cf. Standard and Davis, 1999). Smaller batches means less waiting time. As de Sitter (1994) and authors on Lean Production such as Womack et al. (1990) and Womack and Jones (1996) show, the decrease in waiting time in structures that organize

Organizational structures **89**

around production flows is dramatic. Waiting time is also reduced because planning, making, and supporting are integrated into tasks. In the Buurtzorg case, for instance, team members do their own planning – which is tailored to their own situation. Given their knowledge of the clients they see, and given the fact that they see only a sub-set of the total number of clients, such planning is simpler and takes less time. It also is more relevant – see below.

A related third advantage of low functional concentration is that there are far less routings per production flow, which means less planning and an increased possibility of keeping track of products. If we take the furniture factory as an example, it is easy to appreciate that planning the routings and keeping track of 127 different order combinations in the factory in which tasks are related to all orders is far more complex than planning and keeping track of the order combinations arising in the three parallel production units. As Christensen et al. (2010) argue, in LPVSs a large number of overhead activities become redundant, and the associated costs are much less (pp. 92–93). In all, far less effort is needed to plan and keep track of orders in low parameter value organizations than in those with high values.

The effect of low values of design parameters on the regulatory activities

The control structures of LPVSs are quite different from their HPVS counterparts. They are much simpler, as the level of separation is low. This means that the regulatory and operational aspects are integrated into the same tasks as much as possible. As a result, operational tasks often comprise the regulatory potential needed to deal with the disturbances affecting them. As separation is low, there is also no hierarchy of regulators in ideal typical LPVSs. The control structure is also simpler, because the regulatory tasks are not differentiated into regulatory aspects and parts. That is, they do not comprise different tasks related to setting goals, (re)designing the infrastructure, or operational regulation. They also don't have different tasks for monitoring, assessment, and intervention. And finally, the control structure is simpler because regulatory tasks are not specialized into small tasks having only a small regulatory scope (e.g. dealing with only a small part of the operational process).

As we discussed earlier, the Buurtzorg organization has low values on parameters describing the control structure. Much of the regulatory potential is built into the tasks of caregivers working in the Buurtzorg neighbourhood teams. Moreover, very few managers are operating outside of these teams. Caregivers in the teams have the operational regulatory potential to deal with the disturbances they face. They also have a say in setting and resetting goals and in adjusting the infrastructural conditions to make them fit their work. With respect to operational regulation, all parts of the regulation cycle (monitoring, assessing, and intervening) are part of the caregiver's team tasks. With respect to infrastructural regulation and goal setting, they also contribute to the complete cycle (although resetting goals and changing the infrastructure is not completely left to the teams, as goals and parts of the infrastructure need to be aligned with other teams). Team members have operational regulatory responsibility for the complete process – so there is no specialization of operational regulation.

Now, following the main logic of de Sitter (1994), low values on the parameters relating to the control structure means that, compared to HPVSs, there are fewer relations in the network of tasks. Low specialization, separation, and differentiation lead to structures in which regulation is not broken down into small tasks, into tasks dealing with different regulatory aspect and parts, or into regulatory tasks with a small scope. Instead, the regulatory tasks are as broad as possible (including as many aspects and parts as possible, and having a broad regulatory scope). Moreover, regulation is integrated into operational tasks as much as possible. In all, this leads to a structure with fewer regulatory tasks – and hence to a structure with fewer relations. And, as before, a structure with fewer relations is less disturbance-prone than a structure with more relations.

However, a decrease in the probability of disturbances due to a decrease in the number of relations is not the only reason that the control structure of LPVSs improves *vis-à-vis* the control structure of HPVSs. The second reason has to do with the improvement of the regulatory potential itself. Here, again, the reasoning mirrors the argumentation given in the case of HPVSs. There are several causes for this improved regulatory potential.

To start with, and here we follow de Sitter (1994), low levels of separation ensure the direct involvement of those who regulate with that which is regulated. If regulation is performed by those who also perform the tasks they regulate, there is no delay because operational disturbances can be dealt with immediately. There is no need to process disturbances by means of a network of detached regulators. In a similar vein, regulators (i.e. operational employees with regulatory tasks) can also better appreciate the circumstances in which the disturbance occurs; regulators no longer lack the first-hand information about the nature and the context of the disturbance. Moreover, given low levels of regulatory parameters, employees are allowed to come up with solutions themselves – solutions that are fitting given their context-specific and operational know-how. In such organizations, a low degree of separation, regulatory differentiation, and specialization result in the potential to react to operational disturbances promptly and adequately. Compared to HPVSs, dealing with disturbances is no longer delayed and detached.

Low levels of regulatory differentiation and specialization further enhance the potential to promptly react to disturbances in an adequate way. Low values of parameters related to the production structure enable gaining an overview of the complete process. Low values of regulatory specialization and differentiation ensure that regulatory tasks also have a broad scope. In such a case, for instance, regulatory actions in one part of the process have a better prospect of not being disruptive for the rest of the process. Moreover, given this broad scope, the effect of regulatory actions can be monitored and adjusted.

The caregivers of Buurtzorg are allowed to deal with disturbances themselves the moment these disturbances emerge in the process. Moreover, their regulatory potential covers the complete process. So, in the case of a patient falling ill, a caregiver can, based on her knowledge of the client and the complete care process, understand the disturbance in a relevant way. For instance, she might think that it is likely that the patient has forgotten to take some medication. She could check whether this is so, consult with a doctor about possible solutions, and act accordingly (e.g. administer the medication, monitor some vital functions, arrange transportation to a hospital, etc.).

Having a regulatory overview also supports the possibility to communicate about and jointly deal with problems. As all members of Buurtzorg teams have the same regulatory scope, caregivers can consult each other to discuss care-related problems and solutions. In the example of the patient falling ill because she forgot to take her medication, the caregiver might have checked the intake of the medication and discussed with others in the team what to do. If it turns out that the case is more severe than initially conceived, the team members may back each other up in finding solutions – e.g. one caregiver escorts the client to the hospital, and another caregiver from the team takes on the other duties of the escorting caregiver that day.

In LPVSs, employees also have a broad range of regulatory actions at their disposal – this is quite large, as they are allowed to devise such actions themselves. In HPVSs, the small amount of regulatory actions come at the loss of dealing with disturbances. Contrary to HPVSs, in LPVSs a regulator can chose to deal with a disturbance in one activity by skipping others or performing them more quickly. For instance, in the case of a client for whom washing takes far longer than normal, the caregiver may decide to go on with this activity at the expense of, for instance, house cleaning. The caregiver can decide to do that another day. Such regulatory freedom is not possible in HPVSs. Note that this regulation involves strategic regulation at the team level (as the task targets for one day are altered).

Operational and regulatory overview also support both process and product innovation. Process innovation is easier than in HPVSs, as members are enabled to experiment with changes to operational activities, to learn about and appreciate the consequences of these changes, and to actually change the infrastructure to improve the process. Product innovation is also supported, as it requires an integrated perspective on organizational competencies and market opportunities – see earlier. And, contrary to HPVSs, this integration is much easier to obtain if the scope of regulatory tasks is large and not limited to only a small part or aspect of them. Moreover, as the responsibility for product innovation may be part of operational jobs that connect to clients, such innovations reflect what is going on in the market. In the home care example, for instance, product innovation is also the responsibility of team members, who are thoroughly in touch with their clients and are therefore in a better position to come up with ideas for improving their services and appreciate the effect of certain proposed changes. As an interesting example, Buurtzorg employees came up with the idea to organize a 'rollator race' (which is still held every year) – an idea they claim could only have been thought of given their knowledge of the clients and their regulatory potential to make it happen (Buurtzorg, 2018).

In LPVSs, the potential for regulation by design also increases. Based on an understanding of the complete process, and given the broad scope of regulatory tasks, relevant integral improvements to the infrastructure may be possible. In fact, given low values on all parameters, employees in LPVSs have the time, overview, and regulatory potential to experiment with and learn about new ways of performing operational activities or about the infrastructural conditions supporting these activities. LPVSs seem to enable the natural 'positive infrastructural drift' which comes about when organization members – in communication – gradually learn how to improve (the conditions for) their jobs.

Finally, LPVSs may also have a positive effect on strategic regulation – e.g. setting and (re)setting goals. By having an understanding of the complete operational process and being in touch with the overall goals and environment of the organization, appreciating the effect of a change in goals is much more likely. This improves the prospect of setting and resetting relevant organizational goals.

Low parameter value structures stand a better chance of meeting the two main criteria for organizational adequacy

In contrast to HPVSs, LPVSs have a low probability of disturbances and have the required regulatory potential to deal with them, and because of this, realizing the four basic activities is far less problematic. In this section, we want to show that LPVSs stand a better chance of meeting the two main criteria for structural adequacy – i.e., in contrast to HPVSs, they may

Supporting realizing and adapting the organization's contribution to society

As we discussed earlier, realizing and adapting the organization's contribution to society has been operationalized in terms of quality of organization variables (variables referring to flexibility, control over order realization, and innovation) and quality of work variables (variables related to the well-being of human resources). In this section, we will briefly show that LPVSs support the realization of the variables belonging to the quality or organization and quality of work. We will only give a brief account of these positive effects of LPVSs because the argumentation directly follows from the previous section and basically mirrors the reasoning showing that HPVSs are problematic.

Quality of organization In general, low values on the design parameters lead to shorter production cycle times (and hence more flexibility) and to enhanced control over order realization (two quality of organization variables).

As we discussed earlier, low levels of parameter values result in flows with only a sub-set of the total amount of orders enabling members to have overview of the whole process and to keep track of orders throughout the system. Moreover, low parameter values result in broad, coherent jobs which cover, ideally, the whole process, and have the regulatory potential to deal with the disturbances the moment they occur promptly and adequately. Such jobs decrease the production cycle time (and hence enhance flexibility) in several ways. Shorter production cycle times are possible because the probability of disturbances is lower, and because in operational tasks organization members have the regulatory potential to swiftly detect and deal with disturbances. In addition, if disturbances are detected early and dealt with swiftly and adequately, the probability that the disturbance affects other parts of the network also decreases. So, in LPVSs, the probability that a disturbance creates other disturbances is low (lower than in HPVSs). Moreover, because dealing with disturbances is done by those involved in the process in which these disturbances occur, no time is wasted on understanding the context in which disturbances occurred. On top of that, an overview of the process increases the probability of relevant regulatory actions (i.e. actions that do not impair the whole process) and production planning is much easier. Low parameter values also create the conditions for single-piece (flow) production, which entails far shorter waiting times than in batch and queue production of functionally concentrated structures.

LPVSs also enable a better 'control over order realization' – for comparable reasons. Reliability of production and production times can increase if there are fewer disturbances and if workers have the ability to detect them early and deal with them swiftly and adequately. Similarly, an overview of the complete process, a low probability of disturbances, and the prospect of dealing with disturbances enable keeping track of orders and make planning much easier and more reliable. They also enable product quality control – as, based on their overview and regulatory potential, organization members may detect errors early and have the possibility to repair them in an adequate way.

Finally, LPVSs also positively affect both process and product innovation – as discussed previously. Because of the large scope of operational and regulatory tasks and because of the overview of the production process, process innovations which are not just sub-optimizations may actually be obtainable. Similarly, because of the regulatory integration and lack of operational and regulatory specialization, an integrated perspective on product or goal improvements may be possible. Moreover, the structure of tasks in LPVSs provides the overview and regulatory potential to experiment and learn while performing one's job.

In all, the realization of the quality of organization variables in LPVSs is less problematic than in HPVSs.

Quality of work LPVSs also create opportunities for realizing quality of work variables. As we discussed earlier, quality of work is specified in terms of (1) the degree to which employees can learn and develop while doing their job, (2) the degree to which they feel involved, both socially and intrinsically, and (3) the degree to which they experience job-related stress. As with quality of organization, LPVSs seem to be better equipped to support the realization of these quality of work variables (see de Sitter, 1994; Achterbergh and Vriens, 2010). We will briefly discuss why this is the case.

In contrast to HPVSs, structures with low values on the design parameters offer better opportunities for individual (and collective) learning. Working in teams which have broad, coherent tasks – i.e. tasks that, ideally, cover the complete production process, and have the regulatory potential to detect and deal with disturbances at an operational, infrastructural, and strategic level – offers ample learning opportunities. Because of the involvement in the whole production process and because of the requisite regulatory potential, employees are in a better position to detect errors in the whole primary process and correct them – see the earlier text. Moreover, based on their overview of the process and connection to the output of the process, they can observe and interpret the effect of these corrections in specific circumstances and adjust these actions if needed. Based on their tasks, employees may engage in processes of experimentation in which they can try out and evaluate new modes of doing their job. So, in effect, LPVSs may be said to support the experiential learning cycle of error detection and informed correction – a point also made by others (e.g. Morgan, 1986, pp. 73ff; Anand and Daft, 2007).

By highlighting teamwork in which team members have similar skills and regulatory potential, LPVSs also support learning as a social process in which errors, new modes of behaviour, and their effects may be socially reflected upon. Moreover, LPVSs not only enable learning with respect to conducting primary processes and their operational regulation, they also offer opportunities for learning about organizational goals, output, and infrastructural conditions. In the words of Argyris and Schön (1978), they enable 'single loop' learning – improving primary processes given the goals set for them – as well as 'double loop' learning – learning about the appropriateness of goals, and learning about the conditions (and barriers) for learning. If jobs of employees are visibly connected to the output and goals of the organization, and if employees are granted some strategic regulation, it becomes possible to reflect about the appropriateness of goals and output, and even engage in restating them. Similarly, given their being immersed in the primary process and their potential for regulation by design, employees of LPVSs may not only be good judges of the infrastructural conditions they have to perform their jobs in, they may also engage in constructing and implementing changes to the infrastructure. So LPVSs may enable learning with respect to infrastructures.

As a simple example, consider an employee of the Buurtzorg home care organization. This employee has the relevant skills to perform all care activities and has the regulatory potential at three levels, as described earlier. Moreover, the employee is member of a team of similar employees which provides care for only a sub-set of patients. Because of the connection to only a few patients for which the employee provides all care activities, the employee may engage in a process of caregiving and feedback from patients (and discuss this feedback with team members) and gradually learn how the care can best be provided for these particular clients, given their specific circumstances. The team of caregivers may also learn about the appropriateness of the infrastructural conditions for their work – e.g. about how work may be divided among the team members for a particular period of time. Finally, caregivers may also learn about the appropriateness of the goals set for their work. Given their connectedness with clients, they may, for instance, gradually come to see that besides practical and paramedical care, socio-psychological care is another important goal, and based on their ability for strategic regulation, they may even try to change the set of goals so that the new goal is incorporated.

Besides offering opportunities for learning, LPVSs also support the development of organization members. If development is understood as the accumulation of acquired knowledge in order to be able to better deal with the problems that emerge while doing a job, it may be appreciated that LPVSs support the development of employees. Based on the ideas mentioned previously, it can be appreciated that LPVSs offer care professionals opportunities to develop themselves as professionals (see Vriens et al., 2016). Even if we understand individual development in organizations in an ethical sense, i.e. as developing skills, practical wisdom and moral virtues (we used this description of development in Vriens et al., 2018a; see also earlier in this chapter), LPVSs offer support. As several authors point out, structures with low values on design parameters offer the conditions for this kind of development. They are said to offer so-called 'teleological' conditions (enabling reflection about the appropriateness of goals), 'deliberative' conditions (enabling deliberation about and implementation of appropriate actions), and 'social' conditions (offering a social network in which reflection and deliberation can be made a joint effort) (cf. Vriens et al., 2018a; Breen, 2012).

A similar reasoning applies to the degree of both social and intrinsic job-related involvement of employees (see the explanation earlier) in LPVSs. Being a member of a team of employees which is responsible for realizing a complete (sub-set of) order(s) and which has a joint regulatory potential for operational, infrastructural, and strategic regulation offers opportunities to be 'socially involved' – i.e. to be "actively engaged in a network of social relations associated with the job" (Achterbergh and Vriens, 2010, p. 264). Ideally, goals, infrastructural conditions, and operational regulation are the result of mutual reflection and decision making, implying – even necessitating – active involvement in the team. This was clearly the case in the Buurtzorg home care organization, in which a team of caregivers arrived at their own planning, interacted with each other and other teams to share care-related knowledge, and in which patient well-being was object of joint discussions (cf. Monsen and de Blok, 2013).

LPVSs like the Buurtzorg organization also create chances for 'intrinsic involvement' – i.e. being "able to see and appreciate the point of the task – i.e. its contribution to the process of producing something as well as to the product itself" (Achterbergh and Vriens, 2010, p. 264). In LPVSs, team members are supposed to actively co-contribute to setting goals with respect to the output of a complete product or service, or to designing the infrastructure required to realize the output, as well as to regulate operationally – see earlier. To support this active involvement, LPVSs make sure that employees are in touch with the goals and output of their job. Because employees are in touch with the goals and output of their work, they can actually appreciate what they are contributing to, and because of their *active* involvement, they can also play a part in improving goals and output. In the Buurtzorg organization, this active intrinsic involvement made sure that the care professionals felt that they could do their job as care professionals continuously geared towards the well-being of the patients they looked after.

The last way in which LPVSs support the realization of the quality of work variables is that, contrary to HPVSs, the probability of job-related stress is lower. That is, in contrast to HPVSs, realizing the targets set for a job is less problematic because such jobs face fewer disturbances (the probability of disturbances is lower in LPVSs) and the regulatory potential to deal with these disturbances is built into these jobs. As several authors point out, this situation reduces job-related stress (cf. Karasek, 1979; Christis, 1998).

All in all, LPVSs seem to offer better opportunities for realizing quality of work variables than their HPVSs counterparts. Buurtzorg provides a case in point – Buurtzorg takes pride in the fact that it has been voted the most employee-friendly organization in the Netherlands for several years in a row. Care professionals feel like care professionals again, as de Blok (founder of Buurtzorg) notes (Buurtzorg, 2018).

So, in terms of the model governing the logic of this chapter, LPVSs seem to offer better changes for realizing and adapting the organization's contribution to society (see Figure 3.14). Compared to HPVSs, they have a smaller probability of disturbances (LOW P(D)) in the network and sufficient regulatory potential (ENOUGH RP; left part of Figure 3.14). Realizing these cybernetic desiderata make LPVSs structures with a better prospect of realizing the four basic activities, which, in turn, enables realizing the variables related to quality of organization and quality of work (arrow A in Figure 3.14). And, as the organization's contribution is operationalized in terms of these variables, both realizing this contribution (performing primary processes and their operational regulation) and adaptation (redefining the goals instantiating it) seems more possible than in HPVSs.

LPVSs' potential for reflecting on and adapting organizational interaction premises

The second main criterion for organizational structures is that they enable the reflection on and change of interaction premises – i.e. the organizational goals, the infrastructure, and basic

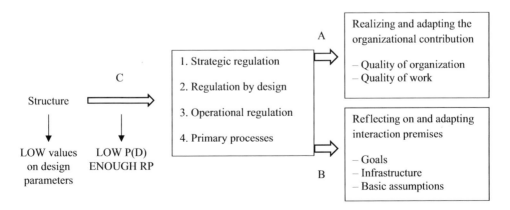

FIGURE 3.14 Low value parameter structures

assumptions (see arrow B in Figure 3.14). We will first deal with goals and infrastructure. After that, we will turn to the prospect of changing basic assumptions in LPVSs.

Reflecting on and changing organizational goals and infrastructure   As we just discussed, LPVSs do a better job of supporting the four basic activities than HPVSs. Therefore, because the activity 'strategic regulation' is better supported in LPVSs, the prospect of reflecting on and changing goals also increases. After all, strategic regulation is about reflecting on and changing goals. A similar reasoning holds for reflecting on and changing the infrastructure. This is exactly what should happen while carrying out the basic activity 'regulation by design'. If this activity is supported adequately, which is the case in LPVS, as we argued in this chapter, then reflecting on and changing the infrastructure is also supported. In all, because the basic activities of strategic regulation and regulation by design are supported in LPVSs, these structures also create opportunities for reflecting on and changing goals and infrastructures.

Reflecting on and changing organizational basic assumptions   As we did when we discussed the effect of HPVSs on reflecting and changing 'basic assumptions', we will first discuss the types of basic assumptions arising in LPVSs. Second, we will discuss the prospect of reflecting on and changing these basic assumptions in LPVSs.

Types of basic assumptions   In contrast to HPVSs, a shared set of basic assumptions with respect to dealing with organizational problems of adaptation and realization is more likely to emerge in LPVSs as employees can, as part of their jobs, develop an idea of the nature of these problems and of their system-wide solutions. In LPVSs, employees are, ideally, in touch with organizational goals and output, and have an idea of how their job relates to these goals and output. Moreover, they have broad tasks and skills, are embedded in a job-related social network, and have the regulatory potential to jointly assess organizational problems and create, discuss, implement, and evaluate solutions to them. And, following Schein, as discussed in Chapter 2, based on these practices, employees may develop job-related basic assumptions. An example may be how assumptions about patient well-being and involvement can emerge in a Buurtzorg-like home care organization. When a team was at one time forced to function with too few members, one employee asked several clients – who lived separately in the same flat – if they would be willing to help each other out in preparing a meal together, under the supervision of the employee. Although the patients were somewhat reluctant at the outset, they found the whole endeavour quite interesting and actually enjoyed preparing the meal together. The employee shared this experience with her team members, and they devised other 'social solutions' in which clients were brought together to help each other out. And even though supervision and individual assistance were still required, engaging clients in this way turned out to be quite successful. The team noted that clients found that these initiatives improved their sense of independence and evaluated these efforts as socially rewarding. Thus, the team developed ideas of the relation between patient well-being and involving and socially engaging clients in activities they wanted help with. These ideas were shared company-wide and formed the basis of many help initiatives. In fact, after several years, the whole idea of the positive effect of client involvement had become so self-evident that most initiatives were based on it, which sometimes meant that individual client needs were overlooked. The point of this example is that the emergence of such job content-related basic assumptions *is* possible in LPVSs as employees have the skill and regulatory potential to change the way they do their work, have the possibility to monitor the results of these changes, and can discuss and evaluate their usefulness with each other. After several successful implementations, team members may develop a shared sense of success of these kind of changes which may affect other work-related initiatives. Although such job-related basic assumptions developed in teams may have their drawbacks, they *can* emerge in LPVSs. Their emergence in HPVSs is problematic.

Besides hinting at the emergence of job-related basic assumptions, we want to take a brief look at three issues related to basic assumptions in LPVSs, just as we did when we discussed HPVSs. We want to address briefly the types of shared assumptions emerging in LPVSs (1) about why jobs are organized in a particular LPV way, (2) about what is needed to perform those jobs, and (3) about the consequences of LPV structures for the working self.

Basic assumptions about why jobs are organized in an LPV way

Thinking of organizations as machines with their many specialized parts serving the efficient realization of pre-determined goals fits HPVSs. Other metaphors, however, may be more suitable for LPVSs. Morgan (1986), for instance, discusses thinking of an organization as an organism as an alternative.[4] This metaphor highlights that organizations should adapt to their environment and need the flexibility to do so. It pictures organizations as learning and adaptive systems, and implies a continuous awareness of the environment and the capacity to change organizational behaviour (and goals). This idea of organizations carries with it the need for infrastructural flexibility: an infrastructure should enable learning and change to support adaptation. This perspective on organizations fits LPVSs in which tasks are in touch with the organization's output and goals (to incorporate the environment), in which task performance takes into account the specific (changing) tasks' circumstances, and in which tasks have the regulatory potential to co-change task goals and conditions. In fact, the organism metaphor allows one to perceive characteristics of tasks in LPVSs as relevant for learning, change, and adaptation. And as these characteristics have 'proven' themselves as helpful in adapting to changing circumstances, they may gradually become part of uncontested basic assumptions about how structures should be designed.

Related to the idea of organizations as adaptive organisms is rejecting organizations as 'inert' systems, but instead embracing them as systems that are changing continuously (cf. Weick, 2000). Instead of viewing organizations as a complex network of intricate parts which, once set in motion, can hardly change direction, organizations can be seen as systems in which continuous experimentation (and hence a kind of structural drift) is going on. This relates to Morgan's (1986) idea of organizations as flux, or Weick's (2000) idea of continuous sense-making. This assumption paves the way for change as a natural phenomenon and helps organization members who share this assumption to understand that they are part of a system that changes continuously, and even that their own task-related experimentation is part of it. This assumption thus helps organization members to see themselves as being actively involved in organizational change. In fact, it prompts them to see themselves as agents of organizational change.

A third set of basic assumptions underlying the design of LPVSs has to do with ideas related to the motivation of organization members. Instead of egocentric motives put forward in agency theory, other perspectives highlight intrinsic individual motivation and responsibility. Such perspectives don't necessitate external control (for instance, supervision and control built into tasks separate from operational work), but allow for teams which control themselves.

Now, as with all basic assumptions, the assumptions mentioned previously affect the way organization members think about how structures should be designed. In this respect, the basic assumptions underlying HPVSs are no different than those in LPVSs. The nature of the assumptions underlying the design of structures does make a difference. And what is relevant in this respect for the purpose of our book: in HPVSs, basic assumptions favour structural reification; in LPVSs, they favour structural change.

Basic assumptions about what is required of employees in LPVSs Other basic assumptions related to organizational structures that may develop have to do with what is required of employees to do their jobs in those structures. In LPVSs, tasks are carried out within teams and have a broad operational scope and regulatory potential at the operational, design, and strategic level. In these tasks, one is an 'active part of a social network' in which one has an operational and regulatory responsibility with respect to organizational output and goals. Being immersed in such tasks, one gradually learns that these tasks require teamwork, dedication, responsibility, and initiative. And, as a result, we may come to expect of ourselves that we contribute to organizational goals and output by showing such teamwork, dedication, responsibility, and initiative.

Basic assumptions about the working self in LPVSs As a result of being immersed in LPVSs, we may also develop assumptions about our working self. In contrast to seeing the working self as being subjected to regimes of trivialization and in contrast to being trapped in hierarchical control systems in which we are forced to see ourselves 'with the eyes of our guards', we may come to see ourselves as individuals whose contribution matters – to ourselves, to our co-workers, and to the environment. In LPVSs, we may develop basic assumptions about being an organization member who can deliver a relevant contribution, and who can develop and grow in the context of our job. Applied to organizations housing professionals, this entails, for instance, that professionals can see themselves *as* professionals – as employees who can develop and apply their specific esoteric skills, knowledge, and experience in order to be dedicated to a particular societal value – or, to put it somewhat more dramatically, as structures that do justice to the 'soul of professionalism' (cf. Freidson, 2001). Once these assumptions of our working self emerge, we may come to expect that our job-related dedication, application of our knowledge and skills, and job-related individual development are (or should be) supported by structures.

As with HPVSs, the basic assumptions described previously (and again, these are just some examples) have an effect on setting goals, designing infrastructures, and how we perform our work. Given the assumptions described previously, LPVS designs put emphasis on *both* quality of organization goals and quality of work. Moreover, these basic assumptions influence design choices in that they favour structures along LPVSs lines. Finally, our idea of how to perform our job and what is required for it is shaped by basic assumptions, as described previously. And, as in HPVSs, once these basic assumptions have emerged, they will serve as a background for all kinds of problems which we may encounter while we perform the four basic activities. In LPVSs, this may lead to monitoring and creating conditions for team-based dedication, initiative, responsibility, and efficiency and lead to keeping parameter values as low as possible. Therefore, these assumptions may result in reinforcing LPVSs.

Reflecting on and changing basic assumptions   At this point, it is worth noting that just as in HPVSs, basic assumptions in LPVSs can also obstruct organizational interaction. In fact, there may even be social processes in LPVSs that enhance the emergence of destructive basic assumption. At times, for instance, team-based interaction may come under the spell of 'group-think' (Janis and Mann, 1977), in which team members develop a strongly held shared understanding of problems and solutions and unintentionally reinforce each other in confirming evidence supporting this understanding and ignoring evidence against it. Basic assumptions are a taken-for-granted background for dealing with organizational problems arising in HPVSs and LPVSs alike, and just as in HPVSs, one needs to reflect on and change them in LPVSs. In this section, we will briefly discuss the prospect of doing so.

Earlier, we discussed several conditions for changing basic assumptions. Let's briefly repeat them:

1. A first condition was that we should become aware of basic assumptions. This entailed that we should systematically reflect on organizational problems and the solutions we come up with. Such reflection requires time, knowledge, and a deep understanding of the problems organizations face and of the solutions proposed to solve them. It also requires being socially connected (within and outside the confines of the organization), which may help to engage in a critical dialogue and jointly discuss the shared background and come up with solutions.
2. A second condition for changing basic assumptions was that it requires experimentation with different ways of approaching organizational problems and discovering that other ways of perceiving them may also work. This, in turn, also requires time, room for experimental manoeuvring, and critical (social) evaluation and reflection on the outcome of these experiments.

In LPVSs, these conditions may be more available than in HPVSs. In LPVSs, tasks have a broad operational and regulatory scope which open up job-related opportunities for reflection and experimentation. Given the broad scope of most tasks, reflection on basic assumptions in the sense of gaining a deep understanding of organizational problems, their causes, and alternative ways of perceiving problems in order to uncover the basic assumptions may be better possible than in HPVSs. Overview and regulatory potential also better enable experimentation and reflection on alternative solutions. Moreover, organization members working in LPVSs are an active part of a social network. And although social biases like group-think may be a problem, this social embeddedness is also necessary for jointly discussing and reflecting on internal and external organizational problems and solutions (cf. MacIntyre, 1999).

So, in all, we argue that LPVSs stand a better chance of realizing and adapting the organization's contribution to society (arrow A in Figure 3.14), as discussed previously. And, as we discussed in this section, we also argue that they may be better at supporting the reflection on and adaptation of interaction premises (see arrow B in Figure 3.14). In such structures, goals and infrastructures are less difficult to change. In addition, reflection on and adapting basic assumptions may be better supported – although, of course, such change remains difficult, given the uncontested nature of these assumptions.

3.5 Summary and conclusion

In this book, we discuss episodic interventions which aim at improving the structure of organizations. Given this topic, we devoted this chapter to discuss what organizational structures are and how they can be improved. This knowledge helps us to appreciate the *object* of such episodic interventions (organizational structures) and, in part, what they aim at (*improved* organizational structures). To provide this knowledge, we first defined organizational structures as a network of related tasks which can be described with scores on seven design parameters. Next, we argued that the contribution of organizational structures was to enable the four basic activities in such a way that these activities could (A) realize organizational variables related to quality of organization and quality of work, and (B) support the reflection on and adaptation in interaction premises. We went on to explain that structures with low values on the design parameters might deliver this contribution better than structures with high values because these structures have a low possibility of disturbances and enough regulatory potential. In this explanation, we first specified the *object* of episodic interventions aiming at improving organizational structures, i.e. we specified what organizational structures are. Second, we tried to delineate the aim of the episodic interventions we're after in this book: improved organizational structures. That is, we tried to explain why structures with low values (that is, as low as possible, given the specific organizational context) are preferred structures.

This last proviso ('as low as possible, given the specific organizational context') is important, and in this conclusion we want to devote some attention to it. Our reasoning with respect to structures (and their improvement) is a normative one: it implies that structures with 'low' values on design parameters are the better ones, if one considers their effect on quality of organization variables, *and* on quality of work variables, *and* on the prospect of reflecting on and adapting interaction premises. In this sense, it foreshadows the aim of episodic interventions into organizational structures as discussed in this book. These interventions should investigate organizational problems in terms of structural deficits – i.e. caused by high values on the design parameters – and look for solutions in terms of lowering these values. In the remainder of this book, this will be a recurrent theme. However, this normative aspect of episodic interventions doesn't mean that design parameters should always have an 'absolute' minimum value (as in the lowest possible value, e.g. the lowest value of functional concentration in the sense of 'every order family should have its own dedicated production flow', or lowest possible operational specialization in the sense of 'one team carries out the entire production process'). Instead, these values should be as low as possible, given the specifics of the organization. In other words, there are limits to lowering the design parameter values, and during an episodic intervention these need to be taken into account.

As an example of such limits, we discussed earlier that lowering functional concentration is bound to the degree of capacity utilization of the emerging flows. This may mean that sometimes an order type cannot have its own flow, but should instead be combined with other order types in a flow. Another example of a limit to lowering design parameter values is the complexity of the primary process. Very complicated processes (e.g. oil refinery) should often be broken down in parts, meaning that some operational specialization may be inescapable. More limits may be given, but the general idea is that given these limits in a specific organizational context, the design parameters should be as low as possible. We will pick up on this issue in Chapter 6.

The overall conclusion of this chapter is that structures with low design parameters are the better structures, and that episodic interventions into organizational structures should take this insight as a normative point of reference.

Notes

1 Actually, comparing levels of functional concentration should not only take into account the number of parallel flows (dedicated to their own order types). It should also take the number of different order types per flow into account. For instance, consider 90 different order types. In this case it is possible (1) to make three flows of 30 order types, or (2) to make three flows of one order type and one flow of 87 order types. Now, the degree to which operational activities are coupled to all order types is (on average) less in the three flows of 30. The overall idea is that the lower the functional concentration, the less the operational activities are coupled to all order types.
2 To be sure, many authors have already written about the lack of opportunities to learn and develop in HPVSs and about the alienation and isolation they lead to (e.g. bureaucratic organizations; Merton, 1957; Mintzberg, 1983; Donaldson, 2001).
3 Remember that the number of order combinations in the HPVS with the same number of orders is 1023!
4 In fact, Morgan (1986) discusses several metaphors which are about adaptation, learning, and change: organizations as organisms, brains, and as flux. Although we understand his reasons for treating these metaphors separately, we prefer to take the more general cybernetic perspective of organizations as 'viable systems' (cf. Beer, 1979), which carries with it a more commonsense idea of organizations as systems that strive for survival and therefore need the capacity to learn, change, and adapt, and refer to this general idea as 'organizations as organisms'.

4

EPISODIC INTERVENTIONS IN ORGANIZATIONAL STRUCTURES

Episodic Interventions in the Structure of Organization

PART I
Theoretical Framework:

– Organizations

– Organizational structure

– (episodic) Interventions

PART II
A 3-D Model of Episodic Interventions:

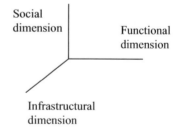

FIGURE 4.0 Roadmap of the book

4.1 Introduction

In the previous two chapters, we introduced our perspective on organizations as social systems conducting experiments with meaningful survival. Moreover, we highlighted the importance of the design of organizational structures for ongoing processes of experimentation. At the end of Chapter 3, it was argued that, because the structure of an organization is such an important condition for the organization's meaningful survival, at some point an *intervention* in this structure may be expedient, or even inevitable.

It is the goal of the present chapter to further explore interventions in organizational structures. In particular, we want to highlight characteristic and relevant features of the type of interventions in organizational structures that will be central in the rest of this book: episodic interventions in organizational structures. At the end of this chapter, it should be clear:

1. how episodic interventions in organizational structures can be defined;
2. how these interventions relate to other types of organizational change;
3. which characteristic features of episodic interventions in organizational structures should figure in a model that can help realize these interventions, i.e. which features are relevant for the 3-D model that is our topic in the second part of the book.

To realize these goals, we first introduce a general understanding of interventions in Section 4.2. Given this general understanding of interventions, Section 4.3 addresses the three topics mentioned above: what are episodic interventions in organization structures, how do they fit into the larger domain of organizational change, and which of their features should be taken into account in the 3-D model? Section 4.4 summarizes the findings of this chapter.

4.2 Interventions: a general understanding

Episodic interventions in organizational structures are only one instance of a much more common practice we call 'interventions'. Because episodic interventions 'inherit' a number of relevant characteristics of interventions, we discuss these characteristics below.

For the purpose of this book, we define an intervention as *a set of coherent activities that involve deliberation and intend to improve the functioning of something relative to some goal*.

Please note that this definition only holds for the purpose of this book, which deals with transformations of organizational structures in order to improve the functioning of organizations. Of course, interventions can have other goals than *improving* the functioning of something. There also may be interventions that aim to *deteriorate* the functioning of something relative to some goal (e.g. bombing a railroad junction in order to deteriorate the functioning of the enemies supply system relative to its goal of staying well supplied) or interventions that aim to *maintain* the functioning of something relative to some goal (e.g. inspecting and, if necessary, oiling a machine in order to keep it running). Because these last two types of interventions are not the topic of this book, they are not included in our working definition of interventions provided in the text.

In order to flesh out our working definition of interventions, some examples may be useful:

1. You find out that the washing machine does not work and someone from the repair service installs a new motor in order to repair it.

In this example, the washing machine is the 'something'. This machine is an artefact built to realize a particular goal: washing laundry. Apparently, the machine has lost its capacity to realize this goal: its current condition does not allow it to function well. In order to improve the functioning of the washing machine, someone from the repair service inspects the machine. Based on this inspection and after going over the options (deliberation), the repair person decides to install a new motor, i.e. this person performs a set of activities with the intention to change the condition for the functioning of the washing machine so that it again can realize the goal of washing laundry.

2. Marc is addicted to drugs and is treated with medication by his psychiatrist.

In this example, Marc is the 'something'. Of course, Marc is not 'just' an artefact, but a living human being. In Marc's case, the goal may not be so clearly defined. Perhaps it is something like, being able to live a normal human life. Apparently, the addiction undermines Marc's capability to realize this goal. Somehow, his condition does not allow him to function well relative to the goal of living a normal life. The treatment with medication is part of a strategy, i.e. a set of coherent activities involving deliberation, performed with the intention to change Marc's condition in order to improve his functioning relative to this goal.

3. According to the board of a chemical company, the R&D department does not contribute sufficiently to the organization's meaningful survival. New departmental targets are set that are more ambitious and new scientists are hired to realize these targets.

In this example, the organization – a social system conducting experiments – is the 'something'. According to the board, the organization does not function well relative to the goal of meaningful survival. In particular, the organization's capacity for innovation (adaptation) is impaired. In order to improve the organization's capacity for innovation, it is considered helpful to reorganize the R&D department. A set of activities is performed with the intention to change the organization's infrastructure in such a way that its functioning relative to the goal of meaningful survival is improved.

From these examples, it can be learned that, in spite of their differences, they describe a 'family' of activities that can be called 'intervention'. More in particular, according to our definition and the examples mentioned above, interventions typically:

A. involve *deliberation* and *intention*;
B. involve a set of *activities* that should be performed in order to make the intervention into a success;
C. presuppose a *goal* of the intervention;
D. presuppose an *object* of the intervention.

Below, we discuss these elements in more detail.

4.2.1 Element A: deliberation and intention

A first characteristic feature of interventions is that they are *intentional* and, as a rule, involve *deliberation*.

Deliberation can be defined as:

> the process through which we decide what to do, or what to believe. When we think about what to do, we are engaged in practical deliberation. Theoretical deliberation is when we think about what to believe, or about which judgement to make.
>
> *(Romein and Roy, 2015, p. 1)*

In line with this definition, deliberation, in our view, involves *explicit weighing* (practical deliberation) and/or *interpretation* (theoretical deliberation): explicit weighing, for instance, of means relative to goals or of goals relative to values; interpretation, for instance, of apparently salient characteristics of a problematic situation. Because deliberation involves explicit weighing and interpretation, it is always 'discursive', 'mediate', and 'indirect'. The contrasting concept to deliberation is intuition. Intuition involves habit and routine (instead of explicit weighing) and immediate 'seeing as' (instead of interpretation). Although action based on intuition also plays an important role in interventions, deliberation-based action plays a role in most interventions.

By 'intentional', we mean that the activities in the intervention are performed with the goal to improve the functioning of something relative to some goal. For instance, Marc's psychiatrist has the goal to improve Marc's quality of life. The prescription of the medication is a means to realize this goal. Please note that intentional activities do not necessarily involve deliberation. For instance, someone may intentionally kill a fly with a newspaper without explicit interpretation of or deliberation about either the goal or the means involved.

4.2.2 Element B: activities in the intervention

In the examples above, *repairing* the washing machine, *treating* someone with medication, or *reorganizing* the R&D department are all intervention activities. Although these activities are quite different in character, they all can be regarded as *implementations* of a solution in order to fix a problem or improve the functioning of something.

'Implementation' is an activity that immediately comes to mind in the context of intervention. However, it actually is only one of four activities that, together, constitute an intervention. These four activities are: *diagnosis*, *design*, *implementation*, and *evaluation*.

In order to give a first impression of these four activities – they will be discussed in more detail in Chapter 6 – it is useful to introduce a basic model for understanding interventions (see Figure 4.1). In this model, we use the main concepts mentioned in our definition and in the examples of interventions provided earlier. According to the basic model, interventions presuppose that:

a. There is something 'S' (e.g. the washing machine) that by means of its activities 'A' (the washing process) can realize some desired effect or goal 'G' (clean clothes).
b. Some current arrangement of factors, the 'current condition', affects S's capacity to perform activities A to realize goal G. We call this current condition 'C1'.
c. There are more or less clear indications (which may prove to be either true or false) that S has problems realizing goal G and that the functioning of S might be improved relative to goal G.

Given this basic model, we can describe the four intervention activities.

Activity 1: diagnosis

Earlier, we spoke about the implementation of a 'solution' to some 'problem'. However, how do we know that there is a problem, and how do we find a solution? Somehow, implementation presupposes an activity that identifies problems and provides a rough indication

106 Interventions in organizational structures

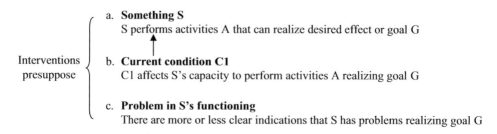

FIGURE 4.1 Basic model for understanding interventions

of possible solutions. This activity is called the *diagnosis*. Typically, a diagnosis is triggered because there are more or less clear indications that something is wrong. The diagnosis, then, identifies problems, analyses what causes these problems, and specifies a solution space.

To *identify problems* in the functioning of S, its current functioning is compared to goal G. To be more precise, a comparison is made between desired effects (goal G) and actual effects of S's behaviour. If there is a difference between these desired and actual effects, S functions either better or worse than specified by goal G. In the latter case, S's functioning may be improved relative to goal G. Apparently, there is something in the current condition C1 that hinders S in functioning as desired. Note that, initially, goal G need not be clearly defined. Therefore, defining goal G may be an important element of the problem identification. Moreover, note that *side effects* of the functioning of S may also be a part of the diagnosis. To this purpose, other goals than goal G should be specified and S's behaviour relative to these goals should also be assessed.

Problems in S's functioning are the point of departure for the *cause analysis*. The goal of a cause analysis is to find out what it is in current condition C1 that hinders S in functioning properly. Here, we only state the goal of the cause analysis. Later, in Chapter 6, we will explain how to perform a cause analysis in the context of interventions in organizational structures. The 'output' of a cause analysis is knowledge about factors in the current condition C1 that cause S to dysfunction. Note that this 'knowledge' is just a *hypothesis* that may be contested and become an object of persuasive discussion, adding to the social complexity of the intervention.

Given the results of the cause analysis, a *solution space* can be specified. To improve the functioning of S, the causes of S's dysfunction should be eliminated. However, an examination of these causes may reveal that some of them cannot be eliminated or are very hard to eliminate, for instance because they are beyond our control or very costly to change. To specify a solution space, the causes that can be eliminated by means of an intervention should be separated from the causes that cannot be eliminated or are too hard to eliminate. The resulting set of causes (those that can be eliminated) by the intervention is called the 'solution space'. This solution space comprises the causes in S's condition that both *should* and *can* be eliminated in order to improve S's functioning relative to goal G. Possible solutions invented by means of the design activity should eliminate these causes. Note that the solution space too is a *hypothesis* with respect to causes that should be eliminated by solutions to the problems in S's functioning. As such, the results of the diagnosis have an *experimental* character.

Activity 2: design

Taking the solution space that is the 'output' of the diagnosis as a point of departure, the goal of the design activity is to invent a solution for the problems in S's functioning. It is the goal of the design activity to invent a new condition for S that enables S to realize goal G. We call this new condition 'C2'. Designing condition C2, as a rule, consists of two sub-processes: (a) constructing possible solutions that fit within the solution space and (b) selecting/composing condition C2 from these possible solutions.

In condition C2, all the (feasible) factors are 'in place' to enable S to function relative to goal G. Once again, note that condition C2 is only a *hypothesis*. It is the hypothesis that implementing C2 will improve the functioning of S relative to goal G. In actual practice, different ideas about condition C2 may be developed, necessitating selection and choice, requiring discussion and persuasion, adding to the social complexity of the intervention.

In addition to the requirement that condition C2 should be able to realize goal G, other requirements may be set as well. Two relevant additional types of requirements are: (1) requirements with respect to S's behaviour relative to *other* goals than goal G, i.e. desired and undesired *side effects* of S's behaviour, and (2) requirements about the implementation of condition C2, *implementation-related requirements*. For instance, in addition to high product quality (goal G), condition C2 should be able to reduce environmental waste (desired side effect), and C2 should be designed in such a way that no members of personnel will have to be discharged as a result of the intervention (implementation-related requirement). Because of these different types of goals, the design of condition C2 may be a quite complex activity involving the joint optimization and explicit weighing of the different types of requirements.

Activity 3: implementation

The output of the design activity is the input for the *implementation* activity. Implementation is an activity that intends to change condition C1 in which S does not function well relative to goal G into condition C2 that allows S to function well relative to that goal. The output of the implementation activity is the new condition C2 for S's behaviour that *per hypothesis* allows S to realize both goal G and possible additional requirements.

Activity 4: evaluation

The evaluation assesses whether the new condition of S, i.e. the condition after implementation, actually realizes goal G, desired side effects, and possible other requirements set for the functioning of S. This evaluation is called *product evaluation*. In addition to this product evaluation, the intervention process may be evaluated (*process evaluation*). To this purpose, it may be useful to specify process goals, for instance goals with respect to time and money spent on the intervention.

In sum, we get four related intervention activities that constitute an intervention: diagnosis, design, implementation, and evaluation. Performing each of these four intervention activities can be regarded as goals *in* the intervention. They are goals in the intervention that should be realized in order to realize the goal *of* the intervention: improving the functioning of S relative to goal G. Because the four activities are all geared to improving the *functioning* of S, we call performing the four activities *function-related* or *functional goals in* the intervention.

TABLE 4.1 Functional goals in the intervention

Functional goals in the intervention that should be realized in order to realize the goal of the intervention	Start intervention: the functioning of something S relative to goal G is affected by a particular arrangement of causal factors called condition C1 + There are indications that S does not realize goal G
Diagnosis	Assessing S's functioning relative to goal G, given condition C1 and finding a solution space 1. problem identification 2. cause analysis 3. specification of solution space
Design	Developing a new condition C2 for S that allows: 1. S to realize goal G (desired effect of the intervention) 2. S to meet additional goals to G (optimizing desired and minimizing undesired side effects 3. for the realization of implementation related requirements Condition C2 is developed by means of the: 1. construction of possible solutions within the solution space 2. selection/composition of condition C2 from these possible solutions
Implementation	Changing S's condition from C1 to C2 in order to improve S's functioning relative to goal G
Evaluation	Assessing S's functioning after implementation relative to goal G (and possible additional goals) (product evaluation) and assessing the intervention process (process evaluation) Finish intervention: something S is in condition C2, enabling S to realize goal G

Together, the activities of diagnosis, design, implementation, and evaluation constitute the *functional dimension* of the intervention (see Table 4.1 for a summary).

Three complications: practice, iteration and recursion

At first glance, diagnosis, design, implementation, and evaluation appear to be sequentially ordered *phases* of the intervention process. It is easy to see why this appears so, since it doesn't seem to make sense to evaluate an implementation that didn't take place, implement a design that wasn't made, or make a design to solve a problem that wasn't diagnosed. As it appears, the 'output' of one activity is the 'input' of the next. However, things are more complicated than this. Three complications are worth discussing: *practice, iteration* and *recursion*.

We all know that in *practice*, all kinds of things may happen that, according to our definition of intervention, do not make sense. For instance, a design may be made in order to solve a problem that was either not carefully diagnosed or not diagnosed at all. More or less well founded opinions about problems and their causes may be taken as a point of departure for the design activity. In general, it is not necessary to 'formally' diagnose a problem in order to develop opinions about problems and their possible causes. Another example may be that a solution is implemented that doesn't result from a 'formal' design. Once again, a formal design is not necessary to implement a solution. As it appears, actual practice may be more varied than our definition of interventions suggests. Perhaps a careful empirical examination of interventions would even show that actual intervention practices *never wholly* conform to our description of the four intervention activities.

Because of this probable gap between actual practices and our definition, it may be asked how the two are related.

A first answer to this question is that our definition is not an empirical, generic, and descriptive definition of interventions. It does not want to capture some common denominator of interventions taking place in actual practice. It is rather an *ideal typical* definition of interventions. As an ideal typical definition, our definition functions as a *normative yardstick* that can be used to 'measure', assess, or guide an endless variety of intervention-like practices. In particular, our ideal typical definition of interventions states that: *if* deliberatively and intentionally changing the functioning of something relative to some goal is considered as a *value*, then a *rational* actor (i.e. an actor that optimizes the activities to realize a given goal) *should* perform the four activities described above.

Given such an ideal typical definition of intervention, it can be used in two ways. First, there is a *descriptive* use. Real intervention-like practices can be selected, identified, and compared to the definition. Based on this comparison, it can be assessed whether these practices are more or less in line with the ideal typical definition. For instance, a researcher interested in intervention practices may use the ideal typical definition in order to identify this type of practices in the endless variety of behaviours going on in organizations.

The second use is *prescriptive*. In its prescriptive use, the ideal typical definition provides us with *goals in* the intervention process that *should* be pursued if we want to deliberately and intentionally improve the functioning of something relative to some goal. For instance, it prescribes that if we want to improve the organization's capacity for innovation, we *should* identify problems in its actual capacity for innovation. In its prescriptive use, the ideal typical definition helps to *guide* our actions towards the goal of improving the functioning of something relative to some goal (e.g. it helps us to guide our actions to develop the organization's innovative capacity). In the rest of this book, both the descriptive and the prescriptive use of the ideal typical definition of intervention are relevant.

In sum, the first answer to the question about the gap between the endless variety of intervention practices and our definition of interventions is that our definition is *not* a generalized description of these practices. It is an ideal type, a normative yardstick (Weber, 1968). And because it is a normative yardstick, it would be rather surprising if the variety of actual intervention practices wholly conformed to it. Actual practices are always more unruly and varied than the ideal type.

Still, this first answer is not wholly satisfactory. The reason for this is that within our ideal typical definition of intervention, the strict sequential order between the activities may be 'broken' because of two factors: iteration and recurrence.

Iteration implies that intervention activities like diagnosis or design are *repeated* during the intervention process (see Figure 4.2a).

We indicated earlier that the results of the four intervention activities should be regarded as *hypotheses* that may prove to be wrong. For instance, during the implementation activity, one may find out that the design is not optimal. An inquiry into the reasons for this suboptimal design may point back to the diagnosis. Due to defects in the diagnosis, causes of the problem were overlooked. As a result, these causes were not added to the solution space and,

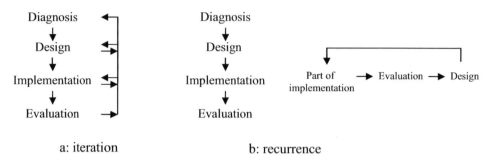

FIGURE 4.2 Iteration and recurrence (example implementation)

for this reason, form no part of the consequent design. At this point, it might be rational to iterate (repeat) both the diagnostic and the design activities. Because such iterations may be the *rational* thing to do if one wants to improve the functioning of something relative to some goal, such iterations are a part of our ideal typical definition of interventions.

Recurrence is a special kind of iteration of intervention activities (see Figure 4.2b). In the case of recurrence, the iteration takes place *within* a particular intervention activity. To give an example, suppose that *during* the implementation of some part of a solution, someone assesses the effects of this implementation on the functioning of something S relative to goal G. Formally, this assessment is a kind of evaluation. Further, suppose that, based on the results of this evaluation, this person adjusts the design of the solution and then continues with the implementation (followed by an evaluation, and so on). In this example, we see an iteration of intervention activities as a part of the implementation activity. Such iterations, we call 'recurrence'. Although recurrence can occur in all four activities in the intervention, it will be more prevalent during the design and implementation activities. Once again, because recurrence may be the *rational* thing to do if one has in mind the goal of improving the functioning of something S relative some goal G, it is part of our ideal typical definition of interventions.

Because the strict sequential order between the activities may be 'broken' on rational grounds, i.e. because iteration and recurrence are a part of our ideal typical definition of intervention, we do not consider diagnosis, design, implementation, and evaluation as 'phases' of the intervention, but rather as 'activities' taking place in the intervention.

4.2.3 Element C: goal of the intervention

The third element of our basic model of intervention is the goal of the intervention. This goal states the *purpose* of the activities in the intervention. It is the proximate answer to the question *why* these activities, and thereby the intervention as a whole, are performed.

To begin with, although we speak of *the* goal of the intervention (singular), this goal actually may include a multiplicity of desired effects (plural). For instance, applied to the functional requirements discussed in Chapter 3, *the* goal of an episodic intervention in the structure of an organization (singular) may be to realize *all* the functional requirements belonging to the quality of organization, the quality of work, and the quality of working relations (plural). Therefore, the goal of an intervention should be seen as a set consisting of one or more variables and their norm values.

With respect to the goal of an intervention, it may be asked where it comes from. At first glance, the answer to this question is quite simple: we want to improve S's functioning relative to some goal G because we *value* goal G. For instance, we want to have the washing machine fixed because we value clean clothes. Apparently, 'clean clothes' fit within a larger web of *ends* and related *values* that 'apply' in a given situation and are developed in our lives with others. Therefore:

a. The activities in the intervention (diagnosis, design, implementation, evaluation) are geared towards the goal of the intervention. This goal is the purpose of these activities.
b. The goal of the intervention, improving S's functioning relative to goal G, presupposes some goal G as a desired effect of S's functioning.
c. Goal G as a desired effect of S's functioning presupposes ends and values that make this effect appear as desirable.

As a consequence of this reasoning, we need to extend our basic model for understanding interventions (see Figure 4.3). If improving S's functioning relative to goal G is at all to appear as a *desired* effect of the intervention, ends and related values are presupposed to make this possible. Ends and values play a necessary role in interventions. Interventions are *value-laden*.

This addition of ends and values to the basic model has at least three relevant implications for our understanding of interventions.

If we reflect on our own lives, we know that in the course of time, ends may change and values may develop. For instance, I may value 'work' quite differently before or after my retirement. And because ends and values may change, develop, or drift into or out of sight in the course of time, one and the same intervention may be valued differently by one and the same person or group of persons at different moments in time. An intervention that once seemed desirable may now seem unimportant (neutral) or even undesirable. As a consequence, it is wise to check the desirability of the intervention not only at its start (during the diagnostic activity), but also as it proceeds. Is improving S's functioning relative to goal G still worthwhile given our present ends and values?

A second implication is that because different persons or groups may have different ends and values at the same moment in time, different persons or groups may value the same intervention differently. One and the same intervention may appear as desirable to one person or group and as neutral or even undesirable to another. Moreover, as the goal of the intervention may consist of multiple desired effects, it may not always be clear how the importance of these effects should be weighted relative to one another. As a consequence, not only may

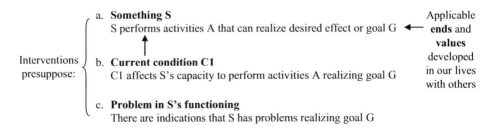

FIGURE 4.3 Extended model for understanding interventions

the results of intervention activities such as 'design' be a topic of disagreement and debate (as indicated earlier), the goal of the intervention, and thereby the intervention itself, may be contested as well. It may be a topic of controversy, and even struggle. Therefore, the goal of the intervention should never be taken for granted. Even in simple cases, it is the outcome of more or less tacit processes of negotiation and agreement. For instance, the mechanic repairing my washing machine may have other ends and values than I have. Still, there is some tacit agreement that the goal of the intervention should be 'improving the machine's capacity to clean dirty laundry'. In more complex cases, the goal of the intervention, and thereby the intervention itself, may remain a topic of struggle during the intervention. So the second implication of adding ends and values to the model is that the goal of an intervention may depend on the dynamics of negotiation and struggle involving the different ends, values, and power resources of parties involved in or affected by the intervention. In short, interventions have an *agonistic* or *political dimension*.

The third and perhaps most important implication is that ends and values are introduced at all. Before ends and values were introduced, both the goal of the intervention (improving S's functioning relative to goal G) and goal G were presupposed as given. *Given* these goals, the relevant issues were at best *instrumental* or *goal rational*: "*If* we want to realize the given *goal* of the intervention, *then* what are the optimal *means* to do this?" (Kant, 2010). Although instrumental reasoning, i.e. reasoning about means *given* some goal, is indispensable in order to perform interventions, it is not the only type of reasoning that is relevant. Another relevant type of reasoning appears on the horizon with the introduction of ends and values into the basic model for understanding interventions. Once ends and values have been introduced, it may be asked how the goal of an intervention fits within the ends and values of particular individuals or groups. And what is more, it may be asked what the *value* of these ends and values is. In the end, it may even be asked how the goal of the intervention relates to what may be considered *ultimate* ends, i.e. ends that are not a means to a higher end, but ends in themselves. Traditionally, such ultimate ends and their relation to more proximate ends are the substance of *ethics*. For instance, in virtue ethics, 'living a humanly fulfilled life' is considered the ultimate end (Aristotle, 1984b) or in Kantian deontology, the ultimate end is to act as a rational and free agent would do (e.g. Kant, 2010). In ethics, then, questions are asked about these ultimate ends and about the fit between some particular end pursued here and now and an end that is considered as ultimate. Therefore, with the introduction of ends and values into the model of interventions, ethical considerations are introduced as well. Intervention-related reasoning (discussion and persuasion) is not only goal-rational, it may also be *value-rational*. This means that both the goal of the intervention and the means to realize this goal may be assessed in the light of what are considered ultimate ends. Examples of such ethical questions are 'Does this intervention disrupt or contribute to the fulfilled life of the parties affected by it?' or 'Are persons figuring in the intervention acknowledged as rational and free subjects, or are they made into "objects" that can be used as mere means to realize the goal of the intervention?' Interventions always have an *ethical dimension*.

4.2.4 Element D: the object of the intervention

To introduce the object of the intervention, it is again useful to return to the basic model. In this model, it was presupposed that there is some set of factors – called the condition – that affects S's capacity to perform activities A that can realize goal G.

To give an example, in Chapter 2 we argued that in the case of organizations, the organizational infrastructure (i.e. its structure, human resources, and technology) is considered as an important factor affecting an organization's capacity to realize meaningful survival. Given the goal of realizing meaningful survival, the organization's infrastructure is viewed as a part of the condition. Of course, other factors may be considered to be a part of the condition as well. For instance, someone may argue that factors in an organization's environment affect the organization's capacity to perform the activities needed to realize the goal of meaningful survival, or the organization's culture may be seen as such a factor. Perhaps there are additional factors, some of them as yet unknown to us, that affect the organization's capacity to perform the activities needed for meaningful survival, factors that for this reason are a part of the condition. In sum, what was called the 'condition' in the model for understanding interventions comprises *all* the factors affecting S's capacity to perform the activities A needed to realize goal G – the known factors as well as the unknown ones. Based on this definition of the condition, the object of the intervention can be defined.

It is the goal of an intervention to improve the functioning of something S relative to goal G. In order to realize the goal of the intervention, the condition affecting S's functioning relative to goal G needs to be changed. This means that factors that *per hypothesis* belong to this condition need to be selected and taken into account in the intervention activities. These factors are the object of the intervention. So the object of the intervention is defined here as those factors that: (1) *per hypothesis* belong to the condition and (2) are taken into account in the intervention activities that are performed in order to realize the goal of the intervention.

For example, a diagnosis may explore whether the structure of an organization is causing its problems with innovation. In this example, the organization's structure is the object of the intervention. It is a factor that *per hypothesis* belongs to the condition affecting the organization's capacity for innovation and is taken into account in a diagnosis in order to improve the organization's capacity for innovation.

Another example might be treating a drug-addicted patient with medication affecting the patient's neurophysiologic system. In this example, the neurophysiologic system of the patient is the object of the intervention. It is a factor that *per hypothesis* is a part of the condition affecting the patient's psychic health and is taken into account in an implementation activity that aims to improve the patient's psychic health. Note that one and the same intervention can take multiple factors into account: for instance, both the structure and the human resources of an organization. If this happens, then these multiple factors are the object of the intervention.

It is important to underline that the object of the intervention is a *hypothesis*. As such, it may be *wrong*. If this is the case, factors that *per hypothesis* are a part of the condition that affects S's functioning relative to goal G, and for this reason are selected as the object of the intervention, actually are *not* part of S's condition. An example of a horrible collection of wrong hypotheses that had a long history of application can be found in the *Malleus Maleficarium*. This fifteenth-century handbook, which supported the interventions of witch hunters, describes "Methods by which the works of witchcraft are wrought and directed, and how they may be successfully annulled and dissolved" (Kramer and Sprenger, 1971, pp. 89ff). It contains all kinds of hypotheses about the negative influence of witches on things we value. For instance, it describes how witches impede and prevent the power of procreation, how they inflict every sort of infirmity, and how they injure cattle in various ways. In general, witches are regarded as factors that belong to the condition affecting procreation and health in plants, animals, and human beings. Because their influence was considered negative, witches became the objects of interventions. For instance, the *Malleus* describes how witches should be detected as actual causes of harm (a kind of diagnosis with the witch as an object), how their influence should be diminished or neutralized (tips for the design of solutions with the witch as an object), or how the proposed solution should be implemented. As a result of the *Malleus*'s wrong hypotheses about factors affecting the procreation and health of different types of living beings, for centuries tens of thousands women (and sometimes men) were made into objects of interventions that involved torture and murder as means of diagnosis and implementation.

With respect to the known and unknown factors that constitute the condition affecting S's functioning relative to goal G, we would like to make three additional remarks that are relevant for understanding interventions.

To begin with, there are two basic types of knowledge about factors affecting S's functioning relative to some goal. The first type is *knowing that*. In this case, someone knows *that* some particular factor affects S's functioning relative to goal G in a particular way. For instance, a cook knows that a pinch of salt makes the soup more palatable. 'Knowing that' may range from experiential knowledge, i.e. knowledge gained by doing, to empirical generalizations resulting from scientific research. The second type of knowledge is *knowing why*. In this case, someone knows what *causes* some factor to affect S's functioning relative to goal G. 'Knowing why', by definition, is scientific knowledge. Both knowing that and knowing why are relevant types of knowledge in the context of interventions. Together, they contribute to the *technical expertise* of the person or group of persons performing the intervention.

Moreover, because multiple known and unknown factors may affect S's functioning relative to goal G, an intervention that has particular known factors as its object may still have unexpected effects on S's functioning. The intervention in the known factors may interact with both known and unknown factors that are not the object of the intervention. These interactions, in turn, may cause the unexpected effects. Therefore, even if our technical expertise with respect to some object of intervention is high, interventions remain experiments that require both continuous monitoring and adjustment, and may teach us new things about (interactions between) factors affecting S's functioning relative to goal G (or other goals, for that matter).

Finally, because (*per hypotheses*) multiple factors can affect S's functioning relative to goal G, it may be decided during the intervention to *change* the object of the intervention. New factors are taken into account and/or old factors are abandoned or eliminated. For instance, an intervention may start with the organization's culture as its object. Later, as the intervention proceeds, attention may shift to the organization's structure. In some cases, such changes are triggered by a lack of success of the intervention. Apparently, the wrong object has been selected or there are other factors affecting S's functioning relative to goal G that override or neutralize the influence of interventions in the current object of the intervention. In other cases, changing the object of intervention may be a part of the intervention strategy. For instance, Marc's psychiatrist may start her intervention with medication affecting her client's neurophysiologic condition. Later on, she may address, as the object of her intervention, factors in Marc's social life. As her intervention proceeds, factors negatively affecting Marc's functioning relative to the goal of living a normal addiction-free life are systematically eliminated.

The discussion of the four central elements of the definition of interventions presented in this section – (1) deliberation and intention, and (2) the activities in (3) the goal of and (4) object of the intervention – allows us to list features of interventions that are relevant for the model supporting episodic interventions in organization structures that is our topic in the second part of the book. These relevant features are:

1. The *deliberative* and *intentional* character of interventions – interventions are not 'routine' activities that can be performed on the basis of intuition alone. They involve explicit weighing of options, and interpretation (practical and theoretical deliberation) and an individual or joint will to improve or fix the functioning of something relative to some goal.
2. The *goal of the intervention* – the goal of an intervention is to improve the functioning of something S relative to some goal G. It states the purpose of the intervention, and is the proximate answer to the question of why the intervention activities are performed. The goal of the intervention presupposes ends and values of the parties involved in or affected by the intervention. These ends and values give interventions both a political and ethical dimension.
3. The *activities in the intervention* – diagnosis, design, implementation, and evaluation are activities that should be realized in order to realize the goal of the intervention. Realizing each one of these activities is a functional goal in the intervention. Together, these four activities constitute the *functional dimension* of the intervention.
4. The *object of the intervention* – the object of the intervention consists of the factors that *per hypothesis* belong to the condition affecting S's functioning relative to goal G and are taken into account in the activities in the intervention.

As a result of the discussion of these four features, we have also found that interventions have an experimental, ethical, social, and political character.

5. The *experimental character* of interventions – the goal of the intervention, the activities in the intervention (including their results), and the object of the intervention are all selections that are made under conditions of uncertainty. They can be regarded as hypotheses that are tested in practice. As such, interventions can be viewed as a kind of experiments.
6. The *ethical character* of interventions – interventions always involve goals. These goals and the means to realize them ultimately may – and should – be judged in the light of 'ends in themselves'.
7. The *social character* of interventions – however 'technical' an intervention may be, interventions always have a social character. The goal of the intervention, its object, and its activities are socially embedded. They either presuppose or consist of interaction (and its premises).
8. The *agonistic/political* character of interventions – the combination of the experimental, ethical, and social character of interventions may lead to a struggle between different points of view that should be managed as a part of the intervention.

Based on this general understanding of interventions, we can now turn to the episodic interventions in organizational structures that are central to this book.

4.3 Episodic interventions in organizational structures

Episodic interventions in organizational structures are only one of many different classes of organizational change. Just as different jobs may require different tools, different types of organizational change may require different conceptual tools to come to grips with them. In order to find out what conceptual tools are needed to deal with episodic interventions in organizational structures, it is useful to further characterize this class of interventions. This section provides such a characteristic by means of an exploration of how episodic interventions in organizational structures fit within the larger domain of organizational change.

To this purpose, a quick glance at Figure 4.4 may be useful. In this figure, episodic interventions in organizational (infra)structures are depicted as a member of the class of interventions in organizational (infra)structures. These interventions belong to the class of organizational interventions. Organizational interventions, in turn, are a particular mode of what we call the 'organizational flux'. To find out what is characteristic of episodic interventions in organizational structures, this section discusses the different classes of organizational change in more detail, starting with the organizational flux.

4.3.1 Organizational flux

In Chapter 2, we argued that organizations are social systems conducting experiments with meaningful survival. As social systems, organizations are involved in a process of continuous 'becoming' that we call *organizational flux* (see Figure 4.4).

In order to explain what we understand by 'organizational flux', it needs to be remembered that we view organizations as social systems that consist of interactions that are 'produced' against a background of interaction premises. These interaction premises function as points of orientation for the production of interactions that both connect with previous interactions and serve as points of departure for future new interactions.

Because interactions are impermanent – they start to disappear the moment they appear – organizations as social systems are under 'continuous construction'. Continuously, new interactions are produced that allow for the production of new connecting interactions. Before

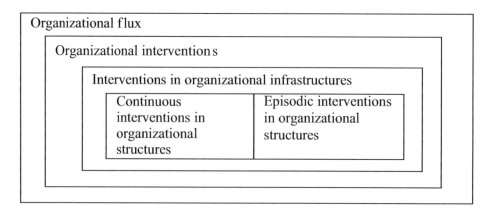

FIGURE 4.4 Modes of organizational change

this production process started, the organization did not exist, and once this process stops, the organization ceases to exist. At the level of their basic elements (i.e. interactions), organizations, as social systems, are involved in a process of continuous 'becoming' or 'renewal', and, in this broad sense, 'change'. At this level, and interpreted in this way, 'change' is co-existent with 'organization'.

Something similar can be said about interaction premises. These premises have a dual character. They not only condition interaction, they are also *conditioned by* interaction. This means that ongoing interaction may explicitly or implicitly change the interaction premises that condition the production of interactions. Interaction premises, therefore, are also continuously involved in a process of becoming.

In combination, both the constant production of new interactions and the explicit or implicit change of interaction premises constitute a continuous 'flow' of change: the organizational flux. And what is more, to the extent that organizations are *social systems* experimenting with meaningful survival, this flux, by definition, *is* the organization. Beyond the organizational flux, there is no change in the organization as a social system experimenting with its own survival.

Of course, it can be objected that organizational change is about changing the behaviours of the members of an organization. What about them? Do these members and their behaviours not change as well? Is organizational change not first and foremost about changing organization members?

Indeed, it is true that the organizational flux presupposes, affects, and is affected by changes in the human beings that are members of the organization. Organizations as social systems would be impossible without the continuous processes of sense-making and micro-adaptation by their members. For this reason, these processes will be quite important in this book. However, it should also be noted that, taken either in *isolation* or as an *aggregate*, individual human beings (or their sense-making and micro-adaptive practices) are neither the organization as a social system nor the organizational flux. Therefore, as long as changes taking place at the level of organization members do not affect the organizational flux, the organization as a social system does not change. Still, we know from experience that local processes of sense-making or micro-adaptation in organizations most of the time, however slightly, do affect organizational interaction or interaction premises, thereby affecting the organizational flux.

A similar objection could be made with respect to the technology that is used in organizations, since organizational change often implies technological change. However, in organizations, technology is not just 'stuff'. It is stuff endowed with social – organizational – meaning. As such, it depends on and plays a role in the social fabric of organizations. Therefore, as long as changes in technology are not somehow reflected in interactions or interaction premises, i.e. as long as they do not affect the organizational flux, nothing is changed in the organization as a social system that experiments with meaningful survival.

Now, if it is admitted that beyond the organizational flux there is no change in organizations as social systems, then it must also be said that if there are different types of organizational change, these different types must be different *modifications* of the organizational flux. So, if we characterize organizational interventions as a particular type of organizational change, it should not be forgotten that these interventions are a *part* of the organizational flux. There is no fundamental opposition between these interventions and the organizational flux. Organizational interventions are a particular modification of this flux.

4.3.2 Organizational interventions

In order to discuss organizational interventions (grey area in Figure 4.5a), we begin with an abridged description of their character. In short, organizational interventions are interventions 'for', 'by', and 'in' organizations. That is, they are interventions 'for', 'by', and 'in' social systems that experiment with meaningful survival. Now, what does this mean?

Organizational interventions are interventions 'for' organizations

In order to explain that organizational interventions are interventions 'for' organizations, it is useful to focus on the goal of these interventions. According to the general definition, all interventions intend to fix or improve the functioning of something relative to some goal. Now, what can be said about this goal in the case of organizational interventions?

If we list some examples, it appears that, in the case of organizational interventions, their goal can be all kinds of (desired) effects of the functioning of organizations. For instance, an organizational intervention can be performed to improve the organization's functioning relative to long-term shareholder value, organizational learning, customer satisfaction, product quality, innovation capacity, short-term liquidity for investors, decreased stress conditions for workers, or even disbanding the organization. Because it is not difficult to go on adding new goals to this list, it is probably impossible to assemble an exhaustive list of goals. As it appears, organizational interventions do not aim to improve an organization's functioning relative to one particular goal. The goal of an organizational intervention can be all kinds of desired effects – i.e. it seems to be *contingent*.

By itself, this contingency of goals is not surprising. As indicated, the goal of an intervention depends on ends and values of parties involved in or affected by that intervention. However, in the case of organizational interventions, these ends and values are tightly interwoven with the 'meaning' that is ascribed in the organization to the organization's experiments with survival. As explained in Chapter 2, this meaning should be regarded as an intra-organizational conception of the organization's contribution to society. It is the organization's answer to the question, 'What is the point of the organization's survival?' In organizations, this meaning results from interaction (that sometimes involves bitter conflict) and is embedded in interaction premises such as the organization's identity, goals, and tasks.

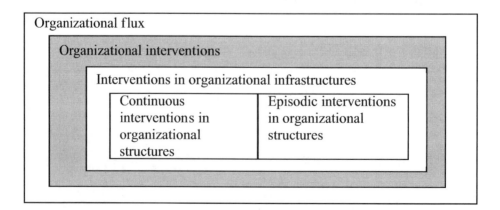

FIGURE 4.5A Organizational interventions

Even a small survey of organizations can reveal that the meaning organizations ascribe to their own survival may vary both within and among organizations. For instance, in *Breaking the Code of Change*, Beer and Nohria (2000, pp. 4ff) distinguish between theory E and theory O organizations. In theory E organizations, meaningful survival is connected to maximizing long-term economic value, while theory O organizations connect meaningful survival with the organization's continued capacity for experimentation. As may be imagined, such different intra-organizational conceptions of what organizational experiments with meaningful survival are about may lead to the adoption of quite different goals of organizational interventions.

However, all of these goals of organizational interventions somehow contribute to meaning that is ascribed intra-organizationally to the organization's experiments with its own survival. To the extent that organizational interventions contribute to the realization of this meaning, they can be said to be interventions 'for' the organization.

Organizational interventions are interventions 'by' organizations

According to our general model, all interventions involve intention and deliberation. This also holds for organizational interventions. However, what makes organizational interventions special is that both the *intention* to improve the functioning of an organization and *deliberations* about this improvement – e.g. deliberations about diagnosis or design or the way they should be organized – become topics of (organizational) interactions that are intended to affect interaction premises. Once this happens, new interactions are produced that have the *intervention* as their explicit topic and theme. Both the intention to improve the functioning of the organization and deliberations about possible improvements become explicit points of orientation for the production of follow-up interactions. Once this happens, interactions may be produced, for instance 'for' or 'against' the intervention or 'for' or 'against' particular results of deliberation. Once the intervention becomes an *explicit* theme in interaction premises, it becomes a truly *organizational* intervention. It becomes a part of the organizational flux. For this reason, it can be said that organizational interventions are interventions 'by' organizations. It is by means of the organization as a social system experimenting with its survival that the organization as a social system experimenting with its survival is transformed.

Of course, the point that both the intention to improve the functioning of the organization and deliberations about this improvement become explicit themes of interaction does not imply that processes of micro-adaptation at the level of individual members of the organization come to a halt. On the contrary, as the intervention becomes an explicit theme in organizational interaction premises, all kinds of interactive processes of micro-adaptation may be triggered that affect the intervention. As a consequence, organizational interventions may have all kinds of unintended (desired and undesired) effects, some of which may become a topic of interaction, while others remain organizationally unnoticed.

Organizational interventions are interventions 'in' organizations

In order to explain that organizational interventions are interventions 'in' organizations, we go back to the general definition of interventions. This definition states that interventions involve the intention to fix or improve the functioning of something relative to some goal. In order to fix or improve this something, the intervention intervenes in some *object*.

As indicated, this object consists of factors that *per hypothesis* affect the functioning of the something relative to the goal of the intervention and are selected to be taken into account in the intervention activities.

Just like all interventions, organizational interventions have such an object. However, what makes organizational interventions special is that their object is *organizational*. By an organizational object, we mean that the object figures in both the organization's experiments with meaningful survival and in organizational interactions and interaction premises. Examples of such organizational objects are the organization's culture, its structure, human resources, and technology.

For instance, suppose that a new piece of equipment (technology) is the object of an organizational intervention that aims to improve product quality. In this intervention, the new piece of equipment is considered in the organization as a factor that positively affects the organization's functioning relative to the goal of high product quality. For this reason, it is taken into account in the intervention activities (such as diagnosis, design, and implementation). However, the new piece of equipment is not just an object of an intervention, it is an *organizational* object.

To begin with, the new piece of equipment figures in the organization's experiments with meaningful survival. It is a hypothesis in that organization that high product quality is relevant to achieve meaningful survival and that the new piece of equipment can help to realize high product quality. As such, the new piece of equipment is a part of the organization's experiments with meaningful survival. Moreover, if the intervention is to succeed, the new piece of equipment should be woven into the fabric of the organization's interaction premises and interactions. For instance, operators should learn to treat the new piece of equipment as 'their' new piece of equipment. They should make it into an 'organizational piece of equipment' by integrating it into their interactive practices. As such, the new piece of equipment should be embedded in interaction premises and ensuing interactions.

Similar examples may be given with respect to organizational interventions that have the culture, structure, or human resources as their object. In each of these cases, culture, structure, or human resources are organizational objects in the dual sense defined above. First, they figure as objects in the organization's experiments with its own survival. Second, actually changing the culture, structure, human resources, or technology of an organization means changing interaction premises and ensuing interactions.

Because objects of organizational interventions are 'organizational' in this dual sense, organizational interventions can be said to be interventions 'in' organizations.

Organizational interventions: functional and social dimensions

In our general model, we indicated that interventions have a *functional dimension*. This functional dimension comprises the activities and their goals in the intervention (diagnosis, design, implementation, evaluation) that should be realized in order to realize the goal *of* the intervention: improving the functioning of S relative to goal G.

Organizational interventions, as a particular subtype of interventions, also have a functional dimension comprising these four activities. For instance, an intervention in the structure of an organization ideal typically involves diagnostic activities that assess what the problems of the organization in realizing goal G are and whether these problems are caused by the organization's structure. Moreover, if the organization's problems are caused by its structure, 'fixing' these problems requires structural redesign and implementation activities. Finally, once the new structure is 'in place', evaluation activities should assess whether the problems have actually been solved by means of the implemented structure. In general, in order to realize the goal of an organizational intervention, the activities that constitute the functional dimension of that intervention should be realized.

In our general model of interventions, we also indicated that interventions have a *social character*. The goal of the intervention, its object, and activities are all socially embedded. They either presuppose or consist of interaction (and its premises). For instance, repairing a washing machine by replacing its motor is not just an intervention in a piece of technology. It also presupposes socially embedded values, goals, and practices of clients and mechanics that are conditions of the possibility of this intervention.

Organizational interventions also have a social character in this 'general' sense. However, because organizational interventions are interventions 'for', 'by', and 'in' organizations, and because organizations are social systems experimenting with meaningful survival, the social character of organizational interventions is of *fundamental* importance to these interventions. Actually, the social character of organizational interventions is so important that in addition to their functional dimension, a separate *social dimension* should be distinguished.

This social dimension is primarily related to the point that organizational interventions are interventions 'in' organizations. As argued, intervening 'in' an organization means intervening in some organizational object – that is, in some object that figures in both the organization's experiments with meaningful survival and organizational interactions and interaction premises. As indicated, examples of such objects are the organization's culture, structure, human resources, and technology. Because these organizational objects are always either instantiated by or related to interactions and interaction premises, organizational interventions always aim at durably changing interaction premises and ensuing interactions.

For instance, intervening in an organizational structure in order to decrease its parameter values, in the end, means changing tasks, and consequent interaction patterns, of organization members. In order to change individual tasks, organization members need to durably integrate or weave new task-related interaction premises into their webs of existing interaction premises. Without this permanent integration of these new task-related interaction premises into the existing repertoire of premises, it is impossible to change the structure of the organization, and thereby to realize the goal of the intervention.

In more general terms, it can be argued that in order to realize the goal of an organizational intervention, some organizational object needs to be changed. In order to change this organizational object, organization members need to durably integrate new interaction premises into their existing repertoires of interaction premises. This, in turn, means that they need to:

1. let go of old interaction premises;
2. adopt new ones;
3. integrate these new interaction premises as points of orientation for their organizational practices.

Therefore, as a complement to the functional dimension – i.e. the dimension that comprises the diagnostic, design, implementation, and evaluation goals that should be realized in the intervention in order to realize the goal of the intervention – a social dimension can be distinguished. This social dimension comprises goals related to the integration of new interaction premises that should be realized in order to realize the goal of the intervention. In sum, relative to the goal *of* the intervention, there are two types of goals *in* the intervention: functional goals and social goals.

Functional goals in the intervention are: performing a diagnosis, making a design, implementing the design, and evaluating the implemented design. Together, these functional goals constitute the functional dimension of the intervention. Realizing these functional goals enhances the probability that: (1) the right intervention object is selected, (2) a design is made that can realize the goal of the intervention, and (3) that this 'right' design is implemented, and (4) actually contributes to the realization to the goal of the intervention, i.e. fixing or improving the functioning of the organization relative to the goal of the intervention.

Social goals in the intervention are: preparing organization members to let go of old interaction premises and motivating them to adopt new ones, searching for and adopting new interaction premises related to the organizational object of the intervention, and integrating these new interaction premises into the repertoire of existing premises. Together, these social goals constitute the social dimension of the intervention. By means of realizing these social goals, the design that is functionally required to realize the goal of the intervention actually becomes a new and well-established social practice in the organization.

It is important to note that the chance of success of an organizational intervention, i.e. the chance that the goal of the intervention is realized, depends on realizing *both* the functional and the social goals *in* the intervention. Not realizing functional goals in the intervention may imply that a design is implemented that does not contribute to the realization of the goal of the intervention. For instance, an organizational structure has been selected that does not improve, but undermines the organization's functioning relative to the goal of the intervention. Although organization members do integrate new interaction premises into their repertoire, these premises do not help to realize the goal of the intervention. By not realizing the functional goals in the intervention, the organization is changed, but it is not necessarily changed in a direction that helps to realize the goal of the intervention. Not realizing the social goals in the intervention implies that organization members do not integrate new interaction premises into their repertoire. The organization as a social system consisting of interactions does not change at all. Therefore, even if a functionally effective design has been found, not realizing the social goals in the intervention implies that this design remains a paper reality. It does not become an organizational – a social – reality.

4.3.3 Organizational interventions in (infra)structures

Organizational interventions in infrastructures have (aspects of) the organization's infrastructure as their object (grey area in Figure 4.5b).

As explained in Chapter 2, an organization's infrastructure consists of its structure, human resources, and technology. This infrastructure is an important condition for the performance of the four activities needed for an organization's meaningful survival: strategic regulation, design regulation, operational regulation, and performing primary activities. As such, the organization's infrastructure can be regarded as an important factor affecting the functioning of the organization relative to its meaningful survival. Because of this importance, the infrastructure of an organization may be taken into account in intervention activities, and thus become the object of an infrastructural intervention.

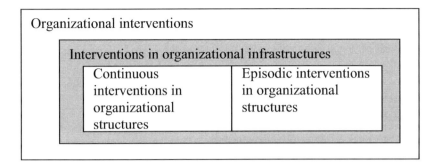

FIGURE 4.5B Interventions in organizational infrastructures

In this book, we only focus on interventions in one of the dimensions of the organization's infrastructure: the organization structure. Because of this focus, from now on we will only discuss (organizational) interventions in organizational structures. The other dimensions of organizational infrastructures (human resources and technology) as well as topics like organizational culture will only be discussed insofar as they are relevant in the context of interventions in organizational structures.

In Chapter 3, organizational structures were defined in terms of the distribution of work. In that chapter, it was also argued that organizational structures are an important condition for meaningful survival. In particular, dependent on the *value* of its structural parameters, an organization is either hindered or enabled to realize the activities necessary for meaningful survival.

High parameter value structures typically *decrease* the organization's capacity for meaningful survival. Because of their structural complexity and hierarchy, high parameter value structures increase the probability of the occurrence of work-related problems and decrease the organization's potential to deal with these problems by means of operational, design, and strategic regulation. Organizations with high parameter value structures face many work-related problems they struggle to deal with because of their lack of regulatory potential. As a consequence, in high parameter value organizations the quality of organization, work, and working relations will be low.

Low parameter value structures typically *increase* the organization's capacity for meaningful survival. They both decrease the probability of the occurrence of work-related problems and increase the organization's potential to deal with remaining problems by means of regulation. As a result, low parameter value organizations create the conditions for a high quality of organization, work, and work relations.

Because the structure of an organization is such a fundamental condition for meaningful survival, it is not surprising that it may be selected as the object of organizational interventions. With regard to these interventions, it is useful to distinguish between *continuous* and *episodic* interventions.

4.3.4 Continuous interventions in organizational structures

In the case of continuous interventions in organizational structures (Figure 4.5c), organization members (not necessarily managers), as a *formal* or *informal* part of their work and on a

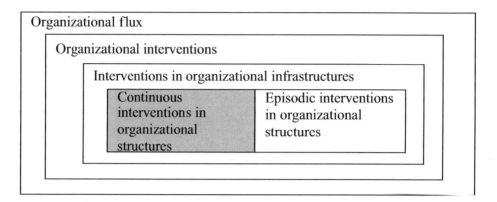

FIGURE 4.5C Continuous intervention in organizational structures

day-to-day basis, monitor the relation between the structure of their work and work-related problems they experience. If opportune, they intervene in their work structure in order to eliminate these problems.

As a rule, continuous interventions in organizational structures have a *local, improving,* and *gradual* character. Organization members locally redefine the structure of 'their' work in order to optimize it relative to some goal. In the course of time and as a result of multiple continuous interventions, the parameter values of (parts of) the organizational structure may change.

Because continuous interventions in organizational structures are realized as a formal or informal part of the daily work of organization members, and because these interventions have a local, optimizing, and gradual character, it is a characteristic feature of these interventions that they are *embedded* in the organization and do *not* require an additional *intervention organization*. By such an additional intervention organization, we mean a temporal organization on top of the organization that is set up especially for the purpose and time of the intervention, comprising, for instance, temporal additional 'intervention tasks' for organization members, intervention managers, intervention teams, project teams, steering committees, external consultants, or crisis managers.

Please note that continuous interventions in organizational structures, in spite of their day-to-day, local, improving, gradual, and embedded character, are still *organizational interventions* – that is, they still are interventions 'for', 'by', and 'in' the organization. As such, they should be distinguished from local initiatives of individual organization members, that are not tied to the 'meaning' of the organization, that are not communicated in the organization as interventions, or that are not carried out by means of interactions that intend to change interaction premises.

In the context of this book, it is relevant to distinguish between continuous interventions in the structure of organizations with *high* and *low* parameter value structures. The reason for this is that continuous interventions in organizations with high parameter value structures may *necessitate* the episodic interventions in organization structures that are the topic of this book, while continuous interventions in organizations with low parameter value structures may *avoid* these episodic interventions. Let us explain.

How continuous interventions in high parameter value structures may necessitate episodic interventions

In organizations with high parameter value structures, organization members typically work in relatively simple production jobs ('workers') or control jobs ('managers'). These production and control jobs are tiny parts of a complex and hierarchical overall structure. In these structures, organization members face a high probability of structure-induced work-related problems that are difficult to regulate.

Because in high parameter value structures separation between production and control is high, the activity of 'design regulation', as a rule, is not a formal part of the task of the workers. Formally initiating and realizing continuous interventions that (re)design the organization's structure is a prerogative of managers who, because of the hierarchy in high parameter value organizations, are quite distant from the primary processes they manage. Because of this distance, managers may have trouble really knowing and feeling the many (structure-induced) problems of workers working in the primary processes. As a consequence, their continuous interventions to improve local work structures, if they happen at all, may well come too late, be ill-directed (not targeting the real problems experienced by workers in the primary processes), or even aggravate the structural causes of the problems, for instance by introducing even more rules or splitting up production tasks in order to further 'simplify' both the work and its management.

'Abandoned' by their managers, workers working in the primary processes of high parameter value organizations may start to perform *informal* continuous interventions in their work structure in order to tackle the problems they experience. They create informal 'coping spaces' as they try to 'work around the system'. However, because of high functional concentration, differentiation, and specialization in high parameter value structures, workers typically have little overview of the complex production process. As a result, informal, uncoordinated, local interventions in work structures may lead to overall sub-optimization. The new informal structures built on top of the old formal structures, although they alleviate local problems, may make the overall network of tasks even more complex than it was before.

In combination, formal and informal continuous interventions in the structure of high parameter value organizations may harbour the danger of a *vicious cycle* that undermines the organization's capacity for meaningful survival (Fruytier, 1994; de Sitter, 1994). In this cycle, work-related problems caused by a high parameter value structure are 'tackled' by uncoordinated continuous interventions that further simplify production jobs (i.e. more differentiation, and specialization) and intensify control (i.e. more hierarchical regulation). As a result of these interventions, the values of the structural parameters gradually increase, i.e. the organization's structure gradually becomes even more complex and hierarchical. This further increases the probability of work-related problems and decreases opportunities for their effective regulation, leading to new work-related problems that require additional interventions, further undermining the organization's capacity for meaningful survival. Ultimately, the organization's capacity for meaningful survival may decrease to the point that an *episodic* intervention in the organization's structure is needed. The aim of this episodic intervention, then, is to reduce the value of the organization's structural parameters in order to improve its capacity for meaningful survival. It is in this way that continuous interventions in high parameter value organizations may *necessitate* episodic interventions in organization structures.

How continuous interventions in low parameter structures may avoid episodic interventions

In organizations with low parameter value structures, organization members typically work in teams that are segments in production flows. These teams work on 'their' coherent contribution to the production activities taking place in 'their' production flow, a flow that is related to a sub-set of the total of the organization's order types. Members of these teams have relatively broad tasks comprising both production and control activities. In low parameter value structures, 'design regulation' is a formal part of the jobs of team members. This means that team members, as a part of their formal tasks, continuously monitor the relation between the structure of their work and work-related problems. As a part of their work, team members initiate and implement local structural changes in order to improve the team's contribution to 'its' production flow.

This type of organization does not have to deal with the problems of organizations with high parameter value structures. Team members themselves initiate local structural change. They do not depend on the initiatives of managers who may be quite remote from the organization's primary activities. Because members work together in teams on coherent contributions to the outcomes of 'their' production flow, they are in a position to oversee what they are doing and assess how local structural changes impinge on the larger processes they are a part of. This reduces the chance of sub-optimization due to local change initiatives. In more general terms, it can be argued that in organizations with low parameter value structures, it becomes possible to harvest the fruits that are usually connected with continuous change in organizations. For instance, local processes of sense-making may be taken seriously, the organization may be said to be in a 'flow' of continuous learning, and it adapts or develops its structure in a more or less organic way. As a result of continuous interventions in the structure of low parameter value organizations, episodic interventions that aim to transform a faulty structure may be avoided.

From what has been said, it may be learned that continuous interventions in organizational structures can have different effects. Dependent on the parameter values of the organizational structure that is in place, these interventions may be either detrimental or beneficial to the meaningful survival of an organization. Ideally, continuous interventions in organizational structures are performed in organizations that have low parameter value structures. In these organizations, these interventions are at the heart of 'organic' processes of adaptation, learning, and development – processes that further improve an organization's capacity to both realize and adapt the goals that are central to its meaningful survival. In practice, however, it is not easy to find organizations that fit this ideal. Many organizations are 'weighted down' by their high parameter value structures. Organic adaptation, learning, and development are difficult to realize in these organizations, and, as argued, continuous interventions in their structures may even aggravate their problems, in the end making an episodic intervention into their structure unavoidable.

4.3.5 Episodic interventions in organizational structures

The rest of this book is devoted to episodic intervention in organizational structures (grey area in Figure 4.5d). This section discusses the main characteristics of these episodic interventions, their triggers and consequent problems, and the three dimensions (functional, social, and infrastructural) needed to deal with them.

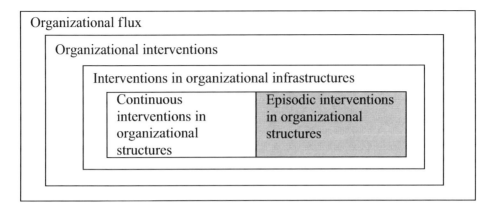

FIGURE 4.5D Modes of organizational change

Episodic interventions in organizational structures: characteristics

In order to characterize episodic interventions in organizational structures, it is relevant to first highlight their *similarities* with continuous interventions in organizational structures. Just like the continuous interventions discussed above, episodic interventions in organizational structures:

1. are a part of the organizational flux;
2. belong to the class of organizational interventions;
3. have the structure of an organization as their object.

Because continuous and episodic interventions in organizational structures are part of the *organizational flux*, they can both be said to be 'emergent'. Viewed from the perspective of the flux, both types of organizational intervention 'emerge' as different interactive practices in the ongoing 'flow' of interactions that constitute the organization as a social system. However, because continuous and episodic interventions in organizational structures are *organizational interventions*, it can also be argued that they both are intentional and involve deliberation. In this way, we break with the idea that continuous interventions are 'emergent' and episodic interventions are 'intentional' (see, for instance, Weick and Quinn, 1999, pp. 365ff, on continuous and episodic change). Instead, we argue that both types of intervention emerge in and are a part of the organizational flux. However, as organizational interventions, they both involve intent and deliberation.

In spite of their similarities, there are also differences between continuous and episodic interventions in organizational structures. Table 4.2 provides an overview.

As indicated in the previous section, continuous interventions in organizational structures are local interventions. Organization members intervene in the structure of their own work. Episodic interventions in organizational structures are more comprehensive than that. These interventions address the structure of large parts of the organization, or even of the organization as a whole. Instead of being local, episodic interventions in organizational structures are comprehensive.

TABLE 4.2 Differences between continuous and episodic interventions in organizational structures

Continuous interventions in organizational structures	Episodic interventions in organizational structures
Local	Comprehensive
Improving	Transforming
Not necessarily coherent	Coherent
Part of the daily activities of workers	Break with daily activities of workers
'Unmarked' in the organization's history	'Episode' in the organization's history
Are performed by means of the organization's current (standing) infrastructure; they do not need an additional intervention organization on top of the organization	Require a temporary and additional intervention organization with its own infrastructure on top of the organization

It is the goal of episodic interventions in organizational structures to transform the functioning of large parts of the organization or of the organization as a whole, i.e. their goal is to have a strategic impact on the organization's functioning. As such, these interventions have a comprehensive and 'transforming' rather than a local and 'improving' character.

In the case of episodic interventions in organizational structures, the transformation of an organization's functioning is realized by means of a comprehensive and transforming intervention. Instead of multiple, local, optimizing interventions that gradually, and not necessarily coherently, change the organization's structure and functioning, episodic interventions in organizational structures attempt to transform the structure and functioning of organizations in the course of a coherent project.

Unlike continuous interventions, episodic interventions in organizational structures are not a 'normal' part of the daily activities of organization members. They rather involve extra activities that should be performed on top of the normal activities in order to make the episodic intervention into a success. For instance, during an episodic intervention, organization members, in addition to their normal work, may be involved in the diagnosis or redesign of their own unit. Because of these extra activities, the episodic intervention will be regarded as an exceptional 'break' with normal ongoing operations.

Moreover, because of their comprehensive, transforming, coherent, and exceptional character, episodic interventions may be viewed as memorable 'episodes' in an organization's history. In organizations, all kinds of stories may circulate that tell their 'history'. Some of these stories highlight phases that are so important for the development of an organization that they are considered as 'episodes' in that history. For instance, stories may be told about the founding phase of the organization, about a phase of extreme adversity, or about the 'reign' of a particular CEO. Because episodic interventions are comprehensive and transforming, and as such have a large impact on the development of an organization, they too may be regarded as 'episodes' in the history of that organization. As 'episodes' in the history of organizations, episodic interventions also have a 'beginning', 'inner structure', and 'end'. This beginning, inner structure, and end are tied to events or developments in the organizational flux that, relative to the episodic intervention, are marked as important or decisive. Please note that the episodic character of an organizational intervention is not just a matter of looking back on the organization's history. At the start of an episodic intervention, the intervention may be introduced as 'episodic'. That is, it may be introduced as a phase in the organization's development during which the organization will go through a comprehensive, transforming, coherent, and exceptional change that will have a beginning, inner structure, and an end.

Finally, because of their comprehensive, transforming, coherent, and exceptional character, episodic interventions in organizational structures, unlike continuous interventions, cannot be performed by the 'standing' organization alone. Instead, episodic interventions in organizational structures require a *temporary* and *additional* 'intervention organization' on top of the organization. The *raison d'être* of this temporary and additional intervention organization is to enable the realization of the *functional* and *social goals in* the intervention and thereby to contribute to the realization of the *goal of* the intervention. An example of such an intervention organization may be a number of project teams that contribute to the diagnosis, design, and implementation of a new organizational structure, and a team of intervention managers that controls and coordinates the project teams.

Please note that an intervention organization has its own *intervention infrastructure*. This intervention infrastructure consists of:

1. an *intervention structure* – the allocation and grouping of intervention activities into intervention tasks that need to be performed in order to realize the functional and social goals in the intervention;
2. *human resources* – the people, including their knowledge, skills, and motivation, required to perform the intervention tasks needed to realize the functional and social goals of the intervention;
3. an *intervention technology* – all kinds of 'means' supporting the intervention, for instance information and communication technology or techniques supporting analysis and design.

The infrastructure of the intervention organization is not just there: it needs to be *designed*. As a consequence, each episodic intervention in the structure of an organization faces *two design challenges* instead of one.

1. the (re)design of the structure of the *organization*;
2. the (re)design of the infrastructure of the *intervention organization*.

On top of these two challenges, the designer of the infrastructure of intervention organization also needs to consider:

3. the *harmonization* of the intervention infrastructure with the infrastructure of the organization – for instance, someone who has a very demanding task in the primary processes of the organization may be overburdened by additional activities in the intervention organization, jeopardizing both these primary activities and the success of the episodic intervention.

Because episodic interventions need an intervention organization, and because this intervention organization has its own intervention infrastructure that needs to be designed, episodic interventions, in addition to their functional and social dimension, also have an *infrastructural dimension*. This dimension refers to the design of the infrastructure of the intervention organization that is needed to realize the functional and social goals in the intervention, and in this way, the goal of the intervention. Because of its relevance for realizing the goal of an episodic intervention, the infrastructural dimension of the intervention organization should be a part of a model that supports the realization of the goal of episodic interventions.

Episodic interventions in organizational structures: triggers

Literature on organizational change and design mentions different triggers of episodic interventions in organizational structures (see, for instance, Nadler and Tushman, 1997; Galbraith, 2000; Ghoshal and Bartlett, 2000). Examples of triggers that are mentioned are the adaptation of strategic goals, problems in an organization's culture, and recurrent problems in the organization's primary processes. Below, we distinguish two groups of triggers. The first group consists of *strategic changes* that, in order to be implemented, require a transformation of the organization's structure. The second group consists of *recurrent* or *engrained problems* that, on closer examination, are caused by the organization's structure.

Strategic changes that, in order to be implemented, require a transformation of the organization's structure constitute the first group of triggers. The most obvious trigger in this group is the adaptation of strategic goals (strategic regulation). By means of their strategic goals, organizations define what their contribution to society is (i.e. what the meaning of their survival is). Examples of 'meaning-defining' strategic goals are the product/service portfolio of an organization, or its desired relations with suppliers of work, resources, and capital. The adaptation of strategic goals may trigger an episodic intervention in an organization's structure because new goals (e.g. new products or services) may require new primary and regulatory activities that, somehow, should be integrated into the processes and structure of the organization. Another trigger within this first group is the introduction of a new technology that is basic to performing core processes of an organization (infrastructural regulation). Just as in the case of the adaptation of strategic goals, the new technology may introduce new primary and regulatory activities that should be integrated into the organization's structure by means of an episodic intervention. A final, perhaps less obvious, trigger within the first group is the transformation of an organization's human resources policy (infrastructural regulation). A fundamentally new perspective on 'people' and 'work' in an organization may involve a new outlook on tasks and the structure in which they are embedded, making an episodic intervention in the structure of the organization opportune.

The second group of triggers of episodic interventions in organizational structures consists of recurrent problems that, on closer examination, are caused by the organization's structure. The most obvious instances of this type of triggers are:

1. recurrent problems in the performance of the organization's *primary processes* and the continuous *operational regulation* that is needed to deal with these problems; as a consequence of these problems and the continuous effort to regulate them, the realization of organizational goals is frustrated;
2. engrained *cultural* problems, such as 'alienation', 'lack of involvement', 'lack of responsibility', 'sluggish bureaucratic behaviour', 'an atmosphere of distrust and blaming others', 'paralysing politics', or 'missing entrepreneurial spirit'; these cultural problems frustrate both the realization and the adaptation of organizational goals;
3. recurrent problems in the organization's *regulatory processes*, i.e. operational regulation, design regulation, and strategic regulation; these regulatory problems hinder both the realization and the adaptation of organizational goals.

The recurrent and ingrained character of these problems suggests that they are *not mere accidents*. On the contrary, it is quite likely that they are *systematically produced* by the organization's flawed infrastructure. A closer analysis, then, may even reveal that the organization's *structure* might well be the cause of these recurrent and ingrained problems. In order to further diagnose and, if necessary, transform this structure, an episodic intervention is staged. In this way, the problems mentioned earlier can be triggers of an episodic intervention in an organization's structure.

Because episodic interventions in organizational structures are often triggered by the three types of problems mentioned above, it is useful to discuss two characteristics of organizations that, because of their problematic structure, need these interventions. These two characteristics are that such organizations face a *problem complex* rather than some isolated problem, and that these organizations have so-called *self-inhibiting structures*.

Problem complexes and self-inhibiting structures

If it is supposed that the structure of an organization is an important cause of the three problems mentioned above, i.e. if it is supposed that this structure is indeed so problematic that an episodic intervention in order to improve it is warranted, then it is to be expected that (1) the three problems mentioned in the previous section occur as a *problem complex* and (2) the organization's problematic structure is more or less *self-inhibiting*.

To start with the first point of the *combination* of the three problems, in Chapter 3 it was argued that problematic high parameter value structures are complex and hierarchical structures. Because of their complexity and hierarchy, high parameter value structures increase the probability of the occurrence of disturbances and decrease the chances to deal with these problems by means of regulation (that is why they are so problematic). As a result, organizations with high value parameter structures experience problems in both their *primary* and *regulatory* processes, i.e. they suffer from *both* the *first* and *third* type of problems mentioned in the previous section. Moreover, the complexity and hierarchy of high parameter value structures reduces the overview workers have over the primary processes they participate in, decreases the insight they have in the organizational goals they contribute to, and 'rob' both workers and managers of the regulatory potential they need to regulate their own work. As a result, a negative *culture* of 'detachment', 'alienation', and 'bureaucracy' may emerge – which is the *second* type of problems mentioned in the previous section. Therefore, it appears that organizations with problematic high parameter value structures will probably suffer from the *three* problems that can be triggers of an episodic intervention in their structure in *combination*. These organizations characteristically face a *problem complex*, consisting of problems in their primary processes, culture, and their regulatory processes, rather than some isolated problem.

To explain the second point of the *self-inhibiting* character of problematic structures, it is vital to understand that episodic interventions in organizational structures are instances of *design regulation*. As argued in Chapter 2, design regulation is one of the four activities that organizations need to perform in order to adapt and realize the goals that constitute the 'meaning' of their survival. By means of design regulation, organizations reshape their infrastructure. Because an episodic intervention in an organization's structure is an activity that aims to reshape the structure dimension of that organization's infrastructure, it is an instance of design regulation.

Given this preliminary remark, the issue of the self-inhibiting character of problematic structures can be addressed. In short, a self-inhibiting structure is a structure that more or less hinders the design regulation – including the episodic interventions – needed to improve that structure. Using this definition as a point of departure, it can be argued that problematic high parameter value structures are self-inhibiting structures. To this purpose, we only need to zoom in on the three problems of high parameter value structures and their combination.

First, as indicated, organizations with high parameter value structures are haunted by recurrent structure-driven problems in their *primary processes*, problems that require continuous operational regulation. Moreover, because of the hierarchical character of high parameter value structures, operational regulation itself requires a lot of effort. Therefore, managers continuously need to deal with both recurrent problems in the primary processes and the problems involved in regulating them. Absorbed as they are in their unceasing attempts at operational regulation, managers have less time and energy to spend on the other types of regulation: design regulation and strategic regulation. As a result, high parameter value structures, because of the continuous effort spent on operational regulation, *indirectly* undermine an organization's capacity for design regulation, and thereby the capacity to perform the episodic interventions needed to improve the organization's own problematic structure.

Second, as argued above, it is quite probable that organizations with high parameter value structures suffer from a *negative culture*, i.e. a culture tainted by detachment, alienation, distrust, blaming, paralyzing politics, etc. As may be imagined, such a culture is not conducive to the episodic interventions that aim to change the organizational structure that contributed to the emergence of that problematic culture in the first place. So, once again, it appears that the organization's high parameter value structure, this time by means of its negative culture, *indirectly* undermines the organization's capacity for the episodic interventions that aim to improve its structure.

Third, 'problematic' high parameter value structures also inhibit an organization's potential for operational, design, and strategic regulation. As such, they not only indirectly inhibit an organization's capacity to perform the episodic interventions that aim to improve its structure, they also *directly* impede an organization's capacity for design regulation, and thereby its capacity for episodic interventions in its structure (because these interventions are instances of design regulation).

Fourth, as argued above, it is probable that organizations with high parameter value structures face the three problems in combination: they face a *problem complex* rather than an isolated problem. This means that in these organizations, the three factors inhibiting their capacity to perform the episodic interventions needed to improve their structure exist simultaneously. Although there may be degrees in the self-inhibiting character of structures, organizations that face structure-driven problem complexes truly have self-inhibiting structures. In these organizations, it will be very hard to successfully perform an episodic intervention that improves the structure that is the cause of its problems.

To conclude this section, it can be argued that organizations with high parameter value structures are *doubly* jeopardized. First, because of their high value parameter structure, these organizations have to deal with a complex of problems that endangers the adaptation and realization of their goals, and in the end jeopardizes their meaningful survival. Because the structure of such organizations has already deteriorated too far, continuous interventions that aim to improve it come too late, and, as argued, may be counterproductive. As a result, these organizations are *most in need* of an episodic intervention in their structure. Second, because of their high parameter value structure, these organizations have quite a low capacity to perform the much-needed episodic interventions in the structure that is at the root of their problems. The high parameter value structures of these organizations are self-inhibiting structures, i.e. they are structures that jeopardize the success of the episodic interventions that are needed to improve them. Thus, we arrive at the paradoxical conclusion that organizations that, because of their high parameter value structure, are *most in need* of an episodic intervention also *inhibit* this intervention the most, making such interventions perilous and very hard to perform. High parameter value structures not only jeopardize the meaningful survival of organizations, they also jeopardize the episodic interventions that are needed to improve these structures. Because of this toxic combination of the *need* for episodic interventions in high parameter value structures and the *inhibition* of these interventions by these structures, it becomes relevant to pay extra attention to this type of episodic interventions. They are the interventions that are both necessary and hard to perform. Therefore, although the 3-D model that will be unfolded in Part II of this book can be used to support episodic interventions that are triggered by both transformational changes and recurrent structure-driven problems, it is actually designed to support the second type of episodic intervention (see dark grey box in Figure 4.5e).

4.4 Harvesting the concepts underpinning the 3-D model

In Section 4.1, three questions were asked: (1) how can episodic interventions in organizational structures be defined, (2) how do these interventions relate to other types of organizational change, and (3) which characteristic features of episodic interventions in organization structures should figure in a model that can help realize these interventions? Here, in the final section of this chapter, we focus on the third question, because answering this question is instrumental for the transition to the second part of the book, in which the layout and use of the 3-D model are explained.

So which are the characteristic features of episodic interventions in organizational structures that should figure in a model that can help realize these interventions? Here are three conclusions.

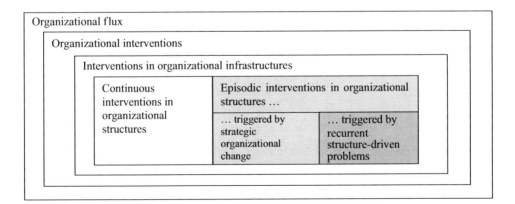

FIGURE 4.5E Episodic interventions triggered by recurrent structure-driven problems

4.4.1 First conclusion: functional, social, and infrastructural dimension

The first conclusion that can be drawn is that episodic interventions in organizational structures are interventions 'for', 'in', and 'by' organizations. The 'for' refers to the *goal of* the intervention, the reason why the intervention is performed. In order to realize the goal of the intervention, the *object* of the intervention, in this case the organization's structure, should be transformed. In order to realize this transformation, at least three dimensions should be taken into account: the functional dimension, the social dimension, and the dimension of the infrastructure of the intervention organization.

The functional dimension refers to activities that should be performed and goals that should be realized in order to transform the object of the intervention in such a way that it can function, i.e. that it can 'work well', relative to the goal of the intervention. The activities that should be performed to this purpose are 'diagnosis', 'design', 'implementation', and 'evaluation'. These activities have their own goals. For instance, the goal of 'diagnosis' is to find problems, to analyse their causes, and to formulate a solution space. These goals are *functional goals in* the intervention.

The social dimension refers to goals that should be realized in order to change the interactions and interaction premises of organization members in such a way that the transformation of the object of the intervention, the organization's structure, becomes an organizational reality. The goals that should be realized in the social dimension are 'motivation', 'adoption', and 'integration'. The social dimension takes seriously the fact that organizations are social systems that consist of interactions which are produced against a background of orientating interaction premises. Motivation, adoption, and integration are *social goals in* the intervention.

Episodic interventions in organizational structures are interventions that require an intervention organization – that is, a temporary organization 'on top' of the organization that can help perform intervention activities. This intervention organization, which in principle can involve all organization members, clients, suppliers, or other parties that have a stake, has its own infrastructure that should be designed. The infrastructure of the intervention organization is the third dimension that has to be taken into account. Just like the infrastructure of the organization, the infrastructure of the intervention organization comprises three aspects: the intervention structure, the intervention technology, and the human resources involved in the intervention.

In an episodic intervention, the three dimensions should be related in such a way that the infrastructure of the intervention organization is designed so that functional and social goals in the intervention can be realized and adapted, thereby maximizing the probability that the goal of the intervention is realized.

4.4.2 Second conclusion

The second conclusion that can be drawn is that episodic interventions have an *intentional* and *deliberative* character. Interventions are not based on routine and intuition alone. They involve setting goals and deliberation about ways to realize these goals. Obviously, their intentional and deliberative character does not mean that interventions evolve in a completely rational and transparent way. Organizations, including the interventions that aim to change them, are social systems conducting *experiments*. This means that functional and social goals in the intervention and infrastructural means to realize them remain mere hypotheses that may need to be revised as the intervention proceeds. Episodic interventions are therefore not 'machine-like' enterprises that can be planned in advance by a small group of experts. Because of their combined intentional, deliberative, and experimental character, a model supporting episodic interventions should allow for situational assessment and flexibility. This means that such a model should: (1) support continuous and local assessments of the progress of the intervention, (2) enable setting and resetting of functional or social goals in the intervention, and (3) allow for designing and redesigning parts or aspects of the intervention infrastructure.

4.4.3 Third conclusion

Episodic interventions in organizational structures can have a profound impact on the lives and aspirations of human beings working together in the particular type of social systems we call 'organizations'. This means that these interventions *always* involve *power* and *politics* (the agonistic side of interventions). Moreover, this means that these interventions also always involve questions related to *morality*. A model supporting episodic interventions in organizations should take both of these features that are inextricably linked to these interventions into account.

Using these three conclusions as a point of departure, the outline of our model can be sketched in the next chapter.

PART II
Designing interventions in organizational structures

5
THE 3-D MODEL IN OVERVIEW

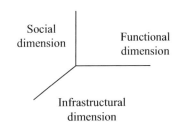

FIGURE 5.0 Roadmap of the book

5.1 Introduction

The three main conclusions from the first part of the book are that: (1) organizations are social systems conducting experiments with their own meaningful survival, (2) low parameter value structures are a necessary condition to successfully conduct these experiments, and (3) changing the parameter values of an organization's structure from high to low requires a particular type of interventions: episodic interventions in high parameter value structures.

These conclusions set the stage for the second part of the book, consisting of Chapters 6, 7, and 8. In these chapters, we discuss the three dimensions of the 3-D model: the functional, social, and infrastructural dimensions.

However, before we enter into a discussion of its dimensions, it is useful to provide an overview of the *whole* of the 3-D model. Providing this overview is the goal of the present chapter. In this chapter, we use insights from the theoretical first part of the book in order to both construct and provide an overview of the 3-D model. This overview, then, will be used as a background for the discussion of the different parts, the logic of use, and the application of the model in the second part of the book. Chapter 5, therefore, is a *transitory* chapter.

In order to both construct and provide an overview of the 3-D model, we depart from the nine features of episodic interventions that, in our view, should figure in a model supporting these interventions. These features were listed in the conclusion of the previous chapter. Episodic interventions:

1. have a *goal of* the intervention;
2. have an *object of* the intervention;
3. have a *functional* dimension;
4. have a *social* dimension;
5. have an *infrastructural* dimension;
6. have a *deliberative* and *intentional* character;
7. are a kind of *experiments*;
8. are *agonistic*, involving *power* relations;
9. have a *moral* aspect.

For the purpose of constructing the 3-D model in the present chapter, we use some of these features as 'building blocks' and others as 'functional requirements'. For instance, the functional, social, and infrastructural dimensions of episodic interventions provide the main building blocks, and taking into account the experimental character of episodic interventions is an important requirement to the functioning and use of the 3-D model. In order to provide an overview of the 3-D model in this chapter, we will proceed in three steps.

In step one, we will discuss the *layout* of the 3-D model. This layout is based on the goal and object of the intervention (features 1 and 2) and their relation to the three dimensions of episodic interventions: the functional, social, and infrastructural dimensions (features 3–5). Section 5.2 discusses the layout of the 3-D model.

In step two, we discuss the *logic of use* of the model. By the term 'logic of use', we mean the underlying principles/procedures that govern the model's application in concrete interventions. This logic of use, in the first place, takes seriously that episodic interventions have an intentional and deliberate character (feature 6). Second, it takes seriously that episodic interventions are a kind of experiments that require continuous assessment and adjustment (feature 7). The 3-D model's logic of use will be discussed in Section 5.3.

In step three (Section 5.4), we summarize the agonistic/power and moral aspect of episodic interventions (features 8 and 9). These aspects, it will be argued, play an undisputable role in the *application* of the 3-D model.

By discussing the 'layout', 'logic of use', and relevant aspects of the 'application' of the 3-D model, we attempt to systematically integrate into the 3-D model the features that, according to the theoretical insights of part one of this book, should be taken into account in a model that supports the performance of episodic interventions in high parameter value structures.

5.2 Layout: the functional, social, and infrastructural dimensions

In order to discuss the layout of the 3-D model, it will be useful to have a look at Figure 5.1. In this figure, the main elements of the model – the functional, social, and infrastructural dimensions – are related to both the goal and object of the episodic intervention.

5.2.1 The goal of the intervention

The *goal of the intervention* provides the answer to the question *why* the intervention is performed at all. In principle, there are two answers to this question: one general and one specific.

The general answer directly relates to the point that episodic interventions are interventions 'for' organizations. This means that these interventions should, somehow, contribute to the meaningful survival of the organization, whatever this 'meaning' may be. This general answer holds for *all* episodic interventions – all episodic interventions should contribute to the organization's meaningful survival.

The second answer is more specific. It states the goal of *this particular* episodic intervention. For instance, it states that *this* intervention should increase the organization's quality of organization by reducing production cycle time from X to Y, by increasing control over production quality from X to Y, and by increasing production flexibility from X to Y.

The specific goal of an episodic intervention is a contingent instantiation of the general goal. It is an *instantiation* because it states what, in the case of *this particular* episodic intervention, 'contributing to the organization's meaningful survival' means. It is a *contingent* instantiation because, unlike the general goal, the specific goal of the intervention is a selection made by the organization – a selection that could have been otherwise. This means

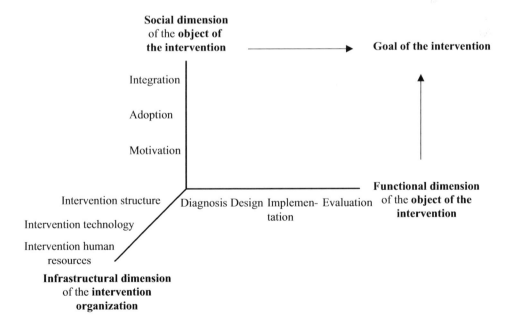

FIGURE 5.1 The 3-D model, its functional, social, and infrastructural dimensions in relation to the goal and the object of the intervention

that different episodic interventions can, and probably will, have different specific goals. In the case of episodic interventions in high parameter value structures, the specific goal of the intervention can be expressed in terms of quality of organization, quality of work, and the organization's capacity to reflect on and adapt interaction premises. From now on, when we refer to 'the goal of the intervention', we mean the *specific* goal of the intervention (unless explicitly specified otherwise).

It is relevant to underline that the (specific) goal of an episodic intervention is not 'ready-made' and 'given' at the start of an episodic intervention. It is formulated and reformulated as the intervention proceeds. For instance, in the early stages of an episodic intervention, e.g. as a part of the diagnostic activity, a first definition of the goal of the intervention may be formulated. As the intervention proceeds, e.g. as a part of the design activity, this first goal definition may be changed or further refined.

5.2.2 The object of the intervention

Episodic interventions are also interventions 'in' organizations. This means that, in order to realize the goal of an episodic intervention, some organizational object needs to be transformed. For instance, in the case of an episodic intervention in a high parameter value structure, the object of the intervention is the organization's structure. That is, in order to improve the organization's functioning, the parameter values of its structure (the object of the intervention) are decreased. In the case of other episodic interventions, this object may be the organization's technology, human resources, or culture. Of course, the transformation of some object, e.g. the organization's structure, may require the transformation of other objects as well, e.g. the organization's technology and/or its human resources. As a result, these other objects become included in 'the' object of the intervention.

In the case of organizational interventions, the object of an intervention has two relevant dimensions: a functional and a social dimension (see Section 4.3.2 on organizational interventions in Chapter 4).

5.2.3 The functional dimension

The *functional dimension* refers to the point that the object of an intervention should be transformed in such a way that it can actually contribute to the realization of the goal of the intervention – i.e. the object of the intervention should be transformed in order to allow the organization to 'work' or 'function' well (hence *functional* dimension). This means that at the end of the intervention, the object should have a design that allows for the realization of the goal of the intervention. In Figure 5.1, the arrow between the functional dimension and the goal of the intervention expresses this point. As argued in Chapter 4, all interventions have a functional dimension.

Applied to episodic interventions in high parameter value structures, the organization's structure is the object of the intervention. At the conclusion of these interventions, the structure of the organization should have a (low parameter value) design that allows the organization to realize the goal of the intervention.

Two requirements should be met in order to increase the probability that the object of the intervention is transformed in such a way that it can contribute to the realization of the goal of the intervention.

The *first* requirement is that *functional goals in the intervention* are realized by means of four intervention activities: 'diagnosis', 'design', 'implementation', and 'evaluation'. Applied to episodic interventions in high parameter value structures, the functional goal of:

1. *diagnosis* is the identification of the organization's current problems in terms of, for instance, quality of organization or quality of work, the analysis of the structure-related causes of these problems, and the construction of a solution space that identifies the parameters of the organization structure that should be changed in order to be able to realize the goal of the intervention;
2. *design* is the invention of a (desired) low parameter value structure that can contribute to the realization of the goal of the intervention;
3. *implementation* is the actual transformation of the current high parameter value structure to the desired low parameter value structure (note that in the case of episodic interventions in organizational structures, design and implementation are often iterative and closely coupled activities);
4. *evaluation* is the assessment of the capacity of the implemented low parameter value structure to actually contribute to the realization of the goal of the intervention.

In Chapter 6, the activities and goals on the functional dimension of episodic interventions in high parameter value structures will be discussed.

The *second* requirement is that diagnostic, design, implementation, and evaluation activities are supported by theory that explains the relation between parameter values of the object of the intervention and values of variables that are used to specify the goal of the intervention. Applied to episodic interventions in high parameter value structures, this means that theory is required explaining the relation between parameter values of the organization's structure and values that are used to measure the organization's performance. Based on such a theory, a structure can be designed that is an instantiation of parameter values that, according to that theory, support the improvement of an organization's performance. In Chapter 3, we unfolded exactly such a theory.

5.2.4 The social dimension

The *social dimension* of the object of an episodic intervention refers to the point that, in the case of organizations, this object always has a social character – i.e. it is socially 'produced' by means of interactions that are performed against a background of interaction premises. For instance, an organizational structure exists by virtue of organization members performing particular task-related interactions based on particular interaction premises. Transforming an organizational structure therefore requires the transformation of both these task-related interactions and the premises that guide their production. Without this transformation of interactions and interaction premises, *nothing* is changed in the organization. Thus, the object of an episodic intervention not only has a functional dimension, it also has a social dimension. This means that at the end of the intervention, the object of the intervention should not only be well-designed (functional dimension), but this design should also be integrated into the interactions and interaction premises of organization members (social dimension).

Applied to episodic interventions in high parameter value structures, this means that in order to realize the goal of the intervention, organization members should irreversibly *integrate* new interactions and interaction premises into their repertoires that (re)produce the organization's improved structure, thereby allowing for the realization of the goal of the intervention. In Figure 5.1, the arrow between the social dimension of the object of the intervention and the goal of the intervention expresses this relation between the integration goal on the social dimension and the goal of the intervention.

This final goal of 'integration', however, cannot be realized instantly. As the episodic intervention unfolds, other prior social goals should be realized as well. First, organization members should develop the *motivation* to change, and second organization members should *adopt* new helping interaction premises and related interaction patterns that enable the realization of the goal of the intervention. Applied to episodic intervention in high parameter value structures, the three social goals in the intervention that should be realized in order to realize the goal of the intervention are:

1. *motivation* – organization members should develop the motivation to:
   a. let go of current and move to new interaction premises and concomitant interaction patterns;
   b. adopt an episodic intervention as the means to do this;
2. *adoption* – based on a justifiable confidence, organization members should adopt new helping interaction premises and interactions that can (re)produce an improved organizational structure that allows for the realization of the goal of the intervention;
3. *integration* – organization members should irreversibly integrate into their repertoires the interaction premises and interactions that both reproduce the organization's improved structure and allow for the realization of the goal of the intervention.

In addition to these three goals, there is a fourth social goal that functions as a continuous background requirement: the *creation and maintenance of change relationships*. In the model, change relationships are considered as a sine qua non for making progress on the three other social goals. Chapter 7 discusses the social dimension of the 3-D model in more detail.

5.2.5 The infrastructural dimension of the intervention organization

Organizational interventions are also interventions 'by' organizations. Generally speaking, this means that organizational interventions evolve by means of organizational interaction both against a background of interaction premises and the organization's infrastructure.

In Chapter 4, we explained that in the case of *continuous* interventions, the infrastructure of the organization provides this background. The infrastructure of the organization provides the background for the interactive transformation of that very infrastructure.

However, we also explained that in the case of *episodic* interventions in high parameter value structures, an 'extra' temporary intervention organization with a separate intervention infrastructure is needed in order to interactively restructure the organization. The high parameter values of the structure of the organization are the reason why this temporary intervention organization is needed. High parameter value structures are self-inhibiting. They are structures that, because of their high parameter values, inhibit the continuous design regulation needed to decrease their high parameter values: the structure of the organization inhibits its own continuous redesign. In order to overcome this self-inhibition, an episodic intervention is required that has its *own* temporary intervention organization. Like all organizations, this temporary intervention organization has an infrastructure, consisting of an:

1. *intervention structure* – the grouping and allocation of operational and regulatory intervention activities into a network of intervention tasks (examples of operational intervention activities are developing motivation and performing a diagnosis; examples of regulatory intervention activities are designing an intervention infrastructure and setting functional or social goals in the intervention);
2. *intervention technology* – techniques or technological means that are used for the purpose of performing intervention activities (e.g. communication techniques, and techniques supporting diagnosis or design);
3. *intervention human resources* – organization members or other participants in the intervention (e.g. consultants, clients, suppliers) that by means of their knowledge, skills, and motivation perform intervention tasks using intervention technology.

As a result, episodic interventions in high parameter value structures have a third dimension. This third dimension is the infrastructure of the temporary intervention organization that is needed to support the episodic intervention. In Chapter 8, we will elaborate this infrastructural dimension of the intervention organization.

5.2.6 Relations between the elements of the model

Given the provisional description of the main elements (goal, object, and the three dimensions) of the 3-D model, we can summarize the relations between these elements.

The goal of the intervention is to improve the functioning of the organization. In order to realize this goal, the object of the intervention – in this case, the structure of the organization – should be transformed. As explained, this object has a functional and a social dimension.

The functional dimension is about transforming the organization's structure in such a way that it allows for the realization of the goal of the intervention – i.e. the organization's structure should be well-designed, and this design should be implemented. In order to realize the required transformation, the organization's structure should be *diagnosed*, *designed*, *implemented*, and *evaluated*. The results of these four activities are the functional goals in the intervention.

The social dimension takes the social character of organizational structures into account. Transforming the structure of an organization means transforming task-related interactions and interaction premises of organization members. In order to transform these interactions and interaction premises, three social goals in the intervention should be realized. Organization members should develop the *motivation* to change, they should *adopt* new helping interaction premises, and they should irreversibly *integrate* these new interaction premises and related interactions into their repertoires of interactions.

Both the functional and the social dimensions of the 3-D model are *goal dimensions*. They specify goals in the intervention that should be realized in order to realize the goal of the intervention.

The infrastructural dimension of the intervention organization specifies infrastructural *means* that are used to realize functional and/or social goals in the intervention. For instance, in the early stages of the intervention, 'performing a diagnosis' and 'developing motivation to change' may be relevant functional and social goals in the intervention. In order to realize these goals:

- intervention tasks should be specified – tasks consisting of activities supporting the diagnosis and/or the development of the motivation to change;
- intervention technology should be selected – techniques supporting the realization of the diagnosis and motivation goal;
- intervention human resources should be appointed – organization members or other parties (consultants, clients, suppliers) performing the specified intervention tasks by means of the selected intervention technology.

In this way, an intervention infrastructure is designed that can help achieve functional and social goals that should be realized in order to arrive at the goal of the intervention. Each time 'old' functional and social goals are realized, new functional and social goals should be set in order to drive the episodic intervention forward. For instance, after realizing the 'diagnostic' and 'motivation' goals, 'design' and 'adoption' may be set as new functional and social goals and an intervention infrastructure can be designed that can help realize these new goals. Ideal typically, this process continues until the 'integration' and 'evaluation' goal are realized and the goal of the intervention is achieved.

Given this summary of the relations between the goal of the intervention, the functional and social goals in the intervention, and the intervention infrastructure, we can take a closer look at the logic of use of the 3-D model.

5.3 Logic of use of the 3-D model

In Chapter 4, we argued that interventions (episodic interventions included) have an intentional and deliberative character: *intentional* because activities in the intervention are performed with the explicit goal to improve the functioning of the organization, *deliberative* because performing these activities involves explicit interpretation of situations and weighing of options.

We also argued that episodic interventions are a kind of *experiments*. This experimental character of episodic intervention is intrinsically linked to their dynamics. Just as in the case of organizing, the experimental character of episodic interventions means that: (1) selections with respect to (functional and social) goals, parts, or aspects of the intervention infrastructure, and operational regulation may prove to be less successful than imagined (they are a kind of hypotheses about what should be successful), and (2) all kinds of factors that are difficult to foresee can (negatively or positively) affect the progress of the intervention. This experimental character of episodic interventions requires that these interventions should be continuously assessed and, if required, adjusted. Assessment and adjustment here means that, if the situation requires this, functional or social goals should be reset, parts or aspects of the intervention infrastructure should be redesigned, and actions to operationally regulate disturbances should be reconsidered.

In order to support continuous assessment and adjustment, the 3-D model should be constructed in such a way that it supports *situational* and *cybernetic deliberation*:

1. *Situational* deliberation means continuous assessment and adjustment, taking into account salient features of the current situation of the intervention and its history.

2. *Cybernetic* deliberation means that continuous assessment and adjustment are related to the main topics of regulation:

   a. setting functional and social goals in the intervention – strategic regulation of the intervention;
   b. designing the intervention infrastructure (and its relation to the infrastructure of the organization) – design regulation of the intervention;
   c. dealing with problems in the primary intervention activities – operational regulation of the intervention.

3. *Deliberation* means that as a part of continuous assessment and adjustment:

   a. the actual status of the intervention is *interpreted* in terms of both progress on the functional and/or social dimensions and (situational) factors that negatively or positively influence progress;
   b. adjustments to functional or social goals, parts or aspects of the intervention infrastructure, and actions that should operationally regulate problems are *weighed* in the light of interpretations of the progress of the intervention and factors affecting progress.

Based on these requirements, it becomes possible to provide a description of the logic of use of the 3-D model.

In order to drive the episodic intervention forward and deal with factors that negatively or positively affect the progress of the intervention, the following five activities should be performed:

1. *Strategic regulation* – select functional and social goals in the intervention.
2. *Design regulation* – build an intervention infrastructure that can perform and regulate (operational, design, and strategic regulation) the operational intervention activities needed to realize selected functional and social goals.
3. *Operational regulation* – manage disturbances of the operational intervention activities (without changing the intervention's design or goals).
4. *Operational intervention activities* – carry out the activities that should realize the functional and social goals.

As a part of the regulatory activities, a fifth activity is presupposed:

5. *Continuously assess the progress of the episodic intervention relative to selected functional and social goals, and dependent on this assessment, perform regulatory activity 1, 2, or 3 (adjustment of goals, infrastructure, or operational regulation).*

These five activities constitute the core of the logic of use of the 3-D model.

An example may help to both clarify what these activities entail and show how they can support the performance of episodic interventions. Let us suppose that in some organization it is decided that an episodic intervention in its structure is warranted. Moreover, the 3-D model is selected as a tool to support this intervention.

At the start of the intervention, an assessment is made of the functional and social goals that already have been realized (activity 5). Based on this assessment, it appears that currently no functional or social goal has been realized (of course, in actual practice, it may be that, for

148 Designing interventions

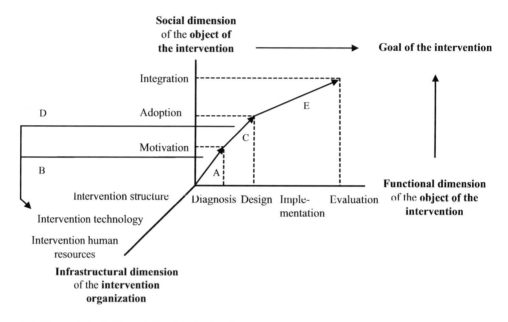

FIGURE 5.2 The 3-D model and its logic of use

instance, a diagnosis has already been made or that organization members already developed the motivation to change).

In order to drive the intervention forward, it is decided that the functional and social goals that are *next in line* to be realized are: 'creating change relationships', 'diagnosis', and 'motivation' (strategic regulation: activity 1; see arrow A in Figure 5.2). From now on, we call the functional or social goals that are next in line to be realized the *proximate* functional or social goals.

In order to be able to realize the selected proximate functional and social goals, an intervention infrastructure is designed that should support the realization and adaptation of these goals (design regulation: activity 2). In particular, this means that an intervention structure is designed and that intervention technology and knowledgeable, skilled, and motivated human resources are selected (see arrow B in Figure 5.2).

As this infrastructure starts to function – i.e. as operational intervention activities are performed that should realize the proximate functional and social goal (performing operational intervention activities: activity 4) – all kinds of things may occur that positively or negatively affect the progress of the intervention. Dependent on the assessment of the intervention's progress (activity 5), it may be concluded that operational regulation (activity 3), design regulation (activity 2), or strategic regulation (activity 1) is required.

For instance, based on continuous assessment, it may appear that realizing the 'diagnosis' goal is negatively affected by a lack of knowledge among some of the participants about what it means to diagnose an organization's structure. In this case, the intervention infrastructure may be redesigned (activity 2) in order to address this knowledge issue. For instance, new participants may be appointed who do have the right knowledge, a consultant may be hired who can support the appointed participants in the diagnostic process, or the appointed participants can be educated so that they can perform this process themselves.

At some moment in the intervention, continuous assessment (activity 5) may show that the proximate functional and social goals have been realized. Now, new proximate functional and social goals should be set in order to drive the intervention forward (see arrow C in Figure 5.2). Based on the assessment, 'design' and 'adoption' are selected as the new proximate functional and social goals. Moreover, it is decided that maintaining 'motivation' remains an important social goal (strategic regulation: activity 1). Given these new proximate functional and social goals, the intervention's infrastructure is adapted in order to enable their realization and adaptation (design regulation: activity 2; see arrow D in Figure 5.2).

Ideal typically, this process of assessing the intervention's progress and adjusting the proximate functional and social goals in the intervention, the intervention's infrastructure, and/or actions to operationally regulate the intervention continues until the 'final' social and functional goals ('integration' and 'evaluation') have been realized (arrow E in Figure 5.2). At this point, a new low parameter value structure (a structure that 'works': functional dimension) has been integrated into the interaction repertoires of organization members (social dimension). This integrated low parameter value structure *per hypothesis* can realize the goal of the intervention.

Please note that this description of the logic of use of the 3-D model is just an example. To begin, the five activities that constitute the core of the model's logic of use can be performed in different orders as required by the actual status of the intervention. Moreover, many alternative trajectories through the 'space' defined by the model's dimensions are possible. For instance, initially only social goals (e.g. 'creating change relationships' and 'developing motivation') may be set as proximate goals in the intervention, or the intervention may fail (the final goals in the intervention 'integration' and 'evaluation' are never realized).

Of course, a lot more can be said about the five activities that constitute the core of the logic of use of the 3-D model. For instance, how should the intervention infrastructure be designed given selected proximate functional and social goals – i.e. what is the relation between selections on the functional and social dimensions and selections on the infrastructural dimension? Who selects the proximate functional and social goals in the intervention, or who designs the intervention infrastructure? What happens if different proximate functional and social goals are set for different groups of participants in the intervention? Which factors can affect the progress of the intervention, and what can be done to deal with them? These questions that further develop and refine the logic of use of the 3-D model will be addressed in Chapter 8. In the present section, we just wanted to outline the basic idea of this logic as a process of continuous experimentation involving continuous assessment and adjustment of the intervention in terms of situational and cybernetic deliberation.

5.4 Application: power and morality

The goal and object of episodic interventions combined with their functional, social, and infrastructural dimensions provided the elements for the layout of the 3-D model. As argued, these elements are inextricably linked to episodic interventions, and for this reason should be part of a model that supports their performance. Something similar can be said about the intentional, deliberative, and experimental character of episodic interventions. Because these three features 'permeate' the dynamics of episodic interventions and their prospects of success, they were selected as points of departure for constructing the 3-D model's logic of use.

In Chapter 4, we also argued that *power* and *morality* are features that are intrinsically linked to episodic interventions. However, power and morality do not add new dimensions to the model's layout. In our view, the functional, social, and infrastructural dimensions are necessary and sufficient. Moreover, power and morality do not add new steps to the model's logic of use. Once again, in our view, the five activities are necessary and sufficient. So, how *do* power and morality figure in the 3-D model?

The simple answer to this question is that, in our opinion, power and morality are features of episodic interventions that should *always* be taken into account when *applying* the model's logic of use, given the model's layout. This means that in *all* assessments with respect to progress on the functional or social dimension and *all* adjustments of functional or social goals, the intervention's infrastructure, or actions to operationally regulate the intervention, issues of power and morality should be addressed. So, although power and morality are no part of either the model's layout or logic of use, this does not mean that they are unimportant. On the contrary, because of their importance and intrinsic relation to episodic interventions, they should be an integral part of the model's application in concrete situations. What this means in practice will be explained in Chapter 8.

5.5 Roadmap of the second part of the book

The rest of the book is organized in order to further explain the layout of the model, its logic of use, and its application-related issues of power and morality. To this purpose, we take the functional, social, and infrastructural dimensions of the model as our point of departure.

The *functional dimension* will be discussed in Chapter 6. In this chapter, we further elaborate what diagnosis, design, implementation, and evaluation entail in the case of episodic interventions in high parameter value structures.

Chapter 7 discusses the motivation, adoption, and integration goals of the *social dimension*. Moreover, this chapter touches on the relation between the 'social goals logic' of the 3-D model and the 'stage logic' of other models of organizational change.

Chapter 8 focuses on the *infrastructural dimension* of the intervention organization, the *logic of use of the 3-D model*, and the application-related issues of *power* and *morality*. To this purpose, this chapter starts with a procedure that supports the flexible design of intervention infrastructures. This procedure systematically relates selected functional and social goals in the intervention to the design of the intervention infrastructure. Second, it addresses factors that can affect progress on the functional and social dimensions – factors that should be taken into account when designing intervention infrastructures. Moreover, it addresses the relation between these factors and the issue of power. Finally, Chapter 8 discusses the three aspects of the intervention infrastructure: the intervention structure, the intervention technology, and the intervention human resources and their relation to the issue of morality.

6

THE FUNCTIONAL DIMENSION

Episodic Interventions in the Structure of Organization

PART I
Theoretical Framework:

– Organizations

– Organizational structures

– (episodic) Interventions

PART II
A 3-D Model of Episodic Interventions:

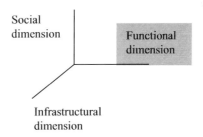

Social dimension

Functional dimension

Infrastructural dimension

FIGURE 6.0 Roadmap of the book

6.1 Introduction

In the previous chapter, we presented an overview of the 3-D model by means of which we approach episodic interventions in high parameter value structures. We stated that this model has a functional, a social, and an infrastructural dimension, and we briefly explained their content. In this and the next chapters, we will explain these dimensions in more detail, starting in this chapter with the *functional dimension*.

As we discussed in Chapter 5, the functional dimension of an episodic intervention in a high parameter value structure is about improving this structure in such a way that the changed structure enables the organization to 'function well' – i.e. the improved structure enables realizing the organization's continuous experiment with its own survival (the ultimate goal of the intervention). In Chapter 3, we unfolded a theory which expresses (1) how organizational structures contribute to 'functioning well' and (2) what these structures should look like in order deliver this contribution. In a nutshell, it was argued that structures should have low parameter values (as low as possible) in order to be able to realize 'quality of work' and 'quality of organization' variables and to enable reflection and change of interaction premises. Based on this theory, it is the goal of the functional dimension to make sure that the current (high parameter value) structure of the organization is transformed into one with values on the design parameters that are as low as possible, to make sure that 'functioning well' is secured.

In order to realize this overall goal of the functional dimension of episodic interventions in high parameter value structures, four activities and their associated goals[1] were identified: 'diagnosis', 'design', 'implementation', and 'evaluation'. Loosely stated (see also Chapter 4), diagnosis is about determining the structure-related causes of current organizational problems; design is about inventing a low parameter value structure that fits the specific organizational context; implementation is about actually transforming the current structure into the desired (low parameter value) structure, and evaluation is about finding out whether the implemented new structure has an improved capacity to support the organization's 'functioning well'. It is the aim of this chapter to elucidate these four activities (and their goals) of the functional dimension of episodic interventions in high parameter value structures.

Based on cybernetics, the overall idea of the functional dimension can also be stated somewhat more formally. In previous chapters, we introduced the relation between structures and the (desired) contribution of the organization to society. We argued that the latter could be operationalized in terms of 'quality of work' and 'quality of organization' variables. Now, if the organization shows undesired behaviour, this implies that one or more of these variables don't reach their associated norm values. And, if one assumes that this undesired behaviour is structure-related (and although there may be other causes, we treat problems as structure-related in this book), then these problems are caused by certain characteristics of the structure and can be dealt with by changing these characteristics. In our reasoning (which is derived from de Sitter's theory – see Chapter 3), these characteristics are described in terms of parameter values: high parameter values are structural characteristics causing problems. Moreover, it is suggested that changing these structures in such a way that these parameter values are lowered will solve problems. So, if P indicates the set of structural parameters and V is the set of variables operationalizing 'functioning well', the main idea capturing the structure dependence of the functioning of organizational is that: $P \rightarrow V$. This formulation provides us with a shorthand for explaining the functional dimension in some more detail. In fact, based on this shorthand, the activities of the functional dimension can be described as follows:

Diagnosis
1. Find out what the problematic organizational behaviour is – that is, find out which $v \in V$ do not meet their desired values.
2. Determine the structural parameters $p \in P$ that cause the problematic values of the v's from step 1.
3. Select those $p \in P$ that need to be changed by a change in structure.

Design	Invent a new structure so that the values of parameters p causing the problematic behaviour in v's (diagnosis step 3) get their 'norm values' (that is, these p's should get such a value that they no longer act as a cause for problems in the v's).
Implementation	Make sure that the current structure is actually transformed into the desired structure (with desired values of all $p \in P$).
Evaluation	Establish whether the change in structure was successful. The main idea here is to find out whether the problematic v's (step 1 diagnosis) are now are no longer problematic v's (and others haven't become problematic), *because* of the new implemented structure with desired p's. Additionally, the evaluation may focus on other (process) criteria describing the intervention success (or failure), such as costs or meeting deadlines.

Given these four activities of the functional dimension, the structure of this chapter is as follows: we devote four sections to discussing the four activities (Sections 6.3–6.5). Moreover, we will explain the four functional activities by referring to a case of a construction firm with a high parameter value structure (this case is introduced in Section 6.2).

Before we start discussing the functional dimension, one important caveat is in order. As we discussed in Chapter 4, episodic interventions are dynamic, iterative, and recursive processes. Therefore, the sequence of goals that need to be realized is not fixed. Moreover, in episodic interventions, functional goals should never be treated in isolation, but in conjunction with relevant social goals. Nevertheless, we will discuss, in this chapter the four functional activities without paying (much) attention to iterations, recursions, or the social dimension (although the intimate relation between design and implementation *is* addressed). The reason is simple: in this chapter, we just want to explain what the functional activities themselves amount to – in later chapters, we will go into the dynamics of realizing the combined goals of episodic interventions.

6.2 Case: a high parameter value construction business

To illustrate the four activities of the functional dimension of episodic interventions in structures with high parameter values, we will refer to a construction firm with a high parameter value structure. The construction firm in this example (which is an actual construction firm one of the authors had to deal with – let's call it 'W') specializes in building projects. It is involved in a few large social housing projects (which aim to build a series of similar buildings) and many small projects (like renovations or extensions) initiated by private house owners. W performs two main services. First, it has the role of main construction contractor. This entails that W is the main contact of a client during a project. Part of this role also entails managing the project and contacting sub-contractors. Second, W has its own pool of masons (20) and carpenters (20) which are assigned to projects and carry out construction work. W employs two construction foremen and one 'overall' project manager. The duties of the overall project manager include reacting to social housing tenders and making construction bids and contracts for private clients (who are often referred to W by architects). After a client has signed a contract, a 'project' is defined and the manager assigns a so-called 'building team' to it. That is, large projects often get a team of four masons and carpenters, small projects mostly get a team of one mason and one carpenter. The mason(s) and carpenter(s) from one team are related to one project at a time – they carry out actual construction work for this project. Each project is supervised by a construction foreman who is responsible for the daily planning, assigns duties to the masons and carpenters, contacts sub-contractors and suppliers, arranges for materials to be at the site, and regulates the project – e.g. monitors progress and reacts to unforeseen circumstances and disturbances. Moreover, the foremen are responsible for training new employees. W only employs two foremen. Each foreman is assigned – on average – to one large project and about six small projects.

W has to pay attention to several variables that are essential for its survival. One set of variables refers to the fact that a project is finished on schedule, within budget, according to planning, and to the satisfaction of the client. Another set refers to being an innovative construction firm – e.g. the degree to which new, sustainable materials can be used, or the degree to which the newest construction management tools are used. Finally, a set of variables refers to being a good employer – e.g. the degree to which employees are satisfied with their work.

Unfortunately, W doesn't score too well on these variables. Almost no projects are finished on time and on budget. Most projects require additional work, and clients are not too satisfied with the quality of the projects. That is, most clients think that the foremen want to finish a project before clients feel that it lives up to quality norms. Much communication is required to convince the foremen that the project isn't finished. Clients are also dissatisfied with the overall communication about the progress of the project, and they are dissatisfied with the way W reacts to requested changes (in fact, it takes a lot of effort on the part of the clients to communicate about these changes and to see to it that they are undertaken). Clients are not supposed to talk to the building team about progress or changes. Instead, they should talk to the foremen, who are, unfortunately, often unavailable. Projects often take longer than planned because the required materials aren't arranged for, because the members of the building team don't know what to do, or because foremen haven't contacted sub-contractors on time. Moreover, if unforeseen circumstances occur (a supplier doesn't deliver, a sub-contractor doesn't show up, material breaks down, or something happens at the construction site), foremen often aren't there to fix them.

These are not the only problems, though. W also experiences problems with innovation and employee satisfaction. W can't keep up with competitor constructors with respect to incorporating the newest sustainable materials and installations. Currently, the foremen lack the knowledge to appreciate the consequences of the use of such materials and installations. For instance, solar energy installations may require different specifications with respect to the roof. As foremen don't have the required knowledge, W has to depend on (expensive) sub-contractors. Finally, W experiences problems with quality of work, as building team members often feel that they aren't being taken seriously. If materials aren't arranged for, if sub-contractors aren't contacted, or if they haven't been given proper instructions, they just can't do their job. As they are on the construction site all the time, the team has to communicate with clients who see that it can't get on with the project. Clients often express their frustration to the team, which causes stress. Also, building team members often find that they can easily fix problems themselves. For instance, they feel that they can very well arrange for the required materials by themselves, or that they can call a sub-contractor who hasn't been contacted by their foreman. Moreover, given the overall planning and specifications, team members can also often make their own daily planning. Team members feel frustrated with not being able to get on with their work: they experience many disturbances which they feel they can solve by themselves, but aren't allowed to. In fact, many team members feel that they don't need a foreman at all, and find that they can carry out many of his tasks. Workers, especially the experienced ones, indicate that the jobs they have to do don't tap into their full potential: not being included in work-related preparation, just receiving orders for the day, and not being able to deal with disturbances themselves not only hinder them in their development, but even feel degrading. As a result, some workers indicate that they don't feel 'connected' to and involved in the project they were assigned to. As one experienced mason remarked:

> I often see what is going wrong, I know how to fix it, but as I am not allowed to do anything and have to wait until the foreman arrives, I feel that I am treated like a child and I don't really feel responsible for the project any more.

Some workers have already left W and gone to a competitor where building teams are granted considerably more regulatory potential.

Foremen also experience a lot of stress. As they are tied to many projects, each having their own specific requirements, they lose track of what is needed in all of these projects. As a result, many things go wrong and they are often too late in reacting to disturbances. Not only does this lead to problems with the main project variables (for which they are responsible), it also causes frustration on the part of the team (with whom the foremen have to deal) and leads to dissatisfied clients (with whom the foremen have to communicate).

Given this description, we will now take a look at the four activities of the functional dimension of episodic interventions. And, while we discuss them, we will *diagnose* the problems of W as problems caused by high parameter values, and *design* as a solution a structure with lower parameter values, briefly discuss its *implementation*, and explain how this implementation may be *evaluated*.

6.3 Diagnosis

The main goal of a diagnosis as part of episodic interventions in high parameter value structures is to find structure-related causes of problematic organizational behaviour. In order to find these causes, a diagnosis has three related sub-goals, which we will discuss in this section:

1. Establish the 'problematic organizational behaviour', or phrased alternatively, perform a 'gap analysis' – i.e. find the gap between desired and actual organizational performance (this gap describes problematic organizational behaviour).
2. Given this gap, the second sub-goal is to establish its structural causes, i.e. find out which design parameters are causes of the gap. As delineated in the theory linking design parameters to organizational behaviour, these design parameters have values that are 'too high'.
3. Given the list of 'troublesome parameters', a third sub-goal is to establish those parameters that should be changed by a change in the structure. This may appear as an odd sub-goal, as one might expect that all troublesome parameters should be lowered by designing a new structure. This sub-goal, however, is about understanding the (high) values of the parameters in context, as it may be that even though a parameter has a high value, its value cannot be lowered given the specific organizational context.

6.3.1 Diagnosis – sub-goal 1: gap analysis

To find the causes of problematic organizational behaviour, this problematic behaviour first needs to be established. We argue that 'problematic organizational behaviour' can be described as not realizing the organization's contribution to society in a proper way. And, as we stated in Chapter 3, this contribution can be cast in terms of variables describing the organization's 'quality of organization' and 'quality of work'. Problematic organizational behaviour, then, can be described as a mismatch between the *desired* values on these variables and their *actual* values. In fact, a gap analysis describes the problematic behaviour in terms of this mismatch: it lists the variables on which there is a mismatch and gives an idea of the degree of the mismatch.

A gap analysis requires the following steps:

1. (Re)formulate the organization's conception of its 'meaningful survival'.
2. Determine the set of variables (V) describing the organization's performance (i.e. those variables operationalizing 'quality of organization' and 'quality of work').
3. Determine the norm value(s) of all $v \in V$ (we will refer to the norm value(s) of variable $v_i \in V$ as $v_i[nv]$).
4. Determine the actual value of all $v \in V$ (we will refer to the actual value of variable $v_i \in V$ as $v_i[av]$).
5. Determine whether there is a problematic difference (an error) between the norm value(s) and the actual value of all $v \in V$ (we will refer to this problematic difference between the actual and norm value of variable $v_i \in V$ as $v_i[e]$)
6. Determine the gap: all $v_i \in V$ for which $v_i[e]$ exists.

Let's briefly examine these steps, given the case of the construction firm presented above.

Step 0: (re)formulate the organization's conception of its 'meaningful survival'

This step should provide an overview of the goals expressing the organization's interpretation of 'meaningful survival' – comprising an idea of its identity and contribution to its environment (see Chapter 2). This conception serves as a background for several selections made during an episodic intervention, as we will see. For instance, it may help in selecting the most relevant 'quality of organization' variables and thus guide diagnosis and design. For instance, W defined itself as a construction firm setting out to incorporate the clients' desires in the best possible way. In this way, it wanted to set itself apart from other construction firms in the region that were a cheaper but had a reputation for being unresponsive to client needs. Given this identity, variables regarding client satisfaction regarding quality and communication seem to be more important than variables expressing efficiency. In a similar way, the identity and ideas about how to serve the environment guide a selection in establishing the severity of problems. So step 0 is needed to provide a background for selections made on the functional dimension. We will indicate its relevance while discussing the activities of the functional dimension when appropriate.

Step 1: determine the set of variables (V) describing the organization's performance

The first step of a diagnosis entails finding the set of variables expressing the organization's performance – i.e. those variables operationalizing 'quality of organization' and 'quality of work'.

To this purpose, we start off from the *general* list of variables expressing quality of organization and quality of work as proposed by de Sitter (1994) and discussed in Chapter 3. For the sake of convenience, this general list is reproduced in Table 6.1.

As we discussed in Chapter 3, these variables are quite general and should be translated to fit the specific characteristics of specific organizations. In the case of the construction firm W, we need to translate the second-level variables from Table 6.1 into variables suitable for W. We will now translate flexibility, control over order realization, potential for innovation, and quality of work for W.

Variables related to flexibility

In order to be flexible (i.e. to be able to adapt to changes in demand which may come about by increased competition or environmental trends), organizations need to realize 'short production cycle times' (the time needed to finish or deliver a product or service), a 'sufficient number of product variations' (the number of different types/versions of products and services), 'a sufficient product mix' (the degree to which any mix of product types/versions can be realized), and 'different volumes' (the degree to which the (mix of) product types/versions can be realized in any volume) (see de Sitter, 1994).

In the case of W, these flexibility variables can be translated in the following way. First, 'production cycle times' have to do with the time needed to finish a construction project. An indicator might be the 'average time to complete projects of type X in days'. In this case, the more specific the degree of detail of X, the more precise the indicator becomes. For instance, the indicator 'the average number of days needed to complete large projects (projects over €100,000)' is of course less precise than 'the average number of days needed to complete a bathroom renovation'.

'Sufficient product variations' can be expressed by the variable 'number of different types and versions of construction projects W is able to offer'. Here, too, the level of detail of the type of products/versions may be important.

'Sufficient product mix' refers to 'the degree to which W is able to deliver different combinations of the construction projects it is offering. So, even though W may offer many types of small renovation projects as well as large social housing projects (sufficient variations), once

TABLE 6.1 General variables expressing quality of organization and quality of work

First level		*Second level*
Quality of organization	Flexibility	Short production cycle times
		Sufficient product variations
		Sufficient product mix
		Sufficient volumes
	Control over order realization	Reliable production time
		Reliable product quality
	Potential for innovation	Strategic product development
		Short innovation time
Quality of work	(Low) levels of absenteeism and personnel turnover	Opportunities to (1) be involved, (2) learn, and (3) develop
		Controllable stress conditions

Source: Adapted from de Sitter (1994, p. 42).

it is involved in a very large social housing projects, there may be no capacity left for realizing small renovation projects. In this case, W cannot realize all possible combinations of construction projects. It may be difficult to express this idea in a set of variables. One possible variable may be 'percentage of the total number of project combinations that can be realized' – but, admittedly, this is a variable that takes some time to calculate. An alternative variable may be 'the number of rejected projects which are part of W's possible projects'.

'Sufficient volumes' refers to 'the degree to which W is able to deliver different combinations of the construction projects it is offering *in any volume*'. In a way, it is a further specification of the product mix variable (also note that if some mix cannot be realized, the volume of at least one project type is 0). Due to capacity reasons (e.g. the number of employees or the number of employees with knowledge of specific projects), the possible number of the same projects may be limited. For instance, given the number of employees, the number of large social housing projects W can participate in is limited. Or, given the limited experience with eighteenth-century carpentry, W can only accept one renovation project of eighteenth-century buildings at a time. Relevant variables may be the 'maximum number of projects of type X if it is the only type of project demanded' or 'number of rejections of additional projects of type X'.

To give the reader an idea of what these variables may look like in other (and more complex) types of business, we also translate flexibility variables for a car manufacturer (mass production) and a nursing home (service industry) – see Table 6.2.

Of course, other and more sophisticated variables may be thought of, but here we just want to illustrate the translation of the general flexibility variables into company-specific ones (as flexibility variables seem to be relatively difficult to translate, we provided examples for other industries, but we will stick to W for examples in the remainder of the chapter).

Variables related to the control of order realization

Control over order realization, in essence, means being able to live up to promises made with respect to product quality and production or delivery time. The two main second-level variables de Sitter (1994) proposes here are 'reliable product quality' (expressing the degree to which one is able to live up to agreed-upon product standards) and 'reliable production time' (expressing the degree to which one is able to produce, deliver, or finish products in the time agreed upon).

The case mentions several translations of these types of variables: the degree to which projects are finished on schedule, within budget, according to planning, and to the satisfaction of the client. These may be further specified, e.g. in terms of 'percentage of the projects ...' (1) '... finished on schedule', or (2) '... within budget'. Other possible variables may be '(average) amount of extra work (e.g. as a percentage of the total project sum)', '(average) number of days beyond schedule (e.g. as a percentage of the total number of days)', '(actual costs / projected costs) * 100%' (as indicator of (not) staying within budget), 'hours spent on repair work', or 'number of times that rescheduling was required'. Also, measures of client satisfaction may be given (e.g. average client scores expressing satisfaction with respect to quality issues). There are many possible variables indicating project quality and project duration – the point is that they should be defined in such a way that they may be used to express both desired and undesired behaviour.

TABLE 6.2 Examples of variables related to flexibility

Flexibility variables	Car manufacturer	Nursing home
Short production cycle times	Average time needed to produce car (of type/version X)	Average time to react to patient call / Average time to perform care activity X
Sufficient product variations	Number of different cars (types/versions) produced	Number of different types of nursing care activities offered
Sufficient product mix	Degree to which manufacturer can realize all distributions of cars (types/versions) – if this variable is OK, the manufacturer will have no trouble switching from, say, 100 cars of type Y and 10,000 cars of type X to 10,000 cars of type Y and 100 of type X	Degree to which nurses can realize all distributions of types of care – e.g. if this variable is OK, the nursing home will be able to take care of 100 patients with different ailments and also, at a later time, 100 patients with the same type of problem
Sufficient volumes	Degree to which manufacturer can realize different mixes of different car types/versions in any volume (additional indicators may be required here, like the maximum capacity)	Degree to which the nursing home can provide care for different numbers of patients at a time – so a sudden increase in the number of patients should not be problematic (here, too, additional indicators may have to do with the maximum hospital capacity)

Variables related to the potential for innovation

De Sitter (1994) operationalizes the potential for innovation into two general indicators: strategic product (and process) development (the degree to which process and product innovations are relevant innovations) and innovation time (e.g. the average time from inception (product idea) to product launch). The degree of innovation relevance may be further specified as, for instance, the number and percentage of successfully adopted process innovations or the number and percentage of successful product innovations. Other specifications may include the degree to which new product or process developments are adopted (or even initiated). The list of possible indicators for 'relevant innovations' doesn't stop here – the innovation literature proposes quite a lot of them (cf. Fagerberg et al., 2005). Here, we just want to give some illustrations.

For the construction firm, two indicators are proposed in the case: the degree to which new, sustainable materials and installations are used in projects, and the degree to which new construction management tools are used.

Variables related to quality of work

Quality of work is expressed by two general indicators: the degree of absenteeism and the degree of personnel turnover (cf. de Sitter, 1994). These are further specified into the degree to which employees can learn, develop, and feel involved, and into the degree to which employees experience work-related stress (de Sitter, 1994; see also Chapter 3). The general indicators can already be translated quite easily – e.g. into 'percentage of days employees stayed home because they reported sick' or 'percentage of employees leaving the company in some time period'. Other indicators may be given by questionnaires on employee satisfaction, which may include scores on items related to learning, development, and involvement like:

1. 'the degree to which I can learn on the job';
2. 'the degree to which I can try new ways of performing my job';
3. 'the degree to which I can develop both my operational and regulatory knowledge and skills';
4. 'the degree to which I am allowed and challenged to apply new knowledge and skills';
5. 'the degree to which I feel socially connected to other employees';
6. 'the degree to which I have knowledge about the goals and output of the organization';
7. 'the degree to which I can influence goals and output of the organization';
8. 'the degree to which I feel an active part of a team';
9. 'the degree to which I am able to see and appreciate the point of my work';
10. 'the degree to which I (as part of my team) can actively contribute to (re)setting goals';
11. 'the degree to which I feel connected to the output of my work';
12. 'the degree to which I feel that I can do my work as a professional'

In a similar vein, indicators for 'experiencing job-related stress' may be formulated, e.g. in the form of direct questions like:

1. 'the degree to which I experience job-related stress';

or in the form of more indirect questions like:

2. 'the degree to which I feel that I can reach the targets set for my work';
3. 'the degree to which I feel that I can deal with disturbances I encounter during my work';
4. 'the degree to which I can rely on my team to deal with disturbances';
5. 'the degree to which I am allowed to think of new ways of dealing with disturbance'.

These are just some examples – and some work is still needed to operationalize such questions (in fact, many such indicators and questionnaires already exist; for a detailed treatment, see Christis, 1998). The idea is that issues like opportunities for learning, development, social and intrinsic involvement as well as experiencing job-related stress, as we outlined in Chapter 3, should be taken as point of departure for delineating quality of work in general. These general indicators (like the questions mentioned previously) can be used in specific contexts directly to obtain an idea of quality of work, but they may also be translated to reflect the specifics of the organizational situation – e.g. (for W): 'the degree to which I am satisfied with the way my building team can react to problems arising at the construction site' or 'During the past year I have considered leaving W', etc.

In all, step 1 leaves us with a set of variables by means of which the (problematic) organizational performance can be captured. Previously, we gave examples of general variables operationalizing quality of organization and quality of work, and gave some hints on how to translate them. We illustrated this translation for the specific situation of the construction firm W. We will refer to some of these translations to further explain the functional dimension. See Table 6.3 for the set of variables (V) we will use to proceed. Please bear in mind that we just want to illustrate the functional dimension, and hence will not produce or use a complete set of variables.

Before we move on to the next diagnosis step, we want to make two final remarks with respect to step 1.

The first is that many variables at many different levels of detail may be produced, and that one may wonder whether the list is ever complete or at the 'proper level of detail'. We'd reply that this may indeed be troublesome, but that the degree of completeness of V may be controlled by the set of goals that was identified in step 0. The goals expressing the organization's interpretation of meaningful survival help to attend to the most relevant variables. As we proposed in step 0, if W sets out to pay close attention to clients' needs as part of its identity, variables expressing the clients' evaluation of the delivered quality may be regarded as particularly relevant.

Moreover, capturing the problematic behaviour in terms of the proper variables is also a matter of experimentation. Some operationalizations may seem straightforward (e.g. 'the average number of days beyond schedule'), but may require some more thought to capture exactly what is going on (e.g. to truly measure the idea that a project is not on schedule, one may get rid of the 'average', or at least compare it with representative other projects). Finally, to control the set V (of variables used in the diagnosis), one may start off with the problematic behaviour and think of variables which capture this behaviour best – so a complete list of variables capturing all aspects of quality of organization and work may not always be required.

TABLE 6.3 The set of variables selected for explanation (second column)

General variables	(Translation of) variables used for 'W'
Reliable production	percentage of construction projects completed according to quality standards
	client satisfaction score with regard to project quality
	percentage of construction projects finished within budget
Reliable production time	percentage of construction projects finished on schedule
Strategic product/process innovation	the degree to which new, sustainable materials and installations are used in projects
Absenteeism	'percentage of days employees stayed home because they reported sick'
Personnel turnover	'percentage of employees leaving the company in the past five years
Learning, development, and involvement	Scores on the following items:
	'degree to which I am satisfied with my work'
	'degree to which I can learn and develop myself as a construction professional while carrying out construction projects'
	'degree to which I feel involved with the output of my work'
Experiencing job-related stress	Scores on the following items:
	'degree to which I experience job-related stress'
	'degree to which I can deal with disturbances I encounter while carrying out construction projects'

A second remark has to do with the type of variables. Previously, we used quantifiable variables, but sometimes these may prove difficult to arrive at. We should stress that all types – different types of quantifiable variables as well as qualitative variables – can be used.

Step 2: determine the norm value(s) of all $v \in V$

Given the set of variables describing (problematic) organizational behaviour (V), the next step is to determine the norm or desired values on these variables. The norm or desired value(s) (we will refer to the norm value(s) of variable $v_i \in V$ as: $v_i[nv]$) – this can either be one value or a set of values; see later in text) is the value (or the set of values) for which it holds: if variable v_i does not have this value (or is not part of this set of values), then the organizational behaviour with respect to this variable is problematic, and if variable v_i does have this value (or is part of this set of values), then the organizational behaviour with respect to this variable is not problematic.

The norm can be one particular value, or may refer to a set of values. For instance, if the variable is 'client satisfaction with respect to project quality' measured on a five-item Likert scale, the norm value of '4' may mean that all scores below 4 are unsatisfactory (and all those above it are OK). It implies a set of norm values covering the interval [4,5] on this scale. Similarly, the variable 'percentage of construction projects finished on schedule' may have a norm value of 95 – implying that all scores in the interval [95, 100] are proper scores, and those below 95 indicate problematic behaviour. Sometimes, one needs two norm values in order to indicate the upper and lower limits of the sub-set of desired values (e.g. if the desired inventory level should be above 100, but below 150, the two norm values are 100 and 150, and there should be some indication that the set of 'desired values' lies between these norm values). However, these are just some 'numerical' considerations with respect to a concept that is intuitively clear enough: the norm value(s) indicate(s) the value (or set of) desired values of the variable, and often (i.e. in the context of the variables in our kind of diagnosis) a set of values is involved.

Given this explanation, the question in step 2 of the gap analysis is to determine the norm value(s). This may not be that straightforward. For instance, what is the desired percentage of the variable 'percentage of construction projects finished on schedule'? Because 100% is unrealistic as one shouldn't discard the fact that there will always be unforeseen disturbances, the question then becomes: What does count as a realistic percentage? One way of approaching this question is to take into account the average percentage in the construction sector, or the average percentage of comparable construction firms. One could also take into account one's own track record (e.g. if this is considerably better than the sector's average). Or take the variable 'the degree to which I experience job-related stress' as measured on a five-item Likert scale. Here, the sector average (if available at all) may not be useable, as other construction firms may find themselves in different circumstances (e.g. maybe the majority are situated in urban regions with more competition, while W is situated in a more rural area). Or maybe the average isn't that interesting because at W, one may think that improving the satisfaction scores *beyond* average is what counts – e.g. because the average is so low that it can be taken as an indication of how poorly the sector takes care of its employees. In fact, this touches upon one very important way of controlling the selection of norm values: the degree to which they reflect the goals which express the organization's idea of meaningful survival. If the well-being of personnel is a relevant goal, then the sector average may not be a relevant benchmark. Similarly, if being responsive to clients' needs is what is intended to set W apart from its competitors, the sector average surely is not a relevant benchmark!

Setting relevant and realistic norm values, then, requires reflection and research: it requires reflection on the company's idea of meaningful survival, an inquiry into comparable settings, and knowledge about what may be expected in the specific company context. Setting norm values may also require experimentation: one may find out that during a gap analysis (or even later in the episodic change process), the norm values aren't set correctly and should be adjusted. It may sometimes even be that one can't agree on exact norm values, and that one finds that what *can* be said is only that the current values aren't good enough and that things should change for the better . . . . In that case, the undesired behaviour is a benchmark for desired behaviour, and reaching desired behaviour may become a matter of several iterations.

In any case, to establish a gap between desired and undesired behaviour, one not only needs a set of variables by means of which behaviour can be described (step 1), but also an idea of the norm values with respect to these variables (step 2).

Step 3: determine the actual value(s) of all $v \in V$

The third step in a diagnostic gap analysis it to determine the actual values of the variables from step 1 (we will refer to the actual value of variable $v_i \in V$ as: $v_i[av]$). This, too, requires some research. In some cases, this may be less demanding than establishing norm values. For instance, for the variables 'percentage of construction projects finished on schedule' and 'percentage of construction projects completed within budget', one 'just' needs to report the actual percentages (given some time period). This requires, of course, that such information is actually available. In other cases, gathering information about actual values of variables may require some more effort. Quality of work indicators (e.g. the 'degree to which I am satisfied with my work' or other indicators mentioned earlier) require valid and reliable operationalization – e.g. by means of some questionnaire. It may not be enough to assume that the indicator 'degree to which I am satisfied with my work' is validly captured by a question which has more or less the same wording and that asking for a score on five-item Likert scale, ranging from 1 to 5, provides valid and reliable information about the indicator. Such matters need additional methodological research. Moreover, finding the actual values of variables requires that questionnaires should be filled out by employees in a proper way, and the information from these questionnaires should be assembled into scores reflecting the 'actual value'. Be that as it may, the third step should yield actual values for the variables from step 1, reflecting the values at the moment of the gap analysis.

Step 4: determine whether there is a problematic difference (an error) between the norm value(s) and the actual value of all $v \in V$

Given the variables by means of which organizational behaviour is described (V from step 1), their norm values (step 2), and their actual values (step 3), it now becomes possible to find out which of these variables are problematic (and to what degree). These variables describe the 'gap' – the problematic organizational behaviour. To establish this gap, one needs to determine for each $v_i \in V$ whether the actual value $v_i[av]$ 'fits' the norm value(s) $v_i[nv]$. In this case, 'fit' can mean 'equals' (if the norm value is singular value) or 'is part of' (if the norm refers to a set of values). In this case, the variable is unproblematic. If $v_i[av]$ *doesn't fit* $v_i[nv]$ (in the same sense as described previously), then we'll say that an error exists with respect to this variable, notation: $v_i[e]$. So, quite simply, suppose that:

v_3 = 'percentage of construction projects completed within budget'

$v_3[nv] = 95\%$ (referring to the interval [95, 100])

$v_3[av] = 90\%$

Then $v_3[av]$ doesn't fit the norm value (set), and therefore $v_3[e]$ exists. V_3 is a problematic variable and part of the set of variables describing problematic organizational behaviour; the 'gap' (see step 5).

In some cases, it may also be possible to determine the size of the error (in the example, the error is 5%), and use this information to prioritize problems (or design solutions) against the background of the goals expressing the organization's interpretation of its meaningful survival. In the case of W, any difference between actual and norm value on variables operationalizing client satisfaction signals a top-priority problem, while a difference of 5% concerning the percentage of projects completed within budget may be less problematic, and even dismissed as not really being a problem.

In the previous text, determining the error appears as an exact science – as a matter of comparing numbers. Although this can be possible, it may also occur that the error is a matter of 'declaring' that there is something wrong with respect to some variable without being able to point at exact numerical values. For instance, one may decide that 'the degree of involvement' is too low after several discussions with key employees (and without further operationalizations and research). Sometimes, such 'declarations' may be enough to continue an episodic intervention.

In all, step 4 leaves us with two sets of variables: those for which an error exists, and those for which there is no error.

Step 5: determine the gap: all $v_i \in V$ for which $v_i[e]$ exists

In this last step, the set of $v_i \in V$ for which $v_i[e]$ exists is confirmed as the gap. This set is taken to describe problematic organizational behaviour. For the sake of illustrating the functional dimension, we will say that all variables listed in Table 6.3 have an error, and hence form the set of problematic variables: the gap (see Table 6.4).

The list of errors in Table 6.4 may be adjusted against the background of the (current and projected) goals of the organization. Some problems may be more pressing than others because they obstruct the most relevant goals of the organization. For instance, at W, one of the main overall goals is to be a good employer, so problems with quality of work may be particularly relevant.

6.3.2 Diagnosis – sub-goal 2: determining structural causes for the problematic organizational behaviour

Given the set of problematic variables from the gap analysis, the next goal of a structural diagnosis is to establish the structural causes of these problematic variables. And, as we discussed, the theory on the relation between structures and organizational behaviour suggests

TABLE 6.4 Result of the gap analysis (the list of $V_i[e]$ – last column)

General variables	(Translation of) variables used for 'W'	Gap
1. Reliable production	1.1 percentage of construction projects completed according to quality standards	$V_{1.1}[e]$ exists
	1.2 client satisfaction score with regard to project quality	$V_{1.2}[e]$ exists
	1.3 percentage of construction projects finished within budget	$V_{1.3}[e]$ exists
2. Reliable production time	2.1 percentage of construction projects finished on schedule	$V_{2.1}[e]$ exists
3. Strategic product/process innovation	3.1 the degree to which new, sustainable materials and installations are used in projects	$V_{3.1}[e]$ exists
4. Absenteeism	4.1 'percentage of days employees stayed home because they reported sick'	$V_{4.1}[e]$ exists
5. Personnel turnover	5.1 'percentage of employees leaving the company in the past five years'	$V_{5.1}[e]$ exists
6. Learning, development, and involvement	Scores on the following items:	$V_{6.1}[e]$ exists
	6.1 'degree to which I am satisfied with my work'	$V_{6.2}[e]$ exists
	6.2 'degree to which I can learn and develop myself as a construction professional while carrying out construction projects'	$V_{6.3}[e]$ exists
	6.3 'degree to which I feel involved with the output of my work'	
7. Experiencing job-related stress	Scores on the following items:	$V_{7.1}[e]$ exists
	7.1 'degree to which I experience job-related stress'	$V_{7.2}[e]$ exists
	7.2 'degree to which I can deal with disturbances I encounter while carrying out construction projects'	

that we look at structural parameters as possible causes. That is, the design theory we outlined in Chapter 3 holds that if structural parameters have values that are 'too high', many organizational problems may be expected. So, in order to find structural causes of problematic organizational behaviour, this design theory suggests finding those structural parameters $p \in P$ that have values that are 'too high' and that can therefore be seen as (partially) causing the problematic values of the variables found in the gap analysis. To find out which structural parameters cause problematic behaviour, the following steps can be identified:

Step 1: Select the set of structural parameters P that may possibly cause the problematic values of the variables establishing the gap. These structural parameters are selected based on some understanding of the relation between structure and (problematic) organizational behaviour.

Step 2: Find out, for all $p_i \in P$, whether p_i is a problematic parameter (a possible cause of problematic organizational behaviour).

Step 2.1: Provide a 'rich description' of the actual, current values of all parameters $p_i \in P$; we will refer to these descriptions of actual value(s) of parameter $p_i \in P$ as: '$p_i[av]$ in context'.

Step 2.2: Determine, for all $v_i \in V$ for which $v_i[e]$ exists whether, based on the design theory connecting parameters to organizational behaviour, it can be expected that $p_i \in P$ (for all i), given its current actual value, is a cause for $v_i[e]$. For every $p_i \in P$ for which this can be expected, we'll say that an error with respect to this parameter ($p_i[e]$) exists (i.e. that the parameter value in context is 'too high' and hence doesn't have its norm value).

Step 3: Establish the list of problematic parameters: all $p_i \in P$ for which $p_i[e]$ exists.

We will now briefly examine these steps and illustrate them based on the construction firm case.

Step 1: select the set of structural parameters P which may cause the problematic values of the gap variables

A structural diagnosis seeks to understand the problematic organizational behaviour (i.e. as described by problematic values of the variables selected to operationalize quality of organization and quality of work – the gap established in the gap analysis) as caused by the organization's structure. More specifically, it identifies characteristics of this structure which may act as such causes. In order to identify these characteristics, one needs to have some understanding of the relation between structure and organizational behaviour. And although different theories about this relation exist (e.g. Thompson, 1967; Galbraith, 1973; Mintzberg, 1983), we select the design theory of de Sitter (1994), which we discussed in Chapter 3, as it is, in our view, the most comprehensive and detailed theory linking structural characteristics (also 'design parameters') to organizational behaviour (i.e. to the variables operationalizing quality of organization and quality of work). Moreover, not only does it seem to be the most comprehensive structural design theory, it has also proven to be a valuable guide in diagnosing and solving structural problems in many organizations (cf. de Sitter, 1994; van Hooft, 1996; Kuipers et al., 2010). As we described earlier, de Sitter (1994) proposes seven design parameters as relevant characteristics of organizational structures (see also Achterbergh and Vriens, 2010, and Chapter 3). He also argues (see Chapter 3) that if these parameters have high values, they may cause problematic values on quality of organization and quality of work variables. Moreover, his theory holds that if these parameters have low values, they contribute to realizing norm values on quality of organization and quality of work variables. In all, we take the design parameters as proposed by de Sitter (1994) as parameters in our structural diagnosis. For purposes of clarity, we list these structural parameters in Table 6.5 (along with some possible indicators; see Chapter 3 for a more comprehensive explanation of these parameters).

Step 2: find out for all $p_i \in P$ whether p_i is a problematic parameter (a possible cause of problematic organizational behaviour)

To establish whether some parameter is a 'problematic' parameter, one might expect a straightforward approach like (1) 'determine the norm value of the parameter', (2) 'determine the

TABLE 6.5 Design parameters used in a structural diagnosis

Parameter	Brief description	Possible indicator
1. Degree of functional concentration	Degree to which operational tasks are related to all (external/internal) orders	Average number of external order types per operational task (e.g. in conjunction with the average complexity of order types – see text); average number of internal order types per operational task
2. Degree of differentiation of operational tasks	Degree to which production, preparation, and support activities are assigned to different tasks	Number of tasks dedicated to production, to support, and to preparation; Number of preparatory or support activities which are not part of operational tasks
3. Degree of specialization of operational tasks	Degree to which operational activities are split up into tasks covering only a small part of the operational process	Number of sequentially coupled tasks in operational process Average cycle time per operational task
4. Degree of differentiation of regulatory tasks into parts	Degree to which regulatory activities 'monitoring', 'assessing', and 'intervening' are assigned to different tasks	Number of tasks dedicated to monitoring, to assessing, and to intervening
5. Degree of differentiation of regulatory tasks into aspects	Degree to which 'strategic regulation', regulation by design', and 'operational regulation' are assigned to different tasks	Number of tasks dedicated to strategic regulation, to design regulation, and to operational regulation
6. Degree of specialization of regulatory activities	Degree to which regulatory activities have only small regulatory scope (i.e. cover only a small part of the operational process, or only a small set of other regulatory tasks)	Number of regulatory tasks
7. Degree of separation of regulatory and operational activities	Degree to which regulatory and operational activities are assigned to different tasks	Number of hierarchical layers Number of operational tasks without regulatory possibility to solve own problems Scores of operational employees with respect to the question whether they have the regulatory potential to deal with their operational problems

actual value', and (3) 'find out whether there is a difference between norm and actual value' – an approach we also used for finding out whether variables describing (problematic) organizational behaviour were in error.

Unfortunately, determining norm and actual parameter values isn't always (or rather, almost never is) a simple exercise. This has to do with two related issues: (1) the problem of operationalizing the parameters into relevant indicators, and (2) the issue of interpreting norm and actual values on these indicators.

The problem of operationalization

In Table 6.5, we gave some examples of indicators of the parameters. These are, however, just examples, and other indicators have also been suggested (e.g. Pugh et al., 1968; de Sitter, 1994). The problem is to find indicators based on which it can be said that the parameters are or are not problematic. If one only relies on 'simple' and/or 'numerical' indicators, a relevant statement about whether a parameter is problematic may be difficult because such indicators often leave out context factors that need to be taken into account. For instance, if functional concentration is operationalized into 'the average number of order types to which an operational task is connected', then one may wonder what a value of '5' means. If the different order types are comparable and don't require too many adjustments to the tasks related to them (e.g. five types of tables only differing with respect to their size), these '5' different order types may be quite doable and may not lead to many problems. However, if these order types are completely different (e.g. tables, armchairs, dining chairs, cupboards, or stools) '5' may be more problematic. In this case, the comparability of order types is a relevant context factor. The complexity of order types (e.g. in terms of the number of different activities required and in terms of the difficulty of these activities and the specialized knowledge needed to perform them) may also be a context factor. If an order type is very complex, adding only one more may already be disruptive. One way of responding to this problem is to try to translate 'all' relevant context factors into indicators as well, and to construct some way of combining them into one overall judgement about the parameter. Although we don't deny that this approach may work in some cases, we think that it may often be (at least practically) unfeasible as the question of whether context factors have been operationalized and combined in a proper way always arises. Instead, we propose to select some indicator that seems 'good enough' (staying as close as possible to the parameter definition we gave in Chapter 3) and interpret its values in context.

The issue of determining the norm and actual values

The issue of parameter operationalization is related to the issue of determining the norm value and, as a result, understanding the difference between actual and norm value. As delineated in the theory on design parameters and organizational behaviour, parameters will cause problematic organizational behaviour if their values are 'too high'. Or, conversely, if they have 'low' values, the parameters will not cause problematic organizational behaviour. So, heuristically, 'low enough' can be set as norm value. However, in Chapter 3, when we discussed de Sitter's design theory, we didn't concern ourselves with issues of operationalization and were content with a general description of the parameters. Based on this description, we introduced 'low' as a norm value. But in the present context, we need to treat such values less heuristically and be somewhat more specific. So what does 'low' (or 'low enough') mean?

One way of answering this question is to point at an 'absolute minimum' for each parameter, given the design theory describing them. For instance, suppose we operationalize functional concentration as the number of order types to which operational tasks are connected. This is high if tasks are related to all order types, and lower if tasks are related to only one or a few order types. Now, given this definition, the lowest possible value of functional concentration describes a situation where every task is related to only one order type. But one may ask whether this 'lowest value' is indeed the best value. It may appear to be unrealistically low and lead to order flows with inefficient capacity utilization. As we argued in Chapter 3, 'low' should be regarded as 'as low as possible' given the specific circumstances. Similar examples could be given for the other parameters. Still, this begs the question, as one may now wonder what the norm value 'as low as possible' means. For a structural diagnosis, it means that in the specific circumstances, if the actual parameter has a value below this norm value, this parameter is still causing problematic behaviour. However tautological and unsatisfactory this description of the norm value may seem, it does present us with an idea of finding out whether a parameter is problematic, even though norm values are difficult to establish. A possible approach is to start off from a description of the actual values of the parameters and try to find out whether these values can be expected to cause problematic organizational behaviour (based on theory and experience) and are actually causing such behaviour (given the expectations and actual problematic behaviour). In this way, an informed, context-specific interpretation of the difference between actual and norm value is given without explicitly stating the norm value in isolation. Such statements are comparable to the judgement of whether a mountain is too steep to climb without equipment, made by an experienced mountain climber. Her judgement 'definitely too steep' is a relevant qualitative normative judgement about the actual level of steepness even in the absence of a precise numerical indicator. Moreover, it is based on her experience (and hence experimentation in similar cases), taking into account contextual factors (such as the absence of ridges or protruding rocks). It is a statement that clearly incorporates a norm value (the acceptable level of steepness) without explicitly stating it.

So, in fact, both of the issues are related, and have to do with incorporating the relevant context. It should be incorporated to (1) capture the essence of the parameter, and (2) understand the difference between actual and norm value (and hence whether a parameter is problematic), in the absence of exact norm values. To deal with this context-specificity in finding out whether a parameter causes problematic behaviour, we propose the following procedure (see the steps mentioned earlier):

Step 2.1: First, a 'rich description' of the parameters and their current values should be given. Here, indicators for the parameters are selected that stay as close as possible to the definition given in Chapter 3. Also, their current values are stated and interpreted in context.

Step 2.2: Second, given this rich description, the design theory connecting parameter values to problematic organizational behaviour in general is used to make a judgement about whether the current problematic effects are indeed related to the actual values of the structural parameters (as derived from step 2.1).

The steps of this approach seek to give an answer to the following question (posed for each parameter):

'Given the actual value of parameter p_i in context, does p_i contribute to problematic organizational behaviour (found in the gap analysis)?'

The first part of this question (the actual value of parameter p_i in context) is derived from step 2.1. The second part (whether the actual value of p_i contributes to problematic organizational behaviour) is derived from step 2.2. The end result of these steps is a table connecting the actual values of the seven parameters in context to the problematic organizational variables (i.e. all variables, operationalizing quality of organization and quality of work for which an error exists: all $v_i \in V$ for which $v_i[e]$ exists – see Table 6.6).

We will now briefly discuss both steps involved in finding out the problematic parameters, using the case of the construction firm.

Step 2.1: provide a 'rich description' of the actual, current values of all parameters $p \in P$

The first step in determining which structural parameters are causes of organizational problematic behaviour is to describe the current values of these parameters in context. And, given our previous reasoning, we will use 'acceptable indicators' for the parameters that stay close to their definitions (without worrying too much about whether these indicators cover all relevant context factors, as these factors will be part of the 'rich description' of the indicators). To illustrate such rich descriptions, we use construction firm W as an example (as described in Section 6.2). Please note that, for the sake of illustration, we will not discuss all parameters in the same level of detail.

Parameter 1: Functional concentration

Definition: Degree to which operational tasks are related to all (internal and external) order types

Indicator: Number of different internal order types (here, different types of projects) to which employees of W doing operational work are related

TABLE 6.6 Connecting the actual values of parameters to problems

		$V_1[e]$	$V_2[e]$	...	$V_n[e]$
$P_1[av]$	Actual degree of functional concentration in context				
$P_2[av]$	Actual degree of differentiation of operational tasks in context				
$P_3[av]$	Actual degree of specialization of operational tasks in context				
$P_4[av]$	Actual degree of differentiation of regulatory tasks into parts in context				
$P_5[av]$	Actual degree of differentiation of regulatory tasks into aspects in context				
$P_6[av]$	Actual degree of specialization of regulatory activities in context				
$P_7[av]$	Actual degree of separation of regulatory and operational activities in context				

Description: Members of the building team (masons and carpenters) are connected to only one project at a time. So, in their case, the functional concentration is low. However, the tasks of construction foremen are related to more projects. On average, they are coupled to one large 'social housing project' and about six small projects at a time. All projects are unique and require different preparatory, support, and regulatory activities. Construction projects are intensive-technology projects (Thompson, 1967), requiring close monitoring of 'feedback' from the project and adjustments to it as it progresses. So, in the case of the foremen, the functional concentration is about half the number of total projects for each of them. This seems to be high, given the nature of construction projects. The overall project manager is also involved in all projects, so functional concentration here seems to be high, too. However, his task is confined to only a small preparatory part of the complete process (bids and contracts, definition of a building team). He is not involved in the continuous monitoring of the parallel projects. Functional concentration may therefore not be too high for the overall planner.

Parameter 2: Differentiation of operational tasks

Definition: Degree to which preparatory, production, and support activities are assigned to different tasks

Indicators:

- number of tasks dedicated to preparation, support and production;
- number of preparatory or support activities that are not part of operational tasks.

Description: In the case of W, building teams carry out production activities. One preparatory activity (making bids and contracts) is the task of the overall project planner. Other preparatory activities are carried out by the foremen (daily planning, assigning duties to building team, arranging for materials to be at the construction site, or contacting sub-contractors). So, even though the number of tasks dedicated to only production, preparation, and support activities may not be high, there is a clear differentiation (this may entail that this indicator for small companies needs to be refined), at least between foremen and building teams. A better indicator in this case may be the number of preparation and support activities that are not part of the operational tasks.

Parameter 3: Specialization of operational tasks

Definition: Degree to which operational tasks cover only a small part of the total operational process

Indicator(s):

- number of sequentially coupled tasks in the operational process;
- average cycle time per operational task.

Description: If one takes the complete construction process as an anchor, a number of specialized tasks can be recognized, as the following separate tasks have been defined and assigned to different parties:

- design: architect;
- technical building plan: sub-contractor;

- initial contact with clients, making bids, making contracts: overall project planner;
- several preparatory activities (which are performed every day): foremen;
- building activities (masonry, carpentry): building team;
- plumbing, electrical mechanics, painting: sub-contractors.

Zooming in on the building team, one can see that their operational tasks cover a large part of the total operational process (they are involved in operational activities from the moment the building team was defined, until the project is finished).

In all, one could say that there are a number of (sequentially coupled) specialized tasks. At the same time, the average cycle time doesn't seem to be that short.

Parameter 1: Differentiation of regulatory activities into parts (monitoring, assessing, acting)

Parameter 5: Differentiation of regulatory activities into aspects (strategic, design and operational regulation)

Parameter 6: Specialization of regulatory activities

Definitions and indicators: see earlier

Description: These parameters don't seem to have high values. However, it is clear that first, the regulatory parts (monitoring, assessment and acting) rest with foremen and not with the building teams.

Second, strategic, design and operational regulation also are assigned to different tasks. Setting overall project goals (project-related strategic regulation) is done by the overall project planner. Also, there is at least one regulation by design activity (construction of building team) which is carried out by the overall project planner. Training new personnel (regulation by design) is the responsibility of foremen. Most operational regulation also seems to be the responsibility of the foremen, although one may imagine that if some small operational problems occur, e.g. if the concrete doesn't have the proper viscosity, the building team has the operational regulatory potential to correct it.

Third, in the case there is some specialization of regulatory tasks. For instance, the overall planner and the foremen regulate a part of the project, and sub-contractors regulate their own contributions. However, many of the regulatory activities (e.g. monitoring the complete process) that are the responsibility of the foremen aren't split up.

Parameter 7: Separation between regulatory and operational activities

Definition: Degree to which regulatory and operational activities are assigned to different tasks

Indicators:

- number of hierarchical layers; number of operational tasks without regulatory possibility to solve own problems;
- scores of operational employees with respect to the question whether they have the regulatory potential to deal with their operational problems (or not).

Description: There seems to be a strict separation between operational and regulatory tasks. The building teams perform operational activities, and although it can be imagined that building teams have some operational regulation (with respect to small operational disturbances), most (operational) regulation is assigned to the foremen. Strategic regulation and regulation by design are not among the responsibilities of the building team. In terms of the indicators, one may find that the number of hierarchical layers is not high. The number of tasks without the regulatory potential to solve their own problems (which holds for task of the building team members) may be relatively high. The score (say, on a five-item Likert scale) on the question whether operational employees lack the regulatory potential to deal with their own problems may be high. Even though there are not many hierarchal layers in W, there seems to be a considerable degree of separation.

Although in a real diagnosis a more detailed and richer description could be given – that is, more context factors could be taken into account to arrive at a better understanding of the current values of the parameters – the previous examples already illustrate that such rich descriptions are more telling than just (numerical) values on a few indicators. Based on these descriptions, we proceed with Step 2.2.

Step 2.2: determine for all $v_i \in V$ for which $v_i[e]$ exists whether, based on the design theory connecting parameters to organizational behaviour, it can be expected that $p_i \in P$ (for all i), given its current actual value, is a cause for $v_i[e]$

To find out whether the actual parameter values in context are problematic, we propose the following procedure.

Repeat for all problems found in the gap analysis:

Take a problem ($v_i[e]$) found in the gap analysis as point of departure and answer the following questions for this problem for each parameter:

- Question 1: Establish, based on design theory, whether a high value on the parameter can be expected to result in the problem, as expressed by $v_i[e]$.
- Question 2: Find out, based on design theory, what problems and issues related to $v_i[e]$ could be expected in the specific context if the parameter had a value that was too high.
- Question 3: Determine whether the expected context specific problems and issues related to $v_i[e]$ do indeed occur in the specific context.

If $v_i[e]$ is to be expected when the parameter has a high value, and if the expected context-specific problems and issues given a (too) high value of the parameter can indeed be found in this context, then we can hypothesize that the parameter contributes to the problem.

If we apply this procedure to all problems found in the gap analysis, we work our way through the cells in Table 6.6 problem after problem. Eventually, this table shows us all the problematic parameters.

We will now briefly illustrate this procedure by discussing one problem found in the gap analysis at W: the problem with reliable production time ($v_{2.1}[e]$ from Table 6.5). In the gap analysis, it was established that production time – the time needed to finish projects – was problematic. That is, too many construction projects aren't finished on time. Given this problem, we now illustrate the answers to the three questions, per parameter.

Parameter 1: functional concentration

Question 1: Can we expect that a high value leads to problems with production time?

Based on the design theory described earlier, it can be expected that too much functional concentration increases the variability of the relations of tasks (too much different content), which, in turn, leads to problems in processing the content in these tasks, and therefore leads to disturbances. Moreover, being connected to too many order types reduces the overview over orders, which may cause delays and disturbances. Delays and disturbances (which have to dealt with) lead to longer production time. So, based on design theory, high functional concentration can be expected to lead to problems with production time.

Question 2: What could be expected in the specific context if the value of functional concentration was too high in relation to production time?

At W, we find that building team members are related to only one order (project), but that foremen and the overall project planner are connected to more/all projects.

If the level of functional concentration of the foremen is too high, we might expect that they will have a hard time planning, monitoring, and reacting to the needs of all individual projects. Especially because every project has its own unique requirements and faces its own unforeseen circumstances, the variability may increase rapidly. Typical consequences of this increased variability include that foremen cannot give all projects the attention they need and will (re)act too late, (re)act improperly, or forget to (re)act at all. Moreover, as foremen lose track of the progress of individual projects and find that they didn't act in a timely or proper way, extra time and communication are required to make up for this.

If the level of functional concentration is too high for the tasks of the overall project planner, we might expect that mistakes are made in making the bids and contracts and/or that producing them takes too long.

Question 3: Do the expected problems and issues occur in the specific context?

We already know that problems with production time (projects that aren't finished on time) are to be expected if functional concentration is high (answer to question 1). Next, we know what high levels of functional concentration would entail in the case of W (question 2). Now, question 3 is about establishing whether the expectations of a (too) high value of functional concentration match the actual situation at W.

Let's start with the tasks of the foremen. We already know from the rich description of functional concentration that the level of functional concentration seems to be high. Here, we want to establish whether it is indeed *too* high, i.e. whether it actually causes the expected problems with production time. Too much functional concentration in the case of the task of the foremen meant that their task was related to too many projects and that they would therefore lose track of projects, and wouldn't be able to give every project the attention it requires. This would lead to disturbances and delays. Now, given these expectations, the following types of questions are relevant for this step in the case of W:

'Do foremen actually lose track of projects?'

'Do foremen actually experience a lack of overview of projects?'

'Are foremen actually unable to pay the required attention to all projects?'

A second type of questions sets out to establish whether there is a link between 'too much variability' and problematic production time. In this case, the relevant questions are:

'To what extent is the delay in projects caused by the fact that foremen lack an overview of projects?'

'To what extent is the delay in projects caused by the fact that foremen are unable to pay the required attention to projects?'

An inquiry into these questions can be realized by analysing the rich description of the actual values of functional concentration and by additional research, e.g. by means of observation, asking foremen and/or asking members of the building teams (perhaps in interviews or by means of closed questions).

A similar approach can be used to investigate the expected effects of too much functional concentration for the overall planner on project delay.

At W, it turned out that foremen do experience too much variability and that the lack of overview and inability to pay the required attention to all projects does lead to stress, delays, and disturbances. However, even though the overall planner was connected to all projects, this didn't lead to stress, delays, or disturbances. Apparently, the complexity of the projects and the fact that they require continual attention at the same time is problematic for the foremen. For the overall planner, projects are less complex (he is mainly concerned with financial and overall planning aspects) and, more importantly, the overall planner is not continuously involved in many projects at the same time – enabling him to process them sequentially. As we discussed, this shows that the same number of projects may have different effects, dependent on additional context-related issues.

Conclusion: Can we hypothesize that the current level of functional concentration is too high (i.e. that it contributes to the problem with production time at W)?

We now know:

- that problems with production time (projects that aren't finished on time) are to be expected if functional concentration is high (answer to question 1);
- which problems and issues (related to production time) can be expected in the specific context if functional concentration has a value that is too high (answer to question 2);
- that the expected problems and issues do indeed occur with respect to the task of the foremen (question 3).

Therefore, based on the answers to the three questions, we can hypothesize that the actual level of functional contributes to delays and hence is too high in the case of W (i.e. related to the task of the foremen).

Parameter 2: differentiation of operational tasks

Question 1: Can we expect that a high value leads to problems with production time?

According to de Sitter's design theory, too much differentiation (separate operational tasks for preparation, production, and support activities) leads to an increase of dependency relations in the network of operational tasks, and because of that, the number of disturbances also increases. Dealing with these disturbances causes delays. So a high level of differentiation of operational tasks can be expected to contribute to the problem that projects take too long.

Question 2: What could be expected in the specific context if the value of differentiation of operational tasks was too high in relation to production time?

In the case of W, a foreman carries out preparatory activities like making a daily planning, arranging for material to be at the site, and contacting sub-contractors. The building team only carries out production activities – but these are dependent on the outcome of the preparatory activities. If one of these preparatory activities wasn't carried out properly (or too late, or not at all), production activities would also be disturbed (e.g. because material wasn't available, or because the planning wasn't good enough, or sub-contractors weren't contacted). Not being immersed in the production activities for which a planning is made or for which equipment is arranged would lead to disturbances, as one might not be able to understand the precise context of these activities. To make up for that, foremen would need to communicate with building team members or visit the construction site regularly, which would take time. Moreover, because production activities are dependent on the preparatory tasks of the foremen, and because members of the building team cannot repair problems in preparatory tasks themselves (by redoing them, e.g. adjust the planning, get other equipment), delays are bound to be expected.

Question 3: Do the expected problems and issues occur in the specific context?

If we look at the case of W, we find that the expectations with respect to the relation between differentiation and production time problems seem to describe what is actually going on. First, from the rich description of the parameter, we already know that the value of the parameter seems to be high. Moreover, if we look at W, we find that foremen do the daily planning for building teams, arrange for material to be at the site, and contact sub-contractors. The production tasks of the members of the building teams are dependent on these preparatory tasks. The main problem seems to be that mistakes are made by the foremen, and that, because building team members cannot carry out these preparatory tasks themselves, they need to wait until the foremen can find the time to redo these tasks. If the daily planning is unsatisfactory – e.g. the planned daily task is finished early – building team members waste their (and the client's) time. The same holds for not contacting sub-contractors or forgetting to take care of the proper material and equipment. Making sure that these mistakes are taken care of also requires a lot of extra communication between the building team and foremen. In all, at W, we find the expected problematic relation between differentiation of operational and project delays.

Conclusion: Can we hypothesize that the current level of differentiation of operational tasks is too high (i.e. that it contributes to the problem with production time at W)?

We now know:

- that problems with production time (projects that aren't finished on time) are to be expected if differentiation of operational tasks is high (answer to question 1);
- which problems and issues (related to production time) can be expected in the specific context if differentiation of operational tasks has a value that is too high (answer to question 2);
- that the expected problems and issues do indeed occur (question 3).

Therefore, based on the answers to the three questions, we can hypothesize that the actual level of differentiation of operational tasks contributes to delays, and hence is too high in the case of W.

Parameter 3: specialization of operational tasks

Question 1: Can we expect that a high value leads to problems with production time?

The design theory we use predicts that too much specialization of operational tasks, just like differentiation, leads to too many dependency relations in the network of operational tasks. The result is that the probability of disturbances increases. And as disturbances need to be dealt with, delays may be expected.

Question 2: What could be expected in the specific context if the value of specialization of operational tasks was too high in relation to production time?

In the case of W, the operational process of construction building has a number of (sequentially coupled) operational activities, which are assigned to different tasks, e.g. the tasks of architect, project planner, foremen, building teams, and different sub-contractors. As these tasks are (sequentially) dependent on each other, problems in one of them will delay and/or cause other problems in subsequent tasks and/or in the final output. One notorious problem in construction projects, for instance, is the planning of sub-contractors. They may be scheduled at a point in time when their services are not yet required, e.g. due to a delay in the construction process, or they may simply not show up at the requested time. Rescheduling the sub-contractor may often be difficult (as the sub-contractor has other obligations), which, in turn, may lead to more delay. And this delay may be a reason for rescheduling other sub-contractors as well .... One way of dealing with this, of course, is to build in slack (cf. Galbraith, 1973), which, however, will come at the cost of other project variables (e.g. completion time) and even company variables (e.g. competitiveness, as the average construction project time may be too long).

Question 3: Do the expected problems and issues occur in the specific context?

The rich description of specialization of operational tasks indicates that, although the cycle time of tasks isn't low, there is some specialization while carrying out construction projects. Next, we need to find out whether the fact that a construction process is split up into sequential tasks (e.g. design, planning, production activities) that are carried out by different parties (architect, foremen, building team, sub-contractors) actually leads to the delays as expected (as given in question 2).

At W, it appears that specialization may indeed cause problems. It often happens that sub-contractors are too late or don't show up at all. In such a case, not only does the sub-contractor who is 'at fault' need to be rescheduled, but often also other sub-contractors that were scheduled later on in the project. This causes a delay, and most of the time such situations are unpredictable and hard to control by W. Even though this is problematic, such problems with sub-contractors often happen and are a 'fact of life in the construction business', according the overall planner at W.

So the expected problems with specialization related to realizing projects on time do indeed seem to occur at W.

Conclusion: Can we hypothesize that the current level of specialization of operational tasks is too high (i.e. that it contributes to the problem with production time at W)?

We now know:

- that problems with production time (projects that aren't finished on time) are to be expected if specialization of operational tasks is high (answer to question 1);
- which problems and issues (related to production time) can be expected in the specific context if specialization of operational tasks has a value that is too high (answer to question 2);
- that the expected problems and issues do indeed occur (question 3).

Therefore, based on the answers to the three questions, we can hypothesize that the actual level of specialization of operational tasks contributes to delays, and hence is too high in the case of W.

Parameters 4, 5, and 6

These don't seem to have high values, according to the rich description.

Parameter 7: separation between regulatory and operational activities

Question 1: Can we expect that a high value leads to problems with production time?

Based on de Sitter's design theory, several problems may be expected if there is a strict separation between operational and regulatory tasks. In general, a high degree of separation causes delays, as regulation isn't taken care of by those who work in the process where the problems occur. Moreover, as discussed in Chapter 3, operationally detached regulation tends to suffer from lacking relevant, context-specific operational information and know-how, resulting in improper solutions to operational problems.

Question 2: What could be expected in the specific context if the value of separation was too high in relation to production time?

At W, we might expect delays, as problems occurring at the construction site are not to be solved by the building teams, but by the foremen, who are not always present. Moreover, as they are not involved in the actual operational construction process, they need to be briefed by the team about the disturbances, which will also take time. The two foremen at W had been construction workers themselves, so they did have the required operational knowledge. In this respect, we won't expect irrelevant regulatory solutions. However, lacking context specific operational information, it may be expected that they come up with solutions that do not fit the specific circumstances, which, in turn, may lead to delays.

Question 3: Do the expected problems and issues occur in the specific context?

From the rich description of the actual value of separation, we already know that it is quite high. To find out whether the expected effects of high separation on production time do indeed occur at W, we need to establish the degree to which the fact that a building team cannot directly solve problems that are encountered during the construction process actually leads to (the expected) delays.

In the case of W, separation was found to affect production time, as many delays occurred because building teams couldn't solve problems themselves – problems that often just required simple acts of regulation (e.g. seeing that material hasn't been arranged for, deciding that it is needed, and driving to the depot to get it). It also leads to problems with respect to production quality, as foremen, because they lack context-specific information, take regulatory decisions that don't do justice to this specific construction context. And, as repairing such mistakes takes time, it also leads to delays. An example of this situation is that at one point in the construction process, tile flooring was planned to be installed, but the building team found that the concrete on which it should be installed was still too moist. They shared this concern with the foreman, who was not on the site. However, he thought that enough time had passed since the concrete was poured that it should be dry enough, so he decided to install the tile flooring anyway. This turned out to be a mistake. In this case, not having enough in situ information may have contributed to problematic regulation. The required rework consumed a lot of time.

Moreover, building teams mentioned that many delays and disturbances could have been prevented or solved if they had the regulatory potential to deal with the disturbances they noted.

Conclusion: Can we hypothesize that the current level of separation between operational and regulatory tasks is too high (i.e. that it contributes to the problem with production time at W)?

We now know:

- that problems with production time (projects that aren't finished on time) are to be expected if separation is high (answer to question 1);
- which problems and issues (related to production time) can be expected in the specific context if separation has a value that is too high (answer to question 2);
- that the expected problems and issues do indeed occur (question 3).

Therefore, based on the answers to the three questions, we can hypothesize that the actual level of separation contributes to delays, and hence is too high in the case of W.

Overall conclusion concerning the problems with production time

The result of considering all the parameters for the problematic variable 'production time' is that we now have an overview of the parameters causing the error on this variable (see Table 6.7).

Following the complete procedure (i.e. for all $V_i[e]$) would yield a complete overview of the problematic parameters – which is the input for step 3.

Step 3: establish the list of problematic parameters: all $p_i \in P$ for which $p_i[e]$ exists

In this step, the result of step 2 is summarized into a final list of problematic parameters – i.e. those parameters of which one assumes, based on the inquiry performed in step 2, that they are causes of the problematic organizational behaviour related to quality of organization and quality of work.

Final remark on the method for establishing the 'problematic parameters'

Before we turn to the last step of the diagnosis, we need to say a few words about how the problematic parameters are determined. The method presented previously contains three sub-steps, but this presentation doesn't mean that these steps should be taken in a strictly sequential order. An actual inquiry into problematic parameters may combine the steps. An example of

TABLE 6.7 Relation of parameters to the concerning the variable production time

		$V_{2.1}[e]$: problems with production time
$P_1[av]$	Actual degree of functional concentration in context	Too high
$P_2[av]$	Actual degree of differentiation of operational tasks in context	Too high
$P_3[av]$	Actual degree of specialization of operational tasks in context	Too high
$P_4[av]$	Actual degree of differentiation of regulatory tasks into parts in context	—
$P_5[av]$	Actual degree of differentiation of regulatory tasks into aspects in context	—
$P_6[av]$	Actual degree of specialization of regulatory activities in context	—
$P_7[av]$	Actual degree of separation of regulatory and operational activities in context	Too high

such an inquiry may be one in which a knowledgeable consultant (that is, with respect to the relation of structural parameters and their effects on organizational behaviour) briefly explains to a team of organization members (working in a problematic structure) how organizational structures may cause problems and guides the team in systematically following and analysing an order as part of their own work. In this analysis, the team identifies delays and disturbances and asks itself (guided by the consultant and the questions discussed in step 2) what their structural causes are. For instance, at W, a building team members and their foreman may be given a short explanation about how structures may cause problems and, next, analyse the delays and problems that occurred during several projects they worked on (of course, more employees can be added, in this case, even all building team members and the two foremen, but here we just provide an example). While discussing delays and problems, the consultant should make sure that the structural parameters are systematically taken into account, in a way the team understands (i.e. by translating the parameters to the relevant context at hand). In this approach, the sub-steps are tackled more or less simultaneously as they move from problem to problem. And, what is more, in this approach, organization members participate in finding and understanding the structural causes of the problems they themselves experience. This paves the way for acceptance and integration of structural changes – an issue we will pick up while discussing the social dimension (Chapter 7) and participation as part of the infrastructure of the episodic change organization (Chapter 8).

6.3.3 Diagnosis – sub-goal 3: selecting parameters that should be lowered by a change in structure

Given the list of 'troublesome parameters', a third sub-goal of the diagnosis is to establish those parameters from this list that should be changed by redesigning the structure. As we indicated, this may appear to be an odd sub-goal, as one might expect that all troublesome parameters should be lowered by designing a new structure. It is, however, possible that some parameter is a cause of problematic organizational behaviour, but that, given the specific organizational context, the parameter cannot be lowered by means of a redesign. In the specific case of W, it seems that the degree of specialization of the operational construction process (including different parties beyond the organizational borders) does have a negative effect, and can cause delays and disturbances. Something similar holds for specialization of regulation, as different parties have their own, disconnected, ways of dealing with their own problems. However, as the overall planner at W remarked, in the current market conditions, it is almost impossible to work without sub-contractors, and make sure that W covers all construction specialities itself. Therefore, even though these two parameters cause delays and disturbances, it can be decided to ignore their specific values in this context.

Another reason for not selecting a parameter has to do with the relevance of the problems it causes (see also step 5 from the gap analysis). If a parameter is only a cause for a (few) minor problem(s), it may be omitted from the final list of parameters that need to be changed.

6.4 Design

Given the outcome of the diagnosis, a list of problematic parameters that should be altered by a change in the organization's structure, we now turn to the next activity on the functional dimension: design. The goal of the design activity is to invent a new structure so that the values of the parameters causing the problematic organizational behaviour are altered in such a way that they no longer act as a cause of organizational problems. In general, the desired structure is a structure with parameter values that are as low as possible, given the specific organizational context. We will call this structure the 'desired structure' (notation: S_d). To design this desired structure, we need a theory describing, in general, what structures with low parameter values look like. Based on de Sitter's design theory, as discussed in Chapter 3, we already have an idea of such structures in general. We also need a theory indicating how to arrive at low parameter values structures – i.e. a theory proposing steps and heuristics guiding us through the design process. In fact, de Sitter's design theory also presents such steps and heuristics, and in this section, we will briefly present them. In this way, we use de Sitter's design theory to arrive at a series of steps which are required for the design activity in episodic interventions in the structure of organizations.

To describe the design activity as part of the functional dimension of episodic interventions in organizational structures, we will first describe the steps of the design activity (and heuristics guiding these steps) in general, based on de Sitter's design theory. Next, we will illustrate how these steps can be carried out to design a desired structure in a particular context, using the case of W.

Before we go into the design activity, we need to say a few words about its relation to implementation – the next activity of the functional dimension. Both activities are closely related. That is, during the design step, parts of the designed structured are often already implemented, and, based on experimentation with implemented parts of the structure, changes often need to be made to the design. So, even though design and implementation can be separated analytically (e.g. by discussing their separate goals and functional steps), they are intrinsically related. We will first cover the design activity and introduce its steps and heuristics, and use this explanation to discuss the mutual dependence of the two activities in the section on implementation.

6.4.1 Steps and heuristics guiding the design activity

From Chapter 3, we know that the ideal typical organizational structure with low parameter values is one in which self-contained task groups operate in autonomous production flows which are dedicated to a (small) sub-set of orders. Ideally, these task groups have the infrastructural means and regulatory potential to contribute (1) to producing the orders in the production flow, (2) to redesigning the infrastructure, and (3) to setting goals (strategic regulation). The steps and heuristics presented in this section will help designers to design a structure that approaches this ideal in a particular context as closely as possible, given that context.

As we discussed in Chapter 3, an organizational structure with low values on design parameters is itself not a source of disturbances and has enough regulatory potential. Based on this idea, the first overall heuristic for building such structures is that one should start with designing the production structure, and after that, one should design the control structure. The reason for this heuristic is that if one first designs the production structure in such a way that it is not a source of disturbances, the control structure can be less complex, as it doesn't need to deal with these disturbances. By properly designing the production structure, the need for regulation is reduced (cf. Galbraith, 1973; de Sitter, 1994), and hence the required regulatory potential (which is what the control structure provides) can be less complex. This logic is a straightforward translation of the cybernetic idea that it makes sense to start with reducing the number of disturbances, and only then implement the required regulatory potential (cf. Beer, 1979; Achterbergh and Vriens, 2010).

Based on this overall heuristic, the design should first focus on the production structure. To design this structure and lower the associated design parameters (functional concentration, operational differentiation, and operational specialization), de Sitter (1994) proposes three consecutive design steps at three different 'structural levels':

1. Parallelization – This step is about identifying (independent) production flows, dedicated to a sub-set of external order types. This is a step at the macro level, as it divides the complete production structure into independent (flow-oriented) units.
2. Segmentation – This step is about identifying relatively independent parts (segments) within the flows identified in step 1. This is a step at the meso level, as it identifies units within the macro level flows.
3. Installing task groups or teams – This step aims to select and equip groups of individuals to realize the output of the segments identified in step 2. This is a step at what de Sitter calls the micro level: the level of teamwork.

The first two steps in this sequence aim to reduce complexity by identifying 'independent units' with as few relations to their environment as possible (i.e. flows aiming to produce a sub-set instead of the total number of orders, and segments realizing, as much as possible, an independent part of the flow). In fact, flows and segments should be designed as 'modular units': they should internally be highly interdependent, but they should have as few relations with other similar units as possible (see Simon, 1962). The task groups, in turn, are units with all the complexity needed to realize the output of segments.

The overall design heuristic entails that the control structure (the network of tasks dedicated to regulation) should be designed after the production structure. To this end (and hence to lower the four parameters associated to regulation), de Sitter (1994) proposes three further consecutive steps, again at three levels. That is, given the outcome of the three steps, one should:

4. Assign regulatory potential to task groups to realize the output of the segments they are tied to. This is a step at the micro level, as it equips task groups with the necessary regulatory potential to realize the output of the group's segment.

    Steps 3 and 4 together lead to self-coordinating task groups or teams – groups with the operational (step 3) and regulatory (step 4) potential to realize their output as independently as possible. In de Sitter's theory, these steps are often taken together.
5. Build in the required regulation between segments to make sure that segments are aligned and can contribute to the output of the flow they belong to. This is a step at the meso level, as it takes care of regulating the integration of flow parts (segments) to yield the flow output.
6. Build in the required regulation between flows to make sure that issues between flows are regulated (e.g. strategic regulation relevant for all flows, or regulation by design for several or all flows, like dealing with shared resources). As this is regulation with respect to the integration of flows, it is a step at the macro level.

184 Designing interventions

The steps aiming at designing the control structure make sure that task groups at the lowest level take care of as many disturbances as possible. Disturbances that can't be dealt with in task groups need to be dealt with by means of regulation between segments (step 5), and the residual variety that can't be dealt with within flows needs to be dealt with at the level exceeding flows (step 6). In this sense, regulation at a higher level takes care of disturbances that can be dealt with at the lower level.

In all, these six design steps reveal a second design heuristic (which is a further specification of the overall heuristic): while designing a structure, one should (given an idea of the goals operationalizing the organization's overall contribution to society):

1. first start at the macro level of the production structure (identifying flows);
2. then move to the meso level of the production structure (identifying independent segments within flows);
3. then move to the micro level of the production structure (and identify the operational requirements of task groups to produce the output of a segment);
4. then move to allocating regulatory tasks at the micro level (and equip task groups with the regulatory potential to realize the segment's outcome);
5. then move to the meso level of the control structure and take care of the regulation integrating segments within a flow;
6. finally, move to the macro level of the control structure and build in the regulation between flows.

We will now briefly examine these six steps.

Design step 1: parallelization at the macro level: finding independent flows in the production structure

The first step in designing the production structure is identifying flows which are dedicated to realizing a sub-set of *external* orders. As we discussed in Chapter 3, the smaller these sub-sets, the lower the degree of functional concentration. Ideally, these flows are independent and have their own dedicated infrastructure needed to realize their own sub-set of external orders. This entails that, ideally, they have their own dedicated 'value chain' (cf. Porter, 1985, which includes activities ranging from contact with clients and suppliers to delivery and service) and their own flow-related production, preparatory, and support functions (low operational differentiation). As de Sitter (1994) puts it, such flows are the smallest organizational units with their own "independent output and profit responsibility".

To understand how sub-sets of orders can be assigned to flows in an adequate way, it is helpful to re-examine the concepts of order and 'order type'. Based on what has been said in Chapter 3, an 'order' can be described as 'a particular (set of) client(s) demanding a particular (set of) product(s) or service(s)'. We also indicated that this 'client' could be an external or internal 'client'; external clients place orders for complete products or services with the organization, while internal clients (e.g. teams or employees in the production process) place orders for particular parts of a product or service (e.g. components, modules, etc.) with previous steps in the production process (cf. de Sitter, 1994). In the current design step (designing macro flows), we will only consider external clients (and the associated external orders and order types). In step 2 about segmentation, we will consider internal clients.

Each order can be described using different order characteristics. Figure 6.1a shows four relevant classes of characteristics, and Figure 6.1b lists several examples of such characteristics.[2] Based on these characteristics, an example of a description of a specific order at some moment in time would be: 'Mr Dupont demanding one luxury dinner table made of oak, which should be ready by next Friday'. Here, 'Mr. Dupont' represents a bundle of client characteristics. He orders only one item, which should be ready by next Friday (demand characteristics). The ordered item is a specific product variation (product characteristic), made of specific material (which implies a supplier who can deliver this material – input characteristic). In a particular period of time, many of such orders can exist, of course, and we will refer to all orders in a particular period of time as the 'total set of orders' (in that time period).

Now, from the total set of orders, an 'order type' can be defined as a sub-set of orders which have one or more of the characteristics (from one or more classes) in common. Examples are:

- all orders having the same type of product;
- all orders demanded by Mr Dupont;
- all orders demanded by wholesalers;
- all orders with products containing raw materials which are bought from the same supplier;
- all orders containing the same product type and form the same area of customers.

In Chapter 3, we used the characteristic 'type of product' to discuss a furniture factory realizing three order types: chairs, tables, and cupboards. Moreover, we used (product-based) order types to discuss functional concentration. In the context of designing organizations, order types which are defined based on product type or type of client/market characteristics as a common starting point (cf. Mintzberg, 1983; de Sitter, 1994). For instance, order types based on type of product or types of clients are often used to identify separate business units (cf. Mintzberg, 1983). However, when designing the production structure at the macro level, it is necessary to see that other sub-sets of orders (order types) besides product- or client-based ones can also be identified by taking other or more characteristics into account.

a	Input characteristics	Product/service characteristics	Demand characteristics	Client characteristics

b	Type of supplier Type of input market ...	Function Family Type Variation ...	Number Order mix Delivery times Delivery address ...	Location Age Social background Income ...

FIGURE 6.1 Order characteristics

In the context of designing the production structure, it is also important to understand that the characteristics to identify order types are chosen for a particular reason: they all represent relevant sources of variation in the production structure – influencing variability. That is, the more orders differ in terms of the characteristics discussed, the more variability is created with respect to production, product development, interaction with the output market (clients), or interaction with input markets (cf. de Sitter, 1994, Chapter 7). For instance, cars and trucks (two product families) vary in terms of production process, product development, and input and output market in such a way that they merit specific attention, and therefore often have their own dedicated business units.

Based on the idea of order type as a sub-set of orders, the following general heuristic can now be derived to identify adequate independent order flows (cf. de Sitter, 1994, although he uses different formulations):

'Define as many flows as possible in such a way that:

1. each flow contains (external) order types which have as few differences (on the previous characteristics) as possible;
2. each flow has a capacity utilization of 80% or more;
3. flows do not share a common resource (like expertise or technology).'

In this heuristic, the overall idea is to make as many independent order flows dedicated to sub-sets of orders as possible, in order to reduce functional concentration. However, 'as many as possible' is limited. De Sitter realizes full well that not every (small) sub-set of orders (e.g. all order types that only differ with respect to product variation) can have its own order flow. He therefore adds three limiting rules of thumb. The first is that the order types should not be 'too' different, or to be more precise, their relative relevant variety (in terms of the order characteristics) should be as small as possible. The less difference, i.e. the more characteristics they have in common, the lower the degree of functional concentration, and hence the less variability and disturbance (see Chapter 3). The second limiting rule of thumb is that a flow should have a capacity utilization of at least 80%, otherwise flows will become inefficient. The third limiting rule of thumb is that flows should not share a resource, to ensure their independence.

So the challenge is to find flows with enough capacity utilization, without shared resources, consisting of order types that are as comparable as possible. To further guide this quest for adequate independent flows, de Sitter suggests that one should start off with characteristics whose variety is most relevant for either production, product development, interaction with input markets, or interaction with output markets. For instance, input characteristics may have a large impact if ingredients or raw materials have to be bought on different markets, requiring a lot of specific knowledge with respect to aspects of the input and reliability of suppliers. If different types of input require their own specific, complex ways of obtaining them, it may be worthwhile to consider input-based order flows in which orders have input in common. Similarly, if different product types differ dramatically in production, flows based on order types may be pursued first. Or, if orders differ primarily based on the interaction with type of clients, client characteristics may be considered first in defining flows. So the characteristic whose variety has the largest impact should be considered as the main characteristic for determining order types. These can be called 'primary order types'. These primary order types may be broken down into smaller order types, based on a characteristic that is ranked second with respect to impact on production, product development, or interaction with input or output market.

So identifying adequate flows may benefit from the rank order of characteristics with respect to their impact. Establishing this impact may be difficult, so de Sitter proposes some guidelines to find this 'impact rank order'. One important criterion for establishing the impact of a characteristic is the influence of clients in the production process. If clients are 'abstract entities' who just buy products without being involved in designing, producing, or otherwise determining them based on their characteristics (like most mass-production products), it often makes sense to start with product characteristics as the main criterion. Only after identifying primary order types based on this criterion (e.g. product type or even variation), secondary order types may be identified based on demand characteristics (e.g. clients demanding products in large volumes versus clients demanding in small volumes; cf. de Sitter, 1994, p. 240). If products or services are co-determined based on client characteristics (e.g. in healthcare the service is healing clients with a particular ailment, or in the construction business the product is, for instance, building a home given the specifications of a client), then it makes sense to start with client characteristics as the main characteristic (e.g. flows in healthcare organized around types of diseases; cf. Christensen et al., 2010). As de Sitter argues, using client characteristics as the main characteristic is often the case in the service industry.

Designing independent flows is a difficult issue and requires much in-depth knowledge and context-specific wisdom. In fact, more could, and perhaps should, be said about it, but in the present context – briefly describing the functional dimension of episodic interventions in organizational structures – we hope that the guidelines will help to understand the idea of parallelization as a first step in designing structures, and we would like to point the reader to more detailed textbooks on the subject (e.g. de Sitter, 1994).

Design step 2: segmentation at the meso level. Identifying relatively independent parts (segments) within order flows

When flows at the macro level have been identified – or when it proves impossible to do so, leaving designers with only one 'macro flow' – one should start with establishing segments within these flows. Segments are relatively independent parts within macro flows which, together, realize the output of the flow. The ideal typical situation (i.e. one with the lowest possible design parameter values) is a macro flow with *no* segments – i.e. one in which one team of employees is responsible for and has all necessary means to perform all preparatory, production, and support activities needed to realize the flow's output. This is, however, often not a feasible option. Identifying segments within a flow is often necessary because the process is too complex for one team. This complexity can manifest itself in many ways, for instance when a process consists of too many different and/or difficult activities, or when the production volume is too high. In terms of the design theory discussed in Chapter 3, due to several context factors (e.g. process complexity or output volume), some degree of operational specialization (and differentiation) is required. To make sure that this degree of specialization and differentiation within a macro flow stays as low as possible, de Sitter (1994) proposes several segmentation guidelines and discusses some segmentation options which are, in his view, suitable given specific process, market, and product circumstances. In the context of this book, there is insufficient space to discuss all these segmentation options in detail. Here, we want to briefly go into the heuristics for segmentation and present some segmentation options and the circumstances in which they seem relevant.

188 Designing interventions

The two main heuristics for identifying segments which can be derived from de Sitter's theory are:

1. Segments should be as 'flow-oriented' as possible. That is, given the macro flow as point of departure, the segments in this flow should have low functional concentration (as low as possible – and here the orders can be internal or external) and low specialization/differentiation (i.e. cover a large part of the operational process – as large as possible). Flow-oriented also means: 'single piece production' as far as possible (instead of 'batch-and-queue' production; cf. de Sitter, 1994, p. 253; Womack and Jones, 1996). Single piece production means that (semi-finished) products (or parts of orders) are passed on directly to the next step in the production process. Batch-and-queue production means that production is carried out in batches. A batch of n semi-finished products is only passed on if all n items of the batch have undergone some production step. In this way, items often need to wait (to be placed in queue) until the whole batch is finished.
2. Segments should be as independent as possible. The coherence between activities *in* the segment should be high, the number of relations *between* segments should be low.

To find adequate segments, de Sitter (1994) further discusses several process and product characteristics based on which he proposes some segmentation options (here, we'll just discuss some of them).

Segmentation option I: product groups

If an organization produces many different products, it may turn out to be impossible to make macro flows for each of these products. Given macro flows for a *group* of products, it may be possible to define segments within these flows in the following way (see Figure 6.2):

1. One segment (A in the Figure 6.2) is dedicated to preparatory activities (e.g. sales, planning, purchase).
2. One segment (B) is dedicated to external logistics and aftersales.
3. In between segments A and B, there are several flow-oriented segments dedicated to making a sub-set of products.

De Sitter (1994, pp. 245ff) calls this way of identifying segments segmentation in terms of 'product groups'. In this case, there is some specialization because preparation, production, and external logistics/aftersales are assigned to different tasks. Moreover, in this segmentation option, preparation and external logistics/aftersales (segments A and B) carry out activities for

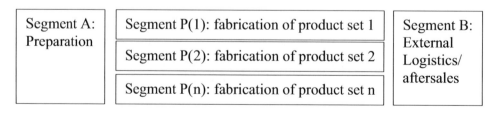

FIGURE 6.2 Segmentation option I: product groups

the total set of products in this macro flow. Segments P(1) to P(n) are parallel, independent production segments which are dedicated to a sub-set of products in this macro flow. So, relative to the orders (products) in this macro flow, preparation and external logistics/aftersales are related to all orders (high functional concentration), but the production segments have lower functional concentration, as they are related to a sub-set of the external orders (products) in this macro flow. The reason for high functional concentration of segments A and B is often that the number of different products makes it impossible to assign these activities to each product set.

Segmentation option II: module groups

If an organization produces many different products, it may be possible to identify production segments such as in option I. However, if it turns out that sales of the different sets of products are unpredictable, the capacity utilization of the different production segments may be either too high or too low. In such a case, it may be an option to construct 'module groups' (if different products have several modules in common; cf. de Sitter, 1994, pp. 249ff). These module groups are segments independently producing a particular (common) part of a product. These modules are later assembled into different final products. So, in this case, specialization is higher than in the production group, as there is now a separate segment responsible for assembly (see Figure 6.3). In this case, independence (and internal coherence) of some of the segments is secured as they are dedicated to a specific part (module) of the product. As we stated earlier, these modules act as 'internal orders'. Relative to these internal orders (placed by the assembly segment), the relatively independent production segments have a low (internal) functional concentration.

In fact, this idea of parallel production flow segments with low *internal* functional concentration need not be restricted to modules which can be assembled into finished products. It may also be possible to find such segments relative to other internal orders. In principle, for each production step, one may consider whether the input it gets from previous production steps may be divided into different order types, which may serve as a basis for internal parallelization.

Segmentation option III: component groups

One special case of parallel production segments based on internal orders is component groups. As de Sitter argues, it is sometimes possible to identify production segments in which different product components are made based on the comparability of process steps and equipment. In such a case, the different components of the set of products that are ordered in some period of time are grouped in terms of their processual comparability (e.g. in terms

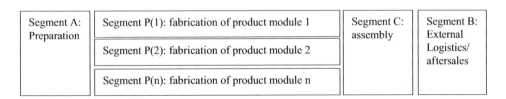

FIGURE 6.3 Segmentation option II: module groups

of the number of shared process steps, or in terms of a sharing a similar amount of time for the same process step). In this case, parallel production segments each process one group of comparable components which are later assembled into final products (see Figure 6.4).

Segmentation option IV: product groups (same product)

Previously, we briefly discussed production segments responsible for one (or a set of) product(s). This may be an option if many different products are made. However, de Sitter (1994, pp. 277–278) also discusses production segments which all make the same product. In such a case, a production structure with a large set of small short-cycle tasks (like tasks in an assembly line) which is dedicated to the production of a high volume of the same product is broken into several segments which all independently make the same product. So, instead of one line of 400 employees each performing one small task assembling 200,000 can openers a year, there can now be 50 groups of eight employees, each assembling 4000 openers. The tasks in the 50 parallel segments can now cover a larger proportion of the complete process.

Segmentation option V: phase groups

The last option for identifying segments we want to discuss is so-called 'phase groups' (cf. de Sitter, 1994, p. 250). If the independence of parallel production segments (or flows) is impossible because of some shared resource (which may be too expensive or too complex to operate to duplicate), a segment operating this shared resource may be identified see Figure 6.5 for an example). In this case, three segments have been identified. Two segments, P(1) and P(2), are each tied to some set of products. These segments share a resource which is operated in the third segment, S. De Sitter stresses that in such cases, one shouldn't make five segments (two product-related segments before the shared resource, one segment operating the shared resource, and two product-related segments after the shared resource). This would increase specialization unnecessarily. In fact, de Sitter recommends keeping all activities (except the shared resource activities) in one segment in order to maintain an overview and responsibility over the production process (see Figure 6.5).

The five segmentation options harbour an additional design heuristic: it is advisable to start with segmentation options I or IV. These options use external order types as a basis, and therefore serve as a means for finding flow-oriented segments that may cover the complete operational process. And, if these don't work out, try to find module or component groups. To find segments that are as 'flow-oriented' as possible, it is advisable to use internal order types that cover large parts of the operational process. Phase groups can be an option for dealing with shared resources in all other forms of parallel segmentation.

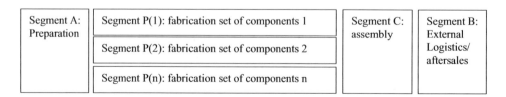

FIGURE 6.4 Segmentation option III: component groups

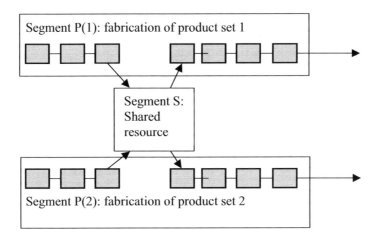

FIGURE 6.5 Segmentation option V: phase groups

Note: The shaded rectangles are different production activities in segments P(1) and P(2).

Again, much more can be said about different possible forms of segmentation, but this falls beyond the scope of this book. Given the two main heuristics and the five general forms of segmentation, we hope to have provided the reader with some ideas about how segments within macro flows might be designed. More detailed ideas can be found in papers and books on 'sociotechnical redesign' (e.g. de Sitter, 1994; de Sitter and den Hertog, 1997) or on lean management (e.g. Womack et al., 1990; Womack and Jones, 1996).

Design steps 3 and 4: designing the production and control structure at the micro level – self-coordinating task groups

Given the flows at the macro level and segments at a meso level, design steps 3 and 4 aim to design self-coordinating teams (or task groups). Such teams are assigned to a segments, and ideally, they can independently realize the segment's output. This entails that they have all the necessary means (in terms of knowledge, skills, and equipment) to carry out all operational (i.e. preparatory, support, and production) activities to realize the output of the segment. It also entails that, ideally, they have the regulatory potential at all levels to deal with problems with the segment's output or to improve realizing it. In designing teams, then, one defines how the segment's output is realized. Designing at the meso level is about designing the external relations of segments. Designing teams is about the 'internal design' of the segments, as de Sitter (1994, Chapter 8) puts it. He describes teams as units at the micro level; at this level, tasks are defined that need to be carried out by team members.

The design of teams includes the design of the *production* structure at the micro level (defining and relating operational tasks at the team level), and it involves the design of the *control* structure at the micro level (defining and relating the required regulatory tasks at the team level). Although these steps can be separated functionally, we will treat them jointly and discuss both 'operational' (production structure) and 'regulatory' (control structure) heuristics for designing teams at the micro level.

Teamwork is a popular theme in organization theory, and has attracted the attention of many scholars and practitioners. Many publications cover the design of effective teams (influential papers and reviews include Hackman, 1987, 2002; Mohrman et al., 1995; Cohen and Bailey, 1997; Mathieu et al., 2008). However, many of these studies don't deal with teams from a *structural* perspective, but go into (social) psychological prerequisites for teamwork. And those that do touch on structural aspects (e.g. sociotechnical theories; see, for instance, Mumford, 2006) often do not embed teams in meso and macro structures. We will use de Sitter's ideas on designing teams, as they are firmly grounded in the sociotechnical tradition and reflect many of the system theoretical notions used for designing teams that have been put forward by others (cf. Morgan, 1986, for an overview of these notions).

Heuristics for designing the production structure at the micro level

De Sitter (1994, p. 296) defines a team as an organizational 'module'. Such a module is an organizational "sub system, which consists of interrelated parts that individually don't have relations with parts of other sub systems" (p. 296; our translation). So the tasks of members of a team (and the tools they use) are interrelated internally, but don't have their own individual relations with tasks of members of other teams. There only exist relations between sub-systems – teams as a whole, not between the individual parts of different teams. Of course, it may be part of a task of a team member to connect to another team, but given the previous description, this connection should only be about the input or output of the team as a whole. So the first overall heuristic for designing teams is that 'teams should have as few interfaces with other teams as possible, and these interfaces should only concern input or output at a team-level, not at the level of individual tasks within the team'.

De Sitter gives a description of teams to stress that teams should have a high internal coherence, but the interfaces with other teams should be as few as possible and only at the team level. In this way, he emphasizes that teams can independently carry out a coherent whole of operational activities (including all preparatory, support, and production activities) and can independently take care of all relevant operational, design, and strategic regulation.

To secure this independence, then, teams should be assigned to a set of activities that are highly interrelated to realize the team output and that have no relations with other activities (except via the output). Criteria for this interdependence are, for instance, if the relation between activities is reciprocal (cf. Thompson, 1967) and/or if activities require much mutual adjustment as a coordination mechanism (cf. Mintzberg, 1983). Securing team independence also means that teams should be assigned the preparatory and support tasks relevant for realizing the team output. Making sure that these two requirements are met can also be seen as a heuristic for designing the production structure at a micro level.

Designing teams also means taking groupwork seriously. That is, the tasks of team members should be defined and interrelated in such a way that communication about and adjustment of tasks becomes possible. In the ideal situation, each team member can perform all activities required in a segment (Emery's redundancy of functions – see, e.g., Emery, 1976), have broad overlapping tasks, and understand the tasks and task requirements of other team members. In this ideal situation, communication about task performance is greatly facilitated, aligning tasks is much easier, and it becomes easier to detect or predict disturbances for all tasks within the team (not just your own task) and to help each other in dealing with disturbances. In this way, de Sitter (1994) (and other proponents of the team idea) argues that groupwork (instead of aggregated individual work) becomes possible. And since segments should be defined in such a way that the internal coherence and interrelations between activities is high, groupwork in the sense as just described, seems to be required. Securing redundancy of functions and broad overlapping tasks provides a final heuristic for designing teams at the micro level.

Again, it should be remarked that more, and more detailed, guidelines help designers to build the micro production structure – and again, we refer the reader to authors who provide more detail (e.g. de Sitter, 1994).

Heuristics for designing the control structure at the micro level

Designing the control structure (in general, not just at the micro level) is about allocating regulatory activities to tasks. As discussed in Chapter 3, there are several relevant distinctions with respect to regulation. First, regulation always implies three regulatory activities: monitoring (the behaviour of some concrete system, in our case an organization or part thereof), assessment (whether the behaviour still complies with a set of norms), and intervention (doing something to make sure that the behaviour will again comply with a set of norms). Second, regulation can refer to three regulatory objects. Strategic regulation is about resetting goals, regulation by design is about changing the infrastructural conditions for organizational behaviour, and operational regulation is about dealing with disturbances, given the goals and infrastructure; it refers to day-to-day regulation of organizational processes. Third, regulation can differ in scope: it can have a small 'span of control' in terms of process, persons or tasks, or it can have a large scope, e.g. covering the complete operational process. And finally, regulation can be more or less part of operational tasks – 'more' when it is part of operational tasks and the hierarchy is flat, less when there is a hierarchy of regulators detached from operational work. Designing the control structure can now be understood as:

1. allocating different regulatory activities to tasks;
2. allocating strategic regulation, regulation by design, and operational regulation to tasks;
3. allocating regulation of a particular scope to tasks;
4. allocating regulation as more or less removed from operational tasks.

As the reader may recall, these four choices in designing the control structure are, in fact, choices with respect to the regulatory design parameters, and we argued that these design parameters should have values that are as low as possible. Now, given the choices made in designing the production structure (flows, segments, and teams) discussed previously, de Sitter proposes three steps for allocating regulatory tasks at the micro, meso, and macro level in such a way that these regulatory design parameters do have low values. And, as discussed earlier, he starts with allocating regulatory tasks at the micro level of teams.

Any form of regulation (dealing with disturbances), at any level, requires (1) relevant, timely, complete, and reliable information about the object of regulation, and (2) the capacity to actually deal with problems. The first requirement is met if the regulator is 'as close as possible' to the object of regulation. The phrase 'as close as possible' implies a proximity in terms of time (there is no delay between the moment of occurrence of a disturbance and the moment of observation, or between the intervention plan and execution) and in terms of knowledge and understanding (the regulator can understand the disturbance in its context, understands its causes and effects, also sees other related disturbances, and can appreciate the virtual and actual effects of regulatory actions). The second requirement is met if the regulator has the knowledge, skills, and resources to actually deal with disturbances. So a first heuristic for allocating regulatory tasks (at the micro, meso, and macro level) is to make sure that regulation is assigned to those who are as close to the object of regulation as possible and to make sure that they have the regulatory potential to deal with the disturbances themselves as much as possible.

At the micro level of teams, this means that teams should, as much as possible, have all the regulatory potential to deal independently with the disturbances they encounter. In particular, teams should have the regulatory operational potential to deal with all kinds of disturbances to realize the segment's output. They should also have, as much as possible, the regulatory capacity to change the segment's infrastructure if that may, in their view, help to better attain the segment's output. This can entail that teams may themselves change the way tasks are divided among members, or may themselves initiate a change in equipment or technology used. Allocating these forms of regulation to teams ensures that those who are involved in operational tasks also have the regulatory potential to deal with disturbances impinging on those tasks. Teams can also have a certain amount of strategic regulation – e.g. they can participate in setting norms for delivery times or cycle times, or they can suggest changes to products based on their segment perspective (cf. de Sitter, 1994, Chapter 8). These forms of strategic regulation, however, require alignment with other segments in the flow (see 'Designing the control structure at the meso level: regulation between segments' later in this section).

Put in terms of the four ways of allocating regulatory potential mentioned previously:

1. teams should, as much as possible, be enabled to perform all regulatory activities concerning the realization of the segment's output;
2. teams should, as much as possible, be allowed to perform operational, design, and strategic regulation;
3. teams should have regulatory potential that covers the complete segment (which should cover as large a proportion of the production process as possible);
4. if teams have the regulatory potential to deal with the segment's output, the distance between regulation and operation is as small as possible.

This way of allocating regulatory potential to teams also ensures that the regulator (the team) is as close to the object of regulation (the process realizing the segment's output – which is carried out by the team itself) as possible, which in turn is required for obtaining relevant, timely, complete, and reliable information (with respect to the segment).

In assigning regulatory potential to teams, it is important to note that this potential should be distributed, as much as possible, among all team members. It should not lead to an in-team hierarchy. By distributing the regulatory potential, one can reap the benefits of joint detection and correction of errors. It should also be noted that the choices made in designing the production structure already set the stage for lowering the regulatory design parameters. For instance, if segments are chosen to cover a large proportion of the operational process, then regulation in segment teams can also have a large scope.

In all, one should, as much as possible, assign the required operational and design regulatory potential to the team to enable it to realize its output by itself. The same holds for assigning strategic regulatory potential to reflect on and suggest improvements of the output. We acknowledge that this is a rather broad heuristic and that it requires context-specific knowledge to determine what should be regulated by teams themselves and what should be handled by extra-segmental regulation. As de Sitter (1994, p. 296) confirms, this is a matter of experimentation.

Designing the control structure at the meso level: regulation between segments

After the teams have been assigned the 'requisite' regulatory potential i.e. the regulatory potential to independently realize, as much as possible, the segment's output, regulatory tasks securing the relations between segments in the flow ('intersegmental regulation' – see Figure 6.6) should be designed.

If the production structure has been designed adequately, segments are as independent as possible, which means that they have as few relations as possible. The required regulation is already decreased by a good design of the production structure (cf. de Sitter, 1994, Chapter 6; Galbraith, 1973). Moreover, if the segments have been assigned the regulatory potential to deal with their own segment-related disturbances, the relations between segments will be less troublesome. In fact, the rationale for designing the control structure is: if it can be regulated in teams, it should be regulated in teams. Nevertheless, segments *are* related in a flow, and these relations should be regulated.

In fact, the relations between segments have operational, design, and strategic aspects. Operational issues that affect multiple segments should be regulated "on-line real-time" as de Sitter (1994, p. 215) puts it, i.e. by means of direct mutual adjustment between teams. If, for instance, the input of some segment doesn't live up to quality standards, a representative of the team may directly consult a representative of the 'previous' team to solve the problem. One heuristic for designing meso-flow regulation, then, is to make sure that operational intersegmental issues are, as much as possible, dealt with by (representatives of) the teams themselves (and not by regulators who act independently from the teams). This ensures the required proximity between regulator and regulated (see earlier text).

To secure the independence of flows, design regulation should as much as possible take place within flows. This means that (re)designing the flow's infrastructure should, ideally, be a matter of flow internal regulation. Part of this regulation by design is assigned to segments (as long as they can still deliver the segment's output). The parts of the infrastructure that can't be

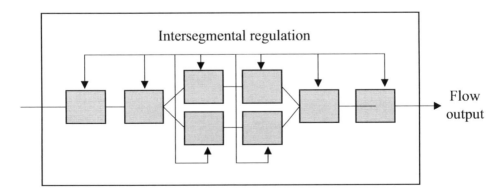

FIGURE 6.6 Regulation between segments

196 Designing interventions

(re)designed without affecting other segments should be subject to intersegmental regulation by design. Examples may be technology connecting the segments (e.g. ICT for monitoring the progress of orders, planning software, or the tools used for the transportation of the output from segment to segment). Another example could be training the skills of representatives of teams and installing procedures for mutual adjustment between teams. Also, the current way of segmentation should be monitored and, if needed, adjusted. Again, those involved in this kind of regulation should, ideally, also be operational members of segment teams, to ensure relevant changes to the infrastructure. Detached regulation by design should be avoided.

Strategic regulation within flows concerns the output of segments as well as the output of the flow as a whole. Segment-related strategic regulation is about (re)setting norms for the segment's output. Such norm adjustment may be needed if it turns out that the old targets are unrealistic. As this may affect other segments, and indeed the output of the flow, it is highly advisable to include representatives of all teams in this kind of regulation. Strategic regulation may also relate to changing the output of the flow in terms of changes to products or services delivered. To the extent that team members have direct relations with the environment of the flow, they should, as much as possible, be involved in such innovative decision making. Moreover, representatives of teams who are not directly related to the environment should also be involved to comment on plans for innovation from their segment-related production perspectives.

Designing the control structure at the macro level: regulation between flows

After regulatory potential is allocated to teams and flows, regulatory tasks concerning the relations between flows should be addressed (see Figure 6.7). The nature of this regulation at the macro level depends on the degree of independence of the flows that are designed. If flows are really self-dependent (and hence share no value chain activities or product development), then inter-flow regulation relates to issues that are not directly tied to orders, e.g. company culture, 'corporate image', investment policies, restructuring initiatives, and some personnel issues (de Sitter, 1994, p. 228). One important issue here is ensuring that flows can learn from each other – e.g. about how structural changes should be carried out or how innovation

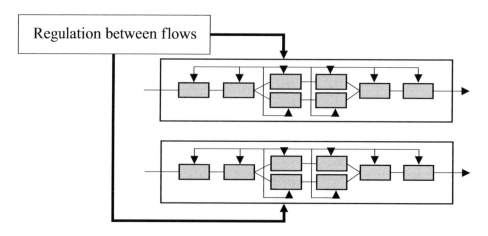

FIGURE 6.7 Regulation between flows

projects can bet set up. Also, the flows themselves (i.e. their viability) should be monitored and, based on the outcome, the collection of flows may be altered. The more independent the flows are, the less they need to be regulated. And where regulation is needed, flow representation is required.

If there is more dependence between flows exits, more should be regulated. For instance, if flows share product development (a common option, as discussed by de Sitter, 1994, p. 240), it is important that representatives from the production segments (from the different production flows) are involved. If flows share a common resource, inter-flow regulation may take the form of on-line real-time regulation between the segments that are directly involved (e.g. directly before the resource, the segment operating the resource, and the segments directly after the resource – which preferably is the same segment as the one before the resource; see earlier text).

Again, much more can be said about regulation at the meso and macro level, but that falls beyond the scope of this book. The heuristics presented in this brief summary give some ideas about how the design step of episodic interventions with respect to designing the control structure should be carried out.

Wrapping it up: heuristics for designing structures

Table 6.8 briefly summarizes the heuristics for designing the production and control structure.

Illustration of the steps of the design activity

To illustrate the design steps, we will revisit the case of the construction firm W, introduced earlier. In previous sections, the problems of W with respect to quality of work and quality of organization have been tied to high values of several structural parameters. In particular, it was found that:

1. Functional concentration was high for the foremen and overall planners, who were involved in many projects. The building team was only involved in one project at a time. Foremen in particular suffered from high functional concentration.
2. Differentiation was high: the building team was only allowed to perform production activities. Foremen (and to some extent, the overall planner) carried out preparatory and support activities.
3. There was some specialization in the complete construction project: architects, planner, building teams, and sub-contractors each had their separate contributions.
4. The separation of regulatory and operational activities was high as the foremen performed all operational activities for the building team.
5. Differentiation of regulation into monitoring, assessment, and intervention was low, but these tasks rested with the foremen, and, because of separation, were removed from operational work.
6. Differentiation of regulation into strategic, design, and operational regulation also seemed low – but building team members had no part in it.
7. There was some specialization of regulation, as the overall planner and foremen regulated their own parts of the process. Also, sub-contractors regulated their own contributions.

Against this background, we can now take a look at the design steps for W.

TABLE 6.8 Design heuristics per design step

Design step	Heuristics
1. Designing the production structure at the macro level: identifying flows	Define as many flows as possible in such a way that: 1. each flow contains (external) order types which have as few differences (with respect to input, product, demand and/or client characteristics) as possible; 2. each flow has a capacity utilization of 80% or more; 3. flows do not share a common resource (like expertise or technology). If products and clients are unconnected (e.g. mass production), start with product characteristics as a base for flows; if they are highly related (e.g. service industry, healthcare), start with client/market characteristics.
2. Designing the production structure at the meso level: identifying segments	1. Segments should cover a large proportion of the operational process (as large as possible), i.e. there should be as few segments as possible. 2. Segments should be as 'flow-oriented' as possible (i.e. low internal or external functional concentration and low specialization/differentiation, and 'single piece production' as far as possible. 3. Segments should be as independent as possible. The coherence between activities *in* the segment should be high; the number of relations *between* segments should be low. 4. Use standard segments as a point of reference.
3. Designing the production structure at the micro level: identifying teams	1. Team tasks are highly related and should have as few interfaces with other teams as possible, and these interfaces should only concern input or output at a team level, not at the level of individual tasks within the team. 2. Teams should be allowed to independently carry out all production, support, and preparation activities needed to realize the segment's output. 3. Team members should have broad, overlapping tasks. 4. Ensure redundancy of functions.
4. Designing the control structure at the micro level: equipping teams with regulatory potential	1. Overall, if it can be regulated by the team, it should be regulated by the team. 2. Teams should, as much as possible, be enabled to perform all regulatory activities concerning the realization of the segment's output. 3. Teams should, as much as possible, be allowed to perform operational, design, and strategic regulation. 4. Teams should have regulatory potential that covers the complete segment.
5. Designing the control structure at the meso level: regulation between segments	1. Make sure that operational intersegmental issues are, as much as possible, dealt with by (representatives of) the teams themselves in an 'on-line, real-time' way (and not by regulators who act independently from the teams). 2. Involve members of teams (or representatives who are part of the team) in design and strategic regulation.
6. Designing the control structure at the macro level: regulation between flows	Involve members of teams (or representatives who are part of the team) in operational, design, and strategic regulation at the macro level.

Step 1: designing the production structure at the macro level – macro flows

At W, the orders are the individual construction projects. There are two main types of projects (large social housing projects and smaller projects). Based on this distinction, it may be investigated whether it is possible to make two general macro flows, and see if both flows can contain all activities to realize their type of output. This would mean that one flow is dedicated to social housing projects (and has someone who monitors and reacts to social housing tenders, and has the personnel to staff these projects), and another flow dedicated to small projects. Whether this is feasible, depends on the projected amount of work in both flows.

For the sake of clarity, we'll assume that there are no macro flows (i.e. no separate *order types*). We'll just assume one macro flow, consisting of individual construction projects as orders. However, we'll use these orders as a base to identify parallel, dedicated sets of activities at the *meso* level – see the next step.

Step 2: designing the production structure at the meso level – segments

If we use individual projects as a base for segmentation, we can identify client-related parallel segments which can have many activities dedicated to these projects (i.e. so that employees performing tasks for one project are not performing tasks for other projects). Ideally, all these individual projects are independent segments that are self-coordinating and have their own preparatory, support, and production activities. One problem may be the activity of the overall planner. There needs to be one point of contact for clients, and only after some deliberation, bidding, and negotiation can a project be defined. So at least some of the 'overall planner' activities need to be shared among project segments.

However, after the definition of a project, it may function as a relatively independent segment, except that sub-contractors also need to be included. One way to include sub-contractors is to see them as relatively independent (external) segments that are inserted into the project flow (see Figure 6.8). In this case, the activities of the building team belong to one parallel segment which, as part of these activities, hires an 'external' segment (a sub-contractors) to do a certain job, and then takes over again (these external segments resemble the phase group discussed earlier). Ideally, the building team segment would carry out the

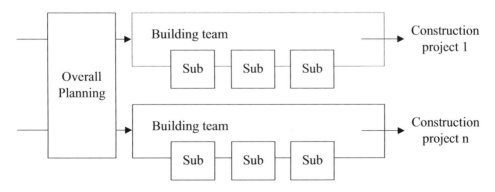

FIGURE 6.8 Segmentation at W (shared overall planner, parallel project segments including 'external' sub-contractor segments)

activities of the sub-contractors itself. It may be investigated whether this can be the case for some activities (perhaps the building team can learn to apply sealing kits or take care of the wooden flooring). However, as this may not be possible for all activities, some form of independence probably cannot be given up.

Steps 3 and 4: designing the production and control structure at the micro level – identifying teams

The building teams should ideally (1) be enabled to carry out all relevant preparatory, production, and support activities to carry out the construction project (except those which are part of the sub-contractors' segments), (2) consist of multi-skilled team members, and (3) have all the regulatory potential necessary to realize the project independently. In particular, teams should be allowed to carry out their own daily planning, arrange for material to be at the site themselves, and contact (and monitor the contributions of) sub-contractors. Moreover, the members should have, as much as possible, all relevant skills and knowledge to carry out project activities. Even though this may be problematic (and is a reason for hiring sub-contractors), knowledge of each other's work is relevant (so, ideally, carpenters have brick-laying knowledge and skills, and masons have knowledge and skills with respect to carpentry). Again ideally, they can also perform other activities to reduce the number of sub-contractors. To adequately monitor the contribution of sub-contractors, team members should preferably have knowledge about the criteria regarding the output of sub-contractors' activities.

Lastly, team members should, ideally, have the regulatory potential to deal with disturbances in projects. This includes all operational regulation (e.g. arrange for different or additional equipment or material in case of problems, make new arrangements with sub-contractors if needed, or discuss problems with clients). It also includes regulation by design (e.g. redefinition of tasks if required, buying new equipment if worn out). It may even refer to strategic regulation, as team members may see that current project goals need to be reset.

Step 5: designing the control structure at the meso level: regulation between segments

In this step, regulation between segments (e.g. between the building team and sub-contractors and the overall planner – or even with the architect) is designed. To instruct and monitor sub-contractors, clear communication between the team and sub-contractors is essential. And, in the case of problems during execution, direct communication is also required. Team members may need to consult with the overall planner in case the project goals need to change. If there are problems with the architectural design, team members also should be allowed to communicate directly with the architect.

At regular intervals, there may also be contact between team members of different construction projects about topics that may be relevant for all projects – e.g. how to deal with uncooperative sub-contractors, or how to use a new kind of equipment. In this case, team members can share knowledge that will help them to better deal with project-related problems. This is, in fact, a kind of regulation by design, which requires intersegmental regulation.

Step 6: designing the control structure at the macro level: regulation between flows

Although we didn't identify multiple flows, some regulatory issues still need to be resolved, for instance training of new personnel and innovation issues. In our case, these could also be discussed in step 5, but as these issues are often relevant across flows, we'll discuss them in step 6. Training of new construction workers can best be taken care of by adding a new employee to a building team and making the team responsible for ensuring that the employee learns the ropes. In due time, the new employee can be assigned (with a more experienced one) to a team. In this way, a kind of apprenticeship is introduced.

Innovation can also to a large extent be a task of building teams. As they are in touch with clients and know, based on being immersed in operational work, what aspects might be improved, they are in a position to come up with project improvements. Team members may also have ideas about the applicability of new technologies or materials in projects – e.g. new durable materials or equipment for solar energy. However, this requires gaining knowledge about such technologies and equipment.

In this section, then, an example of a design is given which follows the six proposed steps. Please note that this is just an example and presents a first, 'ideal' design. In reality, the design is not a one-shot issue, but subject to several iterations. In fact, what often happens, is that during the *implementation* of a design, design steps need to be redone and refined. This is the topic of the next section.

6.5 Implementation

The implementation step on the functional dimension is about the actual transformation of the current high parameter value structure into the desired low parameter value structure, as delineated in the design step. Its goal, then, is to realize a transformed structure, according to the design. Given some design, implementation consists of the following sub-goals:

1. determining the difference between the current structure and the desired structure, as delineated in the design step;
2. defining executable 'implementation' portions – i.e. coherent and manageable parts of the complete structural change;
3. sequencing the portions from (2);
4. actually implementing the 'portions' in the suggested sequence.

Determining the difference between the current and designed structures gives an impression of the 'implementation effort' required to change the structure. This impression can be used as a basis for defining portions and sequencing them: the larger the difference between current and desired structures, the more one needs to portion the implementation. The design theory discussed earlier (in particular, the design heuristics presented earlier) can be helpful to determining the implementation effort: e.g. the more that needs to be transformed at the macro level, the larger the effort.

Defining executable implementation portions (i.e. identifying coherent and manageable parts of the design) is about selecting parts of the structure that can be changed relatively 'independently'. Here, too, design theory may help to identify these parts – for instance, portions can be flows, or segments within flows.

Sequencing the portions is simply about defining the order in which the portions are implemented (e.g. determining which flows should be started first, or what the order of the segments is in a particular flow). As can be appreciated, design theory is helpful for sequencing portions as well.

If we take W as an example, we can briefly discuss the implementation of the design presented in the previous section. This design proposes to lower the values on the design parameters in several ways. However, implementing them all at once would be problematic – not only because it would disrupt the current projects, but also because the effect of the design is uncertain. Therefore, it was decided to select one project as a pilot. This project was assigned to a building team. No foreman was included in the project (although he was available during the whole project in case the pilot didn't work out). The members of this building team were the most experienced employees and had gained some knowledge about each other's work. They were allowed to conduct their own daily planning, which they discussed with the overall planner at the start of the pilot. They were also allowed to carry out preparatory work and deal with disturbances themselves (although they were asked to discuss their solutions at the start of the pilot). Moreover, they were allowed to plan and contact sub-contractors themselves and monitor their contributions. Finally, they were instructed about the fact that even though this was a pilot, they had team responsibility for the output. While the project progressed, the team was gradually given more freedom to do as it saw fit (e.g. after a while, the members didn't have to discuss their daily planning or solutions to problems beforehand). In all, the pilot seemed to work, and it was decided to repeat it for two other projects. In these new projects, the two experienced employees were each paired with another employee to share their experience with the new set up. These teams were also given more internal and external regulatory freedom from the start. Gradually, all employees were introduced to the new way of working. In the end, foremen lost their jobs as foremen and were assigned to the more complex projects. They also were given responsibility for arranging and preparing meetings discussing project issues and innovation. The idea of learning each other's skills was abandoned, as was the idea of doing some of the activities of sub-contractors – although two plumbers were employed by W, to decrease the dependence on external segments.

Although a construction firm is not the most complex of organizations, the sequence of events illustrates how a design gradually gets implemented. We will explore the idea of how to carry out design and implementation in more detail in Chapter 8.

Functionally, there is not much more to say about implementation. The sub-goals seem clear enough. The difficult issues concerning implementation pertain to how these sub-goals can best be realized. However, matters of realizing of the goals and sub-goals on the functional dimension will be discussed in Chapter 8, which deals with the infrastructural dimension. Even so, we would like to end this section with a few remarks on the relation between implementation and other functional activities.

At the start of this chapter, we stated that interventions are dynamic, iterative, and recursive processes. This entails that the sequence of functional goals is not fixed. For instance, during the realization of one goal, it may be found out that the realization of previous goals needs to be redone. We warned the reader that we wouldn't discuss the dynamic relations between realizing functional goals – dealing with the dynamics is the subject of later chapters. However, we want to make one exception and briefly discuss the intimate relation between design, implementation, and evaluation.

We would briefly like to state that, even though there is a clear functional difference (the output of design is, functionally speaking, a plan for structural change, the output of implementation is a transformed structure, which requires the four sub-goals given previously), design and implementation (and evaluation) are tightly interwoven activities, and are therefore difficult to separate in practice.

Their interconnectedness is twofold. First, the six sub-steps for designing a suitable low parameter value structure already imply portions and a sequence in implementation, and hence restrict the degrees of freedom for implementation. It implies, for instance, that there should first be (1) one or more flows, (2) one or more segments within the flow(s), before (3) teams can realize the output of the segment(s). Flows and segments are prerequisites for teams. Similarly, at least one flow, one or more segments within the flow, and a team realizing the segment's output should be available before adding regulatory potential. From this starting point, the implemented structure may gradually gain complexity.

Second, and more importantly, the choices made in the six design steps are uncertain, and their consequences and adequacy can only be appreciated in full after some parts of the design have been implemented. For instance, during design, one may assume that a certain set of products is a basis for a flow, but it may turn out that this flow doesn't meet the capacity utilization criterion. Or it may be that the criteria used for parallelization turned out to be wrong (resulting in flows that are still too complex or too dependent). Finding the right flows is often a matter of experimentation. The same holds for finding as few as possible segments that are as independent as possible. It may turn out that in a particular context, more intersegmental relations need to be allowed than designed, that parallel segments are too dependent, or that segments may be combined into one segment. Similarly, teams may have been designed to do all preparatory and support work, but this may distract them too much from operational work. Or they may have been designed to have multi-skilled members, but that could prove to be a little too ambitious. And finally, including team members in all kinds of inter- and intra-segmental regulation may have the unwanted effect of taking up too much time. In all, given the context, some design choices need to be remade.

Now, because such effects cannot all be foreseen during design, they can often only become manifest after implementation. That is, they become apparent after the evaluation of implemented parts of the design. In fact, as we see it, this experimentation is a necessary part of episodic change – much like experimentation is a necessary part of an organization's 'normal' ongoing infrastructural choices. Therefore, it makes sense to allow for implementation of parts of the design and, based on the outcome of these implementations, to change the design. In this way, implementation and design are highly interwoven activities, making their realization more feasible, but also more complex.

Given the inherent uncertainty of design choices, and hence the interconnectedness between design and implementation, it makes sense to view design and implementation as related in the following way (see Figure 6.9). The starting point for implementation is a 'preliminary' design which is an actual or virtual sub-system of the ideal final design, and ideally contains a flow, some segments, and a team (of course, depending on the organization being redesigned in terms of the values of the structural parameters, this preliminary design can be more or less elaborate). After implementing this preliminary design (based on the implementation steps), one should monitor (evaluate) its effect (and here it should be acknowledged that the effect can be less than expected if other parts of the ideal design haven't been implemented yet). Based on this effect, the implemented preliminary design can be augmented or adjusted.

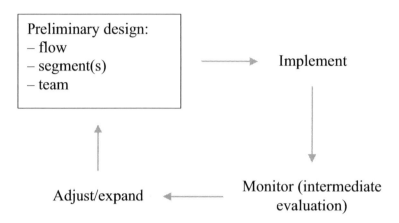

FIGURE 6.9 The relation between design, implementation, and evaluation

Of course, this doesn't tell us yet what the preliminary design should look like and how the implementation steps can best be taken. That is, however, an issue belonging to the infrastructural dimension of episodic interventions. We will pick up on how design and implementation can be tackled in Chapter 8, when discussing the infrastructural dimension.

6.6 Evaluation

The last activity of the functional dimension is evaluation. Its main goal is to establish whether the implemented change of the structure has the desired effect. The desired effect can be thought of in two ways. The main desired effect of the changed structure is, of course, that the problematic variables (as established in the diagnosis) are now no longer problematic (and that others haven't become problematic) *because* of the new implemented structure. The whole idea of changing the organizational structure is to solve problematic organizational behaviour (which is operationalized in terms of quality of organization and quality of work variables), and during the evaluation, this should be established. This kind of evaluation is called a *product evaluation*, and is about determining the effectiveness of the episodic intervention in the organizational structure.

Another type of evaluation has to do with the efficiency of the intervention: this is called a *process evaluation*. Here, one tries to establish whether additional process criteria (like costs or meeting deadlines) are met.

To achieve the evaluation goal, the following steps are relevant:

1. Determine the evaluation criteria ($EC_1...n$) – The *product* evaluation criteria (i.e. those pertaining to the effectiveness of the intervention) are, in fact, the variables describing the organizational performance as determined in the diagnosis. The evaluation criteria relating to the process have to do with the efficient use of resources and reaching deadlines – they refer to the efficient use of elements of intervention project infrastructure. These criteria are not determined during the diagnosis, and should be defined.
2. Determine the norm values ($EC_i[nv]$) and actual values ($EC_i[av]$) of these criteria (norm values for the product evaluation have already been established during the diagnosis).

Norm values with respect to process variables should be determined – and are often determined before the project as well. The actual values of these criteria (i.e. the values of the criteria at the moment of evaluation) still also have to be determined.
3. Determine whether there is a problematic difference (error) between norm values and actual values of the EC's ($EC_i[e]$).
4. Based on the outcome of step 3:

- If there is NO problematic difference, then one should establish whether this is due to the implemented change of the structure (and not due to other circumstances, e.g. an improved economic situation). If no other circumstances can be found, then one can hypothesize that the intervention was successful.
- If there is a problematic difference, then one should try to find out whether the lack of success is due to the implemented structure (and not some other events or circumstances). If no other circumstances can be found responsible, then one can hypothesize that the intervention was unsuccessful.

These steps belong to evaluating a structural intervention, and are relevant after the structure has been changed (ex post evaluation). Of course, evaluations, using the steps, can also be carried out *before* the structure has been changed completely (intermediary evaluation, e.g. to monitor the effect of certain changes while they are being implemented). This kind of evaluation is relevant when monitoring the effect of an implemented part of the design, to be able to adjust the design (see the previous section). It is also relevant for monitoring progress in terms of project duration and budget.

We will now briefly comment on these steps (from ex post and intermediary perspectives).

6.6.1 Step 1: determining evaluation criteria

The criteria used for product evaluation, i.e. the criteria for determining whether the implemented changed structure has the desired effect, are the variables used in the diagnoses for operationalizing the organization's performance. As stated earlier, the whole idea of an episodic intervention is to change the structure in such a way that the organization's meaningful survival, its meaningful contribution to society, is secured. And, as this contribution is defined in terms of quality of organization and quality of work variables, securing the organization's meaningful contribution entails making sure that these variables are within 'norm values'. Now, during the diagnosis, special attention was paid to problematic quality of organization and quality of work variables. The gap analysis revealed these problematic variables, and the episodic intervention is meant to make sure that these variables are no longer problematic. However, the other variables are also relevant, because a change in structure should not mean that, even though problematic variables cease to be problematic, other variables become problematic. So a product evaluation should pay attention to all quality of organization and quality of work variables; it should be established that the problematic variables do indeed cease to be problematic and that other, unproblematic, variables remain unproblematic.

The criteria for process evaluation are used to establish the efficiency of episodic intervention projects, and relate to the use of resources (and budget allocated for these resources) and to the duration of the project (e.g. the allocated time and planning).

For an ex post product evaluation, the quality of organization and quality or work variables should be used. This kind of evaluation determines whether the problematic quality of organization or quality of work variables (as determined in the gap analysis) cease to be problematic because of the changed, implemented structure (and that other variables haven't become problematic because of the change). During an intermediary product evaluation, these variables are monitored while the intervention is going on in order to enable adjustment of certain choices.

In the case of an ex post process evaluation, it is 'simply' established whether an episodic intervention project is finished within budget and time limits, whether it was carried out according to plan. An intermediary process evaluation uses these criteria to monitor whether project progress or budget are still within limits while the project is being carried out. The results of this evaluation can be used to adjust the project – either with respect to norm values of the process criteria or with respect to diagnosis, design, or implementation choices (e.g. to avoid using multi-skilled personnel, as that becomes too costly, or to give up the whole project altogether).

6.6.2 Step 2: determining the norm and actual values of evaluation criteria

Determining the norm values is comparable to setting the norm values discussed in the diagnosis. In fact, most norm values for the variables used in the ex post product evaluation have already been set during the diagnosis stage. The norm values for the process variables may be set at different stages during the project. With respect to norm values used in an evaluation, we'd like to make two remarks.

First, it is important to note is that the norm values for variables used in ex post and intermediary evaluation can change during the project. During the project, it may be possible that one finds out that norm values for the quality of organization or quality of work haven't been set properly and should be adjusted. For instance, at W, the percentage of projects finished within schedule was set at a level that was much higher than the average sector percentage, and was later adjusted to a lower, more realistic level. During a project, norms for process variables may also be reset. If it turns out that the project will not stay within budget or time limits, variables expressing them are often reset.

Second, in intermediary evaluations, norm values that are set for the completed project have to be translated into norm values at the moment of evaluation during the project. These 'translated' norm values express what can be expected at the moment of evaluation; they express project progress towards the final norm values. Translating final norm values into intermediate norm values can be difficult, and is a matter of context-dependent experimentation. However, it can be guided by design knowledge and heuristics presented earlier. For instance, assigning teams to a parallel segment should help to gain an overview and to decrease delays and disturbances. Similarly, after allowing teams to perform preparatory, support, and production activities themselves, it can be expected that delays and disturbances decrease and that absorption of disturbances and quality of work increase. Installing proper intersegmental regulation should have the same effect. So every step in the design and implementation process should produce some improvement (at least in terms of delays, probability of disturbances, absorption of disturbances, and quality of work). During the design/implementation/evaluation cycle (see earlier), the 'minimal' norm values used in monitoring should reflect 'an improvement' compared to the previous situation.

The actual values of the variables in an ex post product or process evaluation are measured after the intervention has been completed. The actual values of variables in an intermediary evaluation are measured at the moment of the evaluation at some time during the project. This can be done at several moments in time – e.g. every time a new part of the design is implemented – or it can even be recorded more often – e.g. if one uses ICT applications to make certain costs of a project visible (like resource expenditures or personnel costs) the moment they occur.

6.6.3 Step 3: determining whether there is a problematic difference between norm and actual values

In an ex post evaluation, this amounts to recording the difference between norm and actual values for all evaluation variables and deciding whether this difference is problematic. If the norms can be set without uncertainty, this exercise seems to be straightforward. However, given the fact that setting norms is an uncertain activity (and that, hence, norms may require adjustment), deciding whether the difference is problematic may require some additional reflection and deliberation. It may be that some norms have been set too ambitiously, and that this is the reason for a difference. In any case, and as a minimum, at least in an ex post product evaluation, one would expect an improvement compared to the old structure.

For intermediary evaluations, determining whether the difference is problematic is even more difficult. These evaluations are meant to record progress, which can be disappointing because the norm values have been set too high. In that case, a result of the evaluation can be that norm values should be adjusted. It can also be a signal of a bad project. Again, most of the time, one would expect some improvement during the project. Its absence requires careful interpretation of the project, based on design knowledge, experience, and comparison with similar projects.

6.6.4 Step 4: finding out whether the intervention is successful

Part of the question of whether the intervention is successful (i.e. that the structure has been changed successfully) has already been addressed in the previous step. If, as a result of an ex post evaluation, it was found that no problematic product of process variables can be found, things look promising. However, it should be ruled out that the positive result has other causes than the implemented change to the structure. Or, which is theoretically less implausible, some research should be devoted to finding out whether other factors than structural factors have contributed to the positive result. Suppose, for instance, that some kind of 'Hawthorne effect' takes place, e.g. with the result that the effort of enhancing the work of employees itself makes that they are more willing to perform well and are feeling more motivated to deal with disturbances. This effect may occlude certain deficits of the implemented structure.

Something similar can be said for a negative result for an ex post product evaluation. It should be ruled out that other than structural factors are still causing problematic behaviour. For one, a structural change should often be accompanied by a change in skills, knowledge, and motivation on the part of human resources and by a change in technology. A change in structure along the lines discussed in this book (i.e. by lowering the value of structural parameters) entails that tasks of employees will become more complex, that additional training will be required, and that more and closer interaction among team members will be needed.

This may not be appreciated by all employees, and may even lead to a loss of motivation. Although in a thorough episodic intervention one should be aware of and deal with this kind of demotivation, it may be a cause of sub-standard organizational behaviour even when structures are changed for the better.

In any case, if there is no problematic difference for all relevant product variables, and no other (extra-structural) reasons for this situation can be found, one may hypothesize that the structural intervention is successful. If a problematic difference is found and no other (extra-structural) circumstances seem to have caused this difference, then one cannot conclude that the intervention is successful.

Things are a little more problematic in an intermediary evaluation. Negative results in particular require careful reflection and deliberation. Norm values may have been set too ambitiously, and sometimes negative results may not be too surprising in retrospect. For instance, demotivation due to resistance or being fed up with too many change efforts may be causing trouble during intermediary evaluations, when measures for reaching goals on the social dimension are still being implemented. However, negative intermediary evaluation results don't need to be problematic – they are (within certain limits) to be expected in an episodic intervention, which is characterized by uncertainty and experimentation. Indeed, they are a natural aspect of such experimentation, and are, in fact, required to further the progress of these interventions.

As a final remark concerning this step, it should be noted that there is a difference between being (un)successful in terms of meeting product variables and being (un)successful in terms of meeting process variables – often effectiveness is more important.

Notes

1 We treat the functional (and social) dimension as a *goal* dimension – consisting of four sub-goals (which, in turn, can be broken down further into sub-goals). In this way, we can set it apart from the infrastructural dimension, which describes the means to realize the goals on the social and functional dimensions. When we use the terms 'activity' or 'step' in this chapter, we intend to refer to a set of sub-goals that need to be realized – however, the use of 'activity' or 'step' is often more convenient and natural.
2 Note that the examples of product characteristics are hierarchically related: a product function (e.g. means of transportation) can have several product families (e.g. cars, trucks, vans) which may have several types (e.g. cars: sedan, station wagon, etc.), each of which may have, in turn, several variations (business, luxury, etc.).

7

THE SOCIAL DIMENSION

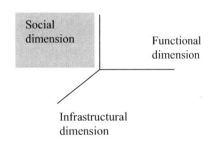

Episodic Interventions in the Structure of Organization

PART I
Theoretical Framework:

– Organizations

– Organizational structures

– (episodic) Interventions

PART II
A 3-D Model of Episodic Interventions:

Social dimension

Functional dimension

Infrastructural dimension

FIGURE 7.0   Roadmap of the book

7.1 Introduction

In the previous chapter, we concentrated on the design of a new and improved organizational structure that can 'function well'. In particular, we discussed the functional activities and goals that should be realized in order to construct a structure that can realize the goal of the intervention. Yet, in the case of *organizational* interventions, such a functional perspective is insufficient to make these interventions a success. Organizational interventions are interventions 'for', 'by', and 'in' organizations as *social* systems. As such, they also have a *social dimension*. In the end, this social dimension is about organization members interactively changing their interaction premises and the interactions based upon them as a result of an intervention.

Applied to episodic interventions in organizational structures, this means that, if the intervention is a success, organization members ultimately (re)produce the improved organizational structure by means of their changed interactions and interaction premises: they actually start to 'live' this improved structure, thereby realizing the goal of the intervention. Without this change of interaction premises and interactions, there is no intervention 'in' the organization or its structure. The organization as a social system remains unaffected and the design of the new structure remains just another plan, however ingenious this design may be.

In this chapter, we focus on organization members changing their interaction premises and interactions in the course of an intervention. However, we do not purport to unravel the full, not yet wholly understood, complexity of these change processes. In line with the logic of the 3-D model, we just concentrate on specifying *social goals in the intervention* that should be realized in the intervention in order to successfully change the structure of an organization and realize the goal of the intervention.

As explained in Chapter 5, it is relevant to know what these social goals are because, together with the functional goals, social goals provide a background for the:

- strategic regulation of the intervention – i.e. formulating particular functional and social goals for parts or the whole of the intervention;
- design regulation of the intervention – i.e. designing an intervention infrastructure (structure, technology, and human resources) that can help realize the formulated functional and social goals;
- actual performance and operational regulation of the intervention – i.e. given the intervention infrastructure, actually realizing the social and functional goals resulting from strategic regulation by means of performing primary intervention activities and managing disturbances when they occur.

In order to unfold the social goals that constitute the social dimension of the 3-D model, the rest of this chapter is organized as follows.

In Section 7.2, we make a first inventory of the three social goals: *motivation*, *adoption*, and *integration*. In Sections 7.3–7.5, we elaborate these social goals by relating them to stage models of change that can be found in so-called 'consultancy-oriented' literature on (planned) change. As a part of this elaboration, we specify social sub-goals, touch on socio-psychological 'drivers' that can help realize social goals, and discuss the relation between goals on the social dimension and goals on the functional dimension of the 3-D model. At the end of Section 7.5, our full inventory of social goals will be presented. Because the consultancy-oriented models of change that are discussed in this chapter are criticized in current literature on organizational change, Section 7.6 is devoted to a discussion of the main lines of these critiques. The purpose of this discussion is to both further clarify the social goals logic that is central in this chapter and distinguish this logic from stage models of organizational change. At the end of this chapter, it should be clear:

1. what the three social goals (and their sub-goals) in the intervention entail;
2. how these social goals relate to:
   - socio-psychological 'drivers' that can help realize them;
   - functional goals in the intervention;
3. how these social goals differ from stage models of organizational change.

7.2 Social goals: a first 'reasoned' inventory

In order to make a first inventory of the social goals that should be realized in the intervention, it is useful to start with the *final* social goal. This final social goal is the social goal that should be realized if the episodic intervention in the organization's structure is to be considered a 'success'. Once we know what this final social goal is, we can go back to the starting point of the intervention and ask what social goals should be realized 'along the way', so to speak, in order to realize the final social goal in the intervention.

From Chapter 6, we already know that, from a *functional* perspective, the episodic intervention is a success if a new and improved organizational structure is implemented that actually supports the realization of the goal of the intervention. From a *social* perspective, the successful implementation of this new and improved structure means that organization members, by means of their interaction premises and interactions, (re)produce this new structure. Viewed from the perspective of individual organization members, this means that they *have irreversibly integrated new interactions and interaction premises into their repertoires that both (re)produce the organization's new and improved structure and allow for the realization of the goal of the intervention*. This 'integration' is the final social goal on the social dimension of the 3-D model. Once integration has been realized, the new improved organization structure that can realize the goal of the intervention is (re)produced by means of the premise-based interactions that constitute the social system.

Please note that the term 'irreversibly' in the definition does not mean that organizational change is somehow stopped or 'frozen'. How can it be? For one, 'being an organization' and 'being in a continuous flux' are the same thing. Moreover, it is a goal of the episodic interventions in organizational structures that are discussed in this book to re-institute the organization's capacity for continuous, 'organic' change. 'Irreversible' therefore does not mean 'absence of change'. It rather means that, once the intervention is successfully concluded, organization members should not, as a consequence of ongoing change, drift back, revert, to their old behaviours – behaviours that, given the goal of the intervention, are unwanted and undermine instead of enable continuous 'organic' adaptation.

Moreover, note that the new interaction premises and interactions that are integrated into the repertoires of organization members can be either *directly* or *indirectly* related to the (re)production of the new structure. An example of interaction premises and interactions that are *directly* related to this structure are the new tasks of organization members and the interactions related to the performance of these tasks. However, new interaction premises and interactions can also *indirectly* relate to the (re)production of the organization's structure. For instance, as a part of their new task, organization members may know that they are expected to:

- operate new *technology* (or operate old technology in a new way);
- apply new task- and technology-related *knowledge* and *skills* (or apply old knowledge and skills in new ways);
- realize new organizational *goals* (or realize old goals in new ways);
- function in a new, for instance, less bureaucratic organizational *culture*.

Therefore, for the purpose of actually realizing the integration goal, interaction premises and interactions that are both directly and indirectly related to the (re)production of the organization's structure should be integrated into the repertoires of organization members.

Finally, note that in this chapter, we concentrate on *organization members* realizing social goals in the intervention. For instance, 'integration' is defined in terms of organization members irreversibly integrating new interactions and interaction premises into their repertoires. However, organization members are not the only parties who may be affected by or involved in the intervention. Other parties, such as 'clients' or 'suppliers', may be affected or involved too. It may even be the case that, if the intervention is to succeed, these parties need to change parts of their behaviour as well. If this is the case, it may be expedient to also specify social goals, like 'integration', for these parties. The social goals discussed in this chapter are selected in such a way that they can also be set for these other parties. So, although in our definitions of the social goals we only mention organization members, these other parties are not excluded from these definitions.

'Integration' is the final social goal on the social dimension of the 3-D model. Given this final social goal, we can now start thinking about social goals that should be realized in order to realize the final social goal.

In order to find out what the *first* social goal in the intervention should be, it is useful to return to the 'old' interactions and their premises before the intervention. Clearly, parts or aspects of these 'old' interactions and interaction premises should differ from the 'new' improved interactions and interaction premises *after* the intervention. Otherwise, no intervention would be needed. In order to bridge this gap between old and new improved interactions and interaction premises, organization members should *change* parts or aspects of their interactions and interaction premises. However, in the case of the high parameter value structures that are the topic of this book, *starting* this change is quite problematic.

Organization members may be so deeply *immersed* in their daily routines that they do not see the possibility, desirability, or necessity of changing the structure of their organization. It is also possible that organization members feel emotionally *attached* to their current behaviours. Even if these behaviours are 'pathological', negatively affecting both individual organization members and the performance of the organization, such feelings of attachment may be quite strong (it is indeed possible to learn to love one's prison). For instance, in the 'hostile' intra-organizational environment of a high parameter value structure, organization members may cherish trusted formal and informal relations with particular co-workers. Actually, these relations may be their last straw. Letting go of the interaction premises and interactions that reproduce these relations may be so daunting that even interventions that promise to transform the structures causing the hostile working environment are regarded with suspicion.

Therefore, if change is to be effected, organization members should first, either by themselves or facilitated by others, develop the *motivation* to change their behaviour. To be more specific, they should develop the motivation to let go of current and move to new interaction premises and interactions. However, in the case of episodic interventions, this 'motivation for change' is insufficient. Organization members should also develop the motivation to change *by means* of an episodic intervention. Organization members should adopt as possible, desirable, and necessary both 'change' and an 'episodic intervention as the means to change'. *'Motivation' to let go of current and to move to new interaction premises and interactions and to see an episodic intervention as the vehicle of change is the first social goal in the intervention.*

In between the two social goals of 'motivation' and 'integration' lies the 'adoption' goal. Adoption means that organization members invent and test *new* helping interaction premises and interactions. That is, they invent and test new interaction premises and interactions that can improve the organization's structure and thereby realize the goal of the intervention. By means of this inventing and testing, organization members should develop a justifiable confidence in the resulting helping interaction premises and interactions, and for this reason, 'adopt' (willingly commit to) them. *'Adoption' therefore means that, based on a justifiable confidence, organization members adopt (willingly commit to) new helping interaction premises and concomitant interactions that can (re)produce an improved organizational structure that allows for the realization of the goal of the intervention.* Motivation, adoption, and integration are the three main goals on the social dimension of the 3-D model (see Table 7.1).

It is not difficult to recognize in the three social goals, the both famous and infamous three-stage model of planned change that, as the story goes, was introduced by Kurt Lewin, and among others, developed by Edgar Schein: *unfreeze, change, freeze* (for a critical analysis unmasking this 'story' as a kind of myth, see Cummings et al., 2016). Roughly speaking, the 'unfreeze' phase of the three-stage model relates to our 'motivation' goal, the 'change' phase relates to our 'adoption' goal, and the 'freeze' phase relates to our 'integration' goal (see Table 7.2 for a Schein-based summary of the three-stage model).

In essence, this seeming correspondence between our social goals logic and, for instance, Schein's three-stage model is to be expected. Arguing that the integration of specific new behaviours (interactions based on interaction premises) into the repertoire of a group of people (refreeze) presupposes both the adoption of this new behaviour (change) and the motivation to let go of old behaviours (unfreeze) seems to verge on the brink of the trivial. For this reason, it is not surprising that authors such as Levy and Merry (1986) and Elrod and Tippet (2002) suggest that quite different kinds of individual or social change, such as

TABLE 7.1 Social goals in the intervention: motivation, adoption, integration

Motivation	Organization members should develop the motivation to:
	– let go of current and move to new interaction premises and concomitant interaction patterns
	– adopt an episodic intervention as a means to do this
Adoption	Based on a justifiable confidence, organization members adopt (willingly commit to) new helping interaction premises and interactions that can (re)produce an improved organizational structure that allows for the realization of the goal of the intervention
Integration	Organization members have irreversibly integrated new interactions and interaction premises into their repertoires that both (re)produce the organization's new and improved structure and allow for the realization of the goal of the intervention

TABLE 7.2 Schein's conception of a three-stage model of the change process

Unfreeze	Creating motivation and readiness to change
Change	Changing through cognitive restructuring: helping the client to see things, judge things, feel things, and react to things differently based on a new point of view
Refreeze	Helping the client to integrate the new point of view

Source: Adapted from Schein (1987, p. 93).

'grieving', 'creative processes', or 'cultural and scientific revolutions', share an underlying three-stage model.

Still, this apparent triviality is deceptive. Particularly in the context of *understanding* the complex processes that underlie social change, it both arouses and deserves suspicion. As a result, there is a quite some literature on three-stage models of change. Grossly speaking, one part of this literature basically *accepts* the three-stage model and attempts to elaborate it by contextualizing its insights or by adding new features, such as sub-stages or socio-psychological insights into 'drivers' of change. Another part *rejects* these three-stage models, for instance, as too simplistic or as favouring top-down and management-driven interventions in organizations. Both parts of the literature are instructive and deserve attention. In Sections 7.3–7.5, we first discuss positive elaborations of the three-stage model in order to enrich our own social goals, then in Section 7.6, we pay attention to the more critical voices in order to further clarify the status and role of 'our' social goals.

7.3 Elaborating the motivation goal

Cummings et al. (2016, pp. 41ff) list a number of appropriations of Lewin's three-stage model in 'consultancy-oriented' literature. In particular, they mention texts by Schein and Bennis (1965), Kolb and Frohman (1970), Tichy and Devanna (1986), Kotter (1995), and Schein (1992). To this list, authors like Perlman and Takacs (1990), Armenakis and Bedeian (1999), and Young (2009) can be added, as they too develop or build upon stage models of organizational change that somehow – correctly or wrongly – refer back to Lewin. It should be mentioned that, according to Cummings et al. (2016, p. 43), such consultancy-oriented appropriations, and not Lewin's initial model, caused the celebrity of the three-stage model while providing the basis for the critique casting doubt on the scientific and practical grounds for this fame.

Be that as it may, some of the appropriations of the three-stage model in the consultancy-oriented literature, in our eyes, still provide insights that are helpful to elaborate 'our' social goals in a way that improves their functionality in the 3-D model. Two types of insights are relevant for our purposes, because some appropriations: (1) provide clues for the derivation of *social sub-goals* that contribute to the realization of the social goals in the intervention, and (2) point to socio-psychological 'mechanisms' or '*drivers*' that may help to realize social goals in intervention. In the rest of this section, we gather these insights in consultancy-oriented appropriations of the three-stage model and use them as an inspiration to elaborate the motivation goal. To this purpose, we turn our attention to what is said about the unfreeze phase in consultancy-oriented literature in order to elaborate our motivation goal. In the course of this elaboration, we discuss: (A) sub-goals within the motivation goal, (B) socio-psychological drivers of motivation, and (C) the relation between the motivation goal and goals on the functional dimension of the 3-D model. In Sections 7.4 and 7.5, the same procedure will be followed in order to elaborate the adoption and integration goals.

7.3.1 A: sub-goals of motivation – creating a sense of urgency and a shared vision

In literature on the three-stage model, some authors argue that, in the unfreeze phase, a felt *need* for change should be created (see, for instance, Lippitt et al., 1958; Kolb and

Frohman, 1970; Tichy and Devanna, 1986; Kotter, 1995; Young, 2009; Armenakis and Bedeain, 1999). In order to be prepared to let go of old interactions and interaction premises, organization members should both understand and feel that change is *urgent*. Note that this understanding and feeling initially may be only *negative* or *abstract* – negative as in, 'We *cannot* carry on like this,' or abstract as in, '*Things* should change over here.' Because negative or abstract feelings of urgency do not yet provide a motivating *positive direction* for change, some authors argue that early in the intervention, a *shared vision* should be created (see, for instance, Tichy and Devanna, 1986; Kotter, 1995). Although, at the initial stage of the intervention, this vision need not (and cannot) be fully developed and detailed, it should still provide a *substantive* and *value-laden* perspective on the future, a perspective that projects the change as both *desirable* and *feasible*. Finally, some authors argue that during the unfreeze phase, *change relationships* should be established. That is, relationships between organization members should be established that can help drive the change forward (see, for instance, Lippitt et al., 1958; Kotter, 1995).

Now, if these insights are applied to the motivation goal, 'experienced urgency' and 'shared vision' seem to fit pretty well. If organization members are to develop the impetus to let go of current and move to new behaviours, and if they are to adopt an intervention as a means to do this, they should indeed understand and feel the need for change (urgency) and develop a shared vision that provides the projected change with a sense of direction, feasibility, and desirability (vision). Included in this shared vision, there should be an awareness that the required change will not 'occur spontaneously' or 'happen anyway' as a result of current ongoing interaction. Organization members should understand that in order to bridge the gap between the current and the desired future situation, a concerted change effort – an episodic intervention – is needed.

Please note that 'sense of urgency' and 'shared vision' are *reciprocally* related. As indicated, the required sense of urgency may initially be more or less negative or abstract. However, it is never wholly so. In order to experience a situation as *undesirable*, there should be some awareness, however vague or inarticulate, of the possibility of things being otherwise and better. There should be notions of what is *desirable*. Of course, such notions may vary among different members of an organization. For instance, in a high parameter value structure, managers may desire to be 'in control' and workers may desire a higher quality of work. Nevertheless, if properly harnessed, ideas about what is desirable may contain relevant materials out of which a new vision of the future may be shaped. In this way, experienced urgency not only *motivates* the creation of a new vision of the future, it also contains *seeds* from which this vision may be created. Conversely, as a shared vision of the future starts to take shape, i.e. as a possible future is projected as more desirable than the current malaise, the experienced sense of urgency starts to lose its negative and abstract character and becomes more positive. The awareness that 'We cannot go on like this' (negative urgency) or that 'Things really have to change' (abstract urgency) is replaced by a felt need to move into the positive and less abstract direction projected by the developing new vision. Thus, the developing sense of urgency feeds the shaping of vision, and the shaping of vision feeds the developing sense of urgency.

'Creating change relationships' is the third element mentioned which, according to some authors, should be a part of the first phase of the intervention. Although we do agree that creating (and maintaining) this kind of relationships is important, we do not add it as a sub-goal of motivation. The reason for this is that we consider 'creating and maintaining change relationships' as a *condition* to realize *all* the goals on the social dimension. As such, creating change relationships is not restricted to the first – 'motivation' – goal. Change relationships should be created and maintained in order to realize the 'adoption' and 'integration' goal as well.

As a kind of 'generic' condition for the realization of goals on the social dimension, 'creating change relationships' can provide a heuristic for the design of the infrastructure of the intervention organization. For instance, in order to build a shared vision of the future (social sub-goal), change relationships should be created. In order to build the relationships needed to formulate this vision, an infrastructure may be constructed: i.e. workers and managers with particular knowledge and skills (human resources) are selected to perform particular tasks in the discussion about the new vision (intervention structure), and technology may be selected to support these discussions (intervention technology). In sum, although we consider 'creating relationships' an important enabling factor, we do not see it as a specific sub-goal of motivation. For the purpose of the 3-D model, we restrict these sub-goals to creating a *sense of urgency* and a *shared vision*. However, we do take up 'creating and maintaining change relationships' as a 'generic' social condition that should be realized in order to realize all three goals on the social dimension.

7.3.2 B: socio-psychological drivers of motivation

Some authors in consultancy-oriented literature also introduce socio-psychological insights in *drivers* that can affect the *action intentions* of organization members and in this way influence processes of unfreeze, change, and refreeze. Examples of such drivers of change are 'feelings of dissatisfaction with the current situation' (feelings related to 'motivation'), 'seeing that current organizational practices are problematic' (cognitions related to 'motivation'), or 'appreciating that work has become more interesting' (feelings related to 'integration').

One of the prominent authors in the consultancy-oriented literature who introduced socio-psychological 'mechanisms', as he calls them, that affect unfreeze, change, and refreeze processes is Edgar Schein (see, for instance, Schein, 1987, 1992). On reflection, the mechanisms mentioned by Schein can be distinguished into different types. The first distinction is that between:

1. *cognition-related* mechanisms – e.g. 'being aware of or knowing that product quality is below standards' or 'understanding why product quality is below standards';
2. *emotion-related* mechanisms – e.g. 'feeling exasperation about current product quality'.

The second distinction is that between mechanisms that are:

1. *individual-centred* – e.g. 'Marc is aware of low product quality';
2. *context-centred* – e.g. 'trusted persons in Marc's immediate organizational context (group) share Marc's awareness of low product quality'.

Based on these distinctions, a two-by-two matrix of types of socio-psychological mechanisms of organizational change (unfreeze, change, refreeze) can be derived (see Table 7.3 for this matrix and an example).

Please note that different values in the cells of Table 7.2 may indeed change the prospects of realizing, for instance, the social goal of 'motivating' Marc to let go of current interaction premises and interactions. For instance, suppose that Marc is:

TABLE 7.3 Examples of types of drivers of organizational change

Drivers	Cognition-related (knowing that/ understanding why)	Emotion-related
Individual-centred	Marc is aware of low product quality	Marc feels exasperated about low product quality
Context-centred	Trusted persons in Marc's team share Marc's awareness of low product quality	Trusted persons in Marc's team share Marc's feelings of dissatisfaction with the low product quality

- not aware of low product quality, or . . .
- that he is aware of low product quality, but quite content with it, or . . .
- that no one in his team agrees with Marc that product quality is low, or . . .
- that distrusted persons in his team share Marc's feeling that product quality is a problem.

In each of these cases, Marc's motivation to actually do something about low product quality may be differently affected.

We consider the distinction between cognition- and emotion-related mechanisms relevant because it is a reminder that the goals on the social dimension, as a rule, cannot be realized by cognition-related drivers alone. As smoking addicts know, information about the harmful effects of smoking does not necessarily remedy the addiction. More in general, and in less extreme cases, it can be argued that, as a rule, behavioural change requires more than 'knowing that' or 'understanding why'. Often (quite strong) emotions are required in order to kick old habits. It seems no coincidence that in Aristotle's treatise on the art of persuasion, both rational argumentation and touching the audience's emotions play a central role. Thus, in order to realize the goals on the social dimension, it is relevant to take into account both cognition- and emotion-related drivers of behaviour (or the intentions to act that that accompany behaviour).

Moreover, within the category of cognition-related drivers, the distinction between 'knowing that' and 'understanding why' is relevant to our purposes. In the context of episodic interventions in organizational structures, experiencing *that* 'things go wrong' does not necessarily imply understanding *why* this is so. Organization members may have all kinds of first-hand experiences – cognitions and emotions – of organizational problems. However, this does not guarantee that they can correctly identify the infrastructural causes of these problems. To this purpose, they need concepts, hypotheses, or theories that, however provisional, help to causally link the organization's performance to its infrastructure. Such concepts, hypotheses, and theories can, in principle, be developed as a part of ongoing organizational practices and learning. However, they also may result from scientific research that is 'imported' into the organization.

Finally, the distinction between individual-centred and context-centred drivers is relevant because it underlines the impact of group behaviour on individual behaviour (see, for instance, Burnes, 2004, p. 981; Coghlan and Jacobs, 2005, p. 450). Even in their paper that is quite critical of consultancy-oriented approaches to the three-stage model, Cummings et al. (2016, pp. 51–52) point to the importance of groups. According to them, it is not individuals and their behaviour, but the group that should be the key unit of analysis, "understanding the force field made up of elements promoting change and elements promoting constancy is key; as is the idea that managing change is more effective if one communicates with and involves the group rather than individuals" (p. 51). According to all these authors, realizing goals on the social dimension primarily means influencing the relation between the dynamics in groups and the behaviours of individuals within these groups.

In sum, in order to realize the social goals – motivation, adoption, and integration – it is relevant to take into account both cognition- and emotion-related drivers, to pay attention to the distinction between 'knowing that' and 'understanding why', and to be sensitive to the impact of group perceptions and behaviour on individual perceptions and behaviour. Taking these points on board is relevant because they can affect the design of the infrastructure of the intervention organization.

After these introductory remarks, we can turn to the drivers that Schein considers important in the *unfreeze* stage of change. Both in his early book on process consultation (Schein, 1987) and in his later work on organizational culture and leadership (Schein, 1992), Schein mentions the following three drivers:

> (1) enough *disconfirming data* to cause serious discomfort and disequilibrium; (2) the connection of the disconfirming data to important goals and ideals causing *anxiety* and *guilt*; and (3) enough *psychological safety*, in a sense of seeing a possibility of solving the problem without loss of identity or integrity.
>
> *(pp. 298–299)*

He discusses these drivers as a part of a process of getting motivated to unlearn old attitudes, perceptions, and behaviours and to learn new ones.

The first driver, *disconfirming data*, is cognition-related (although it may have emotion-related effects). Disconfirming data consist of personal experiences or information from others that 'things are not going well' (negative) or 'could be better' (positive). Examples of disconfirming data in organizations with high parameter value structures are management reports indicating that production or sales targets are not met, customers showing their dissatisfaction with service quality, continuous interruptions of production processes due to planning-problems, high stress-related personnel turnover, or team managers complaining about low personnel involvement. The point of getting '*enough* disconfirming data' is that a state of 'disconfirmation' or 'lack of confirmation' is achieved (Schein, 1987, p. 73). *Disconfirmation* is the actual insight that current behaviour – current interaction premises and interaction patterns – is problematic and should be changed. In our goal-oriented logic, we accept 'disconfirmation' as a state that should be realized in order to achieve the 'motivation' goal. In our view, disconfirmation can and should be both individual-centred ('Marc is disconfirmed') and context-centred (relevant persons in Marc's immediate organizational environment share their disconfirmation with Marc).

According to Schein, disconfirming data and disconfirmation are a necessary but insufficient condition to achieve 'unfreeze'. Disconfirming data may be ignored, denied, or explained away, and disconfirmation does not necessarily trigger action to improve things. For this reason, disconfirming data and disconfirmation should be supplemented by emotions of *anxiety* and *guilt*.

Schein (1987) relates *anxiety* to the emotionally upsetting awareness that, if nothing happens, really important personal *goals* will not be realized now or in the future. For instance, in an organization, a sales person may feel anxious as dramatic decreases in sales may threaten her job security. In later texts, Schein (1992) connects anxiety not only to goals, but more generally to basic assumptions. A feeling of anxiety may be triggered if we become aware that basic, taken-for-granted generative and evaluative assumptions do not seem to work any more. *Guilt*, according to Schein (1987) is related not to goals, but to personal *ideals*. For instance, both the current scope of a nurse's job and the protocols that she is obliged to follow may shatter her ideal of a professionally meaningful job. It is important to underline that in the context of organizational interventions, anxiety and guilt contribute to the social goal 'motivation' by *emotionally* and *personally* – and in this sense, *existentially* – involving organization members in a situation that is not only personally, but also organizationally unwanted. Anxiety and guilt become drivers for organizational change as someone becomes *personally* involved in changing a situation that is *organizationally* unwanted. Because of this personal involvement, this person is more likely to actually pay attention to disconfirming data, instead of ignoring or denying them, or explaining them away.

We accept anxiety as an emotional state that may help to realize 'motivation' in the case of episodic interventions in organizational structures. Guilt, however, is a more complex emotion. According to Schein, the difference between anxiety and guilt is that the former relates to goals and the latter to ideals. We, however, think that there is another difference between anxiety and guilt that is relevant in the context of episodic interventions in organizational structures. Anxiety may be felt about something that is beyond one's capacity and responsibility for control. For instance, on a walk in the open and miles from shelter, one may feel anxious about being struck by the lightning of an approaching storm. Guilt, however, presupposes the capacity and responsibility for control. One may feel guilty about doing (or tolerating) something one could and should have done otherwise. For instance, one may feel guilty about not checking the weather forecast before venturing on a long walk in the open.

If this difference between anxiety and guilt is taken seriously and applied to episodic interventions in organizational structures, it can be argued that workers – as distinct from managers – in high value parameter structures can feel anxious about the organization's performance and structure, but that feelings of guilt seem to be less fitting because, in high parameter value structures, workers neither have the regulatory capacity nor the formal responsibility to intervene in the structure they work in. This structure is designed *for* and not by them. To them, both the structure and the related organizational performance are like the lightning storm that is going to hit the lonely wanderer: a phenomenon beyond one's control that may cause anxiety, but is not a reason for feeling guilt. Therefore, in the case of interventions in high parameter value structures, guilt as a motivating feeling is reserved for those managers who can intervene in and are responsible for the organization's structure and performance (a responsibility that is easily disowned once things go wrong).

Schein mentions a third feeling that is important in the unfreeze phase: *psychological safety*. As argued earlier, feelings of anxiety and guilt may induce organization members to pay attention to disconfirming information. However, 'paying attention' is not the same as 'acceptance', and that is where psychological safety comes in. Psychological safety is needed to decrease the probability of the *non-acceptance* of disconfirming information: "The person receiving the disconfirming information can *accept* it only if it does not involve personal humiliation and loss of face or self-esteem" (Schein, 1987, p. 97). Psychological safety is exactly this: not feeling personally humiliated or not losing face or self-esteem in the face of disconfirming information, anxiety, or guilt. Positively formulated, it is an underlying feeling of *self-worth as a person* in spite of information and feelings indicating that one's current behaviour is unwanted in the light of goals and ideals that are considered important. It is the realization that although one's current *behaviour* is not helpful, this does not mean that one is worthless as a *person*. According to Schein, the absence of psychological safety may turn disconfirming information, anxiety, and guilt into a *personal threat* – a feeling so overpowering that organization members, "will find defense mechanisms that distort or in other ways undo the disconfirming information" (Schein, 1987, p. 98). Facilitators of interventions therefore need to ensure that disconfirming information and feelings of anxiety, or guilt do not end up in a loss of psychological safety in the organization members involved in the intervention (for instance, by reassurance that things will work out or that the problems encountered are not abnormal). We accept psychological safety as a driver contributing to the goal 'motivation' on the social dimension.

A review of Schein's 'mechanisms' reveals that they are formulated in negative terms and primarily contribute to disconfirmation. Disconfirming data, anxiety, guilt, and psychological safety as a safeguard against non-acceptance of disconfirming data all help to present the current situation as unsustainable and motivate organization members to let go of current interaction premises and related behaviours. But what about the more positive motivation to move to new premises and interaction patterns and adopt an intervention as a means to do this? This type of motivation seems to presuppose cognition- and emotion-related drivers that differ from those presented by Schein.

As a starting point, we think that 'confirmation' is presupposed. Confirmation refers to the insight that there is a future – however sketchy – that is worthwhile and can actually be achieved. This prospect of a desirable future situation is the mirror image of the awareness of the undesirability of the present situation that is at the core of disconfirmation. Confirmation should be accompanied by a feeling of 'desire' for that future. Please note that the cognition-related driver 'confirmation' and the emotion-related driver 'desire' work in two directions. First, they can support disconfirmation by providing a desirable alternative to the undesirable present situation, thereby making the acceptance of disconfirming data concerning that situation less threatening. As such, confirmation and desire may contribute to the motivation to 'let go' of old interaction premises and interaction patterns. Second, confirmation and desire result from and reinforce the creation of a shared vision. This vision can motivate organization members to move to new interaction premises and related interactions and find a way (the intervention) to do this. Because of their contribution to the realization of the motivation goal, we add confirmation and desire to our set of drivers.

The mechanisms mentioned by Schein are all individual-centred. However, this does not mean that, in the case of organizational interventions, the social context of these individuals is irrelevant. On the contrary, drivers like disconfirmation, anxiety, guilt, psychological safety, confirmation, and desire may be amplified or attenuated dependent on dynamics in the groups these individuals participate in. For instance, in a group, some organization members may be disconfirmed while others are still confident that the current ways of working are satisfactory. Dependent on how these 'forces' for or against disconfirmation interact, disconfirmation may 'spread' in the group or be contained to a few members. In general, it can be argued that group dynamics – and group interventions – can influence the development of motivating drivers like disconfirmation in individual organization members.

7.3.3 C: motivation and goals on the functional dimension – diagnosis and design

If 'motivation' and its two social sub-goals 'sense of urgency' and 'shared vision' are compared and related to goals on the functional dimension of the 3-D model, it can be argued that there is an 'affinity' between them and the functional goals *diagnosis* and *design*.

As explained earlier, *diagnosis* consists of making a problem inventory, analysing causes, and constructing a solution space.

Given these three sub-goals, diagnosis can, to begin with, be related to the creation of a *sense of urgency*. Applied to the special case of episodic interventions in organizational structures, the problem inventory consists of relating functional requirements to the actual performance of the organization. Actually seeing the gap between these functional requirements and actual performance can contribute to understanding that change is urgent. The same can be said about the cause analysis. Actually seeing the gap between desired and the actual values of the structural parameters can contribute to understanding that structural change is really needed. Both the problem inventory and the cause analysis provide the opportunity to present organization members with disconfirming data. However, diagnosis can also be related to the creation of a *shared vision*. As a part of the problem inventory, a process of strategic orientation eventually leads to the formulation of functional requirements that, in the diagnosis, are used as a norm to assess the actual performance of the organization. However, viewed from the perspective of the social dimension, both the process of strategic orientation and the resulting functional requirements contribute to developing a shared vision that may motivate organization members to change.

Design is about inventing an organizational structure that supports the realization of the functional requirements. As such, design can contribute to further developing the shared vision. In the design process, both the functional requirements and the future structure of the organization are elaborated, making the shared vision more concrete.

It is relevant to emphasize that dependent on the design of the infrastructure of the intervention organization, affinities between the motivation goal on the social dimension and the diagnosis and design goals on the functional dimension may actually become productive for an intervention. For instance, 'sense of urgency' (social sub-goal) may be amplified by means of involving organization members in the diagnosis of their own work (i.e. organization members take on a 'diagnostic' role in the intervention organization). Involved as they are in the diagnostic process, organization members are given the opportunity to find out for themselves 'that' and 'why' current ways of working are not helpful, which is a kind of 'self-disconfirmation' that can effectively drive their sense of urgency. Another example is the development of 'shared vision' (social sub-goal). By giving organization members a 'design' role in the intervention organization, they get the opportunity to develop a vision of their own future work. In short, by means of the design of the intervention organization, affinities between motivation (social goal) and diagnosis and design (functional goals) can be exploited for the purpose of the intervention. Table 7.4 summarizes our elaboration of the motivation goal.

7.4 Elaborating the adoption goal

Adoption is the 'mediate' goal between motivation and integration. Because the adoption goal is closest to the change phase in three-stage models, we use this phase as a starting point

222 Designing interventions

TABLE 7.4 Overview of motivation

Motivation

Organization members should develop the motivation to:

- let go of current and move to new interaction premises and concomitant interaction patterns
- adopt an episodic intervention as a means to do this

A

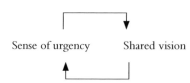

	Creating and maintaining change relationships		
B	**Drivers**	**Cognition-related**	**Emotion-related**
	Individual-centred	Disconfirmation of current interaction/premises	Anxiety
		Confirmation of a worthwhile and achievable future	Guilt (only managers in high parameter value structures)
			Psychological safety
			Desire
	Context-centred	Influence of group dynamics on cognition- and emotion-related drivers	
C	Diagnosis – Design		

Note: A = sub-goals; B = drivers; C = relation to functional goals.

for our elaboration of the adoption goal. Once again, we will elaborate the adoption goal by means of: (A) specifying social sub-goals, (B) discussing socio-psychological drivers of adoption, and (C) establishing the relation between functional and social goals.

7.4.1 A: sub-goals – inventing and testing

According authors who appropriate the three-stage model, the change phase should be seen as a *learning* (and *unlearning*) process in which organization members actually search for and adopt new, helping, interaction premises and interactions and shed old ones (see, for instance, Schein and Bennis, 1965; Schein, 1987; Young, 2009; Schein, 1992; Weick and Quinn, 1999).

'Learning', as seen by these authors, is a process of 'sense-giving and making', of 'exploration', of 'cognitive and behavioural restructuring', of 'searching for and testing new conceptual and behavioural frames' – in our terms, of experimentation in practice.

The goal of this learning process is to find and adopt new, 'helping', 'improved' ways of seeing, interpreting, and interacting that restore functionality and meaning to organizational life. The word 'adopt' here is a sloppy way to say that: (1) organization members *willingly commit* to new helping interaction premises as desirable points of orientation for improved (future) interaction, and (2) this willing commitment is based on a *justifiable confidence* in the efficacy of both these interaction premises and the concepts, theories, and values that support them.

For the purpose of our social goals logic, we agree with this learning perspective. However, it is relevant to add that in the case of episodic interventions in organizational structures and with respect to the social goal 'adoption', learning is not just about experimenting with 'whatever' new, improved perceptions and interactions. In the case of episodic interventions in organizational structures, learning should expressly be concerned with the relation between organizational structure and performance. Organization members who, as a result of 'motivation' and 'diagnosis', have become sensitive to the corrosive effects of high parameter value structures should search for and test new ways of working – new structures – in order to improve the organization's quality of organization, work, and working relations. Only if learning specifically addresses this type of structure-related topics can motivated organization members adopt new helping interaction premises and interactions that are both related to the organization's structure and allow for the realization of the goal of the intervention – which, in the case of episodic interventions in organizational structures, is the core of the 'adoption' goal.

In line with the learning perspective in the change phase, we regard realizing the adoption goal as a process of experimentation in practice. In this process, two sub-goals can be distinguished: *inventing* and *testing*. Applied to episodic interventions in organizational structures, 'inventing' refers to the search for and creation of new interaction premises and interaction patterns that improve the organization's structure relative to the goal of the intervention. 'Testing' refers to all kinds of procedures that may be used in order to assess the efficacy of new interaction premises and interactions that result from inventing.

Initially, *inventing* is propelled by the sense of urgency and the shared vision that compose the motivation goal – that is, 'motivation' functions as a springboard for 'adoption'. In combination, urgency and vision *motivate* the search. Vision *directs* it. Based on the vision, organization members search for concepts, models, theories, or practices that can help to further specify the vision into a more well-defined goal of the intervention. Moreover, using these concepts, models, theories, or practices, organization members invent structural configurations that can realize both this goal and the vision that inspires it. In this way, there is a reciprocal relation between vision and inventing: vision initially directs inventing, and inventing feeds back into vision, reshaping or refining it.

It should be emphasized that 'invention' as the first sub-goal within 'adoption' is not just about searching for helping concepts, models, theories, or practices. Most importantly, it is about *translating* and tentatively *fitting* them to the organizational structure that is the object of the intervention. This means that invention has a *creative* moment. For instance, based on a *general* theory about the relation between organizational structures and performance (a theory like the one presented in Chapter 3), organization members, create *particular* structural configurations that both fit and can be applied to *their* particular processes and problems. This creative moment of invention cannot be avoided. Even if a practice that exists elsewhere – for instance, in another part of the organization or in another organization – is 'copied', the copying involves the translation and fitting of this practice to the structure of the part of the organization that is the object of the intervention.

It might be objected that this description of 'invention' is still quite similar to what has been called 'design' in the previous chapter on the functional dimension. So what is it that makes 'invention' a *social* goal, and not just another description of the functional sub-goal 'design'?

In order to see what is specifically social about 'invention', it is useful to go back to what we mean by 'adoption': organization members 'embracing' – i.e., based on justifiable confidence, willingly committing to – new helping interaction premises as helpful points of orientation for future interaction.

As a sub-goal of 'adoption', 'inventing' should contribute to the emergence of this 'willing commitment' that is based on a 'justifiable confidence'.

This means that by means of inventing, organization members should become *convinced* of the usefulness of these constructs. They should develop *justifiable confidence* in them. This justifiable confidence has both a rational and an emotional dimension. The rational dimension refers to *reasons* that organization members can offer for seeing or accepting particular solutions as useful. The emotional dimension refers to the *faith* they have in these solutions (a faith that may be partly or wholly grounded in the reasons they can offer). 'Inventing', now, means not just 'designing'. As a social sub-goal of adoption, 'inventing' means that organization members develop justifiable confidence in the helpfulness of the solutions they invent, and for this reason adopt them as desirable premises of future interactions.

It should be clear by now that 'inventing', as described here, is quite different from 'coercion'. By coercion, we mean that particular solutions are forced upon organization members from the 'outside', as it were, without giving them the opportunity to convince themselves of their applicability and usefulness. Inventing, on the contrary, is a process in which the organization members who do the inventing *convince themselves* of the applicability and usefulness of particular models and solutions. Of course, inventing does not foreclose that 'outsiders' like consultants, managers, or scientists suggest or even teach organization members possibly helpful models, theories, or practices. What matters is that, in the end, the organization members to whom these suggestions are directed get the opportunity to invent solutions based on these suggestions and be the judge of their applicability and usefulness. Convincing, in the end, is convincing oneself.

In order to be actually adopted, suggestions for new interaction premises and interactions that result from the inventing process should be tested. *Testing* is the second sub-goal within 'adoption'. In organizational contexts, different modes of testing can be used, such as appointing a devil's advocate, systematically debating the pros and cons of a possible course of action, making simulations of solutions in order to get an idea of their effects, examining the effects of comparable solutions in other organizations, or implementing a possible solution in a small part of the organization. As the mode and organization of testing get nearer to the actual work of the organization members who do the testing, more opportunities are created to actually experience and reflect on the tested solution and its effects. Therefore, dependent on the mode and organization of the testing – i.e. dependent on the design of the intervention organization – testing can be a more or less relevant part of the process in which organization members convince themselves of the efficacy of a particular solution.

Inventing and testing are reciprocally related. Positive or negative results from testing can redirect or refine the inventing process, and results from a redirected or refined inventing process provide further input for testing. Because of this reciprocal relation, realizing the adoption goal, as a rule, will imply multiple cycles of inventing and testing. In these cycles, organization members reflect on and refine proposals for new interaction premises, gradually convincing themselves of the usefulness and applicability of the proposals that 'survive' in these cycles.

7.4.2 B: socio-psychological drivers of adoption

In consultancy-oriented literature, different drivers are mentioned that can help propel the second phase of the intervention: the change phase (see, for instance, Schein, 1987, 1992; Kotter, 1995; Young, 2009). These drivers may also apply in the case of our adoption goal.

To begin with, Schein (1987) mentions two drivers of 'change': *scanning* and *identification with a role model*. Both of these drivers presuppose that organization members are unfrozen:

"The effect of unfreezing is to open up the client to new sources of information and new concepts that permit him to look at his situation in new ways, to 'cognitively restructure' it" (p. 105).

Given the results of the unfreeze phase, the change phase, according to Schein, is about learning to see one's situation in a new and helping way, i.e. about *cognitively restructuring* one's situation. Seeing one's situation in a new and helping way presupposes a search for alternative concepts, models, theories, or practices that may shed a fresh and helping light on the situation in which one finds oneself. For instance, someone who has become quite alienated from the organization may learn to see his or her situation as 'open' to new possibilities instead of as 'wretched', 'closed', and 'unchangeable'. Schein calls this cognition-related process of searching for alternative concepts, models, theories, or practices that can help to cognitively restructure one's situation *scanning*.

In our social goals logic, 'scanning' can be a driver that helps to realize adoption. However, applied to episodic interventions in organizational structures, scanning is a somewhat more complicated phenomenon. It refers to: (1) searching for structure-related concepts, models, theories, and applications that can help to improve one's situation, and (2) applying and fitting these structure-related concepts to this situation by creating alternative 'helping' structural configurations. Therefore, in addition to Schein's focus on searching, in our interpretation, 'scanning' also includes the creative moment of 'invention'. Moreover, in addition to Schein's focus on scanning as a predominantly individual process, we would like to emphasize that there is a group component to scanning as well. In the context of organizational interventions, organization members may, together, scan for alternative concepts, models, theories, or applications. Scanning as a social activity can be a benefit, allowing for a more varied search and more rigorous invention. However, as a social activity, scanning, also can lead to tunnel-vision and group think. For this reason, scanning should always be connected to testing.

As indicated, scanning is a cognition-related driver. Schein, however, also mentions a more emotion-related driver in the change phase. He calls this driver: *identification with a role model*. In the context of change, a role model is someone who is considered as 'experienced' or 'wise' and either *introduces* organization members to new values, norms, concepts, models, or theories or *helps* organization members to search for them. A role model is a person whose judgement counts, and, because of that, can convince others to see the world from his or her perspective. Role models may be important because, even if organization members are motivated to search (scan) for new interaction premises, the actual adoption of such premises may be quite a leap of faith. Somehow, organization members need to be able to *trust* the concepts, models, theories, and in the end, interaction premises they adopt. Of course, in an optimal situation, this trust is based on their own experience or knowledge. However, in the case of cognitive restructuring, organization members may lack this experience or knowledge. They typically search for concepts that are *new* (i.e. as yet unknown) to them, and may not find the time to make their own inventions or do their own testing. Therefore, in the absence of first-hand experience and knowledge, organization members can base their trust on the words of someone who they positively identify with as a role model. As will be argued in the next chapter on the infrastructural dimension, this process of identification requires particular skills, knowledge, and a particular ethos on the part of an aspiring role model.

Schein warns that identification with a role model may be a limiting way of learning, focusing "the learner too much on a single source of information" (1987, p. 106). As a remedy, he advises that role models should minimize their own role, point to other possible role models, and emphasize that the view of a role model is just one of many possible views. What really counts is the actual fit between values, norms, concepts, models, or theories suggested by a role model and the situation as experienced by the client. In the end, this fit is to be decided by the client alone.

Schein also compares 'scanning' to 'identification with a role model'. In this context, he remarks that although scanning "may be slower and more difficult than identification, it is more likely to produce an outcome that fits the client's unique situation in that only information that is relevant will be taken in by the client" (1987, p. 106).

We take up 'identification with a role model' as a driver in our social goals logic. However, once again, we would like to point to the importance of groups in the identification process. We admit that identifying with a role model is something individuals do. However, in the context of organizational interventions, 'identification', as a rule, will be a process evolving within a particular group. For instance, some organization members in a group may be taken with a particular consultant, while others in the same group may have grave doubts. Therefore, dependent on the dynamics of the different forces in a group, the identification process can be accelerated, slowed down, come to a halt, or even deteriorate into its opposite of 'dissociation'. As identification processes, in the context of organizational interventions, evolve in groups, it is not improbable that one group's role model, e.g. a role model embraced by the organization's top managers, is another group's nightmare (e.g. a group of workers).

The drivers mentioned by Schein only refer to the sub-goal 'inventing' (and within that sub-goal, they concentrate on 'searching' for new concepts, models, or theories that can support cognitive restructuring). 'Testing' as the other sub-goal of adoption is not explicitly mentioned by Schein. Here, a suggestion made by Kotter (1995) and Young (2009) may be useful. These authors point at the relevance of *quick wins* in the course of the change phase of a three-stage model. A 'quick win' is a solution that is seen to work within a short period of time and can be celebrated as a success by organization members involved in the intervention. It is important that quick wins not only bring organizational benefits. They must be experienced as beneficial at the level of individual members of the organization as well. In the context of testing, quick wins can both cognitively and emotionally drive the adoption of new interaction premises and interaction patterns. At the cognitive level, quick wins bring experience and knowledge about the efficacy of a solution. At the emotional level, quick wins may reduce uncertainty and fear or even introduce trust and hope with respect to the chances of success of the organizational intervention. Although we subscribe to the idea of quick wins, there is one proviso. Quick wins may also blind or distort invention and testing, for instance by focusing solely on short-term financial gains. For this reason, quick wins should always be related to both the object and the goal of the intervention. In the context of episodic interventions in organizational structures, this means that these quick wins should pertain to the relation between changes in the structural configuration of the organization and the quality of organization, work, and working relations.

7.4.3 C: adoption and goals on the functional dimension – design and implementation

'Adoption' as a social goal in the intervention means that organization members accept new interaction premises and interactions in their repertoires that are both related to the object of the intervention and help to realize the intervention's goal. Its two sub-goals, 'inventing' and 'testing', are relevant moments of adoption because, by means of inventing and testing, organization members are given the opportunity to persuade themselves of the efficacy of new interaction premises and interactions relative to the object and goal of the intervention.

Just as in the case of 'motivation', there is an affinity between the social goal 'adoption' and goals on the functional dimension of the intervention. In the case of adoption, the relevant functional goals are *design* and *implementation*.

Design fits particularly well with inventing as a social sub-goal of adoption. As argued, 'inventing' means searching for new concepts, models, theories, and practices and creatively applying (fitting) them to actual work contexts in order to find 'helping' new interaction premises and interactions. In the case of episodic interventions in organizational structures, 'design' is about finding and selecting structural configurations that can help realize the goal of the intervention. As such, 'design' can support 'inventing' by focusing the search (scanning) for helping concepts, models, etc. on the 'object' and 'goal' of the intervention. In this context, models that relate structure to organizational performance may be assessed as more relevant than, for instance, theories about organizational culture.

Implementation has an affinity with testing as a sub-goal of adoption. By means of implementation, organization members can test (parts of) the solutions they have invented. Dependent on the test results (quick wins/losses), organization members may be driven to adopt or not adopt the tested solution.

Here, too, it is important to underline that the design of the infrastructure of the intervention organization is crucial for exploiting the affinities between the social goal of adoption and the functional goals of design and implementation. For instance, dependent on their 'implementation' role in the infrastructure of the intervention organization, organization members may be given the opportunity to experience for themselves the quick wins related to the adoption of particular interaction premises and related interactions. The cumulative elaborations of the motivation and the adoption goal are summarized in Table 7.5.

7.5 Elaborating the integration goal

Freeze is the final phase of the three-stage model ('refreeze' in Schein's terms). Because the term 'freeze' may lead to the misconception that organizational change somehow stops, we use the term 'integration' to refer to the final goal of our social goals logic. 'Integration' means that members of the organization irreversibly integrate new interaction premises and interactions into their repertoires that allow for both the (re)production of the organization's improved structure and the realization of the goal of the intervention.

It should be underlined that 'integration' does not just mean that organization members 'insert' new structure-related interaction premises into their (old) repertoires and interact accordingly. 'Inserting' new interaction premises and interactions, although it is a part of integration, is a too mechanical term for what actually happens as the social goal of integration is in the process of being realized. For this reason, another connotation of the word 'integration' should also be taken into account.

Integration also connotes *synthesis*. Taken as synthesis, 'integration' means that, once the social goal of integration has been realized, organization members have actively shaped their new tasks and found out what it actually means to adequately perform them in the improved structure. In interaction, they have bestowed their new tasks with both organizational and

TABLE 7.5 Cumulative overview of motivation and adoption

Motivation	Adoption
Organization members should develop the motivation to: – let go of current and move to new interaction premises and concomitant interaction patterns – adopt an episodic intervention as a means to do this	Organization members, based on justifiable confidence, 'adopt' (willingly commit to) new helping interaction premises and interactions that can (re)produce an improved organizational structure and allow for the realization of the goal of the intervention

A

    Sense of urgency ⇄ Shared vision   Inventing ⇄ Testing

Creating and maintaining change relationships

B	Drivers	Cognition-related	Emotion-related	Cognition-related	Emotion-related
	Individual-centred	Disconfirmation current interactions/premises Confirmation of a worthwhile and achievable future	Anxiety Guilt (only managers) Psychological safety Desire	Scanning (+ inventing) Quick object- and goal-related, wins (testing)	Identification with role model Quick object- and goal-related, wins (testing)
	Context-centred	Influence of group dynamics on cognition- and emotion-related drivers		Influence of group dynamics on cognition- and emotion-related drivers	
C	Diagnosis and Design			Design and Implementation	

Note: A = sub-goals; B = drivers; C = relation to functional goals.

personal content, style, meaning, and value. By working together, they have developed new practices that (re)produce the organization's improved structure. They have actively synthesized – put together, crafted, assembled – their new tasks into functional and meaningful wholes within the larger context of the organization's structure. By 'doing' their new jobs, organization members have found out how to interact in the new improved structure; they have found out how to operate their task-related technology and how to work together with clients, colleagues, and bosses.

If the social goal of integration is realized, organization members also experience how the new organizational structure helps them to adequately perform their job – experiences that can contribute to the reinforcement of the interaction premises underpinning the (re)production of that structure. However, organization members also inevitably experience the difficulties of their new jobs and possible shortcomings of the improved structure. Dealing with these difficulties and shortcomings is an important part of integration too. If the goal of integration is realized, organization members have regained the task-autonomy that allows them to both accommodate to these difficulties and adjust shortcomings in the organization's structure by means of the continuous interventions that, once again, are enabled by the improved low parameter value structure of the organization.

In this whole complex of integration as inserting/synthesizing the interaction premises and interactions that irreversibly (re)produce the improved structure of the organization, two sub-goals play an important part: *exercising* the job and *reinforcing/adjusting* its underlying interaction premises and interactions.

7.5.1 A: sub-goals of integration – exercising and reinforcing/adjusting

In consultancy-oriented literature on the three-stage model, the 'refreeze' stage is described by authors such as Perlman and Takacs (1990), Kotter (1995), Armenakis and Bedeian (1999), and Young (2009) as, respectively, 're-emergence', 'consolidating improvements and institutionalizing new approaches', 'institutionalization, measurement, reinforcement, and refinement', and as the 'new normal'. Taken together, these descriptions point to two elements of the refreeze stage: (1) the institutionalization of the new work regime as the 'new normal' and (2) the further refinement and reinforcement of this new work regime. In our social goals logic, we translate these two elements into the two sub-goals of integration: 'exercising' and 'reinforcing/adjusting'.

The first sub-goal is *exercising*. The word 'exercising' is used here in its dual meanings: both as *doing* and as *training*. Taken in its fullest sense, 'exercising' refers to the peculiar relation between doing and training that is also relevant in cases of skill acquisition: exercising as *learning by doing*.

Now, if we zoom in on the 'doing' part, then exercising means that organization members actually (start to) use the new (tested) structure-related interaction premises as points of orientation for the production of interactions. They start to perform the tasks they have in the new structure. Inseparably related to this doing is training. As soon as organization members start to 'do' their new jobs, they also start to learn in practice what 'doing' these jobs actually means. As indicated previously, they start to acquire experience and knowledge about how to interact with clients, colleagues, managers, etc. in their new jobs. In this way, they start to flesh out and synthesize the meaning of their new job. By means of 'doing', organization members 'train' themselves, and as a result of training, they:

- learn more about performing their task (What does the task really entail, what is easy about it, what is difficult, what problems are related to it, and how can one cope with these problems?);
- acquire task-related knowledge and develop task-related skills;
- reflexively adjust their task-related interactions to the interactions of parties they work with.

If exercising (doing and training) is successful, organization members both insert the new interactions and interaction premises into and develop their repertoires. As a result, a new pattern of related interactions emerges that both (re)produces the organization's improved structure and realizes the goal of the intervention: the final social goal of integration has been realized.

Training is not only included in doing, it can also either precede or follow doing. This type of training – which is also part of the exercising sub-goal – either prepares organization members to perform their new tasks (training preceding doing) or further qualifies them if their task performance – 'doing' – is not up to standards (training following on doing). Of course, there are all kinds of training methods that can precede or follow the actual doing. Some of them may be quite 'remote' and cognition-related. Others may approach the actual new jobs as closely as possible, for instance training by means of simulation. Two of these latter 'methods' are worth mentioning here.

The first is related to the design of the intervention infrastructure and is explicitly coupled to the type of interventions discussed in this book: episodic interventions that transform high parameter value structures into low parameter value structures. In their 'old' high parameter value structures, organization members, as a rule, have small tasks and few regulatory responsibilities. In their 'new' low parameter value structures, these same members have relatively broad tasks and an array of task-related regulatory responsibilities. Given the gap between their old and new tasks, it is not improbable that organization members need to accustom themselves to these new tasks, for instance because they have 'unlearned' to take responsibility for their own work in the old structure. In order to help organization members to accustom themselves to the requirements of the new low parameter value structure, it may be wise to design their tasks in the intervention infrastructure in such a way these tasks *prefigure* the type of tasks they will take on in the new improved structure of the organization. This means that, in the intervention infrastructure, organization members get relatively broad tasks that honestly involve them in the intervention, making them owners of their part of the intervention. In this way, even before the new low parameter value structure has started to take shape (for instance, during the diagnostic activity), organization members can develop attitudes and skills – like taking initiative, working together, or conferring effectively with others – that they may have 'unlearned' in the old high parameter value structure: attitudes and skills that are indispensable in the new low parameter value structure.

The second 'method' that, in a more or less realistic way, prepares organization members for their new jobs builds upon the relation that can exist between 'testing' as a sub-goal of 'adoption' and 'exercising' as a sub-goal of 'integration'. As mentioned in Section 7.4 about adoption, testing can be done in different ways. One way is to actually experiment with the possible design of a new job or part of the new structure. As a result of this kind of testing, organization members can not only convince themselves of the usefulness of the design (building justifiable confidence in that job or structure), they can also exercise ('do' and 'train' with) the new job or structure. In this way, they can introduce themselves to the requirements set by the new job in terms of knowledge, skills, and practices. As it appears, 'testing' can prefigure the actual 'exercising' of the new job. In this way, testing and exercising can be related. In fact, this relation can also be reversed. Exercising can also be a kind of testing. By actually exercising their new jobs as part of realizing the integration goal, organization members also test themselves, their new job in the network of jobs, and the new network as a whole. If the social goal 'integration' is successfully realized, this exercise-based testing adds to the justifiable confidence of organization members in the new organization structure.

Reinforcing/adjusting the new repertoire of interaction premises and interactions is the second sub-goal of 'integration'. In practice, it is impossible to separate this second sub-goal from the first. Exercising the new task unavoidably means reinforcing or adjusting task-related interaction premises and interactions. By means of the reinforcement of new interaction premises and interactions, more or less stable, practices develop in the organization: the new and improved low parameter value structure is irreversibly reproduced as organization members perform their jobs. However, as a part of 'synthesizing' their new jobs in cooperation with others, organization members also adjust interaction premises and interactions. Adjustment as a sub-goal of 'integration' should be distinguished from the 'organic' adaptations by means of continuous interventions that are re-instituted once the new improved structure is successfully integrated in the organization. Adjustment refers to 'synthesizing' the new job in coordination with other organization members, thereby making the new structure into an organizational reality. Organic adaptation by means of continuous interventions presupposes that this new structure is in place. It presupposes the irreversible integration of the new structure in the interaction premises and interactions of organization members.

7.5.2 B: socio-psychological drivers of integration

In his elaboration of the three-stage model, Schein mentions two socio-psychological drivers of refreezing: the *personal* and the *relational* fit (1987, pp. 110ff). These two drivers neatly fit into the larger context of what Schein understands by refreezing – an understanding that deserves a larger quotation:

> Change can be very fleeting. We all have seen how clients can develop new concepts and points of view during training sessions and then revert immediately to their old point of view when they are back in their home environment if that environment does not support the new point of view. Refreezing is that portion of the change process, then, that embeds the new point of view both in the person's own psychic life space and in his various relationships with significant others.
>
> *(Schein, 1987, p. 110)*

Embedding the new point of view in the person's *own* psychic life space amounts to what Schein calls 'personal refreezing'. If personal refreezing is to be successful, the new point of view needs to fit "comfortably into the person's total self-concept" and should be "comfortably integrated with the rest of his personality" (p. 110). However, this *personal fit*, although a necessary driver, is not sufficient to securely embed (refreeze) the new point of view. 'Relational refreezing' is needed as well:

> Even if the idea fits into the client's own personality and self-concept, it is possible that it will violate the expectations of significant others around the client – his boss, peers, and subordinates – to a sufficient degree that they will either not reinforce it or actually disconfirm it.
>
> *(Schein, 1987, p. 111)*

Apparently, in addition to a personal fit, there should also be a relational fit. The client's behaviour should fit, be accepted as legitimate, in his or her behavioural field. If this acceptance is withheld, the client, according to Schein, needs to retrain the significant others in this field, making them the object of a change programme that changes their expectations of the client's behaviour. In this process of relational refreezing:

> The consultant or managerial change agent plays a critical role [. . .] in being for a time the only person who may be reinforcing the new point of view and behaviour, helping the client to become comfortable enough with it to sustain himself in other encounters.
>
> *(Schein, 1987, p. 111)*

If we apply Schein's ideas about refreezing to both our social goals logic and the episodic interventions in organizational structures that are the topic of this book, they appear helpful in some respects and unhelpful in others.

Let us start with the unhelpful bit, or to put it in more friendly terms, the bit that does not neatly fit the interventions in organizational structures that are discussed in this book.

Based on the quotation at the start of this section, it can be argued that Schein's idea of 'refreeze' seems to presuppose that clients adopt a *new* (changed) point of view and then go back to their *old* (unchanged) environment. If that environment does not support the new point of view, there is indeed a fair chance that clients regress to their old point of view and its related behaviours (e.g. a treated alcohol addict going back to her old cafe). Nothing would have been gained. Refreezing, interpreted as embedding the new point of view 'in the person's own psychic life space and in his various relationships with significant others', in this case, really seems indispensable.

Applied to the episodic interventions that are central in this book, this image of 'refreeze' and its contribution to the success of the intervention would be fitting in the following example. Suppose that some organization has a high parameter value structure. As a consequence of this structure, organization members have developed different kinds of pathological outlooks and practices that culminate in what is diagnosed as a 'negative culture'. For instance, due to the complex and bureaucratic structure, organization members are not involved in their work any more (not seeing the point of it), tend to blame others when things go wrong (and a lot of things do go wrong), informally work around problems instead of addressing them, and continuously complain about and distrust their managers. Some of them have even become so alienated that they often report sick or behave as a kind of 'walking dead' in the organization. Now, moreover, suppose that in order to address this 'negative culture', an episodic intervention is staged. This intervention consists of a set of training sessions. In these sessions, organization members in small rotating groups re-learn how to work together, face problems instead of looking away, and trust one another. After some time and due to excellent process consultation, both their outlook on their work (their point of view) and their practices actually change. So they get their training certificates and go back to work. However, the *structure* of their work has not changed. It still is that old complex, bureaucratic, high parameter value structure from before. No wonder that, within months, organization members, working in their old pointless jobs, confronted with the same old problems, and managed by managers with the same old management problems, start to relapse to their old practices; acting as if nothing happened. Now, this is the kind of intervention that is described by Schein, the kind of intervention in which clients with a *new* point of view go back to their *old* environment; the kind of intervention in which 'refreeze' and its socio-psychological drivers are really essential, but, in our opinion, quite hopeless.

Given this example, it should also be clear why the episodic interventions that are central in this book do not neatly fit the kind of interventions described by Schein. The episodic interventions discussed in this book are episodic interventions in the structure of organizations. If these interventions succeed, organization members do not go back to their old environment, to their old high parameter value structure. Instead, they *change* the structure (and the technology and human resources systems related to its (re)production) that was the cause of their problems in the first place. 'Refreezing', here, does not mean embedding the new point of view and behaviour in the old structure. It rather means (re)producing the *new* structure *by means of* the new point of view and its related practices – an endeavour that, in our opinion, is still difficult, but much more hopeful.

In spite of this important difference between the interventions envisaged by Schein and the episodic interventions in organizational structures discussed in this book, his ideas about 'refreeze' can still help to elaborate the integration goal in our social goals logic. In fact, his ideas about refreeze are helpful in two ways.

First, they are helpful in that Schein, too, emphasizes the importance of what we have called the 'irreversibility' of the integrated interaction premises and interactions – i.e. organization members should not drift back to their old behaviours, thereby (re)producing the old high parameter value structure. As indicated, refreeze does not mean that change somehow stops. On the contrary, *because* change continues, clients can regress to their old behaviours, and this is what should be prevented by refreeze.

Second, Schein's ideas are helpful in that they point at both the multi-level character of refreeze – the level of *persons* and the level of *relations* between persons – and the importance of a personal and relational fit as drivers of refreeze. In order to explain how Schein's distinction between personal and relational refreezing may be helpful to further elaborate the 'irreversible integration of interaction premises and interactions', it is useful to further zoom in on the integration process.

If episodic interventions in the structure of an organization are to be successful, we have argued, organization members should irreversibly integrate new interaction premises and interactions into their repertoires that are both related to the (re)production of the organization's structure and allow for the realization of the goal of the intervention. This integration is a more complex phenomenon than first meets the eye. In order to explain what it entails, we take Schein's hint to heart and distinguish between to levels:

1. *personal integration* – i.e. integration of interaction premises and interactions in the repertoires of individual organization members;
2. *relational integration* – i.e. integration of interaction premises and interactions into the pattern of repertoires of *related* organization members.

Personal integration, in the first place, means that 'old' interaction premises and interactions in the repertoire that are *directly* related to the (re)production of the structure of the organization are replaced by 'new' ones. This implies, for instance, that organization members *willingly accept* their new tasks as an interaction premise and interact accordingly. However, given the direct and indirect relation between interaction premises and interactions and the (re)production of organizational structures, this interpretation of integration is incomplete. What should be added is that organization members also integrate into their repertoires new interaction premises and interactions that are *indirectly* related to the (re)production of the organization's new structure. For instance, they should also *willingly accept* into their repertoires interaction premises and interactions related to the technology or the knowledge and skills that are required to perform their new tasks. That is, they should both know and accept that, in line with their new task, it is expected of them that they operate task-related technology in task-related way and exercise particular task- and technology-related knowledge and skills.

Second, in order to be able to meet these expectations and actually perform the expected interactions, organization members should learn both what their new tasks actually entail and what it means to operate the technology that is related to those tasks. Moreover, they should acquire the knowledge and develop the skills related to their new tasks and their related technology. 'Integration', therefore, is supported by indispensable *learning* and *training* processes that enable organization members to actually perform the task-related interactions prescribed by their task-related interaction premises. As such, task-related learning and training drive the process of integration.

Third, 'integration' means that new interaction premises and interactions and new task-related knowledge and skills are *accommodated* both to each other and to 'old' interaction premises and interactions that are not an object of the intervention. If integration is successful, accommodation contributes to the development of a *coherent* repertoire of interaction premises and interactions (as well as supporting knowledge and skills) that enables organization members to *adequately* perform their new tasks in the (new) network of tasks. An example of accommodation may be someone whose new task brings more and new responsibilities that require additional knowledge and skills. However, the organization's dress code was not an object of the intervention. Accommodation, now, is about fine-tuning and adjusting the new responsibilities to both the required knowledge and skills needed to fulfil the new responsibilities and the dress code: 'Should I dress differently now I have more responsibilities in the organization?' It is about developing a coherent repertoire of interaction premises and interactions, a repertoire that is needed to perform the new task in a way that is accepted as 'adequate' in the organization.

This last point, of performing the new task in a way that is accepted as adequate in the organization, brings us to the other level of integration: integration at the level of the pattern of related repertoires of organization members.

Until now, it appeared as if 'integration' only pertains to the repertoires of interaction premises and interactions of individual organization members. However, 'integration' involves more than this. In organizations, organization members are supposed to work together in a network of related tasks. In this network, organization members depend on others in order to adequately perform their tasks. This dependence relation implies that organization members, in the course of integrating new structure-related interaction premises and interactions into their (individual) repertoires, should also adjust their own repertoires to the changing repertoires of organization members they are supposed to work with in the new structure. In more mundane terms, 'integration' also means that organization members need to learn to work together in the new structure. The social goal of integration can only be considered a success once this process of adjustment between repertoires of organization members actually allows them to adequately perform their task in the new organization structure.

As it appears, the integration of new structure-related interaction premises and interactions is a complex phenomenon. It at least involves the four following 'moments' that may be conceptually distinguished, but cannot be separated in reality:

1. willingly accepting new structure-related interaction premises and interactions, i.e. of interaction premises and interactions that are *directly* and *indirectly* related to the (re)production of the organization's structure;
2. acquiring knowledge and developing skills needed in order to be able to actually interact according to new structure-related interaction premises;
3. accommodating 'new' and 'old' interaction premises and interactions as well as knowledge and skills into a coherent repertoire that allows for adequate task performance;
4. adjusting repertoires of related organization members so that they can perform their new tasks in the network in a way that is accepted as adequate in the organization.

These processes are driven by what are called 'personal fit' and 'relational fit' (Schein, 1987). Personal fit means that organization members experience that their new job better fits their goals and aspirations than their old job did: the new job is seen as an improvement. Relational fit means that organization members see that relevant others (co-workers, other professionals) also experience their new jobs as an improvement. These others confirm what organization members experience, thereby enforcing the personal fit.

7.5.3 C: integration and functional goals – implementation and evaluation

Just like 'motivation' and 'adoption', 'integration' also has an affinity with activities and goals on the functional dimension. The relevant activities here are 'implementation' and 'evaluation'.

'Implementation' makes sure that the current high parameter value structure is actually transformed into the desired low parameter value structure. As such, 'implementation' is the functional counterpart of the social 'integration' goal. If the two are combined into one formula, it can be said that by means of 'implementation' and 'integration', interactions and interaction premises are changed in such a way that the new low parameter value structure becomes a durable organizational reality.

'Evaluation' primarily checks whether the change in the organization's structure was successful – that is, it checks whether the problems that were diagnosed are solved because of the transformation of the organization structure. Dependent on how the 'evaluation' is organized, it can have an effect on 'integration'. In order to explain why, it is useful to point to two drivers of 'integration' that were mentioned previously. These two drivers are the personal fit and the relational fit. The personal fit entails that organization members see that the new structure better fits their goals and aspirations than the old one. The relational fit entails that organization members see that relevant co-workers have similar experiences.

Now, if the evaluation is organized in such a way that organization members can participate in it, they are given the opportunity to reflect on the success of the episodic intervention, and thereby become aware of their improved working situation. This awareness, in turn, can support both the personal fit and relational fit. In this way, there may be an affinity between 'evaluation' on the functional dimension and 'integration' on the social dimension. As a conclusion of this section, Table 7.6 presents the elaborated goals on the social dimension of the 3-D model.

7.6 Learning from critique: clarifying the role and status of the social goals

At the end of Section 7.2, we said that the three-stage model of change not only inspired authors to develop it further, we also indicated that it was criticized in literature on organizational change. In this section, we want to survey this critique in order to further clarify the role and status of the goals on the social dimension of the 3-D model.

For the purpose of a *survey* of the critique, an article by Burnes (2004) is helpful. In this article, Burnes provides an overview of the main lines of critique on Lewin's Planned Change approach – of which, according to Burnes, the three-stage model is a part. In his article, Burnes discusses the main lines of critique ranging from the eighties to the turn of the century (1980–2000). Moreover, based on an exposition of Lewin's ideas and ideals, Burnes attempts to respond to these main lines of critique, thereby re-appraising Lewin's Planned Change approach.

In order to contextualize both his overview and responses, Burnes starts with a rough sketch of new and relevant approaches to organizations and organizational change in the literature in the period discussed by him. In his view, three new approaches are particularly relevant because they are both influential and quite critical of Lewin's approach: the *Culture-Excellence School*, the *postmodernists*, and the *Processual approach*.

According to proponents of the Culture-Excellence School:

> the world is essentially an ambiguous place where detailed plans are not possible and flexibility is essential. [. . .] They argue that change cannot be driven from the top but must emerge in an organic, bottom-up fashion from the day-to-day actions of all in the organization. Proponents of Culture-Excellence reject as antithetical the Planned Change approach to change . . ..
>
> *(Burnes, 2004, p. 988)*

Postmodernists underline both the socially constructed character of organizational life and the importance of power in organizations. In combination, social construction and power can make organizations into vehicles of domination, for instance by letting managers or consultants invent solutions *for* instead of together *with* organization members. However, social construction and power can also be used in more democratic ways, for instance by making processes of construction "open and available to all", organizations can create, "opportunities for freedom and innovation rather than simply further domination" (Hatch, 1997, pp. 367–368, cited in Burnes, 2004, p. 989).

TABLE 7.6 Cumulative overview of the goals on the social dimension

	Motivation	Adoption	Integration
A	Organization members should develop the motivation to: – let go of current interaction premises and move to new ones and concomitant interaction patterns • adopt an episodic intervention as a means to do this	Organization members, based on a justifiable confidence, adopt (willingly commit to) new helping interaction premises and interactions that can (re)produce an improved organizational structure and allow for the realization of the goal of the intervention	Organization members have irreversibly integrated new interactions and interaction premises into their repertoires that both (re)produce the organization's improved structure and allow for the realization of the goal of the intervention

Sense of urgency → Shared vision → Inventing → Testing → Exercising → Reinforcing / Adjusting

B. Creating and maintaining change relationships

Drivers	Cognition-related	Emotion-related	Cognition-related	Emotion-related	Cognition-related	Emotion-related
Individual-centred	Disconfirmation of current interactions/premises Confirmation of a worthwhile and achievable future	Anxiety Guilt (only managers) Psychological safety Desire	Scanning (+ inventing) Quick object- and goal-related wins (testing)	Identification with role model Quick object- and goal-related wins (testing)	Experiencing the new structure as personally beneficial (quality of work): personal fit Acquiring cognitions and developing skills that support interactions in the new structure Accommodating the old and the new Joint development of skills supporting cooperation in the new structure Seeing that others experience the new structure as personally beneficial: relational fit	Return of hope Desire to further integrate the new structure into the repertoire Development of a new elan
Context-centred	Influence of group dynamics on cognition- and emotion-related drivers		Influence of group dynamics on cognition- and emotion-related drivers			

C	Related functional goals	Diagnosis and Design	Design and Implementation	Implementation and Evaluation

Note: A = sub-goals; B = drivers; C = relation to functional goals.

'Processualists', as Burnes calls them, "reject prescriptive, recipe-driven approaches to change and are suspicious of single causes or simple explanations of events. Instead, when studying change, they focus on the inter-relatedness of individuals, groups, organizations and society". The Processualists consider the Planned Change approach as too prescriptive, doing injustice to the complexity of real processes of change that are always an "untidy cocktail of rational processes, individual perceptions, political struggles and coalition building" (Burnes, 2004, p. 989).

> In spite of important differences, the three approaches, according to Burnes, share a basis that underpins the main lines of critique of the Planned Change approach (including its three-stage model). In one way or another:
> The newer approaches tend to take a holistic/contextual view of organizations and their environments; they challenge the notion of change as an ordered and linear process; and there is an emphasis on change as a continuous process which is heavily influenced by culture, power, and politics.
>
> *(2004, p. 990)*

In addition, Burnes remarks that the three approaches do not stand in isolation. They are supported by new perspectives on the nature of change in organizations. In this context, he refers to the emergence of the punctuated equilibrium model and the continuous transformation model, which relieve the earlier incremental model of organizational change, and to increasingly popular complexity theories of change.

Against the incremental model – which claims that organizations only change part by part, in small steps, and one problem and goal at a time – the punctuated equilibrium model argues that in organizations, "relatively long periods of stability (equilibrium periods) [. . .] are punctuated by relatively short burst of fundamental change (revolutionary periods)" (Romanelli and Tushman, 1994, p. 1141, cited in Burnes, 2004, p. 990). Against both the incremental and the punctuated equilibrium models, the continuous transformation model, then, argues that "in order to survive, organizations must develop the ability to change themselves continuously in a fundamental manner" (Burnes, 2004, p. 991). Complexity theories of change go even further by arguing that organizations, in order to survive, should permanently operate 'on the edge of chaos':

> If organizations are too stable, nothing changes and the system dies; if too chaotic, the system will be overwhelmed by change. In both situations, radical change is necessary in order to create a new set of order generating rules which allow the organization to prosper and survive.
>
> *(ibid, p. 991)*

In sum, just like the Culture-Excellence School or the postmodernist and Processualist approaches, both the continuous transformation model and complexity theories of change underline the ubiquity and necessity of change in organizations as well as at its complexity and unpredictability.

Against the background of his overview of these new and relevant theoretical models, Burnes then formulates what he sees as the four main lines of critique of Lewin's approach. Viewed from these new positions, Lewin's approach:

1. is "too simplistic and mechanistic for a world where organizational change is a continuous and open process" (Burnes, 2004, p. 992);
2. is "only relevant to incremental and isolated change projects and is not able to incorporate radical, transformational change" (p. 993);
3. underplays "the role of power and politics in organizations and the conflictual nature of much organizational life" (p. 994);
4. advocates "a top-down, management driven approach to change", and ignores "situations requiring bottom-up change" (p. 995).

In order to learn from these main lines of critique and further clarify the role and status of the social goals in the 3-D model, we will proceed in two steps. First, we will relate our perspective on organizations and change to the models and theories discussed by Burnes. As it appears, we agree with these models and theories in seeing change in organizations as ubiquitous, complex, and inherently unpredictable. Moreover, we agree that change involves processes of social construction and power. However, we do not agree that this forecloses the possibility and relevance of episodic interventions in organizational structures. Second, we will discuss 'our' social goals in relation to the four main lines of critique distinguished by Burnes.

7.6.1 Models of organizational change and our perspective on organizations and change

In Chapters 2 and 4, we introduced our view of organizations and organizational change. In this view, organizations are social systems conducting experiments.

As social systems, organizations are in continuous flux. Interactions are continuously 'produced' against a background of interaction premises that continuously change by means of interactions. 'Being an organization' and 'being in this continuous flux' are the same thing. Please note that, defined as continuous flux, 'change' in organizations is neither good nor bad, it is just what it means to be an organization: if the flux stops, the organization as a social system stops.

By means of the interactions and interaction premises that constitute the flux, organization members give meaning to the organizational world they inhabit. This meaning-giving process can be viewed as a process of social construction. In interaction, concepts, models, theories, and ways of working are adopted that allow organization members to make sense of and interact in the organization they are a part of. Position, power, interests, and perceptions play an important role in these processes of social construction. As a result, the organizational flux is so complex that the actual processes by means of which an organization (re)produces itself as a social system can never be fully expressed in that organization: the processes of self-production (autopoiesis) of an organization as a social system are intransparent to that organization as a social system (Luhmann, 1984). Thus, in our view, complexity, uncertainty, unpredictability, and intransparency go hand in hand with organizing as a social phenomenon. All of this we share with the Culture-Excellence School, the postmodernists, and the Processualists.

In Chapter 2, we also argued that organizations are not 'just' social systems. They are a particular type of social systems that 'survive' by means of adapting and realizing their 'meaning' (that is, their particular contribution to society that can be operationalized in terms of organizational goals). To this purpose, organizations perform primary processes, operationally regulate these processes, strategically formulate their meaning, and design their own infrastructure by means of design regulation. Once again, all these processes are inescapably complex, involving uncertainty, unpredictability, and intransparency. That is why we called organizations 'experiments'. In interaction, strategic, design, and operational selections are made that can be seen as experiments with the meaningful survival of the organization. At this point, we agree with the continuous transformation model. Organizations should be able to continuously and 'organically' adapt themselves – i.e. they should be able to continuously and 'organically' experiment with their own meaningful survival.

Because the experimental character of organizations is unavoidable – i.e. organizations cannot 'abolish' experimenting without abolishing themselves – it is important to improve the conditions for the processes of continuous experimentation. This means that conditions should be created for the performance of primary processes and continuous interactive operational, design, and strategic regulation. In Chapter 3, we argued that the organizational infrastructure, and in particular the organizational structure, is such a condition. Dependent on the values of the parameters of their structure, organizations are either facilitated or inhibited in their processes of continuous experimentation. Low parameter values, it was argued, attenuate the probability of disturbances and amplify chances for regulation. As a result, low parameter value structures facilitate the experimental adaptation and realization of organizational goals. High parameter values amplify the probability of disturbances and attenuate chances for regulation. Thereby, they inhibit processes of experimental adaptation and realization.

Of course, organizational structures are no exception as far as continuous change is concerned. They too are a part of the organizational flux, and just like all interaction premises, organizational structures also change in the course of unfolding organizational interaction. In Chapter 4, we discussed a possible result of these processes of change: the gradual change or drift of the parameters of organizational structures to ever higher values, for instance as a result of work being split up further in order to 'simplify' it or the introduction of additional procedures, rules, and regulations in order to regain 'control' over the organization's performance and workers. As a result of these processes of structural drift, the production structure becomes more complex and the control structure gets more bureaucratic, gradually undermining the organization's potential for continuous and 'organic' adaptation. These processes of structural drift (which are processes of continuous change), in the end, can lead to a situation that fundamentally endangers the meaningful survival of the organization and requires a fundamental transformation. After a (dynamic) 'equilibrium' period in which the parameter values of the organization's structure has gradually drifted to ever higher values, a 'burst' of fundamental change is needed that restores the organization's potential for continuous transformation by reducing the values of its structural parameters. Therefore, at this point, we agree with the punctuated equilibrium model. And what is more, insofar as organizational structures are concerned, we do not necessarily see a contradiction between the continuous transformation model and the punctuated equilibrium model. *Because* organizations need to be able to continuously adapt themselves (continuous transformation model) and *because* the values of the parameters of organizational structures may gradually increase as time goes by, a fundamental change reducing these parameter values may sometimes be needed (punctuated equilibrium model). Apparently, in the case of organizational structures, it can be argued that the truth of the punctuated equilibrium model goes hand in hand with and presupposes the truth of the continuous transformation model.

This book is about the episodic interventions in organizational structures that, as punctuations in a dynamic equilibrium, may be needed in order to restore an organization's potential for continuous adaptation, or to put it in our own words, to restore an organization's potential to carry on its experiments with meaningful survival. As such, these interventions do not just aim for 'organizational change'. 'Change' is ubiquitous in organizations, and, as argued, may even lead to the gradual deterioration of their structure and their demise as organizations. Instead, these interventions aim to *develop* organizational structures. That is, they aim to *enhance the structural conditions for organizational experimentation, i.e. for processes of the continuous realization and adaptation of meaningful survival in complex and changing environments.* Thus, because of our subscription to the continuous transformation model, we think that episodic interventions in organizational structures may be relevant and, in some cases, badly needed.

As indicated previously, we also subscribe to the thesis that organizations are inherently complex, unpredictable, intransparent, and construction-, perception-, power-, and interest-dependent. These characteristics of organizations do not make episodic interventions in organizational structures less relevant. However, they do make these interventions hard to perform. As argued in Chapter 4, episodic interventions in organizational structures themselves are a kind of experiments. Models supporting these interventions should incorporate that point. They should incorporate the point that organizations function in complex institutional contexts, that change in organizations is not an ordered and linear process, and that change is continuous and heavily influenced by culture, power, and politics. It is in this spirit that we discuss the four main lines of critique distinguished by Burnes to further clarify the status and role of our goals on the social dimension.

7.6.2 Our social goals logic and the four main lines of critique

Before we begin our discussion of the four main lines of critique, it should be made clear that in his paper, Burnes (2004) intends to re-appraise the Planned Change approach in the light of new critical models of organizations and organizational change. To this purpose, he identifies four main lines of critique on the Planned Change approach that, according to him, follow from these new models. Then he discusses how a conception of the Planned Change approach that does justice to Lewin's original ideas and ideals can cope with these main lines of critique.

In this sub-section, both our goal and strategy differ from the goal and strategy selected by Burnes. It is not our goal to re-appraise the Planned Change approach. Rather, we want to further clarify the role and status of 'our' goals on the social dimension of the 3-D model. To this purpose, we discuss the four main lines of critique insofar as they pertain or can be related to these social goals. Moreover, we use this discussion to further clarify the role and status of these social goals. So it is our strategy to treat the four main lines of critique on the Planned Change approach as possible lines of critique on our social goals logic and learn from them.

Critique 1: the social goals logic is too simplistic and mechanistic

The first main line of critique is that the Planned Change approach is "too simplistic and mechanistic for a world where organizational change is a continuous and open process" (Burnes, 2004, p. 992).

It is not difficult to see how this line of critique relates to our social goals logic. Actually, in his paper, Burnes himself provides a clue to this relation as he quotes Kanter et al.:

> Lewin's model was a simple one, with organizational change involving three stages; unfreezing, changing, refreezing... This quaintly linear and static conception – the organization as an ice cube – is so wildly inappropriate that it is difficult to see why it has not only survived but prospered... Suffice it to say here, first that organizations are never frozen, much less refrozen, but are fluid entities with many 'personalities'. Second, to the extent that there are stages, they overlap and interpenetrate one another in important ways.
> *(Kanter et al., 1992, p. 10, quoted in Burnes, 2004, pp. 988–989)*

It is not difficult to relate this critique to our social goals logic, for, in order to elaborate this logic we borrowed insights from consultancy-oriented interpretations that build upon the three-stage model. For this reason, 'our' logic may also be too simple a model of organizations and organizational change. Therefore, a further clarification of the role and status of our social goals logic is in order. To this purpose, we first discuss the 'simplicity' argument, then we go into the question of 'stages and their overlap or interpenetration'.

To start, we want to underline that, as we see them, organizations are neither ice-cubes nor liquid entities with many 'personalities'. We rather view organizations as a particular type of social systems that are in a continuous flux. This makes organizations into complex, intransparent, and largely unpredictable phenomena. Hence our suggestion to interpret organizations in terms of experiments with meaningful survival. However, if pressed to choose between the 'liquid entity' and the 'ice-cube' metaphor, we would choose the former one, and to be fair, as Burnes (2004) argues, Lewin's own ideas about group dynamics also forbid him to interpret organizations or organizational behaviour as being 'unfrozen' and 'refrozen' ice-cubes in the sense implied by Kanter et al.

Given our view on organizations, we also agree that it is probably hard to capture actual processes of organizational change in terms of a three-stage model like Lewin's unfreeze, change, and freeze. Organizational changes in general, and episodic interventions in organizational structures in particular, are much more capricious and open-ended than that. Probably none of these interventions will neatly or even by approximation fit Lewin's three-stage model. As an empirical model of episodic interventions in organizational structures, Lewin's three stages seem to be quite inadequate.

Now, how does this reflect on 'our' goals on the social dimension? Are they also inadequate as an empirical model?

Our answer to this question would be 'Yes.' As an *empirical model* of episodic interventions in organizational structures, 'motivation', 'adoption', and 'integration' are indeed too simple. However, we would immediately add that, in the 3-D model, it is not the *role* of 'motivation', 'adoption', and 'integration' to function as an empirical model of these interventions. We do not see 'motivation', 'adoption', and 'integration' as a generalized and simplified empirical description of how episodic interventions in organizational structures actually evolve in organizations. We rather interpret them as *navigational coordinates* that can help steer these interventions. That is why we do not speak of social *stages*, but of social *goals*. And that is also why we do not speak of a three-stage *model*, but of a social goals *logic*.

Now, what does it mean that our social goals function as navigational coordinates? As explained in Chapters 4 and 5, the 3-D model is designed to support episodic interventions in organizational structures. Moreover, the 3-D model takes seriously that these interventions are a kind of experiments. Because organizations are continuously evolving, complex, intransparent, and unpredictable phenomena, the 3-D model does not consider performing episodic interventions in organizations as controlled and orderly affairs, as straightforward cases of 'unfreezing', 'moving', and 'refreezing', it rather sees them as complex processes of experimentation.

In order to support these processes, we proposed in Chapter 5 an 'experimental', 'situational', 'cybernetic', and 'reflective' logic that basically consists of the following activities:

1. strategic regulation – select functional and social goals in the intervention;
2. design regulation – build an intervention infrastructure that can perform and regulate (operational, design, and strategic regulation) the primary intervention process needed to realize selected functional and social goals;
3. operational regulation – manage disturbances of the primary intervention process (without changing its design or goals);
4. primary intervention process – the process that should realize the functional and social goals.

As a part of the regulatory activities, a fifth activity is presupposed:

5. assess the progress of the episodic intervention relative to selected functional and social goals, and dependent on this assessment, perform regulatory activity 1, 2, or 3.

In this logic, 'selecting social goals' is a reflection on 'what' one wants to realize with 'whom' in order to realize the goal of the intervention (for instance, 'motivating' the organization's management to consider the organizational structure as the object of an intervention). Based on selected social (and functional) goals, it becomes possible to think about the intervention infrastructure that can help realize them. Moreover, it becomes possible to execute and steer one's actions, and, if necessary, to adapt the selection of both goals and the intervention infrastructure.

Of course, the selection of particular social goals does not make an episodic intervention into an orderly and controlled affair. In principle, endlessly many unforeseen developments can either disturb or support the realization of these goals. Moreover, as the circumstances require this, the goals themselves may need to be reselected too. It is rather the other way around. Because goals (in our case, social and functional goals) have been selected, 'developments' can appear disturbing or supportive. 'Disorder' and 'order' appear in the light of these goals.

To borrow the metaphor of the organization as a 'liquid entity' used by Kanter et al., setting social (and functional) goals in the case of episodic interventions is like sailing on an unruly sea, full of unpredictable currents, vortices, and winds that, in combination, continuously drive the ship off course. In order to know at all whether the ship is on or off course, navigational coordinates that constitute this course are needed (coordinates that may be reset as the situation requires this). Moreover, in order to steer the ship, even without exactly knowing the complex, intransparent, and unpredictable forces that drive the ship off course, once again, these navigational coordinates are needed.

Social (and functional) goals in the 3-D model have exactly this role and status. They are not an empirical model of the sea that is being navigated; they are not an empirical model of the organization as a continuous flux. Neither are they an empirical model of the actual trips that are made on this sea; neither are they an empirical model of organizational change in general or episodic interventions in organizational structures in particular. They rather are temporary prescriptive constructs that can help navigate this sea; social (and functional) goals are *temporary prescriptive constructs* (this is their *status*) that *help perform and regulate episodic interventions in organizational structures* (this is their *role*). In the case of episodic interventions in organizational structures, we need these temporary prescriptive constructs *because* of the *complexity* of organizations and organizational change, *not* because of their *simplicity*.

As to the second point of 'stages' and their 'overlap' and 'interpenetration', it can be argued that the social goals logic, although it does not provide an empirical stage model of episodic interventions in organizational structures, still treats these interventions as if they consist of a simple set of goals that *should* be realized in a particular sequence: 'motivation', 'adoption', 'integration'. However, inspired by Kanter et al. (1992), it can be asked, 'Why at all a sequence of goals and why no interpenetration or overlap?'

To this question, we have two answers: (1) 'Yes, the social goals logic involves a sequence of social goals; however, this sequence is conceptual rather than empirical, and what is more, setting and realizing these social goals in actual practice are anything but simple and straightforward,, and (2) 'Yes, between the setting and realization of social goals, different kinds of overlap and interpenetration are possible.'

In order to explain the first answer, it is useful to ask what it *means* to perform a *successful* episodic intervention in an organizational structure. In our view, the answer to this question is that organization members have irreversibly integrated new interactions and interaction premises into their repertoires that are related to the interactive (re)production of the organization's improved structure and allow for the realization of the goal of the intervention. For instance, if the goal of an episodic intervention is to transform an organization's structure in order to restore its capacity for continuous and 'organic' transformation, then we consider this transformation successful if organization members have integrated the structure-related interaction premises and interactions into their repertoires that allow for the realization of this goal.

The observant reader will immediately see that our definition of a 'successful episodic intervention in an organizational structure' is equal to what we understand by 'integration' as the final goal in our social goals logic: 'integration' is nothing more or less than the conceptual articulation of what we understand by a 'successful episodic intervention in an organization's structure'. Now, what does this mean?

To begin with, it means that we do not see 'integration' as the *empirical* final *stage* of episodic interventions in organizational structures. Empirically, these interventions can end in all kinds of ways. Some of them are a success. Some of them are a total failure. Some of them end up somewhere between success and total failure. Some of them end in a bang, others in a whimper. Therefore, the assertion that 'integration' is empirically the final stage of episodic interventions in organizational structures contravenes available evidence, and, for this reason, is untenable.

But if 'integration' is not empirically the final stage of episodic interventions in organizational structures, then what is it?

As indicated, 'integration' is the conceptual articulation of what we understand by a successful episodic intervention in an organization's structure. Therefore, *if* a 'successful episodic intervention in the structure of an organization' is the goal, *then*, by definition, this means that 'integration' is what one is after. And what is more, under the condition that 'success' is the goal, 'integration' is not just one of many goals within the episodic intervention, it is the *final* goal. Once 'integration' has been realized, the episodic intervention, by definition, is concluded successfully.

Thus, for our purposes, 'integration' is not empirically the final stage of episodic interventions in organizational structures. It is *conditionally* and *conceptually* the *final goal* of these interventions. That is, given the condition that one wants to make these interventions successful (which is exactly what the 3-D model aspires to contribute to), then, by definition, 'integration' is the social goal that, *finally*, should be achieved. In the sequence of social goals, 'integration' is conditionally and conceptually the final social goal in the intervention.

A somewhat similar reasoning holds for 'adoption' as a mediate social goal between 'motivation' and 'integration'. Here, it is relevant to ask the question, 'Why is a successful episodic intervention in the organization's structure needed?' To this question, we would answer, 'Because *current* structure-related interaction premises and interactions do not allow for the realization of the goal of the intervention.' That is, there exists a *gap* between (unwanted) *current* structure-related interaction premises and interactions that do not allow for the realization of the goal of the intervention, and *future*, yet unknown, *desired* structure-related interaction premises and interactions that do. Under the condition that one wants to make the episodic intervention a success, this gap should be bridged by inventing and testing structure-related interaction premises and interactions that do allow for the realization of the goal of the intervention. This is what the social goal 'adoption' entails. Therefore, just like 'integration', we do not consider 'adoption' as an empirical stage in the intervention process. We see it as a social goal that should be realized under the condition that an episodic intervention in the structure of the organization is needed. And, what is more, it is not just any social goal, *conceptually* it is the *mediating* social goal – that is, the social goal that mediates between an unwanted current situation and a, yet unknown, future desired future situation.

'Adoption' conceptually not only presupposes that some current 'situation' – i.e. the current dynamics of structure-related interaction premises and interactions and their effects on the performance of the organization, for instance, in terms of quality of organization, work, and work relations – is unwanted, it also needs this situation to be seen both as 'unwanted' and requiring an episodic intervention that should be made into a success. This is what the social goal 'motivation' entails. So, once again, we do not see this social goal as an empirical stage of intervention processes as they really occur, but as a goal that should be realized if, in the end, the intervention is to be a success.

To sum up: yes, there is a sequence. However, this sequence is not an empirical sequence of stages. It is rather a conditional and conceptual sequence of social goals that *should* be realized *if* an episodic intervention in the structure of an organization is:

1. to be made into a success – final social goal, integration;
2. actually needed – mediate social goal, adoption;
3. to be seen as actually needed – immediate social goal, motivation.

246 Designing interventions

As such, we consider the social goals as conditional, conceptual, prescriptive constructs that can be used as navigational coordinates in order to perform and regulate the intervention. Given the 'fluidity', complexity, intransparency, and unpredictability of organizations, both setting and sailing along these navigational coordinates are anything but simple or straightforward. The capricious courses that episodic interventions in organizational structures actually take can testify to this.

Now, if there is a conceptual sequence of social goals, what about their 'overlap' and 'interpenetration'?

To start answering this question, it is useful to refer back to the elaboration of the social goals in Section 7.3, where we discussed a set of social sub-goals and argued that, between these sub goals, interdependency relations may exist (see Figure 7.1). In *practice* and as far as *goal setting* and *realization* are concerned, these interdependency relations allow for both overlap and interpenetration.

By *overlap*, we mean that, in a particular time frame, different social goals may be *set* either (a) in the same group or (b) across multiple groups engaged in an episodic intervention. An example of (a) may be a group that works on the 'adoption' of suitable solutions and at the same time strives to maintain its 'motivation'. This group may even see the continued realization of the motivation goal as a precondition for the realization of the adoption goal. In that group, overlapping goals have been set. An example of (b) would be two groups involved in one intervention. In a particular time frame, one of these groups has set the adoption goal, the other the integration goal. Thus, a patchwork of overlapping social goals may be set across multiple groups participating in the same episodic intervention. As a corollary to this definition, 'overlap' can also mean that, in a particular time frame, different goals may be *realized* or *fail to be realized* either in the same group or across multiple groups engaged in an episodic intervention. For instance, in one and the same group and in a particular time frame, both the realization of the 'adoption' goal and the continued realization of the 'motivation goal may be jeopardized. Or, across multiple groups, different social goals may be in different stages of realization.

By *interpenetration*, we mean that, in a particular time frame, the realization of one goal can affect the realization of another, either (a) within a particular group or (b) across multiple groups. An example of (a) would be a particular group that has set 'adoption' as its social goal. However, for some reason, this group fails to invent and test successful solutions to its problems. That is, this group fails to realize the adoption goal. Because and to the extent that the group is unable to come up with viable solutions, its shared vision of a better future (sub-goal of 'motivation') starts to crumble as well, undermining the continued realization of the motivation goal. Apparently, in this group, the failure to realize the adoption goal affects – interpenetrates with – the continued realization of the motivation goal. An example of

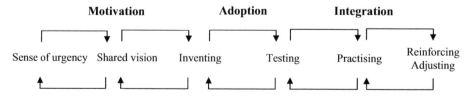

FIGURE 7.1 Interpenetration and overlap between social goals

(b) would be two groups involved in an episodic intervention. One of these groups realized its integration goal and thereby positively affects the motivation of the other group. Thus, the realization of a social goal may interpenetrate across groups. As it appears, as far as 'setting' and 'realizing' social goals are concerned, social goals can indeed overlap and interpenetrate 'in important ways', both in a particular group and across multiple groups.

In order to summarize the lessons that can be drawn from the first line of critique, it can be said that in the 3-D model, the social goals do not have the status and role of generalized empirical descriptions of the stages of episodic interventions in organizational structures. They are temporary prescriptive constructs that can help perform and regulate these interventions. As such, the social goals should be regarded as a conditional and conceptual sequence of goals. Under the condition that the episodic intervention is to be a success, 'integration' is the final goal; under the condition that the episodic intervention is actually needed, 'adoption' is the mediate goal, and under the condition that the episodic intervention is actually to be seen as needed, 'motivation' is the immediate goal. With respect to goal setting and goal realization, social goals can overlap and interpenetrate both within and across groups. Moreover, social goals can be set at different levels of aggregation: from the level of the episodic intervention as a whole to the level of groups of individuals or individuals participating in the intervention. In this way, a complex patchwork of social goals can be set in an episodic intervention that, to add to the complexity, in one and the same time frame, may be in different phases of realization. Finally, setting and realizing social goals in an episodic intervention is anything but straightforward or simple. Both organizations and episodic interventions in organizations are inherently complex social phenomena. Social goals can help to navigate this complexity, but they cannot remove it.

Critique 2: the social goals logic is only relevant to incremental and isolated change programmes

According to the second main line of critique, Lewin's Planned Change approach, including its three stages, is only suited to deal with incremental and isolated change programmes – that is, with separate change programmes that proceed part by part, step by step, and problem by problem.

We will begin with the issue of incremental change. Once again, it is not difficult to see how this critique might affect our social goals logic. We propose this logic as part of the 3-D model that is designed to support episodic interventions in organizational structures –; interventions we characterize as '*transformational*' (see Chapter 4). If it is true that the social goals logic is only relevant to incremental change, how, then, can it support transformational – yes, even revolutionary – change?

In order to address this question, it is relevant to start by clarifying what we mean by 'transformational', since this term may mean different things.

To our intents and purposes, the term 'transformational' refers primarily to the intended *impact* of the intervention, and secondarily to the *way this impact is realized*.

As to their impact, episodic interventions in organizational structures are called 'transformational' because they aim to have a strategic impact on the organization's functioning. As such, these interventions have a comprehensive and 'transforming' rather than a local and 'improving' character. 'Transformational change', here, is contrasted to 'optimizing change'. The episodic interventions in organizational structures that are the topic of this book may even be called 'revolutionary' cases of transformational change because they aim to realize this strategic impact by literally 'turning around' the values of the parameters of an organizational structure from 'high' to 'low'.

As to the way this strategic impact is realized, episodic interventions in organizational structures can also be called 'transformational' in order to distinguish them from multiple continuous interventions that, in the course of time and as a more or less contingent and aggregate effect, also may turn around the values of the structural parameters of an organization. In contrast to such aggregates of continuous interventions, episodic interventions in organizational structures are a *coordinated* and *sustained* effort that aims to transform the structure of an organization, an effort that requires an intervention organization to support it and is experienced as a more or less coherent episode in the organization's history. Instead of multiple, local, optimizing continuous interventions that gradually, and not necessarily coherently, change the organization's structure and functioning, episodic interventions in organizational structures are also called 'transformational' because they attempt to transform the structure and functioning of organizations in the course of one coherent project.

In order to address the question of 'incremental' and 'transformational' change, it is relevant to also specify what we do not mean by 'transformational'.

In our vocabulary, 'transformational' (or 'revolutionary', for that matter) does not mean that episodic interventions in organizational structures 'happen overnight' or in a 'flash'. On the contrary, these interventions take time, sometimes even years, and are performed part by part, step by step, and goal by goal. For instance, an episodic intervention in the structure of an organization may start in some team or some department, and then gradually involve more and more parts of the organization. Alternatively, such an intervention may start at the top of the organization and then cascade down to its business units, the departments of these units, and the teams within these departments. Defined in this way, episodic interventions in organizational structures have an 'incremental' and 'iterative' character that does not contradict the also 'transformational', or even 'revolutionary', nature of these interventions.

The social goals logic is intended to support this incremental and iterative change within the larger context of a transformational episodic intervention. For this reason, it enables the *flexible* application and use of the social goals. Social goals can be set and reset as the situation requires, and they can be set at different levels of aggregation (at the level of individuals, groups of individuals, etc.). As such, these goals can be used to perform and regulate the episodic intervention as a change process that is at the same time incremental and transformational.

The second point that is raised is that the social goals logic is only relevant to 'isolated change programmes'. This point is correct. Indeed, the 3-D model is designed to facilitate episodic interventions in organizational structures as 'isolated' change programmes. It is not designed to 'coordinate between' or 'preside over' a whole portfolio of change programmes in the 'environment' of the episodic intervention.

However, this does *not* mean that the 3-D model is *blind* and *non-responsive* to other concurrent activities in the organization – concurrent activities that, in addition to ongoing primary processes and continuous interventions, may include other episodic interventions. As will be made clear in the next chapter on the infrastructural dimension and the relations between functional, social, infrastructural dimensions of the 3-D model, these other concurrent activities need to be taken into account when (1) setting functional and social goals and (2) designing the intervention infrastructure. For instance, when designing 'tasks' in the intervention organization (structural aspect) and allocating organization members to these tasks (human resources aspect), one needs to take into account that the organization members allocated to these tasks may also have tasks in the ongoing primary processes of the organization and may be involved in other organizational interventions as well. In this way, the infrastructure of the intervention organization can be designed in order to coordinate ongoing activities in the organization in which the episodic intervention is performed with ongoing activities in the episodic intervention.

Critique 3: the social goals logic underplays the role of power and politics in organizations

Previously, we argued that organizations are a particular type of social systems. Moreover, we indicated that power and politics play an important role in these social systems. As a part of the organizational flux, power relations – for instance, hegemonic power relations invested in the organization's culture – are (re)produced and transformed by interactions and interaction premises, and vice versa, interaction premises and interactions are (re)produced and transformed against a background of power relations. As a consequence, interaction premises (and concomitant interactions) are often the topic of organizational politics. For instance, as part of this politics, plans regarding the strategy, structure, human resources policy, or technology of the organization may be heavily contested, and their acceptance or non-acceptance can make or break brilliant careers. Of course, power and politics are also reflected in episodic interventions in organizational structures, since these interventions too are 'part' of the organization as a social system and one of the 'modes' of the organizational flux.

Now, if power and politics are important factors both in organizations as social systems and in the episodic interventions that aim to transform their structure, it is to be expected that these factors play an important role in a discussion of the social dimension of these interventions. However, if we take a look at the social goals and their elaboration, it appears that power and politics are not mentioned at all. Obviously, the social goals logic must underplay the role of power and politics in organizations.

In order to address this point, it is once again helpful to zoom in on the role and status of the social goals. Previously, we argued that these goals are temporary prescriptive constructs that can help to perform and regulate episodic interventions in organizational structures. For instance, in the course of an episodic intervention and in a particular group, the social goal 'motivation' and the functional goal 'problem inventory' are set. Based on these goals and an assessment of the group's progress, an intervention infrastructure is selected. That is, *in situ* decisions are made about who is to be involved in what role in order to realize the social and functional goal, which techniques supporting communication and analysis may be helpful to this purpose, and what knowledge and experience are needed. Given this intervention infrastructure, the group starts work. After a while, an assessment is made. Is the group actually in the process of realizing the social and functional goals that were set? Unfortunately, the answer to this question is 'No.' No real progress has been made.

At this point it may be asked *why* no progress has been made. And the answer, of course, may be: because the power and politics that are always involved in interventions obstructed the realization of the social and functional goal. However, the answer also may be: because participants in the intervention have quite different outlooks on the organization, or because group cohesion was too low (or too high), or because the required theoretical knowledge about organizational structures was lacking, or because a facilitating consultant failed to actually 'facilitate' the group, or because group members developed a considerable dislike for each other, or because an inappropriate technique supporting the problem inventory was selected, or because of some other factor, or because of any combination of these factors.

In fact, all kinds of interdependent factors can affect the realization of social and functional goals in an episodic intervention, power and politics being (important) among them. It is impossible to foresee all these factors and their interrelations beforehand and 'calculate' their possible and actual effects on the realization of social and functional goals. For this reason, we did not even try to include all these factors and their possible effects in the social dimension of the 3-D model, however important these factors are. Instead, by formulating social goals, we constructed the model in such a way that, by means of setting social goals, organization members become *sensitive* to the influence of factors like power and politics on the realization of these goals. Social goals, therefore, are prescriptive and *sensitizing* constructs that can help perform and regulate episodic interventions in organizational structures.

By setting social goals like 'motivation', 'adoption', or 'integration' – goals that, in the end, conceptually relate to the 'success' of the intervention in terms of 'integration' – and by keeping score of the realization of these goals in practice, organization members can assess the progress they make relative to the intervention's final goal: 'integration'. Given their assessments, they can inquire into factors that helped or prevented their making the desired progress. In the course of this inquiry, they can develop hypotheses about the actual causes that affected their progress – for instance, the abuse of power by coalition X, Y getting ill, consultant Z lacking relevant knowledge, Q providing dysfunctional support, etc. Based on these hypotheses, they can act, for instance by resetting social or functional goals (strategic regulation), reconfiguring the infrastructure of the intervention organization (design regulation), or otherwise dealing with the disturbing factor (operational regulation).

In sum, it is not because we underplay the importance of power and politics in episodic interventions in organizational structures that these factors are not mentioned in the discussion of the social goals and their elaboration. On the contrary, we fully acknowledge their importance. However, in actual practice, there are other, possibly interrelated, factors besides power and politics that can also impinge on the realization of social (and functional) goals in these interventions. Social (and functional) goals in the intervention have the function of making organization members situationally *sensitive* to the actual influence of such factors. Given their assessment of the actual progress of the intervention relative to these goals, organization members can make a *situational* analysis of the causes of insufficient progress and act on it.

Critique 4: our social goals advocate a top-down, management-driven approach to change

One of the most damning critiques of the Planned Change approach is that it is top-down and management-driven. Planned Change, as this critique holds, is not initiated, performed, and regulated by organization members working in the primary processes, it is initiated, performed, and regulated 'for' them by their managers. These managers and their minions (consultants, experts, facilitators, human resources personnel) are the 'change agents'. The organization members working in the primary processes are the 'change recipients'.

'Intervening', then, consists of change agents more or less subtly forcing change recipients 'top-down' to conform their behaviour to some preconceived 'blue-print' masterplan.

As it appears, this fourth line of critique takes the issue of power and politics one step further. Power and politics are not only factors that *influence* the realization of social and functional goals, and thereby of the goal of the episodic intervention. Episodic interventions *themselves* are political and reproduce the dominating power of the organization's management.

Once again, it is not difficult to see how this critique relates to the social goals logic. The only questions one needs to ask is: 'Who calls the shots?' – for instance, 'Who sets social and functional goals in the course of the intervention?' or 'Who designs and redesigns the intervention infrastructure that should realize these social and functional goals?' If the answer to such questions is 'The organization's management,' then our approach – including its social goals logic – would certainly be top-down and management-driven. Hatch's concern that episodic interventions in organizational structures contribute to 'domination' in organizations would be warranted in this case. However, if we can show that the 3-D model provides opportunities to make processes of construction 'open and available to all', then his concern can, perhaps, be taken away.

Now, before we address this issue head-on, it is relevant to reflect on the type of episodic interventions discussed in this book. This book is about episodic interventions in organizational structures that aim to restore an organization's potential for meaningful survival by transforming the parameter values of its structure from 'high' to 'low'. This means that an organization with a complex production structure and an impressive, powerful, and politically (over)active bureaucracy is turned around into an organization with a relatively simple production structure and decentralized decision making authority. Ideally, organization members in the 'new' low parameter value structure have broad tasks that are related to the organization's 'meaning' – tasks that they can regulate themselves. The design of these tasks allows organization members to understand their role in and contribution to the organization's meaning, to regulate their own work and working relations, and to do this with others in their team. In this way, structural conditions are created for the actual participation of organization members in ongoing 'bottom-up', 'worker-driven' continuous interventions or 'construction processes', as Hatch would have it. Therefore, before addressing the issue of the allegedly 'management-driven' and 'top-down' character of our social goals logic, one should keep in mind that it is perhaps the most important goal of the type of episodic interventions discussed in this book to make processes of social construction, sense-making, learning, and continuous improvement more 'open and available to all', managers and other organization members alike. Of course, this does not eliminate the role of power and politics in organizations. However, it considerably changes the playing field.

Moreover, before addressing the question 'Who calls the shots?', it is relevant to take a closer look at the social goals logic itself.

Each of the social goals that are part of this logic are formulated in such a way that organization members, right from the start, should be engaged in the episodic intervention: 'motivating' themselves for the intervention, inventing and testing ('adopting') solutions for themselves, and 'integrating' (exercising and reinforcing/adapting) these solutions in their own work. What is more, the social goals were formulated in such a way that it is not 'coercion' and 'outsiders' (change agents), but organization members participating in the intervention that are central. In addition, it appeared that the 'affinity' between social and functional goals can help here, because, dependent on the design of the intervention infrastructure, organization members can participate in diagnostic, design, implementation, and evaluation activities. As argued, this allows them to develop their own solutions to their own problems. In this way, they can convince themselves of:

- the urgency and desirability of the intervention – 'motivation' in combination with 'diagnosis' and 'design';
- the possible efficacy of the solutions they invented and tested themselves – 'adoption' in combination with 'design' and 'implementation';
- the actual benefits of the selected solutions – 'integration' in combination with 'implementation' and 'evaluation'.

Therefore, insofar as the *primary activities* in the episodic intervention – that is, the activities that actually realize the functional and social goals in relation to the goal of the intervention – are concerned, the social goals logic does not advocate a top-down and management-driven approach. On the contrary, it encourages the active engagement of organization members in these primary intervention activities.

For this reason, the social goals logic also flat-out rejects the whole image of a group of 'change agents' (managers, consultants, 'facilitators') top-down forcing another group of 'change recipients' to adopt some pre-conceived master plan. Given the social goals logic, it can be argued that, if the distinction between 'change agent' and 'change recipient' is useful at all, it should refer to *roles* that, as the intervention proceeds, can change – turning organization members sometimes into change agents, sometimes into change recipients, and sometimes into the recipients of a change they themselves instituted as agents.

Now, if the social goals logic does not advocate a top-down and management-driven approach with respect to the primary intervention activities, what, then, about the *management* or *regulation* of these primary activities? That is:

- Who sets the social and functional goals (strategic regulation in the intervention)?
- Who designs the intervention infrastructure (design regulation in the intervention)?
- Who assesses the intervention's progress and acts once disturbances occur (operational regulation in the intervention)?

This is the question of 'Who calls the shots?' This question still hovers over our discussion like a big black bird. A suspicious mind could, for instance, argue that 'engaging personnel' in the primary intervention activities is just one more trick of a management that has found new, more advanced, and indirect ways of dominating 'its' workforce in order to 'drive' the intervention forward. Although 'personnel' participate in the actual diagnostic, design, implementation, and evaluation activities, the organization's management, by setting 'participative' social and functional goals and by designing a 'participative' intervention infrastructure, still decides *that* participation is the way forward and *who* participates in the intervention organization *in what role* and under *which conditions*. In this indirect way, the social goals logic can still favour a top-down and management-driven approach – however, now not with respect to the primary activities in the intervention, but with respect to the strategic, design, and operational regulation of these activities. So is it management that, according to the social goals logic, in the end, calls the shots?

There are at least two possible answers to this question. The first is the 'principled' answer. The second is the answer that takes into account the complexities of life in organizations with high parameter value structures.

We start with the principled answer. No, the social goals logic does not necessarily imply that management sets the social and functional goals, designs the intervention organization, and assesses the intervention's progress and acts on disturbances. Fundamentally, the social goals logic just specifies goals *that* should be realized in the intervention in order to make it into a success. It does not specify *who* should set these goals, either for parts or for the whole of the intervention. For instance, it is fully possible to make the 3-D model available to *all* organization members (not just to managers), and give them the opportunity to also participate in the regulation of the intervention. For instance, organization members may be given the opportunity to set social and functional goals with respect to the intervention in 'their' part of the organization. Moreover, given these goals, they can design the infrastructure of 'their' part of the intervention organization in order to realize the goals they themselves set. Finally, they can keep score of their progress and act if this is needed. Just as the level of separation between 'production' and 'control' in an organization structure may be 'low' (providing organization members with *task autonomy*), the level of separation between 'intervention' and 'control' may be low in an intervention structure (providing organization members with *intervention task autonomy*). There is nothing in the social goals logic that enforces or advocates a high level of separation or prevents a low level of separation. As such, this logic does not advocate a top-down, management-driven approach, either with respect to the primary intervention activities nor with respect to their regulation.

This is the principled answer, but what about real organizations? Or, more specifically, what about real organizations with high parameter value structures: organizations with often complex and powerful bureaucracies? In these organizations, it cannot be denied that managers, not workers, have the *formal* task of initiating and regulating organizational interventions. Although workers in high parameter value structures can, and actually do, act as change agents, pressing or persuading, and in this sense 'driving', the organization's management to initiate change, as a rule, the formal decision to start an episodic intervention in order to change the organization's structure is reserved to the organization's management. So it is to be expected that episodic interventions aiming to change the structure of these organizations are formally initiated at the top and driven – in the sense of regulated – by their managers.

Please note that here, the top–down and management-driven character of episodic interventions is a feature of the organization in which these interventions take place rather than an implication or effect of the use of the 3-D model or its social goals logic. In organizations with high parameter value structures, it is difficult, if not impossible, to avoid managers taking fundamental formal decisions about the initiation of episodic interventions and their social and functional goals as well as about the design of the intervention infrastructure. In these organizations, it is initially less important *that* managers take these fundamental decisions; it is more important *what* decisions they take. Are these decisions the outcome of a habitual 'managerial' reflex to be and to stay in what they see as 'control'? Or are these decisions in line with the participative approach of the 3-D model, and do they prefigure the autonomy provided by the low parameter values of the structure that is the intended outcome of the intervention?

If managers 'adopt' an intervention that reduces the parameter values of the structure of their organization (adoption goal) – that is, if they, for whatever reason, are convinced of the value of restoring the organization's potential for continuous adaptation – they should also be able to understand the value of a more participative approach to the intervention itself and restrain their 'old' managerial reflexes. They should be able to see that changing the organization's structure starts with changing their own behaviour, and not with forcing others to change theirs.

So does the social goals logic advocate a top-down, management-driven approach? We think it does not. An important goal of the structure-related episodic interventions it supports is to restore the organization's potential for continuous interventions. This potential for continuous, local, optimizing, bottom-up interventions (that require task autonomy) is regarded as a value by the 3-D model. Moreover, with respect to both the *primary intervention activities* and their *regulation*, the social goals logic does not advocate a top-down or management-driven approach. Although in the type of organizations that are the subject of the interventions supported by the 3-D model, managers, as a rule, call the shots, both the social goals logic as well as the 3-D model support an approach that allows organization members to participate both in the primary intervention activities and their regulation, making processes of organizational transformation 'open and available to all', as Hatch would have it.

7.7 Conclusion: social goals in the intervention

Episodic interventions in high parameter value structures are interventions 'by' and 'in' organizations. This means that, as a result of the intervention, interactions and interaction premises that are directly and indirectly related to the (re)production of the organization's high parameter value structure are interactively changed in such a way that the new low parameter value structure becomes an organizational reality.

In order to change these interactions and interaction premises, social goals in the interventions should be realized. In the 3-D model, three social goals are distinguished: 'motivation', 'adoption', and 'integration'. Each social goal has its own sub-goals (e.g. 'motivation' has 'urgency' and 'vision' as sub-goals). Sub-goals are related in such a way that consequent sub-goals can both be built upon and reinforce the preceding sub-goal. For instance, 'vision' (consequent) can both be built upon insights that are a part of 'urgency' and further reinforce 'urgency' (precedent). In this way, social sub-goals are intrinsically related.

In organizations, there are socio-psychological 'drivers' that can help realize social goals. These drivers may be either 'cognition-related' (e.g. 'disconfirmation') or 'emotion-related' (e.g. 'anxiety', 'desire'). As such, these drivers are in line with two of the means of persuasion that can be found in classical rhetoric: 'logos' (cognition-related) and 'pathos' (emotion-related). Moreover, drivers may be either individual- or context-centred.

From a closer analysis of the critique of stage models of social change, we learned that the social goals that are a part of the 3-D model:

1. are not an empirical description of stages of episodic interventions – Social goals are prescriptive constructs that can help navigate the complexity of episodic interventions (without negating or eliminating this complexity). These prescriptive constructs can be set for/by different participants in the intervention (e.g. intervention teams, individuals).

2. can support both incremental and transformational change – Transformational here means the transformation of the organization's structure from high to lower parameter values. Incremental here means that the change process by means of which this transformation is effected is an incremental change process.
3. as prescriptive constructs, can sensitize participants in the interventions to all kinds of factors – including power and politics – that can affect the progress of the episodic intervention (in terms of realizing functional or social goals).
4. do not prescribe or 'enforce' a top–down or 'blue-print' approach of episodic interventions – Social goals may be set by an intervention team for that intervention team (local autonomy). Moreover, social goals may be set and reset as the intervention evolves (muddling through).

8

THE INFRASTRUCTURAL DIMENSION

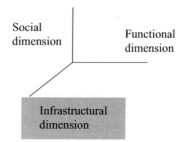

Episodic Interventions in the Structure of Organization

PART I
Theoretical Framework:

– Organizations

– Organizational structures

– (episodic) Interventions

PART II
A 3-D Model of Episodic Interventions:

Social dimension

Functional dimension

Infrastructural dimension

FIGURE 8.0 Roadmap of the book

8.1 Introduction

In the previous two chapters, we discussed the functional and social dimensions of the 3-D model. These dimensions specify goals in the intervention that should be set for parts or the whole of the intervention in order to realize its goal. In addition to the two goal dimensions, an *infrastructural dimension* is needed. This infrastructural dimension is relevant because episodic interventions, as a rule, require an intervention organization. Earlier, we defined this intervention organization as a temporary organization, on top of the 'standing' organization, that is devoted to the actual performance and regulation of the episodic intervention.

Just like any other organizations, intervention organizations have their own infrastructure and hence their own infrastructural dimension. This intervention infrastructure consists of: (1) an intervention structure – the network of intervention tasks needed to realize and adapt functional and social goals in the intervention; (2) intervention technology – the technology or techniques supporting the performance of intervention tasks by human resources; and (3) knowledgeable, skilled, and motivated human resources (organization members, consultants, facilitators, stakeholders) who, supported by intervention technology, perform intervention tasks.

It is the purpose of an intervention infrastructure to enable the realization and adaptation of functional and social goals in the intervention.

In the intervention structure, operational and regulatory intervention activities are grouped and allocated into a network of intervention tasks. Examples of operational intervention activities are: 'performing a diagnosis', 'creating change relationships', 'making a problem inventory', or 'testing a particular new way of working'. Examples of regulatory intervention activities are: selecting functional or social goals that should be realized next, designing parts or aspects of the intervention infrastructure, or dealing with disturbances that occur during the intervention.

In addition, intervention technologies or techniques should be selected that can support the performance of intervention tasks. For instance, *Group Model Building* (Vennix, 1996) may be selected as a technique in order to 'test' a new way of patient scheduling.

Finally, knowledgeable, skilled, and motivated human resources should be selected or trained who can use the selected intervention technologies or techniques in order to perform the required intervention tasks.

In short, in order to enable the realization and adaptation of functional and social goals, an intervention infrastructure should be designed.

Like all design regulation in organizations, designing an intervention infrastructure is a kind of experiment. Based on selected functional and social goals, an intervention infrastructure is designed that will require redesign as the intervention unfolds, for instance because new functional or social goals are set or because unforeseen problems or opportunities occur. As a consequence, the design of the intervention infrastructure is not static, but dynamic. It develops along with the intervention.

Given the experimental and dynamic character of the design of intervention infrastructures, it is impossible to appoint one particular infrastructure as 'the' blueprint intervention infrastructure that should be used in order to realize functional and social goals in the intervention. However, we can develop a procedure supporting the flexible design of intervention infrastructures that is as simple as possible. This procedure should at least meet two requirements.

First, it should help 'translate' functional and social goals that are set as the intervention proceeds into a design of an intervention infrastructure that can realize and adapt these goals – i.e. they should relate the infrastructural dimension of interventions to their functional and social dimensions. Only in this way can an intervention infrastructure be designed that enables the realization and adaptation of functional and social goals.

Second, the procedure should help adjust the design of the intervention infrastructure to problems and opportunities as they actually occur. Only in this way can the intervention infrastructure address experimental demands of episodic interventions in organizational structures and enable flexible responses to what the world might throw at it.

We can also describe what the three aspects – structure, technology, human resources – of the intervention infrastructure entail. Here, at least three questions are relevant. First, what do we understand by an intervention structure, by technology supporting the intervention, and by the knowledge, skills, and motivation of the human resources performing the intervention? Second, what topics regarding intervention structures, technology, and human resources are relevant to discuss in the context of episodic interventions in (self-inhibiting) organizational structures? Third, how are the structural, technological, and human resources aspects of the intervention infrastructure related to the procedure that supports the design of the intervention infrastructure – i.e. how can these aspects of the intervention infrastructure actually be designed?

Consequently, this chapter consists of two main divisions. The first introduces a procedure supporting the design of flexible intervention infrastructures (Sections 8.2 and 8.3). The second discusses the three aspects of the intervention infrastructure – intervention structure, technology, and human resources – and their relation to the procedure (Sections 8.5–8.7). The two main divisions of this chapter are separated and joined by Section 8.4, where factors that can affect the progress of episodic interventions are discussed. These factors should be taken into account in the design of the three aspects of intervention infrastructures. Section 8.8 reflects the findings of this chapter.

8.2 A procedure supporting flexible design regulation: function and 'glue'

Before we explain the procedure that can support the flexible design of the infrastructure of an intervention organization, it will be useful to address two questions.

The first is about what this procedure should do, what its function is. The answer to this question is that the procedure should support two types of design regulation: 'goal-driven design regulation' and 'improvement-driven design regulation'. The crux of both types of design regulation (and the procedures supporting them) is that selected goals on the functional and social dimensions are, somehow, translated into a design of an intervention infrastructure that can realize and adapt these goals.

The second question we want to address in this section pertains to this *translation issue*. Translating functional and social goals into an intervention infrastructure presupposes that the two goal dimensions of the 3-D model can be meaningfully connected to its infrastructural dimension. The second question is about how this connection can be made. It is about the 'glue' that connects goals on the functional and social dimensions to the design of the infrastructure of the intervention organization. The answer to this second question is that the interactions needed to realize selected functional and social goals provide this glue.

8.2.1 What the procedure should do: goal- and improvement-driven design regulation

In a trivial sense, we already know what the procedure should do: it should support the flexible design of intervention infrastructures that enable the realization and adaptation of functional and social goals in episodic interventions in organizational structures.

In order to find out what this entails, we need to take a closer look at what it means to flexibly 'design' intervention infrastructures. We need to take a closer look at the role of 'design regulation' in the experiments that episodic interventions in organizational structures are. To this purpose, a quick reminder of the logic of use that was developed in Chapter 5 may suffice. As argued there, this logic presupposes the following activities in the intervention:

1. Strategic regulation – select functional and social goals in the intervention.
2. Design regulation – build an intervention infrastructure that can perform and regulate (operational, design, and strategic regulation) the operational intervention processes needed to realize selected functional and social goals.
3. Operational regulation – manage disturbances of the operational intervention process (without changing its design or goals).
4. Operational intervention process – this process should realize the functional and social goals.

As a part of the regulatory activities, a fifth activity is presupposed:

5. Continuously assess the progress of the episodic intervention relative to selected functional and social goals and, dependent on this assessment, perform regulatory activity 1, 2, or 3.

From these activities, two types of design regulation can be derived: *goal-driven* and *improvement-driven* design regulation.

Goal-driven design regulation relates to the selection of new 'proximate' functional and social *goals* in the intervention to the design of an intervention infrastructure that can realize these goals (note that the term 'proximate' here refers to functional and social goals that are 'next in line' to be realized). As discussed in Chapter 5, at the start of an episodic intervention, 'diagnosis' and 'motivation' may be selected as proximate functional and social goals. Later, as the diagnosis and motivation goals are realized, 'new' proximate goals (e.g. design and adoption) may be selected. Ideal typically, this process of selecting new proximate goals in the intervention continues until the final functional and social goals (evaluation and integration) are realized. Each time new proximate functional or social goals are selected, design regulation should, if required, translate these new goals into an intervention infrastructure that enables the realization and adaptation of the selected proximate goals.

Improvement-driven design regulation relates to *improvements* of the intervention infrastructure as the episodic intervention unfolds, *given* selected proximate functional and social goals. Some of these improvements may be required because of *problems* that occur. Other improvements may be related to *opportunities* that present themselves. In sum, the two types of design regulation required for the flexible design of intervention infrastructures are goal- and improvement-driven design regulation. If our procedure is to support such a flexible design, it should be able to cover these two types. This is *what* the procedure should be able to do.

8.2.2 Looking for 'glue': 'what', 'how', and 'who' of interaction

Before we can turn our attention to the question *how* goal- and improvement-driven design regulation can be realized, i.e. what the procedures for goal- and improvement-driven design regulation look like, we need to address the issue of the connection between the two goal dimensions of the 3-D model and its infrastructural dimension.

As indicated, a procedure for the flexible design of intervention infrastructures should enable the translation of selected functional and social goals into an intervention infrastructure that supports the realization and adaptation of these goals. But how is this 'translation' possible? How can dimensions as diverse as the functional, social, and infrastructural dimensions be connected in a way that results in an intervention infrastructure that actually supports the realization and adaptation of functional and social goals? What 'glue' can connect these dimensions in a way that is useful for the desired flexible design of such an infrastructure?

In order to solve this 'glue problem', it will be useful to re-examine our description of organizational interventions. 'Organizational interventions', we indicated, are interventions 'for', 'in', and 'by' organizations. Until now, the 'for' – the goal of the intervention relative to the organization's meaningful survival – and the 'in' – the object of the intervention and its relation to the interactions and interaction premises that (re)produce it – have had the lion's share of attention. Now it is time for the 'by' to take centre stage.

That organizational interventions are interventions 'by' organizations simply means that interaction is needed in order to realize functional and social goals in the intervention (and, thereby, the goal of the intervention). Interaction is a necessary 'ingredient' of all organizational interventions. No organizational intervention, including the episodic interventions that are the topic of this book, can succeed without it. That is also why in Chapter 7, 'creating and maintaining change relationships' was described as an important 'generic' social goal that supports the realization of the 'motivation', 'adoption' and 'integration' goals. Change relationships are an important social condition for the interactions by means of which organizational interventions actually take shape.

Now, how can this insight that organizational interventions are interventions 'by' organizations be of help? An example may be instructive.

Suppose that in some episodic intervention, 'making a problem inventory' is the 'proximate' – i.e. next to be realized – functional goal. Moreover, suppose that 'making a problem inventory' should contribute to the social goal 'motivation' – i.e. making the problem inventory should motivate organization members to let go of current and move to new interaction premises and concomitant interaction patterns and adopt an intervention as a means to do this. Given the selected proximate functional and social goals, goal-driven design regulation should 'translate' these goals into an intervention infrastructure. Based on the idea that organizational interventions are interventions 'by' organizations and therefore involve interaction, this 'translation' may benefit from asking the following questions:

> Question 1: *What* topics should be interactively addressed in order to realize the proximate functional and social goal? For instance, in order to develop the required motivation by means of making a problem inventory, variables and norms should be specified that can be used for the purpose of establishing the gap between norms and facts.
>
> Question 2: *How* should one interactively address these topics in order to realize the proximate functional and social goals? For instance, should interaction aim at divergence and confrontation, or convergence and harmony; should interaction aim at precision and detail, or approximation and general outline; should interaction aim at rapid results, or allow for thorough deliberation; should interaction be formal, or informal?
>
> Question 3: *Who* should be involved in interactions about what selected topics in order to realize the proximate functional and social goal? For instance, should all organization members be involved in all the interactions about 'making a problem inventory', or should particular members be selected to participate in particular interactions?

Questions like these provide important clues for the design of an intervention infrastructure that can support the interactions needed to realize and adapt the proximate functional and social goals in the intervention. They provide a link between proximate goals on the functional and social dimensions of the 3-D model and selections on its infrastructural dimension.

What-questions

'*What-questions*' about topics that should be interactively addressed in order to realize proximate functional and social goals provide a first indication of operational intervention activities. Operational intervention activities are activities that should be performed in order to realize proximate functional and social goals. Examples of operational intervention activities are discussing the organization's meaning in the context of a diagnosis, working together on the design of the production structure of some part of the organization, or discussing differences and commonalities in order to create change relationships. As a rule, operational intervention activities can be derived by: (1) decomposing selected proximate functional and social goals into sub-goals, and (2) asking what should actually be done – i.e. what topics should be interactively addressed – in order to realize these sub-goals. Deriving operational intervention activities is relevant because it is a first step towards the design of the *structure* of the intervention organization. Just like the structure of another organization, the structure of an intervention organization consists of a production and a control structure. The production structure of an intervention organization can be defined as the grouping and allocation of operational intervention activities into a network of intervention tasks relative to (proximate) functional and social goals in the intervention. In order to be able to group and allocate operational intervention activities into intervention tasks, one needs to know what these operational intervention activities are. 'What-questions', i.e. questions about topics that should be interactively addressed in order to realize proximate functional and social goals, can help to make an inventory of operational intervention activities, and for this reason are a first step towards designing an intervention structure.

How-questions

'*How-questions*' refer to *how* the topics resulting from the what-questions should be interactively addressed in order to realize (proximate) functional and social goals. How-questions are primarily about *required modes of interaction* (see van Amelsvoort, 1998, who discusses most of the modes mentioned below). Should interaction be:

1. participative, and if so what type of participation is required – should it be active (co-decision, co-creation), or more passive (consultation or just being informed)?
2. technically informed, or based only on common sense reasoning (technical knowledge or skills)?
3. carefully planned in terms of rules, procedures, and goals, or should interaction be free and open-ended (planning)?
4. detailed and precise, or should it aim for outline and approximation (detail)?
5. formal, or informal (formalization)?
6. slow-paced, or quick (speed)?
7. convergent, or divergent (convergence)?

Reflecting on required modes of interaction may help because, in combination with the topics of interaction, these modes provide clues for the design of the *structural*, *technical*, and *human resources* aspects of the intervention infrastructure. For instance, in the context of making a diagnosis, it may be decided that the organization's function should be discussed (what-question). Asking how this topic of 'function' should be discussed can be helpful. For instance, if it is concluded that function should be discussed in outline and in a participative way, aiming for convergence, it becomes possible to select the techniques that can support the required interaction.

Who-questions

'*Who-questions*' are questions about persons who should be involved in operational intervention activities in order to realize (proximate) functional and social goals in the intervention. Who-questions, therefore, refer to the human resources aspect of the intervention infrastructure. For instance, once it is established that the organization's meaning should be discussed in a participative way, using a particular technique, it becomes possible to ask who should be involved in these discussions. Once this selection issue is resolved, it also becomes possible to reflect on the human resources support measures that may be required to develop the knowledge, skills, or motivation of the selected organization members to actually use the selected technique in the interactions about the selected topic (in the example, the organization's meaning).

8.3 Goal- and improvement-driven design regulation: procedures

Therefore, perhaps it *helps* to take seriously that organizational interventions are interventions 'by' organizations, since the interactions – in terms of topics (what), modes (how), and participants (who) – that are needed to realize proximate functional and social goals in the intervention provide a starting point for the design of the structural, technical, and human resources aspects of the intervention infrastructure. As it appears, these interactions provide the 'glue' we were looking for; they can help to meaningfully connect selected goals on the functional and social dimensions of an episodic intervention to the design of its infrastructural dimension. Based on this idea, we will develop our step-by-step procedures for goal- and improvement-driven design regulation.

8.3.1 Goal-driven design regulation

The procedure for goal-driven design consists of two parts. The goal of the first part is to establish what should be done in order to drive the episodic intervention forward: what is the required intervention effort in the next phase of the intervention? In order to establish this effort, three steps are needed:

> Step 1: Assess the current status of the intervention in terms of functional and social goals that have been realized.
>
> Step 2: Select desired proximate functional and social goals that should be realized in order to drive the intervention forward.

Step 3: Determine the gap between the current and desired status of the intervention in terms of functional and social goals.

Once the gap between the current and desired status of the intervention is established, it becomes possible to ask what-, how-, and who-questions. What topics should be interactively addressed in order to close this gap, how should these topics be addressed, and who should be involved in addressing these topics? Answers to these questions provide a first indication of operational intervention activities, intervention techniques, and intervention human resources that are needed to close the gap between the current and the desired status of the intervention. Based on this first indication, a design for an intervention infrastructure can be made that should support the activities needed to close the gap between the current and desired status of the intervention. This is what steps 4 and 5 are about.

Step 4: Reflect on what topics should be interactively addressed in what way and by whom in order to close the gap between the current and the desired status of the intervention in terms of functional and social goals.

Step 5: Design the infrastructure of an intervention organization that can support the activities that should be performed in order to close the gap between the current and the desired status of the intervention, i.e.:

5.1: design an intervention structure;

5.2: select the intervention technology/techniques;

5.3: select human resources and human resources support measures.

In order to explain what the five steps entail, we start by presenting an example. Based on this example, we (A) illustrate steps 1–4 and (B) add comments in order to amend the simplicity of the example and make that step applicable to more complex situations. Because the topics that constitute step 5 will be discussed in separate sections (intervention structure in Section 8.5, technology in Section 8.6, and human resources in Section 8.7), step 5 will only be discussed in outline in this section.

Example: cardiology department

Suppose that in some hospital, the quality of cardiac care is far below standards. Mortality rates are unacceptably high, patients and their families complain about the quality of pre- and post-operative care, and normal working relations are undermined by chronic communication problems both among surgeons and between cardiac specialists and nurses. As a result, absentee and personnel turnover levels are higher than in the rest of the hospital. After yet another grave incident, the National Health Supervisory Authority decides to temporarily close down the hospital's cardiac care facility. In an attempt to improve the situation, the hospital's board of directors decides that an episodic intervention is needed. To this purpose, a senior consultant with an excellent track record in the field of hospital care is hired. In order to guide her through the strategic part of goal-driven design regulation, this consultant uses the 3-D model and reflects on the following questions.

Step 1: Assess the current status of the episodic intervention in terms of functional and social goals that have been realized

Explanation of step 1 in terms of the hospital example

In order to assess the current status of the intervention, the consultant interviews different parties that are involved in or affected by the intervention: the board of directors, some of the members of the cardiology department, and other hospital staff who have dealings with the department. As a result of these interviews, she concludes that no goals on the functional dimension have been realized yet. Although the report of the supervisory authority specifies a number of problems, no diagnosis has been made. On the social dimension, she concludes that, forced by the report of the supervisory authority and the subsequent closing down of the department, the board of directors and most members of the cardiology department have already developed a sense of urgency. However, at present, this sense of urgency is still 'abstract' ('Things should change around here') and 'negative' ('We cannot go on like this'). As it is, neither the motivation goal nor the change relationships needed in order to make progress in the intervention have been realized yet.

Comments on step 1

With respect to the assessment of the current status of the intervention, no less than four comments are in order. The first comment is a quite complex one. It is about the relation between episodic interventions and their organizational pre-history. It is about what happens before the 3-D model is selected as a technique that can support the episodic intervention. The other comments are more straightforward. The second is about what it means to specify the current status of the intervention in terms of functional and social goals. The third comment is about the 'subject' of the assessment, i.e. who assesses the current status of the intervention. The last comment touches on how the assessment is performed, i.e. it touches on assessment techniques.

Comment 1: the pre-history of episodic interventions and their infrastructures Let us start with the convoluted issue of episodic interventions and their organizational pre-history. In the example, it seems as if the episodic intervention starts when the hospital's board decides to hire a consultant. However, on closer examination, things are more complicated than this. Episodic interventions, particularly those in organizations with high parameter value structures, as a rule, have long and complex pre-histories that consist of critical events, processes of issue selling and agenda setting, and power struggles between agents pushing for and against change. Because of the intransparency of organizational processes of self-production, attempts to reconstruct these pre-histories remain selective and fragmented views on the genesis of episodic interventions. As a result, it is hard, if not impossible, to pinpoint the beginning of episodic interventions in a 'historical' or 'reconstructive' sense. Their myriad roots go deep into the organization's history, and it always seems possible to refer to yet other events or processes that eventually led to an intervention.

Still, episodic interventions can be said to begin in another, 'formal', sense. In some phase of an organization's history, the possibility and usefulness of an episodic intervention may become an explicit issue in interaction. At some point, it may even be formally decided that an episodic interaction needs to be performed. Once this happens, the goal of 'performing an episodic intervention' can become an interaction premise that actually guides the production of intervention-related follow-up interactions and interaction premises that, together, constitute the ensuing episodic intervention, making the intervention into an organizational reality.

In the case of the episodic interventions in (hierarchical) organizations with high parameter value structures, the formal decisions that bootstrap episodic interventions into organizational existence, as a rule, are the prerogative of the organization's (top) management. So, although these episodic interventions may have long pre-histories involving all kinds of organizational agents, at some point they become an explicit issue of formal decision making in managerial circles. Once this happens, and more importantly, once 'performing an episodic intervention' becomes an interaction premise that guides the production of intervention-related interactions and interaction premises, these interventions can be said to begin in a formal sense. Of course, this managerial start of the episodic intervention does not exclude that change agents at the 'bottom' of the organization may have pushed for change. Moreover, it does not necessarily imply that the intervention itself will be pursued in a 'top-down' manner.

In general, it can be argued that episodic interventions have long and complex pre-histories. In spite of this, it is still possible to meaningfully speak about their 'start' by referring to the phase in which the goal of performing an episodic intervention becomes a formal interaction premise guiding intervention-related follow-up.

Moreover, just like episodic interventions, intervention infrastructures have a history – i.e. their design is not something that happens in a flash of God-like creation. Intervention infrastructures are more organic than that. They 'grow' out of the infrastructure of the organization, attain a more or less separate existence, and once again 'merge' with the infrastructure of the organization.

In the example, the hospital's board, as part of its task in the infrastructure of the organization, takes the decision to appoint a consultant to a particular intervention task. Technically speaking, this decision is an act of design regulation with respect to both intervention human resources and the intervention structure, since by means of its decision, the board appoints a consultant (intervention human resources) to perform the intervention task of preparing the intervention (intervention structure). As such, the board performs a task that can be seen as a precursor of the intervention infrastructure. In general, it can be argued that intervention infrastructures grow out of, and therefore have a pre-history in, the infrastructure of organizations.

Of course, this pre-history can influence the design of the intervention infrastructure. However, as will be shown, it does not determine this design. On the contrary, it is highly probable that mature intervention infrastructures that are based on the 3-D model have features that are quite the opposite of the complex and hierarchical structures of the organizations that are the object of the episodic interventions that try to change these structures.

Given the pre-histories of episodic interventions and their infrastructures, it is likely that, before the 3-D model appears on stage, all kinds of design decisions have already been made. As a matter of fact, the selection of the 3-D model is itself an instance of design regulation: the model is selected as a technique that is a part of the intervention technology. This means that the use and application of the 3-D model in a particular episodic intervention has a history too. Both the goal- and improvement-driven design of the intervention infrastructure discussed in this section presuppose that the 3-D model, in some way and for some reason, has been selected. As such, designing an intervention infrastructure by means of the 3-D model necessarily presupposes some preceding, more or less embryonic, intervention

Comment 2: specifying the assessment of the current status   The second comment is about the assessment of the current status of the episodic intervention in terms of functional and social goals that have been realized.

In the example, the consultant concludes that the intervention is still in its infant stage: no diagnosis has been performed, no change relationships have been created, and although the crisis contributes to a sense of urgency, this sense of urgency is still abstract and negative. Because the intervention is in its infant stage, the consultant's assessment is still quite general (for instance, because no diagnosis has been made yet, it is not relevant to ask what parts and aspects of the organization have been diagnosed). Still, for the purpose of goal-driven design regulation, it might be relevant to further specify the assessment of the current status of the intervention. In the case of assessing the realization of *functional* goals, this specification entails:

1. *sub-goals* of the main goals diagnosis, design, implementation, and evaluation – e.g. the sub-goals of the diagnosis goal are problem inventory (PI), cause analysis (CA), and defining a solution space (SS);
2. *parts* of the organization that realized particular functional goals or sub-goals – e.g. a team within the cardiology department has been diagnosed, but the cardiology department itself or the hospital as a whole have not been diagnosed;
3. *aspects* of the organization that have been diagnosed, designed, etc. – e.g. the organizational structure, its technology, its human resources, and its culture.

This further specification is relevant because, in a possible next step of the intervention, it may be useful to include other sub-goals, parts, or aspects as well. For instance, after a diagnosis of the culture of the cardiology department, it may be decided that a diagnosis of its structure may also be useful.

In the case of *social* goals, it also might be relevant to specify both social sub-goals and socio-psychological drivers. Moreover, it might be useful to specify persons or groups that realized these sub-goals. For instance, it might be useful to ask whose change relationships are sufficient for the purpose of performing intervention activities, who developed the motivation for change, or whose behaviour was disconfirmed.

In order to address these questions, an overview might be made of relevant groups in the intervention. These groups are parties that are or should be involved in the intervention or are affected by the intervention. Examples of such groups are the members of the cardiology department, the board of directors, or the nurses within the cardiology department. Making an inventory of these groups is itself an experimental activity. In the example, the consultant, for instance, did not differentiate between different types of members of the cardiology department. However, it might be relevant to distinguish between doctors, nurses, and supporting staff or between older and younger members of the department's personnel. Moreover, the consultant did not include the department's patients or their representatives in the list of parties involved. On reflection, and as the intervention proceeds, she might consider it useful to add new groups to her list or remove old parties from it. Given this second comment, it may be helpful to use Table 8.1 for the purpose of assessing the current status of an episodic intervention.

TABLE 8.1 Current status of the intervention

Current status				
Functional (sub-)goals: realized				
	Diagnosis *PI – CA – SS*	*Design*	*Implementation*	*Evaluation*
Part/aspect	—	—	—	—
...	—	—	—	—
Part/aspect	—	—	—	—
Social (sub-)goals: realized				
	Creating change relationships	Motivation Urgency – Vision	Adoption Inventing – Testing	Integration Exercising – Reinforcing/ adjusting
Board	No info	Urgency (abstract/ negative)	—	—
Cardiology Dept	No info	Urgency (abstract/ negative)	—	—
Group n	No info	—	—	—

In Table 8.1, we find that in the hospital case and on the functional dimension, no part or aspect of the organization has been diagnosed, designed, implemented, or evaluated. On the social dimension, there is no information available about the quality of current change relationships. Apparently, both the board (group 1) and members of the cardiology department (group 2) experience an abstract and negative sense of urgency (as part of motivation). Given this overview, the consultant might decide to do some further research into the change relationships between and within the groups involved.

Comment 3: who assesses the current status of the episodic intervention In the example, it is the consultant who is assigned to facilitate the episodic intervention. As indicated, this assignment is an act of design regulation on the part of the hospital's board. The consultant, then, selects the 3-D model as a tool (which is an act of design regulation, too), and starts assessing the current status of the intervention in terms of functional and social goals that have been realized. In technical terms, this assessment is an activity aimed at the goal-driven design regulation of the intervention infrastructure. Of course, the 3-D model does not prescribe that a consultant should be selected to perform this goal-driven design regulation. Other persons or parties can perform this activity as well. For instance, some group that performs operational intervention activities, e.g. by participating in a diagnosis, can assess its own progress on the functional and social dimensions in order to specify what functional and social goals should be realized next. In this case, this group not only performs operational intervention activities, it also performs regulatory intervention activities (in this case, goal-driven design regulation). Later in this chapter, as we discuss the intervention structure, this topic of the regulatory autonomy of individuals or groups participating in an episodic intervention will be taken up again. Here, we just want to underline that the activity of goal-driven design regulation can be performed by all kinds of persons or groups in the organization.

Comment 4: how the current status is assessed   The fourth comment refers to the interviews that the consultant uses in order to assess the current status of the intervention. Of course, 'interviews with relevant parties' is only one technique to find an answer to assess the current status of the intervention. Group discussions, document analysis, observation, or even a survey involving all organization members are examples of techniques that can be used as well. In general, all kinds of techniques can be used in order to find answers to the questions that support goal-driven design regulation. The selected techniques should be seen as part of the technical aspect of the infrastructure of the intervention organization.

Step 2: Select new proximate functional and social goals that should be realized in order to drive the intervention forward (this is the desired proximate state of the intervention)

Explanation of step 2 in terms of the hospital example

Based on her assessment of the current status of the intervention, some extra research on current change relationships, and discussions about the next step in the intervention with both the board of directors and members of the cardiology department, the consultant decides that 'creating change relationships' should be a 'social' priority. In particular, change relationships should be developed both within and between the cardiology department and the hospital's board. Moreover, the social goal 'motivation' should be served by developing a vision for the cardiology department. This vision, should make the existing sense of urgency less negative and abstract. Moreover, it should contribute to a positive desire for change. Both the hospital's board and all the members of the cardiology department are included in this 'vision' goal. Functionally, a start should be made with the first part of the diagnosis: an inventory of the problems of the cardiology department. To this purpose, a start should be made on defining diagnostic variables and norms that can serve as a basis for a problem inventory. Because there is a possible affinity between developing a vision and specifying diagnostic variables and their norms, realizing the (social) vision goal should go hand in hand with specifying the (functional) variables and their norms.

Comments on step 2

As a first comment, it should be stated that the three last comments on step 1 also hold for step 2. Applied to step 2, this means that:

1. (new) desired proximate functional and social goals should be further specified, in terms of sub-goals, parts, and aspects – e.g. what parts and aspects of the organization should be diagnosed or who should develop change relations;
2. other parties than the consultant can select the new proximate goals in the intervention;
3. other techniques than 'discussions with some of the parties involved' can be used for the purpose of selecting these new proximate functional and social goals.

For the purpose of keeping track of the selected proximate functional and social goals (the desired status of the intervention) Table 8.2 may be useful. Applied to the hospital example, this table can be filled in as follows. Functionally, an inventory of the problems

TABLE 8.2 Desired status

Desired status				
Functional (sub-)goals: realized				
	Diagnosis	*Design*	*Implementation*	*Evaluation*
	PI – CA – SS			
Part: cardiology dept/aspect	Problem inventory of cardiology department: define variables and norms	—	—	—
…	—	—	—	—
Part/aspect	—	—	—	—
Social (sub-)goals: realized				
	Creating change relationships	Motivation Urgency – Vision	Adoption Inventing – Testing	Integration Exercising – Reinforcing/adjusting
Board	Create change relationships	Urgency/desire (positive) Create vision	—	—
Cardiology dept	Create change relationships	Urgency/desire (positive) Create vision	—	—
Group n	No info	—	—	—

of the cardiology department should be made (PI). Socially, change relationships should be established both within and between the hospital's board and the cardiology department. Moreover, these groups should start working on the creation of a vision that outlines the future of the cardiology department. This vision should also contribute to making the experienced sense of urgency less abstract and negative.

The second comment we want to make is about different 'modes of planning' of episodic interventions. In the example, proximate functional and social goals are selected that define the desired next step in the episodic intervention. However, 'defining the desired next step' is only one mode of planning. In actual practice, different modes of planning can be applied (and even be combined) in episodic interventions. Three of these modes are discussed here: simple planning, intervention programmes, and intervention projects.

Simple planning is the basic mode. In the case of simple planning, proximate functional and social goals are set for one or more organizational aspects, parts, or groups. In this way, only the desired next step in the episodic intervention is specified. This mode of planning is applied in the hospital example. In the example, defining variables and norms that can be used as the basis for a problem inventory is set as a proximate functional goal. Moreover, building change relationships is set as a proximate social goal for both the hospital's board and the cardiology department. Finally, creating a vision and developing a positive sense of urgency are selected as proximate social goals for both the board and the cardiology department. Simple planning differs from more advanced modes of planning because *only* proximate functional and social goals are set, i.e. goals that are next in line to be realized. For this reason, simple planning is closest to the situational character of episodic interventions: i.e., as the intervention evolves, new proximate functional and social goals are set.

Planning becomes more complex as *sequences* of proximate functional and social goals are set for one or more organizational aspects, parts, or groups. For instance, *first* the board of directors should develop the motivation for change and adopt a macro solution for the organization's problems, *second* selected 'pilot' teams involved in the operational activities of the organization should develop a motivation for change and both adopt and integrate their solutions for the problems they diagnosed, *third* all other teams in the organization should follow the example of the pilot teams.

In this more complex case, an *intervention programme* may be developed. Such a programme is an 'overarching plan' that provides an 'outline' of the episodic intervention. The programme is overarching because it includes all the functional and social goals that should be realized in the intervention, starting with 'diagnosis' and 'motivation' and ending with 'evaluation' and 'integration'. The programme is only a plan in outline because it does not provide a detailed specification of the goals and means involved in the intervention. Given the programme's outline, more detailed proximate functional or social goals may be selected as the episodic intervention unfolds. In this way, it becomes possible to take into account the salient features of the actual problems or opportunities that present themselves in the course of the intervention. As such, an intervention programme still combines planning with the experimental character of episodic interventions.

Intervention projects go one step beyond intervention programmes. In the case of intervention projects, functional and social goals are defined in terms of well-specified 'deliverables' that should be realized at particular pre-specified moments in time by particular human resources against particular costs. In order to make and manage the intervention project, project management tools seem to be indispensable. Most of the available tools focus on functional goals, risks involved in the intervention, and the organization, resources, time, and information needed to realize these goals. Social goals (and their relation to functional goals) are a blind spot of most project management tools. Intervention projects are farthest removed from the situational character of episodic interventions. Both the blindness of project management tools to the social dimension of episodic interventions and their focus on (if not obsession with) detailed planning and control can do these interventions more harm than good because they suggest 'control' where there is in fact 'muddling through'. Still, some of the techniques supporting intervention projects can be relevant in the context of episodic interventions in organizational structures.

As indicated in Chapter 7, independent of the mode of planning, the total portfolio of organizational activities, i.e. ongoing operational and regulatory activities in the organization and other interventions or projects, should be taken into account when selecting (sequences of) new proximate functional and social goals in the intervention. In this way, both the feasibility of actually realizing these goals and the total workload of organization members can be kept in check.

Step 3: Determine the gap between the current and desired status of the intervention in terms of functional and social goals

Explanation of step 3 in terms of the hospital example

Given the results of step 1 (current status) and step 2 (desired status), the consultant determines the gap between the current and the desired status of the intervention. In this way, she gets an impression of the required proximate *intervention effort*, i.e. of what should be done next in order move the intervention forward. Figure 8.1 depicts this effort.

In Figure 8.1, applied to the hospital example, the black dot stands for the current status of the intervention. It indicates that, except for an abstract and negative sense of urgency (U), no functional or social goals have currently been realized. The black square stands for the

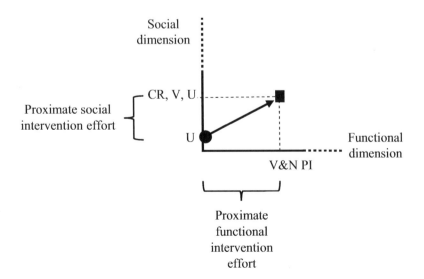

FIGURE 8.1 The required proximate intervention effort

desired status of the intervention. It indicates that on the functional dimension, variables (V) and norms (N) should be selected for the purpose of a problem inventory of the cardiology department. This problem inventory is a first step towards a diagnosis of the department's organization structure. On the social dimension, the square indicates that change relationships (CR) should be created and a vision (V) of the future should be developed that can make the existing sense of urgency (U) less abstract and negative, or even better, turns it into a desire for change. The arrow stands for the proximate intervention effort. As indicated by the curly brackets in the figure, the intervention effort can be analysed into a proximate functional and social intervention effort. By determining the gap between the current and desired status of the intervention, the consultant gets an overview of who should move from what current situation to what desired situation. This overview provides a point of departure for asking questions about what topics should be interactively addressed, in what way, and by whom in order to actually realize the required progress.

Comment on step 3

We want to underline, once again, that for the purpose of determining the intervention effort, *specificity* is required: what precisely is the gap between the current and the desired status of the intervention? Because, in the example, the intervention is still in its infant stage, specifying the intervention effort seems a somewhat trivial exercise. However, as the intervention proceeds, more parts or aspects of the organization may become the object of the intervention and more groups may become involved in it. As this happens, keeping track of the gap between the current and desired status of the intervention becomes a more complex job. Table 8.3 nay be used for charting an overview of the proximate intervention effort.

Step 4: Reflect on what topics should be interactively addressed in what way and by whom in order to close the gap between the current and the desired status of the intervention in terms of functional and social goals

Explanation of step 4 in terms of the hospital example

In order to answer the 'what', 'how', and 'who' questions that function as 'glue' between the two goal dimensions of the 3-D model and its infrastructural dimension, the consultant summarizes the findings of step 3. Based on this step, she knows that on the functional dimension, variables and norms should be specified for the purpose of a problem inventory of the cardiology department. On the social dimension, change relationships should be created both between and within the hospital's board and the cardiology department. Moreover, a vision should be formulated that can help to make the existing sense of urgency more positive (less negative and abstract). Both this vision and the positive sense of urgency should be shared by the board and the members of the cardiology department. Based on her summary, the consultant starts by asking 'what-questions'.

What-questions She begins by asking what topics should be interactively addressed in order to specify the required variables and norms on the *functional dimension*. This is the list of topics she comes up with:

TABLE 8.3 Required proximate intervention effort

Desired status

Functional (sub-)goals: realized

	Diagnosis PI – CA – SS	Design	Implementation	Evaluation
Part: cardiology dept/aspect	No problem inventory → Problem inventory of cardiology department	—	—	—
…	—	—	—	—
Part/aspect	—	—	—	—

Social (sub-)goals: realized

	Diagnosis	Design	Implementation	Evaluation
	Creating change relationships	Motivation Urgency – Vision	Adoption Inventing – Testing	Integration Exercising – Reinforcing/adjusting
Board	Weak change relationships → Strengthened change relationships within the board and between the board and the cardiology department	Abstract and negative sense of urgency → Positive sense of urgency/desire for change No vision → Shared vision for the cardiology department	—	—
Cardiology dept	Same as group 1	Same as group 1	—	—
Group n	—	—	—	—

1. the current function of the cardiology department – i.e. its current products and services and their contribution to the hospital's function;
2. relevant developments in the cardiology department and its environment;
3. based on 1 and 2, the desired function of the cardiology department and its contribution to the hospital's function;
4. requirements for the functioning of the cardiology department – in terms of quality of organization and quality of work – given its desired contribution to the hospital's functioning.

On the *social dimension*, the consultant decides that the listed 'functional' topics can also serve as a basis for creating a vision. In her view, this vision should specify both 'what' (function) and 'how good' (functional requirements) the department's future contribution should be. Because these topics are already covered by her list, she does not add new topics. Moreover, because the vision of the department's future should be a first step in turning the abstract and negative sense of urgency into a (positive) desire for change, the consultant does not add new urgency- or desire-related topics to her list. Finally, the consultant reflects on topics that should be discussed in order to create change relationships. After consultation with members of the groups involved (both of the board and the cardiology department), she decides that the process of vision creation itself can perhaps contribute to the creation of change relationships. She hopes that by means of the process of envisioning a shared and brighter future (instead of by raking up old stories about what went wrong), people can start to learn to know and perhaps even trust one another. For the time being, she does not select extra topics that should be discussed in order to create change relationships.

After inspecting the topics on her list and the relation of these topics to proximate functional and social goals in the intervention, the consultant understands that she has chosen a strategy that attempts to realize proximate social goals by means of the realization of proximate functional goals. Given this dependency relation, a lot comes down to *how* the functional topics on her list will be discussed and *who* will be involved in these discussions.

How-questions   In order to address the 'how-questions', the consultant starts by reflecting on the required modes of interaction mentioned earlier (level of participation, technical content, planning, etc.):

1. Because the process of vision creation should lead to a vision that is shared by parties affected by the intervention, she decides that *participation* should be high – organization members should be enabled to co-create a vision on their shared future.
2. With respect to the *technical* content of the process of vision creation, the consultant appreciates that, on the one hand, the 'functional' topics on her list should be discussed in the correct sequence. This presupposes technical expertise both about what these topics mean (e.g. what the functional requirements quality of organization and quality of work mean) and how they contribute to the functional goal of defining variables and norms and the social goal of building a shared vision. On the other hand, organization members participating in the vision creation process should not be hindered by these technical aspects. They should be as free as possible to discuss the future of the cardiology department.

3. In the consultant's view, the combination of technical constraint and interactive freedom implies that the discussions should be *planned* in such a way that they help organization members to meet the required technical standards, for instance by means of discussion formats and facilitators that can explain the underlying 'logic' of these formats. However, the facilitators should interfere as little as possible in the input that is being generated by the participants in the discussions.
4. As to the level of *detail*, the consultant knows that defining variables and norms for the purpose of a gap analysis requires detail. However, she also understands that in this early stage of the intervention and given the high level of participation, it is neither possible nor desirable to try to attain this required level. In her view, the social goals of creating a shared vision and creating change relationships prevail over the functional goal of defining variables and norms. More detailed variables and norms can still be developed in the future.
5. Although, in a sense, the intervention has already started, the goal of 'performing an episodic intervention' is not yet a shared interaction premise in the hospital. The consultant decides that the process of vision creation also should contribute to this *formal* introduction of the intervention to the organization. This means that it should be formally acknowledged and explicitly backed by the hospital's board of directors. However, with respect to the process itself, the consultant decides that it should cut through the 'normal' formal relations within the hospital, providing hospital members with the opportunity to also discuss the cardiology department's future with people they seldom meet in their daily work. Given the formats that are needed to safeguard the quality of the vision creation process, facilitators should take care that these discussions are as informal as possible.
6. *Speed* is essential, according to the consultant. Not only should the start of the vision creation process not be delayed (in order to exploit the existing sense of urgency), the process itself should not take more than two or three *intensive* meetings.
7. Because creating change relations and formulating both a shared vision and shared variables and norms are the social and functional goals of this part of the intervention, interaction should be aimed at *convergence* and harmony, rather than divergence and struggle.

Who-questions In order to specify *who* should be involved in the vision creation process, the consultant once again reflects on the proximate functional and social goals in the intervention: formulating (shared) variables and norms, creating change relationships, and creating a shared vision. Given these goals, she can start to ask questions:

- Who should share the variables and norms?
- Who should create relationships that are conducive to change?
- Who should share the vision?

On reflection, she decides that all the members of the cardiology department should be involved in realizing all three goals. The same holds for the board of directors. Moreover, because the cardiology department has all kinds of working relations with other departments in the hospital, key members of these other departments should at least be involved in the creation of change relations and the vision creation process. In order to identify these key members, the consultant analyses the department's working relations and selects members of related departments that cooperate intensively with members of the cardiology department.

Comments on step 4

Because the 'what', 'how', and 'who' questions provide the glue that links the two goal dimensions of the 3-D model to its infrastructural dimension, and for this reason are pivotal for the design of the intervention infrastructure, it will be useful to reflect on the example. So, in addition to the comment that 'specification' is required and that other 'subjects' than the consultant can address the three questions, we would like to make four comments. The first is about using affinities between the functional and the social dimensions. The second comment is about variety. The third is about the order of asking the questions. The last is about what is achieved and what is not achieved by addressing 'what', 'how', and 'who' questions.

Comment 1: affinities between proximate functional and social goals   In the example, the consultant exploits affinities that can exist between realizing proximate functional and realizing proximate social goals (possible affinities between functional and social goals are discussed in Chapter 7). As indicated, her strategy is to realize all proximate social goals by means of realizing the proximate functional goal in the intervention. In order to make this strategy work, she carefully reflects on the 'how' and 'who' questions. 'Who' should discuss the topics ('what') that are functionally relevant in what way ('how') in order to *also* realize the proximate social goals?

In practice, it is indeed a valid strategy to exploit possible affinities between realizing functional and social goals, for instance for efficiency purposes. However, exploiting such affinities may also come at a cost or be counterproductive. For instance, the consultant wants to exploit interactions about the functional topics on her list in order to create change relationships. In her view, no extra topics need to be addressed that solely focus on change relationships. This may be a risky strategy – for instance, because relationships within the cardiology department may have been damaged in the past to an extent that bars fruitful discussions about the department's future. In this case, an alternative strategy would be to address this damage; now, the consultant should add social relationship-related topics to her list of functional topics, making her answer to the 'what' question more complex. It is this complexity that is the topic of the next comment.

Comment 2: variety: topics, modes, and groups   In the hospital example, the consultant's strategy to pursue the realization of proximate social goals in the intervention by means of the realization of the proximate functional goal attenuates the complexity of her deliberations. With regard to the 'what' question, only functional topics appear on her list. Moreover, she decides that all these functional topics can and should be addressed in the same way ('how': high participation, speed, convergence, etc.). Finally, in the consultant's view, all the parties involved ('who') should discuss the same topics in the same way. However, in practice, things may be more complex than this.

To begin, we already saw that it is not always possible or desirable to exploit affinities between functional and social goals. This means that, concerning the 'what' question, different topics related to different functional and social goals may appear on the list: 'topic variety'.

Moreover, these different topics may require different modes of interaction. For instance, given particular proximate social goals, interaction about one topic may require more participation than another: 'mode variety'. Finally, as in the example, different groups may be involved ('group variety'), and it is not unimaginable that these groups should interact about different topics in different modes. Together, topic, mode, and group variety can make deliberation about the 'what', 'how', and 'who' questions more complex than in the hospital example.

Moreover, the three types of variety can lead to sequencing and coordination issues. For instance, the consultant could have decided that the topic of the desired function of the cardiology department should be discussed (and resolved) by the hospital's board (this is the third 'functional' topic on her list). Given the decision of the board, the members of the cardiology department then formulate requirements for the functioning of the cardiology department (the final 'functional' topic on her list). In this example, topic and group variety together lead to a *sequence* of proximate functional (and social) goals in the intervention. Moreover, they introduce the issue of *communicating* (*coordination*) the decision of the hospital's board on the desired function of the cardiology department to the members of that department.

Comment 3: the questions and their order In the example, the consultant addresses the questions in a particular order. Given the proximate functional and social goals, she first addresses the 'what' question, then the 'how' question, and finally the 'who' question. With respect to the 'what' question, she starts by asking what topics should be interactively addressed in order to realize proximate *functional* goals. And with respect to the 'how' question, she starts with 'participation' and ends with the question about 'speed'. Now, it can be asked whether this particular order of asking these questions is mandatory.

To begin with the order of 'what', 'how', and 'who' questions, it is indeed advisable to start with the 'what' question, then to proceed to the 'how', and finally deal with the 'who' question. However, this order should only be used as a rule of thumb. In some cases, it may be useful to go back from the 'who' to the 'how' and even to the 'what' – for instance, because an interaction mode has been selected ('how') that on closer examination does not fit with a particular group that is involved in the interaction ('who'), e.g. because it is too complex or too simple. Still, as a rule, starting with the 'who' question is not advisable. In principle, the proximate intervention effort and related 'what' and 'how' questions should be leading, not 'who' is available or, for whatever other reasons than 'what' and 'how', desirable as a participant in the intervention.

Moreover, with respect to 'what' questions, it is useful to start with topics that should be interactively addressed to realize proximate functional goals and then go on to the 'social' topics. In this way, it is easier to find and exploit affinities between realizing proximate functional and social goals. Once, again, this order should only be considered as a rule of thumb.

Finally, with respect to the 'how' questions, it can be useful to play with their order and to weigh their importance. In the example, the consultant starts with the required level of participation and later deals with the question of detail. Because she wants a high level of participation, she decides to pursue less detail in the formulation of variables and norms. Now, suppose that she had started her deliberations with the issue of detail: a high level of detail is required. Later on, she would have come across the question about the required level of participation. In this case, it is not unimaginable that the consultant, because of her earlier decision about the required high level of detail, would have decided to make the intervention less participative. As it appears, a decision about an earlier question now functions as a constraint on a decision about a later question. Although this type of constraint is not necessarily wrong, it should, of course, not be dictated by the contingent sequence in which the 'how' questions are addressed.

For this reason, it is important to see the 'how' questions as both separate and interconnected items. As separate items, they should be addressed in isolation (against the background of the topics and the proximate functional or social goals they are connected to). To this purpose of seeing them in isolation, it may help to play with the sequence in which they are addressed. As they are interconnected, there may be tensions between decisions on some items (e.g. participation and speed: high) and decisions on other items (e.g. detail: high). In this case, it is relevant to weigh these decisions against the background of the proximate and social goals in the intervention.

In general, we want to once more underline the experimental character of organizing. This experimental character also holds for addressing the 'what', 'how', and 'who' questions. In this light, going through these questions is not a linear process, but an iterative one.

Comment 4: what is and what is not achieved by deliberation on 'what', 'how', and 'who' questions   Addressing 'what', 'how', and 'who' questions is a crucial step towards a design of an intervention infrastructure that can realize and adapt proximate functional and social goals. The questions provide a first indication of:

- operational intervention activities (activities that should be performed in order realize proximate functional and social goals);
- techniques that can support the performance of operational intervention activities;
- who should be involved in performing these operational intervention activities.

However, addressing the 'what', 'how', and 'who' questions still leaves a lot of design issues unanswered. For instance, how should operational intervention activities be clustered into a network of intervention tasks, what about supporting and regulatory intervention activities and their clustering into tasks, and what about the technology supporting the regulation of the intervention or the selection of experts that can facilitate the intervention process? Apparently, a fifth step is needed.

Step 5: Design the infrastructure of an intervention organization that can support the realization and adaptation of (proximate) functional and social goals

Step 5.1: Design an intervention structure

Step 5.2: Select the intervention technology/techniques

Step 5.3: Select human resources and human resources support measures

Step 5 is about designing the three aspects of the intervention infrastructure: its structure, technology and techniques, and its human resources and human resources support measures.

Because each of these aspects is the topic of a separate section (Sections 8.5–8.7), we will not go into the design criteria that hold for these aspects here. However, we can summarily describe the design selected by the consultant in the hospital case.

After considering the 'what', 'how', and 'who' questions, the consultant decided to organize two large-scale meetings. The goal of the first meeting was to discuss the current function of the cardiology department, relevant developments in its environment, and its desired function. The second meeting was devoted to the desired function and the department's functional requirements. The meetings were organized in order to introduce these functional topics in way that was as 'natural' as possible (avoiding the explanation of all kinds of concepts and theories). Participants in the discussions were the members of the hospital's board, the cardiology department, and selected members of other departments in the hospital. As a consequence, all these participants had an operational task in this part of the episodic intervention. The meetings were facilitated by consultants who had sufficient knowledge of (1) the 'functional' topics that were at issue in the meetings and (2) the dynamics affecting the realization of the social goals connected to these meetings. The function of these facilitators was to support the participants in their reflections on the department's future. The last part of the second large-scale meeting was devoted to the goal-driven design regulation of the intervention. In this context, participants were asked to assess the process and results of the large-scale meetings. Moreover, they were asked to select new proximate functional and social goals in the intervention. Finally, given their views on the required intervention effort, they were asked to outline the next step in the intervention. In this way, participants were not only involved in operational intervention activities, they also contributed to the intervention's regulation.

8.3.2 Improvement-driven design regulation

During an episodic intervention, all kinds of *problems* or *opportunities* may present themselves that affect the intervention's progress.

In the case of *problems*, some of them may be dealt with by means of operational regulation. In this case, functional and social goals as well as the intervention infrastructure remain unchanged. Other problems may require the adjustment of functional or social goals by means of strategic regulation. For instance, because of a major problem, 'creating change relations' may be selected as a new social goal instead of the old, apparently difficult to achieve, adoption goal. This selected new goal, then, may require a redesign of parts or aspects of the intervention infrastructure in order to realize it. In this case, the problem is tackled by goal-driven design regulation. Finally, some problems may occur that specifically require a redesign of the intervention infrastructure *given* selected proximate functional and social goals. In this case, the intervention infrastructure is improved by means of design regulation in order to deal with these problems. So this final case is an instance of improvement-driven design regulation. For instance, during an intervention, a power struggle may develop between the organization's middle management that feels threatened by an attempt to restructure the organization and a group of change agents that wants to carry on restructuring the organization. Currently, the intervention infrastructure is insufficiently equipped to deal with this problem, for instance because conflict management skills are lacking. Based on an analysis of this problem, it may be decided to hire specialized consultants and temporarily add them to the intervention infrastructure.

It is also possible that, as the intervention unfolds, *opportunities* present themselves, e.g. in one of the intervention teams, a particular design tool worked especially well or a consultant was hired that appears to have exceptional skills in motivating people. In order to exploit such opportunities it can be useful to redesign parts or aspects of the intervention infrastructure, e.g. to introduce the tool in other intervention teams as well. In some cases, exploiting opportunities may trigger goal-driven design regulation – i.e. as the opportunity presents itself, new proximate functional or social goals may be set that are more ambitious than the goals that were selected previously. Given these more ambitious goals, a redesign of the intervention infrastructure may be made that maximally exploits the opportunity. However, it is also possible that, *given* the selected proximate functional and social goals, the opportunity only triggers an adaptation of the intervention infrastructure. In such cases, the design regulation is improvement-driven.

In sum, in order to deal with problems or exploit opportunities, it may be useful to improve the design of the intervention infrastructure *given* selected proximate functional and social goals. Because improvement-driven design regulation can be triggered by either problems or opportunities that have presented themselves, there are two (structurally quite similar) procedures for this type of design regulation. We start with improvements of the intervention infrastructure in the face of *problems* that present themselves. Three steps are involved:

Step 1: Assess the actual or projected progress of the intervention relative to selected proximate functional and social goals.

Step 2: If progress is worse than required (deviates negatively from proximate functional or social goals), search for and analyse the causes of insufficient progress.

Step 3: If required, redesign the intervention infrastructure in order to either attenuate the causes of the disappointing progress or amplify the infrastructure's capacity to deal with the problematic effects of these causes.

In order to establish causes of insufficient progress, it should be noted that these causes may stem from:

1. *the standing organization* or its *environment* – e.g. a demoralized work force, distrust between organization members, a bureaucracy that obstructs change, institutional factors that obstruct change;
2. *the intervention process* and the *intervention organization* – e.g. starting the design activity without a proper diagnosis, selection of a consultant who has no design experience, or selection of inapt intervention techniques;
3. *the relation* between the organization and the intervention organization – e.g. overburdening organization members with intervention activities on top of their normal activities.

In order to exploit *opportunities* that present themselves, three similar steps to the ones mentioned previously are required. In this case, actual or projected progress that is better than specified by the proximate functional and social goals functions as a trigger of a possible redesign of the intervention infrastructure. To recap, the three steps involved are:

Step 1: Assess the actual or projected progress of the intervention relative to the selected proximate functional and social goals.

Step 2: If progress is better that specified (deviates positively from proximate functional or social goals), search for and analyse the causes of this more than satisfactory progress.

Step 3: If desirable, redefine functional or social goals in the intervention and redesign the intervention infrastructure in order to exploit the causes of more than satisfactory progress in order to realize these new goals.

Together, the two procedures for improvement-driven design regulation discussed here and the procedure for goal-driven design regulation discussed earlier can be used as heuristics that support the flexible design of intervention infrastructures. 'Flexible' here means that these procedures allow for the continuous:

- *assessment* of the progress of the intervention in terms of proximate functional and social goals that have been realized;
- *adaptation* of proximate functional or social goals and/or the intervention infrastructure that is needed to realize and adapt these goals.

As such, these procedures take seriously the experimental and thereby situational, deliberative, and cybernetic character of episodic interventions.

Instead of selecting an intervention infrastructure and rigidly sticking to it, the procedures can help to flexibly make sense of and respond to problems and opportunities as they happen in the intervention. In this way, it becomes possible to avoid the intervention infrastructure turning into a straitjacket that obstructs instead of supports the progress of the intervention. Instead, the intervention infrastructure can remain responsive to the huge variety of basically unpredictable events that can affect the intervention's progress.

Now, for the purpose of continuously *assessing* the intervention's progress and *adapting* functional or social goals in the intervention and/or the intervention's infrastructure, it is useful to have prior knowledge of factors that may possibly affect the intervention's progress. For instance, suppose that in some episodic intervention it is difficult to realize the social goal of developing a shared 'vision'. Given this slow progress on the social dimension, it may be asked *why* progress is slow and *what* may be done about it. In order to search for *actual* causes that stand in the way of making progress in this particular intervention, it may be helpful to have some prior knowledge of factors that can *possibly* affect the progress of episodic interventions. Based on this prior knowledge, it becomes possible to search for *actual* causes of slow progress in this particular intervention. Once these actual causes are found, the intervention infrastructure can be (re)designed in order to deal with them. As it appears, the (re)design of intervention infrastructures can benefit from prior knowledge of factors that can affect the progress of episodic interventions. That is why we examine these factors in the next section before we turn to the issue of the design of the intervention structure (Section 8.5), its technology (Section 8.6) and human resources (Section 8.7).

8.4 Factors affecting the progress of episodic interventions

In Chapters 5 and 7, we indicated that all kinds of factors can affect the progress of episodic interventions. In these chapters, we also promised a more thorough examination of these factors. In this section, we will do our best to fulfil this promise. To this purpose, we first devote a few words to why we think it is *relevant* to pay attention to these factors in the present chapter on the design of the infrastructural dimensions of the intervention organization. Second, we introduce a *problem* regarding these factors and present our strategy for *coping* with it. Third, we examine the *factors* themselves. Finally, we turn to the issue of *power and politics* in episodic interventions.

8.4.1 Relevance

There are at least two reasons why we consider a closer examination of factors affecting the progress of episodic intervention as relevant.

The first reason is quite general. When discussing the 3-D model with both students and practitioners, there always was one question that cropped up sooner or later: 'Where are power and politics in your model?' We even incorporated this question into an examination of a course on the 3-D model by asking, 'If you were pressed to add a new dimension to the given dimensions of the 3-D model, what would that dimension be (explain your answer)?' Almost all students answered: 'I would add a power dimension.' They supported their answer by making the point that organizational life in general and episodic interventions in particular are inevitably agonistic. For this reason, they argued that a model that claims to support episodic interventions in high parameter value structures cannot negate power and politics. On the contrary, such a model should make power and politics a central issue by devoting a separate dimension to them: the 3-D model should be a 4-D model.

Of course, the students (and practitioners) are right. Power and politics are intrinsically related to both organizations taken as social systems that experiment with meaningful survival and the episodic interventions that attempt to change these organizations. As such, power and politics figure in at least two ways in episodic interventions. First, they play a role in the interactive processes in which proximate functional and social goals are set and adapted and intervention infrastructures are (re)designed. So the interactive *adaptation* of functional and social goals and the infrastructural means to realize them have a power aspect. Second, once functional and social goals are set and an infrastructure is in place that is geared to realize them, power and politics can affect the *realization* of these functional and social goals.

Therefore, there is no disagreement about the pervasiveness and possible impact of power and politics on the progress of episodic interventions. However, once their importance is granted, it can be asked, 'Importance for what?' And *our* answer would be, 'For realizing and adapting functional and social goals *in* the intervention, and thereby, for realizing the goal *of* the intervention.' So, given the logic of the 3-D model, power and politics are important. But they are important as factors that: (1) can affect the progress of episodic interventions and, for this reason, (2) should be taken into account when designing the intervention infrastructures that can support the realization and adaptation of functional and social goals.

And what is more, power and politics are not the only factors that are important in this way. There are many more. Think, for instance, of the role played by basic assumptions, ingrained routines, or emotional attachments to current organizational practices. And, as will be argued later in the text, these other factors are intertwined with power and politics in such a way that, as a generic denominator, 'power and politics' may be too crude to be helpful when assessing or adjusting an episodic intervention.

So the first reason why we think it is relevant to discuss factors that can affect the progress of episodic interventions is just to make the point *that* there are factors that:

- are neither to be found on the goal dimensions of the 3-D model (functional or social goals in the intervention) nor on its infrastructural dimension (intervention structure, technology, or human resources);
- are still *crucial* for the progress and success of episodic interventions.

By means of the procedures for goal- and improvement-driven design – procedures that take the experimental character of episodic interventions seriously – the 3-D model is explicitly designed to deal with these factors. In this sense, these factors are already a part of the 3-D model: not of its layout or of its logic of use, but as a part of *applying* this logic in concrete situations.

The second reason for discussing factors that can affect the progress of episodic interventions is more specific. It concentrates on the particular role that knowledge of these factors can play in application of the 3-D model. For, if what has been said about power and politics (and other factors as well) is true – i.e. if it is true that there are factors that can affect the realization and adaptation of functional and social goals in the intervention and for this reason should be taken into account in the design of the intervention infrastructure – then goal- and improvement-driven design should benefit from knowledge of these factors.

In the case of *goal-driven* design regulation, knowledge of these factors can be applied to scan the organization for their actual presence. If desirable, functional or social goals can be set to accommodate for the presence of these factors and/or an intervention infrastructure can be designed that allows to cope with their effects. For instance, suppose that a particular deep metaphor, e.g. the machine metaphor, is a factor that can negatively affect the progress of an episodic intervention, and further suppose that this metaphor is indeed 'active' in the organization in which the intervention takes place, then functional or social goals in the intervention may be set in such a way that the presence and influence of this metaphor can become an explicit topic of interaction, at least opening up the conceptual space to start seeing the organization in other ways.

In the case of *improvement-driven* design regulation, knowledge of factors that can affect the progress of episodic interventions can be used to search for and analyse causes of unexpected slow or rapid progress (step 2 of the procedures for improvement-driven design). Moreover, knowledge of these factors can be used for the purpose of redesigning the intervention infrastructure (step 3 of the procedures).

8.4.2 A problem and a coping strategy

After having established the general and particular importance of factors that can affect the progress of episodic interventions, nothing would be more natural than to start discussing them. However, there is a problem here. In Chapter 7, we indicated that there is such a large variety of interrelated factors that it is difficult to provide a comprehensive overview of them.

One strategy to cope with this variety may be to categorize factors. For instance, it can be argued that factors that can affect progress exist in:

1. *the environment* of the organization – e.g. there are institutional factors that can slow down or speed up the progress of episodic interventions (see, for instance, Vermeulen, 2011);
2. *the organization* – e.g. particular basic assumptions structuring interaction in the organization may slow down or speed up progress;

3. *the intervention organization* – e.g. power struggles within the intervention organization may affect progress;
4. *the relations* between the organization and the intervention organization – e.g. organization members may be overburdened by intervention tasks on top of their normal organizational tasks.

Although such a 'localization' of factors can certainly be useful as a heuristic for a 'hunt' for actual causes of slow or rapid progress in an intervention, it is still quite crude. Moreover, why 'localize' factors? Why not 'temporalize' them by making a distinction between (inherited) factors that existed before the intervention and factors that develop once the intervention is under way? Or why not make a matrix combining 'localization' and 'temporalization'? Or why not add new distinctions to the matrix, e.g. between 'cultural' and 'infrastructural' factors? For more creative minds than ours, the possibilities are almost endless. And finally, what about the cells of the matrices that are produced in this way? Would their exploration not land us with the huge variety of factors that can affect the progress of episodic interventions that was the problem in the first place?

Given this problem of a stand-off between the desirability and complexity of knowledge about factors affecting the progress of episodic interventions, one of the main messages of this book may provide a helpful coping strategy. This message is that is not always productive to talk about 'change' in general. It might be relevant to specify the kind of change and the kind of circumstances under which that kind of change takes place. This is one of the reasons why this book is not about 'change' in general, but about 'episodic interventions in high parameter value structures'.

Therefore, given the message and the topic of this book, it is perhaps possible to limit the list of all possible factors that can affect progress to factors that are related to the high parameter value structures that are the object of episodic interventions in these structures. These factors should *always* be taken into account when designing the intervention infrastructure for this type of interventions. Therefore, below we cope with the problem of finding factors that can affect an intervention's progress by listing some of the factors (our list is not exhaustive) that are to be expected in the case of episodic interventions in high parameter value structures.

In Chapters 3 and 4, we dwelt on the problems of high parameter value structures. For instance, in Chapter 3, we argued that organizations with high parameter value structures have difficulties realizing the required quality of organization and work. In Chapter 4, we pointed to the self-inhibiting character of high parameter value structures. 'Self-inhibition', it was argued, means that the high parameter values of the structure of an organization inhibit the design regulation – including the episodic interventions – needed to redesign the structure of that organization. The organization's structure stands in the way of the design regulation needed to improve that structure: the structure is self-inhibiting.

Now, self-inhibition is an *underlying* factor that *systematically* causes problems in episodic interventions that have the improvement of organizational structures as their goal. In Chapter 4, this underlying factor was analysed into direct and indirect problems affecting design regulation (see Section 4.3.5). However, although helpful, this distinction between direct and indirect problems still remains somewhat general and abstract.

In order to find more concrete factors that can explain deviations from the desired progress of episodic interventions, it useful to examine how the *knowledge*, *skills*, and *motivation* of organization members (individuals and groups) working in high parameter value structures can affect the realization of proximate functional and social goals. Based on the results of this examination, factors can be found that can be used to: (1) explain negative or positive deviations in the intervention's progress and (2) design the intervention infrastructure in such a way that the knowledge, skills, and motivation of organization members are improved or supported.

8.4.3 Factors affecting progress: knowledge, skill, motivation

For the purpose of our examination of factors affecting progress, we depart from an ideal typical high parameter value structure. In this structure, we find functionally concentrated departments, relatively small operational tasks, and a complex hierarchy of specialized managerial tasks (a complex structure with simple tasks). Given this high parameter value structure, we ask how it affects and may be affected by the knowledge, skills, and motivation of individual or groups of organization members who are involved in realizing the functional and social progress in the intervention (see Figure 8.2).

Of course, in addition to the knowledge, skills, and motivation of human resources, technology can be a factor that affects the progress of an episodic intervention in high parameter value structures. Take, for instance, expensive and inflexible ICT systems that are tightly coupled to the *existing* production and control structure. The sheer presence of such systems can cripple initiatives to change the organization's structure or become an obstacle in the design stage. In spite of the possible presence of these technical factors, we will focus on the human factor.

Knowledge

High parameter values of organizational structures can affect and be affected by knowledge that is relevant for realizing and adapting functional or social goals in at least five ways: (a) departmental focus, (b) social distance, (c) aspectual refraction of problems and solution, (d) structure blindness and economies of scale, and (e) deep metaphors. As such, these knowledge-related factors should always be taken into account when applying the procedures for goal- and improvement-driven design regulation to concrete episodic interventions.

Departmental focus

Workers (including professionals) working in the primary processes of high parameter value structures have relatively small jobs in functional departments that are coupled to all orders (note that, in this way, high parameter value structures tend to de-professionalize

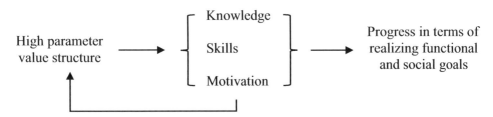

FIGURE 8.2 High parameter values, knowledge, skills, and motivation and the intervention's progress

professionals). As a result, workers focus on their own jobs and have limited knowledge of the production processes they participate in, let alone of the relation between these processes and the different orders they contribute to. Moreover, because workers are focused on their tasks in their functional departments, it is difficult to stay in touch with the goals that constitute the organization's meaning (see de Sitter, 1994; Achterbergh and Vriens, 2010; Vriens et al., 2018b).

Managers of primary processes in high parameter value structures are focused on running and optimizing their own functional departments. This departmental focus can have negative effects on the overview managers have of the production processes and their relation to orders. Moreover, their focus on departmental goals can negatively affect their knowledge of and involvement in realizing the goals that constitute the organization's meaning.

Still, in episodic interventions in organizational structures, and particularly in more participative designs of these interventions, shared knowledge about both organizational goals and the relation between production processes and orders is required, for instance in order to participate in the diagnosis or redesign of these processes (functional dimension). On the social dimension, knowledge about the realization of goals that constitute the organization's meaning is important because this knowledge can contribute to the development of both a sense of urgency (e.g. vital goals are not realized) and a vision on the organization's future (discussions about the organization's meaningful survival).

Social distance

In high parameter value structures, separation between operational and control tasks is high. High separation can imply that workers (including professionals) and managers come to live in what seem to be almost different worlds. Workers are immersed in their world of daily activities and problems. Managers live in their world of targets and strategies (including their underlying theories and conceptual frameworks needed to realize these targets). As a result, there may be quite a social distance between the knowledge, language, and experiences of workers and managers in high parameter value structures. For instance, a professional working in a school may define a problem with a pupil in professional and existential terms, taking seriously the school's contribution to *this* pupil's life. A manager working in this school may see this problem as one of the many problems on her list and define it in the statistical terms of the school's quality system and its application.

As can be imagined, the social distance between the knowledge, language, and experience of workers and managers in high parameter value structures can affect the realization of functional and social goals in episodic interventions. For instance, overcoming this distance by creating a basis for mutual understanding and trust – creating change relationships – can considerably slow down processes of realizing functional or social goals in the intervention.

Aspectual refraction of problems and solutions

In high parameter value structures, not only is separation between operations and control high (leading to social distance), specialization *within* control is high, too. This means that in these structures, all kinds of managers at different levels (operational, design, and strategic regulation) focus on different *aspects* of the regulation of primary processes and the infrastructures needed to realize them (de Sitter, 1994). For instance, some managers focus on regulating quality, others on human resources, yet others on procurement and logistics, on ICT, costs, finance, corporate social responsibility, and so on. The management of each of these different aspects requires its own conceptual frameworks, theories, professional training, and experiences. As a result, aspectual managers will be inclined to see organizational problems and their solutions in terms of the conceptual frameworks, theories, training, and experiences that belong to their particular managerial task. In this way, one and the same structure-driven problem may be refracted into many different problems. For instance, long production cycle times that *per hypothesis* are due to a high parameter value structure, may be interpreted by:

- human resources managers as caused by low worker involvement and motivation;
- quality managers as caused by high reworking rates due to all kinds of quality problems in the production process;
- ICT and communication managers as caused by a lack of communication between workers and managers.

And in a way, each of these groups of managers is right, for if the problem of long production cycle times is truly driven by the organization's high parameter value structure, it is likely that, after they have done their own research, the human resources managers will find that worker involvement and motivation are actually low, the quality managers will find that there is indeed a lot of reworking going on, and the ICT and communication managers will find that communication is indeed problematic. As a consequence, a basically structure-driven problem is refracted into so many aspectual problems.

Moreover, based on their findings, the different managers will start to search for solutions within their respective aspectual knowledge domains. So the human resources managers will come up with human resources solutions, the quality managers with quality solutions, and so on. Although each of these solutions may suppress or partly address the problems, their structure-driven root cause is not resolved. As a consequence, a solution that should have been structure-related is refracted into so many aspectual partial solutions.

This aspectual refraction of problems and solutions may be quite problematic as far as the functional dimension of the 3-D model is concerned because it stands in the way of a diagnosis and redesign of the organization's structure. On the social dimension, aspectual refraction also causes problems because differences in the backgrounds (conceptual frameworks, theories, professional training, and experiences) of managers involved in the intervention may stand in the way of a productive dialogue about the problem and its structure-related causes and solutions.

'Structure blindness' and preference for economies of scale

Structure blindness and a preference for economies of scale can even amplify the effects of refraction, negatively affecting progress on both the functional and the social dimensions.

'Structure blindness' means that managers in high parameter value structures are *unaware* of the relation between the organization's structure and its overall performance. For instance, they do not know what a structure is (e.g. confusing structures and processes), what the parameters of a structure are, or how a structure's parameter values are related to organizational performance. And what is more, they may be *unaware of their unawareness*.

This 'double unawareness' makes it difficult to even start seeing organizational structures as both a root cause of and root solution to a variety of organizational problems (affecting diagnosis and design on the functional dimension). Moreover, because of their double unawareness, managers, on the social dimension: (1) do not have the concepts and theories to discuss the organization from a structural perspective and (2) do not start searching for these concepts and theories. Creating the required types of awareness – both *that* and *how* structures matter – can considerably slow down progress on both the functional and the social dimensions.

'Preference for economies of scale' means that managers in high parameter value structures do have ideas about the relation between structure and performance. However, they see this relation as quite opposite to the ideas expressed in Chapter 3. Instead of advocating 'economies of flow' (building flows and integrated tasks), these managers advocate 'economies of scale'. This means that they think that functional concentration, separation, and specialization in the production structure make work more, instead of less, efficient (see Christis et al., 2018, for an exposition and critique). For instance, they argue that by separating 'making' and 'supporting' activities into functionally concentrated production units (making) and shared service centres (supporting), both the efficiency of production and the productivity and quality of support will increase (for an explanation and critique, see van Laar et al., 2016). Deeply rooted ideas supporting economies of scale can even be more damning for progress on the functional and social dimensions than structure blindness. To actually make progress, not only should the conceptual and theoretical presuppositions underlying the economies of scale perspective be (cognitively) dismantled, but also deeply rooted (emotional and social) attachments to these concepts and theories should be overcome.

Please note that, unlike the first three factors – departmental focus, social distance, and refraction – the factors structure blindness and economies of scale are not primarily caused by high parameter value structures. It is rather the other way around. Structure blindness and preference for economies of scale contribute to the development of high parameter value structures (that, in turn, may enforce structure blindness or a preference for economies of scale). In the case of structure blindness, the organization's structure is not an explicit issue for managers. As a consequence, it can drift virtually unnoticed to ever higher parameter values. In the case of economies of scale, the high parameter values of the organization's structure probably result from interventions by managers, engaged as they are to improve the efficiency and quality of the organization by means of their economies of scale agenda.

Deep metaphors (as an example of basic assumptions)

All kinds of basic assumptions – such as institutional practices inherited from the organization's field, basic valuations with regard to the desirability of conserving or changing the organization, or deeply held beliefs about the role of organizational structures – may either stand in the way or speed up the progress of an episodic intervention in a high parameter value structure. Because it is impossible to discuss all these basic assumptions, we will pick just one example: deep metaphors that can be linked to high parameter value structures.

According to Grant and Oswick (1996, p. 1), metaphors play an important role in our everyday lives because they allow us to understand relatively complex phenomena (e.g. human knowing) in terms of more familiar phenomena (e.g. the input, throughput, and output of computers). This general relevance of metaphors also holds for organizations (see, for instance, Morgan, 1986). In organizations, metaphors can become 'generators of meaning and action'. For instance, once organization members see their organization as a machine, it is probable that they start to act accordingly, which, in turn, reinforces their way of seeing.

Deep metaphors are metaphors which determine, "centrally important features of the idea or object being examined" (Schön, 1993, p. 149, cited in Grant and Oswick, 1996, p. 6). Based on deep metaphors – e.g. the organization as a machine – all kinds of *surface metaphors* can be derived, e.g. the consultant as a 'fixer' of technical problems instead of a 'healer' of organizations (on the distinction between deep and surface metaphors, see, for instance, Døving, 1996, pp. 185ff; Marshak, 1996, p. 154). Together, deep and surface metaphors can constitute more or less coherent *metaphorical fields* that structure processes of sense-making in organizations.

Two features of deep metaphors are particularly important in the case of episodic interventions: their *one-sided* character and their *out-of-awareness* character (see Marshak, 1996, p. 150). The one-sided character of (deep) metaphors relates to the point that they allow us to see some unfamiliar phenomenon A in terms of a relatively familiar phenomenon B. As such, metaphors highlight particular B-like (e.g. machine-like) characteristics of phenomenon 'A' (organizations) while leaving other C- and D-like characteristics (e.g. organism-like, arena-like characteristic) in the dark. The out-of-awareness character of deep metaphors means that deep metaphors as a rule are part of the basic assumptions of organization members, and as such implicitly structure the production of interactions and interaction premises. Organization members use metaphors in their interactions, but they are neither aware of the use they make of these metaphors nor of the effects this has on the organization that is constituted by means of their interactions.

Together, the one-sided and out-of-awareness characters of deep metaphors can affect episodic interventions in high parameter value structures in two ways: they can affect the *results* of intervention efforts (e.g. a diagnosis or a design) and they can affect the handling of the intervention *process*.

Results As argued in Chapter 3, it is not unimaginable that in organizations with high parameter value structures, deep metaphors are 'in use' that highlight the machine- or pyramid-like character of organizations. Because of their one-sidedness, these metaphors leave other characteristics of organizations in the dark. However, these other characteristics may be quite relevant for diagnostic or design purposes. For instance, due to the machine metaphor, organization members may see the organization as a 'steady state' machine, blotting out its goal-generating and goal-adapting character. Such a one-sided and possibly out-of-awareness machine perspective can influence the results of both diagnosis and design, for instance by emphasizing the efficiency and effectiveness of *current* production processes and leaving out relevant functional requirements related to their adaptation.

Process The one-sided and out-of-awareness character of metaphors can also affect the intervention process and the way it is handled. An example may help. Suppose that in some high parameter value organization the machine metaphor is prevalent. It is not unimaginable that in that organization, the intervention is seen as a more or less technical process of diagnosis, design, implementation, and evaluation that 'repairs' a structure that is 'broken'.

Because of the (deep) machine metaphor, the functional dimension of episodic interventions is highlighted and its social dimension remains in the dark until it is too late. Now, suppose that, after the intervention has started to go pear-shaped because of this one-sided interpretation, a consultant is hired who sees the organization both as an ever-changing social 'flux' and as an 'arena' in which power interests clash. Given these metaphors, it is to be expected that this consultant will focus on the social dimension of the intervention, neglecting its functional dimension. Once again, this one-sidedness will have grave effects on the intervention process and its ultimate result. And things become even more complicated once organization members (machine metaphor) and the consultant (flux metaphor) start to talk to each other. In the beginning, it will seem as if they are discussing different worlds, and soon they will be immersed in a time-consuming process in which metaphors need to be recognized, repudiated, reframed, replaced, released, or reintegrated (see Marshak, 1996, pp. 157ff, on dealing with deep metaphors in organizations).

Skills

High parameter value structures also affect the skills of organization members. Some of these skills may be *needed* to realize progress on the functional and social dimension. However, high parameter values may tend to undermine the development of these skills. Other skills that do develop in high parameter value structures can *stand in the way* of the intervention's progress. 'Problem solving' and 'cooperation' are examples of the first type of skills. 'Skilled incompetence' is an example of the latter type.

Problem solving

In high parameter value structures, differentiation between 'making', 'supporting', and 'preparing' and separation between 'operations' and 'control' are high. For workers (including professionals), high differentiation and separation imply that they largely depend on others ('support people' or managers) to solve their problems for them. Because problem solving by means of continuous and local design regulation is not a part of their task, workers are not encouraged to engage in problem solving activities as a part of their daily work. As a consequence, it is difficult to develop work-related problem solving skills. It may even be possible that, given the structure of their jobs, workers 'unlearn' to solve problems for themselves, accustomed as they are to others solving their problems for them. Still, problem solving skills, in particular skills in solving problems by means of continuous and local design regulation, can be relevant in the case of episodic interventions in organizational infrastructures

Cooperation

In episodic interventions that aim to reduce the parameter values of an organization's structure, cooperation across departments and managerial aspects as well as cooperation between workers and managers are highly relevant. For instance, as a part of the design of a production flow, workers and managers from different departments may need to cooperate in order to specify the tasks of teams within that flow. However, 'departmental focus', 'social distance', and 'aspectual refraction' may stand in the way of developing the skills that are needed for this type of 'unit- and aspect-spanning' cooperation.

Skilled incompetence: a high parameter value variant

As explained earlier, in high parameter value structures, the probability of structure-driven disturbances (P(D)) is high and the regulatory potential (RP) to deal with these disturbances is low. This brings organization members (workers and managers alike) into an awkward and frustrating situation. On the one hand, they are confronted with many, often recurring, disturbances – high P(D). On the other hand, they have difficulties regulating these disturbances – low RP –, and thereby performing their tasks as is expected of them. Because organization members cannot *deal* with disturbances by means of operational or design regulation, they develop *coping* strategies that, instead of addressing the underlying structure-related problems, tend to reproduce them. For instance, organization members may become skilled at:

- *accepting* problems as a 'normal';
- releasing frustration by *informally complaining* about problems (without doing something about them);
- *explaining* away problems;
- *hiding* problems from others;
- *working around* problems;
- *exporting* problems to other persons/units in the organization;
- *blaming* others as the cause of problems;
- *stop caring* about/*becoming indifferent* to problems (alienation).

Such coping strategies are a kind of *defensive routines* as defined by Argyris, i.e. actions or policies "designed to avoid surprise, embarrassment, or threat", but also actions that "prevent learning and thereby prevent organizations from investigating or eliminating the underlying problems" (1986, pp. 75–76; particularly the second part of Argyris' definition is relevant here). As these coping strategies develop, organization members become more and more *skilled* in behaviours that make them *incompetent* to address and solve the structure-driven problems that cause the development of these skills (see Argyris, 1986, on skilled incompetence). Organization members are caught in a cycle of structure-driven problems that trigger the development of skills that make them incompetent to address and solve these problems, thereby conserving or even reinforcing the high parameter value structure that caused these problems in the first place (see Figure 8.3).

In the case of episodic interventions in high parameter value structures, the skilled incompetence of organization members can obstruct progress both on the functional and on the social dimensions, particularly in the early stages of the intervention, because organization members have 'unlearned' to address and solve problems by examining their underlying causes.

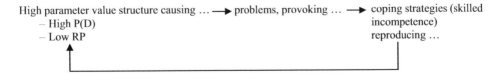

FIGURE 8.3 Skilled incompetence in high parameter value structures

Motivation

The high parameter values of an organization's structure, in combination with the aforementioned factors, also can influence the motivation of organization members to participate in an episodic intervention that aims to reduce these values. Please note that the term 'motivation' here has a broader meaning than in Chapter 7 on the social dimension. In this section, it refers to a general willingness to participate in an episodic intervention in the organization's structure (not just to the first goal on the social dimension). With respect to motivation, we want to point at four factors: (a) 'reluctance', (b) 'departmental focus again', (c) 'personal loss', (d) 'rootedness'.

.Reluctance

In high parameter value structures, it is to be expected that decisions to episodically intervene in the organization's structure are taken by higher-level managers. These managers may be reluctant to take the decision to intervene in the organization's structure. This reluctance may have all kinds of causes, such as aspectual refraction of problems and causes, or structure blindness. However, it may also be caused by an awareness of the sheer impact that episodic interventions in organizational structures have on organizations and the people working in them. As may be clear from Chapters 2 and 3, the organizational structure is *basic* to the functioning of an organization because it relates its human resources and technology to the processes that realize and adapt the goals of that organization. Changing the organization's structure means changing all these relations, which is a daunting project with a risky outcome. For this reason, it is understandable that managers try all kinds of other interventions – e.g. improving leadership, changing appraisal and reward systems, introducing technology, changing culture – before choosing their weapon of last resort: an episodic intervention in the organization's structure.

Departmental focus again

On top of reluctance, focus on departmental instead of organizational performance can frustrate the motivation to intervene in the organization's structure. In high parameter value structures, managers of functionally concentrated departments have a tendency to be focused on the performance of their own department, for instance because their rewards are based on departmental performance. As a result, these managers are motivated to optimize departmental processes, sometimes at the expense of other departments or even the clients of the organization. This motivation for local departmental optimization comes at the cost of the motivation to reduce the functional concentration of the organization as a whole and thereby improve its overall performance.

Personal loss

High parameter value structures have evolved hierarchies on top of functionally concentrated units. Changing the parameter values of these structures from high to low means tearing down these hierarchies and units in favour of semi-autonomous production flows. This prospect may be threatening to managers who have devoted an important part of their life and career to advancing through the ranks, acquiring their position in the hierarchy. What will be their place in the new low parameter value structure? Is there a place at all? Apparently, an episodic intervention reducing the parameter values of the organization's structure may result in a personal loss for the managers affected by the intervention, undermining their motivation to support the intervention.

Rootedness

Even in high parameter value structures, organization members may learn to live with and work around the daily problems caused by these structures (see also the earlier comments on skilled incompetence). They may learn to hate some co-workers and trust others, and they may learn to love their shared hatred and trust. In this way, organization members may become rooted in the high parameter value structures they inhabit. Sharing hardship, enemies, friends, obligations, promises, rights, and duties can forge strong emotional relations that make organizational life bearable (see, for instance, Hirschhorn, 2000, on structures as moral orders). An episodic intervention that threatens to disturb this known and trusted web of relations, uprooting organization members by 'forcing' them to embrace a new and uncertain future, may be an unwelcome prospect undermining motivation for change.

Although the list of factors presented here is both incomplete and skewed (it particularly deals with factors that *impede* progress on the functional or social dimension), it still provides some insight into the type of problems that may be encountered when intervening in high parameter value structures. As indicated, foreknowledge of such factors can be helpful because it can be used for the purpose of the assessment and (re)design of intervention infrastructures. Of course, there are also factors that *facilitate* the progress of episodic interventions in high parameter value structures. For instance, the suffering of production managers, workers, and clients because of these structures may overcome the motivation issues discussed previously. Or the power that top managers have in these structures can help to get these interventions going (episodic interventions in high parameter value structures are virtually impossible without the backing of top management). However, as the argument stands: high parameter value structures are self-inhibiting, and this means that the factors impeding progress probably outweigh the factors facilitating it.

8.4.4 Power and politics

Having almost reached the end of this section, still nothing has been said about power and politics. How can this be? Was their importance not underlined in Chapters 4, 5, and 7, and in Section 8.4.1?

On reflection, however, a counter-question can be asked: 'Were power and politics not, in some way or other, at issue all the time?'

Take the 'aspectual refraction of problems and solutions'. Here, different groups of aspectual managers develop their own aspect-related definition of a problem that *per hypothesis* is structure-driven. Moreover, in line with their aspectual problem definitions, each group comes up with its own aspect-related solution. The resulting problem definitions and their solutions may easily become the focus of a power struggle between groups of aspectual managers. In this power struggle, *not only* the problem definitions and their related solutions may be at stake, *but also* the power of the different groups of aspectual managers. As it appears, 'aspectual refraction' becomes a vehicle for exerting (and increasing) power.

Or take the influence of deep (and related surface) metaphors. The one-sided and out-of-awareness character of deep metaphors can exert a hegemonic power over the sense-making processes of organization members, 'gently forcing' a particular 'view' of organizational events on organization members while excluding alternative views.

Or take the lack of motivation of middle managers or professionals to change the current way of working in a high parameter value structure. This lack of motivation may well end up as passive or active resistance to the episodic intervention. And once again, the stake of this struggle is *not only* the immediate point of contest – in this case, the role and status of 'the' middle manager or 'the' professional – *but also* the power of the groups that are involved in the struggle.

On closer examination, it doesn't seem difficult to connect each of the factors mentioned previously (as well as other contingent factors that can exert their influence on the intervention's progress) to the topic of power and politics in organizations. And what is more, we would like to suggest that making this connection is more useful than referring to power and politics as generic and separate factors affecting the progress of episodic interventions.

In the first place, connecting power and politics to factors that can affect the progress of episodic interventions seems to do justice to the *pervasiveness* of power and politics. Instead of making them into 'separate' factors that exist besides other factors that are then presumed to be 'power and politics-neutral', power and politics become an aspect that pervades *all* these factors – factors as diverse as 'departmental focus', 'skilled incompetence', or 'rootedness'.

Second, by connecting power and politics to factors that can affect progress, the *analysis* of these factors as well as of power and politics in organizations can win. Instead of just saying that one should take power and politics into account (which is both true and a cliché) or that, for instance, 'aspectual refraction' impedes progress on the functional or social dimension, it becomes possible to make the connection between a particular factor such as aspectual refraction and power and politics and ask questions like 'Who are involved?', 'What is at stake for them?', 'What power resources and strategies are used?', 'How intense is the struggle?', and 'Who is winning and who is not?' By making this connection, the analysis of the factor 'aspectual refraction' can win. This factor is not just naively taken at face value, but explicitly related to possible underlying power relations between different groups of aspectual managers. And what is more, by making the connection, the analysis of power and politics also wins. Power and politics are not just taken as a generic influences. They are connected to factors (in this case, aspectual refraction) that actually affect the progress of the intervention.

In fact, by making the connection, power and politics become something 'in between' a *dimension* of the 3-D model and just one of the *factors* (besides others) that affect progress on the functional or social dimensions: they become inescapable aspects of *all* the factors that affect the intervention's progress.

We think that this does justice to the role of power and politics in organizational interaction. *All* interaction in organizations can be viewed from the perspective of 'power and politics', be it in terms of hegemonic power or in terms of the power and politics of particular groups or individuals who want to maintain or increase their power. As such, *all* the factors that can affect the intervention's functional or social progress have a political or power aspect and should be treated as such. In this way, power and politics are an integral part of the *application* of the 3-D model, leaving intact both its layout and logic of use:

- In our view, the layout can be left intact because in order to support the flexible design of intervention structures, no more is required than goal dimensions that allow for the specification of what goals should be realized and an infrastructural dimension that allows for the specification of the infrastructural means that should help realize these goals. In our view, the functional and social dimensions are necessary and sufficient to define the goals that should be realized in the intervention in order to realize the goal of the intervention. The infrastructural dimension, then, can be used to specify the infrastructural means. A fourth dimension devoted to power and politics is not required for the purpose of flexible design.
- The logic of use can be left intact because the five activities that constitute its core are necessary and sufficient for the continuous assessment and adjustment of the intervention. In our view, no additional activities devoted to power and politics are needed here.

Still, as indicated in Chapter 5, *given* the layout of the 3-D model and *given* its logic of use, power and politics, because of their pervasiveness, should *always* be factored in when *applying* the model's logic of use in concrete episodic interventions. This means that actual assessments of the intervention's progress and actual adjustments of either proximate functional or social goals or the intervention's infrastructure should *always* take power and politics into account, not as generic phenomena, but as unavoidable aspects of *all* the factors that can affect the intervention's progress.

This final reflection on the role of power and politics in the 3-D model completes this section on factors that can affect the progress of episodic interventions.

Given this reflection, we now turn to the design of the intervention infrastructure itself. In the next three sections, we will examine the three aspects of this infrastructure more closely: the intervention structure is discussed in Section 8.5, its technology in Section 8.6, and its human resources in Section 8.7. Each of these sections is organized in the same way. The first sub-section discusses what the aspect entails, the second discusses relevant topics related to the design of that particular aspect, and the third relates these topics to the procedures for goal- and improvement-driven design regulation.

8.5 Intervention structure

In this section, by an intervention structure, we mean the *grouping and allocation of intervention activities into a network of intervention tasks that is related to both proximate functional and social goals in the intervention as well as to the structure of the organization*. Let us start by explaining what this definition means.

8.5.1 Intervention structure: explaining the definition

Basic to the definition of the intervention structure is the concept of *intervention activities*. Intervention activities are activities that *aim to contribute to the realization or adaptation of functional or social goals in the intervention*. Two types of interaction activities can be distinguished: (1) operational and (2) regulatory.

Operational intervention activities directly aim to contribute to the realization of functional or social goals in the intervention. As such, they are the counterpart of operational activities in the organization, for these activities directly aim to contribute to the realization of the goals that constitute that organization's meaning. Examples of operational intervention activities are:

creating change relationships, participating in the diagnosis of the current structure of the organization, facilitating the search for new concepts and models that can help to deal with problems in the organization, or testing a new procedure that should contribute to solving these problems.

Regulatory intervention activities aim to regulate operational intervention activities. As may be clear by now, these regulatory intervention activities can be distinguished into: (1) *strategic regulation* of the intervention, selecting functional and social goals in the intervention, (2) *design regulation*,: constructing an intervention infrastructure that can realize selected functional and social goals, and (3) *operational regulation* of the operational intervention activities, dealing with disturbances that occur as the intervention proceeds, given both the intervention infrastructure and selected functional and social goals.

Operational and regulatory intervention activities can be grouped and allocated into *intervention tasks*. Just as in the case of the tasks that constitute the structure of organizations, intervention tasks can be performed by different types of 'capacities', for instance individual participants in the intervention (e.g. organization members, hired consultants, but also clients or suppliers can perform intervention tasks), intervention teams (e.g. scrum teams), work groups, steering committees, or the intervention organization as a whole can perform intervention tasks. As an intervention unfolds, one and the same capacity can perform different intervention tasks. For instance, at the start of the intervention, the task of an intervention team may consists of diagnostic activities; later on, it may consist of activities related to design and testing. In this sense, the intervention task of a capacity can be dynamic (see the discussion in Section 8.5.2 of the functional dynamics of intervention activities).

Based on the allocation and grouping of intervention activities into tasks, a *network* of related intervention tasks comes into existence. This network is the intervention structure. Just as the structure of the organization is related to orders, the structure of the intervention organization is related to functional and social goals in the intervention: it links the intervention technology and human resources to the activities (grouped and allocated into the network of intervention tasks) needed to realize proximate functional and social goals in the intervention. On top of this, the network of intervention tasks is related to the structure of the organization because organization members working in the organization can also have tasks in the intervention structure. When designing intervention structures, it is useful to take both relations into account. We will now discuss what these relations entail and how they affect the design of intervention structures.

8.5.2 Intervention structure: design-related topics

In this section, we will discuss four topics related to the design of intervention structures. However, before we start, we would like to repeat a cautionary remark. Because episodic interventions are a kind of social experiments, it is impossible to prescribe one particular design as 'the' design. Designers should be *free* to design intervention structures as required by the situation as they see it and given the proximate functional and social goals that have been set. However, this freedom is not absolute. It should be *constrained* by principles that govern design regulation. These constraining principles should be seen as *enabling* constraints. They are principles that enable the design of structural configurations that support social experimentation. Based on the findings of Chapter 3, we already know what these principles are. However, in this section we aim to gear them to the particular case of the design of intervention structures and develop some heuristic principles (HPs) that can support their design.

In this way, we intend to shed some light on the design of intervention structures that support the realization and adaptation of functional and social goals in the intervention.

To this purpose, we will now discuss the intervention structure and its relation both to the structure of the organization and the realization and adaptation of functional and social goals in the intervention. Moreover, we want to devote some words to the design of the role of consultants in the intervention and the relation between the design of intervention structures and morality.

Intervention structures and their relation to organizational structures

Previously, we mentioned that the intervention structure is related to the structure of the organization. This relation exists because organization members performing activities in the organization are also involved – in some way – in intervention activities that aim to change the work they do in the organization. This involvement gives rise to two issues deserving attention: *participation* and the resulting *addition* of and *overlap* between activities in the organization and activities in the intervention organization.

Participation

It is easy to understand why members working in an organization are in some way or other involved in intervention activities that aim to change their work, since we already know that organizational interventions are interventions 'in' and 'by' organizations.

As argued in Chapter 4, the 'in' is related to the object of the intervention. This object always has a social dimension. This means that changing the object, e.g. changing the structure of an organization, always means changing the object-related interaction premises and interactions of organization members. And what is more, if the intervention is to succeed, organization members need to change these object-related interaction premises and interactions in such a way that the functional design of the object of the intervention (functional dimension) is interactively made into an organizational reality (social dimension). Only then can the goal of the intervention be achieved.

The 'by' is related to the point that in order to change object-related interaction premises and interactions, interaction is needed. The 'by' therefore always implies the interactive involvement of organization members whose work will be changed by means of the intervention. If organization members are to 'integrate' the new way of working into their interaction repertoire, they somehow need to be interactively involved in the intervention.

If the 'in' and 'by' are combined, it can be argued that successful organizational interventions interactively change the object-related interactions and interaction premises of organization members in such a way that the functional design of the object of the intervention is interactively realized. From this combination, it can be learned that organization members are involved in organizational interventions in at least two ways. If the intervention is to succeed, organization members need to:

1. change their object-related interaction premises and interactions in such a way that the functional design of the object of the intervention is interactively realized;
2. be involved in interactions that aim to change these object-related interaction premises and interactions.

This double involvement of organization members is a feature that is *inextricably* linked to organizational interventions – i.e. no organizational intervention can be performed successfully without it. Taken in this basic and minimal sense, *all* organizational interventions are 'participative'; they all somehow presuppose the 'involvement' of organization members in interactions that aim to change both their interaction repertoires and the interaction premises supporting these repertoires.

Usually, however, the term 'participation' is not used in this basic and minimal sense. Instead, 'participation' is seen as a *variable* that allows for *degrees*.

In this less basic and minimal sense, the degree of participation generally refers to the direct and active involvement in the intervention of the persons: (1) who experience or contribute to some problem and/or (2) whose behaviour should change in order to solve that problem. A high degree of participation, then, allows these persons to directly and actively contribute to the intervention activities that are needed to solve the problem. The 'objects' of the intervention also are the 'subjects' that intervene. In the case of a low degree of participation, these persons are only basically and minimally involved in intervention activities needed to solve the problem. They are the 'objects' of the intervention. 'Others' solve the problem for them. These 'others' are the 'subjects' that intervene.

In the less general case of episodic interventions in high parameter value structures, we are dealing with organizations that, because of high separation between operation and control, ideal typically allocate activities related to strategic and design regulation to 'managers' and 'staff'. In these organizations, they are the 'subjects' that intervene. Persons working in the primary processes of the organization (workers, professionals, operational managers), in these structures, ideal typically, are the 'objects' of these interventions.

Therefore, in the case of episodic interventions in high parameter value structures, the level of participation may be called 'low' if only 'managers' and 'staff' (possibly helped by consultants) or consultants (instructing managers and staff what to do) perform the intervention activities that are needed to transform the work of organization members who perform the primary processes of the organization. In this case, the work of these workers is transformed by these managers or consultants. The workers' involvement in the intervention is limited to the basic and minimal level discussed previously. Participation is called 'high' if workers working in the primary processes of the organization perform the intervention activities needed to transform their own work. In this case, the workers' involvement in the intervention, their participation, far surpasses the basic and minimal level.

In order to speak in a more sophisticated way about participation, it is relevant to take four interrelated factors into account: (1) *who* is involved (2) in *what* intervention activities, (3) is this involvement *indirect* or *direct*, and (4) is the *mode* of involvement more passive or active?

As to 'who' is involved, we already indicated that it is relevant, in high parameter value structures, to distinguish between:

- organization members (and consultants) predominantly performing activities related to the strategic and design regulation of the organization – e.g. top managers or support staff dealing with design regulation;
- organization members predominantly performing activities related to the primary processes of the organization – workers, professionals, and operational managers; we will call them 'workers' for short.

The level of participation increases as more 'workers' are involved in intervention activities. Note that as the level of participation increases, the involvement in the intervention of organization members performing strategic and design regulation in the organization may decrease. But also note that this decrease does not necessarily mean that their control over the intervention diminishes, since they may still be involved in crucial intervention activities, for instance, related to the strategic or design regulation of the intervention.

The first factor, 'who is involved', directly refers to the second: 'in what intervention activities are participants in the intervention involved'? Based on the 3-D model and its underlying cybernetic logic, different types of intervention activities can be distinguished. First, 'workers' may be involved in operational intervention activities that aim to realize goals on the functional and/or social dimensions. For instance, they may be involved in 'diagnostic' activities or in activities that should lead to 'integration'. Second, 'workers' may be involved in activities pertaining to the regulation of the intervention: operational, design, and strategic regulation. In general, it can be argued that the level of participation increases as more workers are involved in more operational and regulatory intervention activities.

The third factor is about how 'workers' are involved in the intervention. Is their participation representative or direct? In the case of participation by representation, selected organization members working in the primary processes of the organization are involved in the intervention organization in order to (more or less actively) bring in the viewpoints or interests of their co-workers in the intervention process. This intervention process, however, is performed by others. In the case of direct participation, organization members working in the primary processes of the organization are themselves more or less actively involved in the performance of intervention activities that are needed to change their own work. As the involvement of organization members working in the primary processes of the organization becomes more direct, the level of participation increases.

The fourth factor, the 'mode' of participation, ranges from passive to active participation (see also de Sitter, 1994, Chapter 8). That is, organization members can be interactively involved in intervention activities in order to:

- be *instructed* to follow up on the results of intervention activities performed by others – e.g. doctors and nurses are instructed to take up their new tasks in the organizational structure that was designed by others (passive);
- be *informed* by others – e.g. consultants sharing the findings of the diagnosis with the doctors and nurses (passive);
- be *queried* for information that is used by others in the intervention – e.g. extracting information from doctors and nurses that can be used for the purpose of a diagnosis of the functioning of their ward (passive);
- be *consulted* by others – e.g. asking the opinion of doctors and nurses with regard to particular design options (passive);
- *give advice* to others – e.g. give advice (asked or unasked) about a next step in the implementation (active);
- *perform* intervention activities – e.g. doctors and nurses making a design for their own department (active);
- *co-decide* on the result of an intervention activity – e.g. co-deciding that this particular part of the design will be implemented (active);
- *decide* on the result of an intervention activity – e.g. deciding on the next proximate functional and social goals (active).

The level of participation increases as the mode of participation becomes more active.

Taking these four factors into account, it can be said that participation is *minimal* if only consultants and/or organization members who predominantly perform activities related to strategic and design regulation in the organization are actively involved in intervention activities that change the work of others in the organization. These 'others' are the organization members who predominantly perform activities related to the primary processes of the organization. In the case of minimal participation, these 'others' are not even represented in the intervention organization. Moreover, their mode of involvement remains only passive.

Participation can be said to be *maximal* if all organization members who normally work in the primary processes of the organization are directly and actively involved in the intervention activities that are needed in order to transform their own work in the organization.

Of course, in actual practice, the level of participation will be somewhere in between the minimum and maximum described here. The minimum and maximum are only ideal typical descriptions. Moreover, in practice, levels of participation may vary as an intervention proceeds (e.g. starting with low and ending with high levels of participation).

Please note that participation of organization members working in the primary processes of the organization is only one form of participation. Other parties that are affected by or have an interest in the intervention may also be involved. Examples of such parties are clients, suppliers, or interest groups. For this reason, it is perhaps better to speak of different types of participation: of 'worker' participation, 'client' participation, 'supplier' participation, 'interest group' participation, etc. For each type of participation, then, high to low levels can be distinguished by applying the interrelated factors mentioned previously. For instance, the level of client participation increases as more clients are directly and more actively involved in more intervention activities. Given these additional types of participation, our definition should be expanded to comprise parties such as clients, suppliers, and other interest groups as well. The level of participation, then, increases as more 'workers', 'clients', 'suppliers', and 'other parties that have an interest' are involved directly and actively in more intervention activities.

As may be imagined, high levels of participation can have positive effects on realizing functional and social goals. For instance, on the functional dimension, experiences of clients or work-related knowledge and skills of organization members participating in the intervention may be indispensable to improve the quality of a diagnosis or design. On the social dimension, high levels of participation can help to realize the motivation, adoption, and integration goals as organization members participating in the intervention contribute to the design and development of their own work in the new organization structure.

However, high levels of participation also can invoke some of the knowledge-, skill-, and motivation-related problems mentioned earlier (introducing problems related to power and politics as well). Moreover, high levels of participation can make the intervention structure and its relation to the organization in which the intervention takes place more complex. Thus, participation also can also be a source of problems. From our discussion of participation, a first structure-related heuristic principle (HP_s) can be formulated:

> HP_s 1: Intervention structures should be designed to take advantage of positive effects of participation, while keeping down (1) the complexity of the intervention structure and (2) possible adverse effects of addition and overlap of intervention tasks and tasks in the organization.

The first issue of keeping down the complexity of the intervention structure will be discussed further below in the sub-section about the relation between the intervention structure and functional and social goals in the intervention. The second issue of 'addition' and 'overlap' is the topic of the next sub-section.

Addition and overlap

Because organization members working in the primary processes of the organization can, and probably will, play a more or less direct and active role in the intervention organization (worker participation), the structures of the two organizations are related. Two basic relations between these two structures are relevant to discuss: (1) in some cases, intervention activities are *added* to 'ongoing' activities that are performed in the organization, and (2) in some cases, goals in the intervention and goals of the organization *overlap* in one and the same activity – the activity, at one and the same time, is an intervention activity and an ongoing activity in the organization.

Addition Many of the intervention activities that constitute the intervention structure will be 'added' to 'ongoing' tasks that organization members already have in the organization, e.g. a bank employee performing intervention activities 'on top of' her ongoing banking tasks. In the case of these 'added' intervention activities, attention should be paid to the *affinity* between intervention activities and ongoing tasks. More specifically, attention should be paid to:

- how ongoing tasks in the organization equip organization members for their intervention activities – e.g. how can this bank employee, because of her involvement in the banking process, be of special value in, for instance, diagnostic or design activities?
- how intervention activities equip organization members for their possible new ongoing tasks in the structure of the organization that results from the intervention – how does this bank employee, because of her involvement in diagnostic activities, acquire new knowledge or skills, e.g. new communication and analytical skills, that she will need in order to perform her new task in the restructured bank?

The use of these affinities between intervention activities and ongoing activities in the old or new organization is one of the factors that can contribute to the success of more participative intervention structures. In particular, participative intervention structures that *foreshadow* the new low parameter value structure of the organization are helpful here. In these intervention structures, organization members can both become acquainted with and acquire skills that are relevant to the type of work that they are expected to do in the new structure.

Moreover, in the case of 'added' intervention activities, attention should be paid to the total *workload* of organization members. As the episodic intervention proceeds, the involvement of organization members in the intervention can vary. At any point in time, the addition of intervention activities to 'ongoing' tasks can overburden organization members who are involved in the intervention. Continuous attention and care for the total workload of these organization members is one of the factors that can prevent the failure of more participative intervention structures.

Overlap It is also possible that intervention goals and goals of the organization overlap in one and the same activity. The activity is part of the structure of both the intervention and the organization.

Activities realizing the 'integration' goal are a good example. As explained in Chapter 7, 'integration' is all about organization members 'synthesizing' their new job. It is all about constructing or crafting the new job and finding out how it fits into one's own working life and the working life of others. The way to do this is to actually perform the new job, to actually work together in the new structure, thereby making this structure into a new organizational reality. In this case, one and the same activity – performing one's job in the new structure – can serve the purposes of:

1. the *organization* – the activity contributes to the realization of goals that constitute the meaning of the organization;
2. the *intervention* organization – the activity contributes to the realization of the social 'integration' goal in the intervention.

Seen from one perspective, this activity is an 'ongoing' activity in the new structure of the organization. Seen from another perspective, it is an intervention activity in the intervention organization.

It is relevant to take overlap into account because, in the first place, one and the same activity may be evaluated in terms of different norms – in this case, norms related to the goals of the 'standing' organization and norms related to the social goal of 'integration'. In the course of time, the prevalence of these norms may change. At first, the 'integration' goal may prevail, later on, the organizational goals. Second, because of the possible overlap of intervention goals and organizational goals in one activity, it may seem as if the intervention organization has already ended, while in fact organization members are still performing intervention activities. Particularly at the start and at the end of an episodic intervention, participants in the intervention may perform intervention activities that overlap with their activities in the organization.

From our discussion of addition and overlap, we can take away two heuristic principles that can support the design of intervention structures:

> HP_s 2: The design of intervention infrastructures should take into account possible advantages resulting from activities that organizational members:
>
> - perform in the old organization and activities they perform in the intervention organization;
> - perform in the intervention organization and activities they will be performing in the new organization (foreshadowing).
>
> HP_s 3: In the case of addition, the design of intervention infrastructures should take into account the total *workload* of organization members performing tasks in both the organization and the intervention organization.

Intervention structures and their relation to functional and social goals

Previously, we discussed participation in the context of the relation between the organization's structure and the structure of the intervention organization. We saw that the level of participation increases as more 'workers' (including professionals and operational managers) working in the primary processes of the organization are directly and actively involved in more intervention activities. Moreover, we indicated that 'worker participation' is not the only kind of participation. 'Clients', 'suppliers', or 'other parties that have an interest' can also be involved in episodic interventions, making these interventions more participative. In addition to these parties that increase the level of participation, other parties that do not necessarily increase the level of participation will also be involved in episodic interventions – e.g. organization members performing activities related to strategic and design regulation in the organization (managers and staff) and consultants. And this list of parties that can be involved in episodic interventions is probably incomplete.

As more and more workers, clients, suppliers, and other parties with an interest are involved in an episodic intervention, not only its participative character, but also its *complexity* increases. More and more parties with different backgrounds and interests are involved in possibly interdependent activities that should realize functional and social goals, increasing the need for interaction and coordination. This mounting complexity, of course, may endanger the success of the intervention. One way to decrease this complexity is to pay attention to the intervention's structure: to the way intervention activities are grouped and allocated in a network of intervention tasks:

> HP 4_s: The intervention structure should be designed to decrease the complexity introduced by high levels of participation.

Now, we already know that it is the function of intervention structures to support the realization and adaptation of proximate functional and social goals in the intervention. To this purpose, these structures should be designed in such a way that they:

A   support *all* the intervention activities needed to actually realize and adapt the required functional and social goals – this introduces the topics of the *functional dynamics* and *experimental character* of intervention activities in relation to *planning* and *design*.
B   attenuate (preferably: minimize) the probability of disturbances caused by the intervention structure and amplify (preferably optimize) potentials for regulation of the intervention given the required levels of participation – this introduces the topics of *participation* in relation to *parameters of intervention structures* and their *desired values*.

Below, we first discuss 'A' and 'B' and their related topics in order to derive additional heuristic principles that can support the design of intervention structures. Second, we provide three examples of intervention structures that are applications of these heuristic principles.

A: intervention activities, functional dynamics, experiment, planning, and design

Intervention structures should support the performance of *all* the operational and regulatory intervention activities related to the realization and adaptation of proximate functional and social goals in the intervention, because it is by realizing and adapting these goals that the goal of the intervention is formulated and realized.

Now, we already know that, as an episodic intervention proceeds, new proximate functional and social goals are selected, setting the course for the step-by-step realization of the final functional and social goals: 'evaluation' and 'integration'. This step-by-step selection of new proximate functional and goals during the intervention, of course, also has consequences for the intervention activities that should be performed in order to realize these goals. Each time new functional and social goals are selected, new intervention activities need to be performed in order to realize these goals. For instance, in the early stages, intervention activities related to 'diagnosis' and 'motivation' may be required; later on, activities related to 'design' and 'adoption' may become relevant. Therefore, as proximate functional and social goals change during the intervention, the intervention activities needed to realize these goals also change. Please note that this dynamic character of interaction activities is not due to *contingent* problems or opportunities that present themselves during the intervention, it is a *necessary* consequence of the *function* of the intervention structure itself: supporting the performance of all the intervention activities needed to realize and adapt changing proximate functional and social goals – intervention activities are *functionally* dynamic.

We also know that episodic interventions are a kind of experiments. Proximate functional and social goals are set, and, given an intervention structure supporting the realization and adaptation of these goals, intervention activities are performed to realize these goals. However, all kinds of contingent problems and opportunities may present themselves, requiring additional operational or regulatory intervention activities. This means that at the start of an episodic intervention, it is not yet known what 'all' the intervention activities are that should be performed in order to realize all the proximate functional and social goals of the intervention. What intervention activities are needed in what exact sequence only becomes clear as the intervention unfolds itself.

Given the functional dynamics and experimental character of intervention activities, *planning* and its relation to the *design* of intervention structures become relevant. Earlier, we discussed three modes of planning: simple, programme, and project planning.

Applied to the design of intervention structures, *simple planning* entails that each time new proximate functional or social goals are set, the operational intervention activities that should realize these goals are specified and allocated to a network of operational intervention tasks. Given this network of operational intervention tasks, the activities needed to regulate the realization and adaptation of the operational intervention tasks are specified and added to the network. In this way, the intervention structure develops 'organically' as the intervention proceeds, accommodating problems and opportunities as they present themselves during the intervention. As indicated earlier, simple planning, including the design of the intervention structure, is most in tune with the experimental characteristic of episodic interventions. Here, it can be added that simple planning fits in well with the functionally dynamic character of intervention activities.

In the case of *programme planning*, an *overarching* sequence of functional and social goals is specified involving one or more aspects, parts, or groups in the organization. Ideal typically, this sequence is predefined by the order of proximate functional and social goals that should be realized in order to make the episodic intervention a success. Given this overarching sequence, the intervention structure (including its dynamics) can be designed in *outline*. For instance, it may be specified that first, groups of organization members are involved in realizing particular 'diagnostic' and 'motivation' goals. Then, small groups 'design' and 'implement' their part of the new organizational structure, thereby also realizing the 'adoption' goal. Finally, groups of organization members 'integrate' and 'evaluate' the new structure they themselves designed. In literature on episodic interventions, different intervention programmes have been described ranging from highly participative to top-down and expert-driven. For a helpful overview, see van Amelsvoort (1998), who (among other programmes) discusses: 'blueprint', 'expert', 'de-blocking', 'cascading', and 'collective' programmes. Because intervention programmes are overarching and in outline, the intervention structure should be micro-designed as the intervention proceeds. This micro-designing can be done in the mode of simple planning with respect to selected functional and social goals with respect to parts and aspect of the intervention.

Although *project planning* is not fully excluded by the logic of the 3-D model, it is still the planning mode that is least compatible with the experimental character of episodic interventions. Project planning treats a fundamentally experimental process as if it can be planned and designed both in advance and in detail. Because project planning is most out of tune with the experimental character of episodic interventions, we will not further pursue this mode of planning here. This means that our discussions will only apply to simple and programme planning.

From this discussion, we can take away a heuristic principle that can support the design of intervention structures:

> HP_s 5: In the case of episodic interventions in high parameter value structures, the design of intervention structure should be in the mode of either simple or programme planning. In the case of programme planning, the micro-design of the intervention structure should be in the mode of simple planning. A detailed structural design in the project planning mode is unadvisable (if not impossible) in the case of episodic interventions in high parameter vale structures (particularly in large interventions).

B: attenuation, amplification, parameters, and participation

Just as in the case of the structure of an organization, the structure of an intervention organization should not be a source of disturbances. Moreover, just like the structure of an organization, the structure of an intervention organization should facilitate regulation. This means that intervention structures, just like the structures of organizations, should be designed in order to (1) preferably minimize the probability of structure-related disturbances and (2) optimize structure-related potentials for regulation.

In order to design intervention structures that can meet these two requirements, it will be useful to take a closer look at the parameters of intervention structures and their desired values. For purposes of convenience, four structure-related parameters are discussed here:

1. functional concentration;
2. specialization of operational intervention tasks;
3. separation between operational and regulatory intervention tasks;
4. specialization of regulatory intervention tasks.

Of these four parameters, functional concentration is the most important. Unfortunately, it is also the parameter that is hardest to articulate in theoretical terms, while in practice, i.e. when applying the 3-D model, it seems relatively easy to keep levels of functional concentration down. So it is with some reluctance that functional concentration is discussed here. Readers who are interested in the practical implications of this discussion are advised to skip on to the discussion of the related heuristic principles (HP_s 6–8).

Functional concentration In general, functional concentration refers to the relation between operational tasks and orders (see Chapter 3). If all operational tasks are (potentially) related to all orders, then the level of functional concentration is high. If operational tasks are only coupled to a sub-set of all orders, functional concentration is low.

In order to apply this general definition to episodic interventions in high parameter value structures, we first need to specify what an 'order' is in the case of these interventions. Now, in Chapter 3, we defined an order as a specific individual demand for a product or service. So what are the 'products' or 'services' produced by episodic interventions in high parameter value structures?

To answer this question, we need to look at what should be achieved by the intervention. Here, it is useful to make a distinction between what should be achieved *ultimately* and what should be achieved *along the way*.

What should be achieved *ultimately* is that organization members (but also clients, suppliers, and other stakeholders) previously working in or with the high parameter value structure of the old organization have integrated the new low parameter value structure into their interaction premises in such a way that, by means of their interactions, the new structure becomes an organizational reality and the goal of the intervention can be realized. What should be ultimately achieved is that groups of organization members work together in the functionally de-concentrated, semi-autonomous teams that constitute the new organization structure. These groups of organization members, doing what they should be doing in the flows and teams of the new structure, are the 'orders' that should ultimately be 'produced' by the intervention. If clients, suppliers, or other stakeholders working with the new low parameter value structure are also involved (participate) in the intervention, they can be added to this definition of orders.

If we look at what should be achieved *along the way*, we can say that groups of organization members should be transformed (or better, transform themselves) in such a way that the proximate functional and social goals in the intervention that hold for them are realized. What should be 'produced' along the way are 'groups of organization members who are transformed in such a way that the proximate functional or social goals that hold for them are realized'. So these 'transformed groups' are the orders along the way. Once again, to this definition, groups of clients, suppliers, or other stakeholders that participate in the intervention can be added.

Given our discussion thus far, functional concentration refers to the relation between operational intervention tasks and groups of organization members who are transformed by the intervention in such a way that they realize proximate or ultimate functional or social goals that hold for them. If all operational intervention tasks are (potentially) related to all these groups, then the level of functional concentration is high. If operational tasks are only coupled to sub-sets of these group, functional concentration is low.

Although these definitions better specify what the 'orders' are, it has to be admitted that they are still quite hard to understand (and therefore useless in practice). To further clarify the definitions, attention should be paid to two issues related to the 'orders' – issues that have a bearing on what low and high functional concentration in the case of episodic interventions mean.

The first issue is that the groups of organization members (and possibly clients, suppliers, and other stakeholders) mentioned in the two definitions of 'orders' are not involved in the intervention process in the same way that, for instance, 'tables' and 'chairs' are involved as the orders of a furniture making process. The difference is that, in the case of episodic interventions, the 'orders', i.e. the groups that ultimately or along the way should change their organizational behaviour, are also *involved* in the intervention process as *co-creators* of their own changed behaviour. Leaving behind old interaction premises and patterns, adopting new ones, and integrating new interaction premises and patterns is not just any transformation process, it is first and foremost a process of *self*-transformation that requires the involvement of the person or persons who are being transformed. That is why we argued previously that all episodic interventions are 'participative', at least in a basic and minimal sense. Therefore, in the case of episodic interventions, 'orders' and 'co-creators of orders' coincide in the groups of 'human capacities' that should have changed their behaviour after the conclusion of the intervention. Based on this insight, a heuristic principle with respect to low functional concentration and ultimate orders of the intervention can be formulated:

> HP_s 6: In order to keep the level of functional concentration low, the groups of organization members (and/or clients, suppliers, etc.) that ultimately should perform the interrelated jobs in the flows and teams of the new organization structure should, as much as desired levels of participation allow, be involved in the operational intervention activities needed to create their *own* flows and teams; intervention activities should be allocated to them in order to allow them to become the co-creators of their own flows and teams.

However, at this point, the second issue immediately becomes relevant.

This second issue relates to the point that, at the start of an episodic intervention in a high parameter value structure, it is seldom known what groups of organization members (and clients, suppliers, etc.) are going to work together in the flows and teams of the new organization structure. So it is seldom known what the ultimate 'orders' are. Of course, it is known *that* at the end of the intervention, groups of organization members should have integrated new interaction premises into their repertoires, allowing them to work together in the flows and teams of the new low parameter value structure. However, *who* is going to work with *whom* in what flow or team is seldom known at the start of an episodic intervention. This seems (and only *seems*) to undermine the heuristic principle formulated previously (HP 5). For how can we allocate operational intervention activities to groups of organization members working in flows and teams that have not yet been designed?

This not knowing at the start of an episodic intervention what the ultimate 'orders' are has two implications for designers of intervention structures who want to keep the level of functional concentration low.

First, intervention structures should be designed step-by-step (possibly given some overarching programme). So this is where the 'orders along the way' become relevant. That is, in order to keep functional concentration down, each time new proximate functional and social goals are set (new 'orders along the way' are defined), new operational intervention activities should be defined and grouped into tasks that, given the desired level of participation, are allocated to the groups of organization members who, given the proximate functional and social goals, should change their outlook or behaviour according to these functional and social goals.

To give an example, at the start of an episodic intervention, it may be decided that particular groups of organization members should experience how complex their high parameter value organization actually is (e.g. as a part of the 'diagnosis' and 'motivation' goals). To this

308 Designing interventions

purpose, operational intervention activities are allocated to these groups. For instance, they map their network of work-related dependency relations and analyse how this network hinders them doing their work properly (i.e. how the network is both a source of work-related problems and hinders their regulating these problems). By means of this intervention structure, each group of organization members becomes the co-creator of its own transformation in terms of the functional and social goals that should be realized for that group (which is the 'order along the way' that should be produced): particular intervention tasks are coupled to sub-sets of orders:

> HP_s 7: In order to keep the level of functional concentration low, each time new proximate functional and social goals are set, operational intervention activities should be defined and grouped into tasks that, as much as desired levels of participation allow, are allocated to the groups of organizational members (clients, suppliers, etc.) that should change their outlook or behaviour according to these proximate functional and social goals.

By means of the seventh heuristic principle, operational intervention tasks are coupled to the realization of proximate functional and social goals that are set for particular groups of organization members.

But what about the sixth heuristic principle? Is it superseded by the seventh? We think not. There is a second implication of not knowing at the start of an episodic intervention what the ultimate 'orders' are. For, as intervention structures are designed step-by-step in such a way that they can realize proximate functional and social goals, the ultimate orders, i.e. the flows and teams that should result from the intervention, also, step-by-step, come more clearly into sight as proximate functional and social goals are realized. Gradually, it is becoming clear who are going to work together in these flows and teams, and for this reason should be involved in their design.

To give an example, suppose that in some organization with a high parameter value structure, groups of organization members working in the functionally concentrated departments of that organization, as a part of 'diagnosis' and 'motivation', map and analyse the network of interdependency relations they are 'trapped' in (see Figure 8.4a). Further suppose that, as a result of this analysis, these organization members have started to understand both *that* they work in a high parameter value structure and *what* the adverse consequences of this are. Now, as a part of proximate 'design' and 'adoption' goals, organization members from different functional departments are grouped into intervention teams that consider the possibilities for the design of flows (see Figure 8.4b). Finally, as 'implementation' and 'integration' goals are also set, relevant members of the intervention teams are given the opportunity to design and experiment with 'their' new flow structure, for instance by moving their equipment from the old functionally concentrated setup to a prospective order-related flow and micro-designing their flow-related tasks (Figure 8.4c).

In this example, organization members are involved in operational intervention tasks in such a way that they, *because* of their involvement:

- can *understand* the reasons for the design of both the new low parameter value structure and the part of the new structure (flow, team) they will be working in;
- as much as levels of participation allow, are the *co-creators* of the flow and team they will be working in.

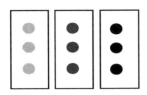 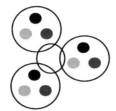 

8.4a Groups of organization members in their functional departments mapping and analysing the complexity of dependency relations in the old structure

8.4b Groups of organization members from different functional departments discussing the possibilities of flows in intervention teams

8.4c A selection of members from the intervention teams designing and experimenting with a prospected order-related flow

FIGURE 8.4 Example of a dynamic intervention structure

In practice, this means that organization members (clients, suppliers, etc.) are involved in all operational intervention activities (from 'diagnosis' and 'motivation' via 'design', 'adoption', and 'implementation' to 'integration' and 'evaluation'). However, in order to keep functional concentration low, they are not involved in all operational intervention tasks with respect to all parts of the old or new organization. As the intervention proceeds, they are involved in those operational intervention activities that are geared to functional and social goals pertaining to 'their' part of the organization. At the start of the intervention, the main point of reference will be the part of the old organization they *are* working in. Of course, this does not imply that organization members working in some part of the organization cannot work together with members from other parts, for instance on diagnostic activities. What is important is that they are able to see how 'their' part of the organization contributes to the organization's problems. Later, as the outlines of the new organization structure become clear, the main point of reference will be the part in the new structure that they *will be* working in. In this way, the sixth and seventh heuristic principles can be connected to each other, leading to an eighth heuristic principle:

> HP$_s$ 8: In order to keep functional concentration down, operational intervention activities should, given desired levels of participation, be defined and grouped into tasks that enable organization members (clients, suppliers, other stakeholders) to:
>
> • understand the reasons for the design of both the new low parameter value structure and the part of that new structure (flow, team) they will be working in;
> • be the *co-creators* of the flow and team they will be working in.

This long, painstaking, theoretical exposition has a relatively simple counterpart in practice. It is part of the logic of the 3-D model to ask 'what', 'how', and 'who' questions given particular proximate functional and social goals in the intervention. By carefully answering these questions, there is a high probability that activities that need to be performed in order to realize these proximate functional and social goals ('what') are allocated to organization members or other parties ('who') who are also mentioned in these goals; thereby involving them in some way or other ('how') in the intervention. In this way, these organization members contribute to the realization of proximate functional and social goals that pertain to themselves – they become the co-creators of their own projected transformation.

Specialization of operational intervention tasks Specialization of operational intervention tasks refers to the coherence and variety of operational intervention activities that are comprised in intervention tasks. If intervention tasks only comprise a small part of the operational intervention activities needed to realize proximate functional and social goals in the intervention, then the level of specialization is high. If all operational intervention activities needed to realize proximate functional and social goals are comprised in intervention tasks, then the level of specialization is low. For instance, suppose that a group of workers or professionals is involved in diagnostic activities in order to realize the proximate functional goal 'diagnosis' with respect to some part and aspect of the organization (e.g. the diagnosis of 'control over quality' in their own department), then specialization is high if the different operational intervention sub-activities that are needed to realize this 'diagnosis' goal – i.e. making a gap analysis, making a cause analysis, and formulating a solution space – are allocated as tasks to sub-groups of these workers or professionals: one group making a gap analysis, the other analysing causes, and yet another formulating a solution space. Specialization is low if this group of workers or professionals performs the required diagnostic sub-activities as a group.

Please note that the parameter 'specialization of operational intervention tasks' presupposes that proximate functional and/or social goals have already been allocated to groups of organization members (or other parties) involved in the intervention. That is, *given* some level of functional concentration of operational intervention activities, specialization *further* subdivides operational intervention activities and allocates them as specialized tasks to sub-groups. Moreover, as the specialization of operational intervention tasks increases, i.e. as more related operational intervention activities are distributed as specialized tasks to more groups of organization members (or other parties), more dependency and coordination relations between these groups come into being, amplifying the probability of disturbances:

> HP_s 9: In order to minimize the probability of structure-related disturbances, the specialization of operational intervention tasks should be kept as low as possible.

Separation between operational and regulatory intervention tasks Separation refers to the extent to which coherent regulatory intervention activities are integrated in intervention tasks. The object of these regulatory activities may be (1) 'disturbances' (operational regulation), (2) relevant parts or aspects of the intervention infrastructure (design regulation), or (3) relevant proximate functional and/or social goals (strategic regulation). Separation is high if intervention tasks comprise only a few or no regulatory intervention activities that are geared to the operational intervention activities contained in those tasks. Separation is low if regulatory intervention activities that are geared to the operational intervention activities contained in intervention tasks are integrated into these intervention tasks.

By keeping down the level of separation, dependency and coordination relations between (separate) operational and regulatory intervention tasks are reduced. This attenuates the probability of the occurrence of structure-related disturbances. Moreover, by integrating regulatory intervention activities into intervention tasks, groups of organization members (and/or other parties) are enabled to regulate with respect to the intervention tasks they perform – their structure-related potential for regulation is amplified:

HP$_s$ 10: In order to minimize the probability of structure-related disturbances and to optimize structure-related potentials for regulation, the level of separation between operational and regulatory intervention activities in intervention tasks should be kept as low as possible.

Specialization of regulatory intervention tasks Specialization of regulatory intervention tasks refers to the coherence and variety of regulatory intervention activities that are comprised in a particular intervention task. Specialization is high if intervention tasks comprise only different parts (e.g. only 'monitoring', 'assessing', or 'intervening') or aspects (e.g. only 'operational', 'design', or 'strategic') of regulation. Specialization is low if different parts or aspects of regulation are integrated into intervention tasks. Once again, it can be argued that more specialization increases the number of dependency and coordination relations between intervention tasks, increasing the probability of structure-related disturbances. Moreover, more specialization decreases structure-related potentials for task-related regulation:

HP$_s$ 11: In order to minimize the probability of structure-related disturbances and optimize the structure-related potentials for regulation, the specialization of regulatory activities in intervention tasks should be kept as low as possible.

Based on these considerations, two ideal typical intervention structures can be distinguished: the low and the high parameter value intervention structure. Moreover, it can be argued that, in the case of the low parameter value intervention structure, the probability of structure-related disturbances is minimized and the potentials for structure-related regulation are optimized, thereby increasing the probability of realizing both proximate and ultimate functional and social goals. In practice, the ideal type of the low parameter value intervention structure, for good or bad reasons, will only be approximated by real intervention structures. Of course, this does not undermine the prescriptive status of this ideal type as the summation of heuristic principles that should guide the design of intervention structures.

In order to illustrate the application of the heuristic principles discussed previously, three examples of intervention structures will be discussed in the next sub-section.

Examples of intervention structures From what has been said until now, we know that the design of intervention structures can be related to both simple and programme planning. In the case of simple planning, the intervention structure is (re)designed 'along the way' as new proximate functional or social goals are set or problems or opportunities present themselves: the intervention consists of a succession of (possibly parallel) *simple designs* of intervention structures that are geared to the realization of proximate functional and social goals in the intervention. In the case of programme planning, an intervention structure for the whole intervention is specified in outline: the *programme design*. This programme design, then, is detailed and, if necessary, adjusted as the intervention proceeds by means of simple planning and design.

Moreover, we know that intervention structures can be described in terms of (1) desired levels of participation and (2) the values of the parameters of the intervention infrastructure. Levels of participation may range from low to high, and they may be either fixed

312 Designing interventions

or varying. In the latter case, levels of participation vary as the intervention proceeds – for instance, an intervention starts with low levels of participation, gradually involving more and more organization members working in the organization's primary processes, clients, etc. in the intervention.

Finally, given the heuristic principles developed previously, we know that, *in the case of episodic interventions in high parameter value structures*, both fixed low levels of participation and high parameter value intervention structures should be avoided:

- Fixed low levels of participation neither do justice to the *impact* of these interventions (transforming the work of virtually all organization members), nor to the point that this transformation primarily is a process of *self*-transformation requiring the active involvement of organization members working in the primary processes of the parts of the organization that are being changed.
- High parameter value intervention structures increase the probability of structure-related disturbances and decrease structure-related potentials for regulation, thereby undermining the realization and adaptation of proximate goals in the intervention.

Based on these findings, a table can be constructed combining participation (fixed/changing, low/high) and parameter values of the intervention infrastructure (high/low). In the cells of this table, examples of possibly useful simple and programme designs can be mapped. Below, we discuss three of these examples (see Table 8.4).

Large group simple design

The *large group intervention* is a highly participative simple design geared to the realization of particular proximate functional and social goals in the intervention.

In a large group intervention, the whole 'system' is involved in the intervention – that is, many or all organization members and possibly other relevant stakeholders participate.

In a relatively short time (two to four days; Worley, et al., 2011, p. 405), these participants work together (sometimes in varying sub-groups) in order to realize particular functional or social goals. Bunker and Alban (1992, p. 589) mention 'creating organizational visions' (future searches), 'redesigns', 'conflict resolution', 'promoting workplace reform', and different kinds of 'learning' as goals that can be pursued by means of large-scale interventions. In a later publication, other goals are added, such as, 'trans-organizational development', 'citizen engagement', and 'scenario planning' (Bunker and Alban, 2005).

TABLE 8.4 Examples of simple and programme designs

			Parameter values of the intervention structure	
			High	Low
Level of participation	Fixed	Low	To be avoided	To be avoided
		High	To be avoided	Large group (simple design) Micro-macro (programme design)
	Varying		To be avoided	Macro-micro (programme design)

'Large' is defined in different ways: in quantitative terms, e.g. as groups comprising 50–500 (Bunker and Alban, 1992) or even 2000 people (Worley et al., 2011, p. 405), and in qualitative terms, e.g. as groups that are so large that face-to-face contact between all participants in the group becomes impossible.

The agenda of large-scale interventions may range from rigid and formal to loose and informal (Worley et al., 2011, p. 405). Axelrod (1992), for instance, seems to propose a more rigid and formal format. In his discussion of the redesign of an organization by means of a large-scale intervention, he points to four core elements of this intervention:

1. the 'enabling' element of the large scale intervention, consisting of: (1) the steering committee that, in our terms, takes care of the intervention's strategic and design regulation, and (2) the data assist team that processes the information that is generated as the intervention proceeds;
2. four conferences that constitute the core of the large-scale intervention – the 'visioning', 'customer', 'technical', and 'preliminary design' conferences;
3. 'walkthrough presentations' designed to share the results of the conferences as they unfold;
4. implementation of the design – "where new organizational units develop their team structure" (p. 504).

In addition to these core elements, Axelrod (1992, pp. 505–506) stresses the importance of the careful and detailed *planning* of the conferences ("Every exercise and expected outcome must be thought through"), the *structuring* of the intervention ("The conferences must have structure, including participant workbooks that outline tasks and activities"), the *pacing* of the conferences (taking into account "that tasks requiring more than 1 hour to complete were difficult for most sub-groups" and that not all sub-groups can complete the same task in the same time), *data reporting* (limiting the time allowed to sub-groups to report on their results and preventing fatigue and boredom as a result of reporting), *conference summaries* (keeping track of the outcomes of the conferences), *internal resources* supporting the work in the conferences, *multimedia and play* in order to keep the conferences lively and creative, and *pre-conference preparation* (ensuring the contribution of each conference to the main goals of the large-scale intervention).

As may be imagined, large-scale interventions can be particularly useful in the early and later stages of episodic interventions in high parameter value structures, as large groups of organization members need to be motivated for the intervention or as the intervention needs to be evaluated. In the middle stages, as smaller groups of organization members work on the design and implementation of 'their' part of the organization, some of the principles of large-scale interventions may still be applicable, but, as a rule, the size of these groups will be too small to speak of 'large' groups.

Micro-macro programme design

The *micro-macro programme design* is a *fixed high-level participatory programme design* that, given the commitment of the organization's top management, starts in one or only a few selected organizational units at the micro level of the organization and then step-by-step involves more units in the intervention. A version of a micro-macro programme design was developed, applied, and tested by Offereins (Offereins and Fruytier, 2013).

In the case of a micro–macro programme, organization members working in the few selected units at the micro level of the organization are given the opportunity to develop an ideal vision of their own work. Moreover, they are empowered to (re)structure their work in accordance with the vision they have developed. This restructuring consists of getting rid of local and inter-local structural arrangements that hinder their working according to their vision (e.g. functional concentration, specialization of operational tasks, separation between operational and regulatory tasks). It aims to create the positive conditions for implementing the vision. Dependent on the intervention's success, more and more units may be selected and involved in the intervention, going through similar processes of self-transformation to the first selected units.

Viewed from a *functional perspective*, micro–macro programmes seem to flout the design precedence rules which specify that:

1. the first step of a structural redesign should be 'outside-in' – reasoning from the organization's environment to its structure;
2. the second step should be the design of the production structure, starting at the macro level, then proceeding to the micro level;
3. the third step should be the design of the control structure, starting at the micro level, proceeding to the macro level.

However, on closer examination, it appears that micro–macro programmes can exist in harmony with these design precedence rules. Particularly, the first two precedence rules are relevant to discuss here.

In the case of the first, the 'outside-in' precedence rule, 'outside-in' can be interpreted as 'starting with a strategic orientation on developments in the organization's environment'. In high parameter value structures, this strategic orientation, as a rule, is the prerogative of the organization's higher management, which, as the argument goes, is best 'equipped' to perform this orientation. Given this interpretation, micro–macro programmes indeed seem to violate the precedence rule. In a micro–macro programme, workers or professionals working in the selected units of the organization do not start their intervention with a strategic orientation on the organization's environment.

However, the 'outside-in' precedence rule can also be interpreted in another way. It can be interpreted as: 'thinking about what ideally can and should be done in order to create value for clients one has to deal with in one's work on a daily basis'. This is also an 'outside-in' reasoning. However, this 'outside-in' reasoning starts with the ideas and actual experiences of organization members working in the primary processes of the organization. Based on their experiences, the micro–macro programme challenges these members to imagine what can and should be done for their clients in terms of creating value. Workers and professionals involved in the day-to-day handling of clients should have the prerogative to adopt this type of 'outside-in' reasoning.

A similar argument can be made with respect the second step, the macro–micro design of the production structure. Here, it is relevant to ask *why* the design of the production structure should start with the organization's macro structure. The answer is: functional de-concentration. In order to functionally de-concentrate the organization's structure, one should start at the macro level by designing production flows relative to sub-sets of the total of the organization's orders. Once (macro) flows have been designed, their segments (meso) and teams (micro) can be designed.

Here too, it can be argued that higher management should have the prerogative to design the structure of the organization at the macro level, since it is higher management that is responsible for the structure of the organization as a whole and has the best overview over the organization's product portfolio.

However, again, a counter-argument can be provided. If functional concentration, in essence, is about grouping activities into relatively independent flows that can coherently service particular orders, then it can also be argued that organization members working in the primary processes know best:

- which complex (inter)dependency relations in the current structure hinder their creating order-related value;
- how activities should be rearranged into a more simple structure consisting of relatively independent flows that can best create the required value.

As long as both the organization's current structure and its order portfolio are not too complex, it seems quite possible for organization members working in the primary processes to design its macro level flows.

As it seems, there need not be a conflict between micro-macro programmes and the design precedence rules. *Conceptually*, the two issues are distinct. Design precedence rules are about the order of design questions that should be tackled, not about who should tackle these questions. For instance, if a design precedence rule states that the organization's production structure should be designed starting at the macro level, this does not imply that the organization's higher management should make the macro design. However, in *practice*, we may be used to judging that organization members working in the organization's primary processes are less equipped to perform some of the steps prescribed by the precedence rules. Yet, as has been argued, this may be a prejudice. Micro-macro programmes suggest that these members can and should play an important role in the design process. Given the backing of the organization's top management, the early, active, and leading involvement of 'workers', 'professionals', and 'operational managers' in the design of the new structure may even be key to the success of an episodic intervention.

Macro-micro programme design

Macro-micro programme designs are examples of *'varying' programme designs*. Macro-micro programmes allow for increasing levels of participation as the intervention proceeds. In a sense, these programmes are the mirror image of micro-macro designs.

In the case of a macro-micro programme, top managers start with an exploration of developments in organization's environment, the development of a vision on the organization's future, and the formulation of functional requirements for the organization. Based on the functional requirements, the organization's overall performance is diagnosed. If the outcomes of the diagnosis suggest that a structural redesign is required, the managers of the organization's macro-level units are involved in the intervention.

At the level of these units, the vision, functional requirements, and diagnosis are discussed. The outcomes of these discussions become the topic of a dialogue with the organization's top management. Given the results of this dialogue, it may be decided to make a first draft of the design of the organization's macro structure – of its order-related flows.

Given the first draft of the organization's macro structure, organization members working in the primary processes of the organization are involved in the intervention. In small intervention teams, they diagnose (parts or aspects of) their own work, relating problems found at the micro level to problems found at the macro level. Dependent on functional and social goals that are set, these intervention teams can consist either of members of the same organizational unit or of members from different organizational units.

The outcomes of the diagnoses performed by the intervention teams may shed a new light on the proposed draft of the organization's macro-structure (its projected flows), requiring adjustments. These adjustments are discussed both at the level of the organization's top management and at the level of its units. The result of these discussions, an adjusted draft of the organization's macro-structure, becomes the starting point for further design and implementation.

To that purpose, intervention teams are assembled consisting of organization members who will be working in the primary processes of the projected flows. These teams are involved in the design, implementation, and evaluation of organizational structures at the meso and micro level of the organization (segments and teams). Of course, it may be decided not to build all the projected flows at the same time. For instance, to start with, one flow may be selected as a 'pilot', thereby reducing risk and providing learning opportunities.

Just like micro-macro programmes, macro-micro programmes break up the whole of the episodic intervention into a set of smaller ones that are performed by intervention teams consisting of organization members working in the organization's primary processes. In this way, the total complexity of the episodic intervention is reduced. Just like teams, segments, and flows in organizations absorb particular 'parts' of the total complexity an organization has to deal with, intervention teams that are part of the intervention organization absorb 'parts' of the total complexity of an episodic intervention.

Consultants: facilitating, directive, combinatory

We already know that consultants may be involved in intervention activities. However, nothing was said about possible *roles* of consultants in episodic interventions. Still, particularly in the case of episodic interventions in high parameter value organizations, the role of consultants may be quite important.

This importance is partly due to the 'functional complexity' of these interventions. Changing the structure of an organization requires a lot of knowledge about and experience with (1) organizational structures and their relation to meaningful survival (knowledge of the type that was discussed in Chapter 3) and (2) activities and goals on the functional dimension of an episodic intervention that should be realized in order to turn a high parameter value structure into a low parameter value structure (knowledge of the type that was discussed in Chapter 6). Because this knowledge and experience are not always available in an organization that is being restructured, external consultants may be needed.

However, functional complexity is only one side of the coin. The other side is 'social complexity'. Episodic interventions in high parameter value structures require the transformation of deep-rooted interaction patterns and premises under the often toxic conditions of self-inhibiting structures. Facilitating and guiding this transformation require knowledge and skills that, once again, are not always available inside the organization that is being transformed.

Therefore, besides other reasons for bringing in external consultants, e.g. as harbingers of bad news, accomplices of the organization's management, or expensive pets of the board of directors, the functional and social complexity of episodic interventions in high parameter value structures may be a good reason to hire outside help.

Now, although a lot more can be said about the roles of consultants in episodic interventions – either from a *prescriptive* perspective, specifying what consultants *should* do, or from a *descriptive* perspective, describing how consultants *actually* behave – we just want to discuss three roles that are related to the functional and social complexity of episodic interventions in high parameter value structures. These are the facilitating, directive, and combinatory roles. As will become clear shortly, the main difference between these roles is the way consultants deal with the conceptual models and techniques that are needed to transform the parameter values of organizational structures from high to low (models and techniques that are primarily related to the functional dimension, as discussed in Chapters 3 and 6).

In a *facilitating* role, consultants consider episodic interventions as processes in which organization members, both individually and in groups, transform their own basic assumptions, interaction premises, and interaction patterns. These processes of self-transformation are seen as learning processes. In the course of these learning processes, organization members together:

- find out what kind of 'helping' questions they should answer for the purpose of the next step in their processes of self-transformation;
- search for conceptual models and techniques that can help them to answer these questions;
- apply these models and techniques to their own situation in order to find the answers to the questions they consider as helping.

Based on both their search and answers, organization members:

- check whether they asked the right questions or selected the right models and techniques;
- transform their own organizational outlook and/or behaviour.

It is the role of the consultant to facilitate these learning processes by providing and maintaining conditions that engage organization members in them, monitoring the social dynamics of learning, and, if required, intervening in these dynamics. Yet, to the extent that they are facilitators, consultants should abstain from bringing in their own questions, conceptual models, techniques, applications, and answers. Because consultants operating in the facilitator role support organization members in their processes of self-transformation, this role may be quite suited to dealing with the social complexity of episodic interventions. This is the strong point of the facilitator role. However, it may take quite some trial and error before organization members come up with the conceptual models and techniques that will actually help them to transform the parameter values of the organization's structure from high to low. This is the weak point of the facilitator role.

In a *directive* role, consultants bring in their own conceptual models and techniques as they see fit in order to answer the questions they consider as helping. Moreover, they themselves apply these models and techniques to parts or aspects of the organization. Finally, they use the answers they find in order to direct organization members (often, but not necessarily, the organization's management) to transform the organization's structure in a particular direction.

These organization members, then, support or perform the required transformation processes. In the literature, this directive role is sometimes called the 'expert' role. We do not use this term because it might suggest that directive consultants are 'experts' and facilitator consultants are not. Of course, this is wrong. Dependent on their knowledge, experience, and skills, both facilitator and directive consultants can be experts in what they do. They just differ in what their expertise is. Directive consultants (if they are experts in what they do) may be highly effective in dealing with problems related to the functional complexity of episodic interventions in high parameter value structures. This is their strong point. However, they leave the social dimension of these interventions almost untouched. This is their weak point.

In a *combinatory* role, consultants bring in the conceptual models and techniques they consider relevant, given the stage of the intervention (given proximate functional and social goals that should be realized). However, combinatory consultants facilitate both organization members working in the organization's primary processes and their managers to:

- understand the function and logic of these models and techniques relative to the selected proximate functional and social goals in the intervention;
- apply these models and techniques to their own (part of) the organization;
- actually use the results for the purpose of their own self-transformation.

Because this combinatory role literally combines expertise with respect to the functional and social complexity of episodic interventions, it may be argued that this role should be preferred over the other two. We, at least, think it should. However, we also think that, given the experimental character of episodic interventions, consultants should not dogmatically stick to one particular role. The three roles are there to be played:

> HP_s 12: Although episodic interventions in organizational structures probably require combinatory consultants, facilitating and expert consultants also have a role to play. Consultants should be able to assess the role they play and, if required, either change it or call in assistance from others.

Given their assessments of what is right or wrong, useful or useless in a given situation, consultants, as a part of the ongoing experiment they too are involved (not to say, immersed) in, should have the courage to either call for assistance from others or change the role they play in an episodic intervention.

Intervention structures and morality: virtuous intervention structures

The last design-related topic we want to discuss pertains to the relation between the design of intervention structures and morality. In Chapter 4, we argued that episodic interventions always have a moral dimension. Moreover, in Chapter 5, we argued that this moral dimension should be a part of the application of the 3-D model. So here we want to raise the question how the design of intervention structures can be related to morality.

In order to answer this question, we will refer to earlier publications of ours on the relation between organizational structures and virtue ethics in organizations (see Achterbergh and Vriens, 2010; Vriens et al., 2018a). In these publications, we argued that the structure of an organization should be designed in such a way that it enables persons affected by that organization (e.g. clients or organization members) to 'live a fulfilled life'. In virtue ethics, living a fulfilled life means developing oneself *as* a human being to the best of one's ability. Applied to our active lives with others, this means that we develop the capacities that characterize us as human beings – i.e. *reason*, and in a derivative sense, *desire* – in a virtuous way, disposing us to choose what is right for the right reasons in a given situation. In virtue ethics, this acquired disposition to choose what is right for the right reasons is called 'moral character'.

Moreover, in these publications, we argued that low parameter value structures support organization members in applying and developing their moral character. These structures not only improve the *performance* of organizations in terms of functional requirements, they also enable human beings to develop and apply their moral character, which is our virtue ethics-inspired interpretation of morality. For this reason, episodic interventions that attempt to transform the parameter values of the structure of an organization from high to low already contribute to morality as conceived by us.

In the present sub-section, we want to make a similar argument with respect to intervention structures. Intervention structures should not only help organization members to realize and adapt functional and social goals, they also should be designed to enable participants in the intervention to apply and develop their moral character – they should be 'virtuous intervention structures'.

Of course, we know that developing a moral character (1) involves the *whole* range of human activities (not only one's work, let alone an episodic intervention as part of this work) and (2) takes the *whole* span of a human life (not only one's working life, let alone an episode in this working life during which an intervention is performed). So it could be argued that, given the 'limited' character – both in range and span – of an episodic intervention, it is not really relevant to pay attention to creating the teleological, deliberative, and social context for the application and development of moral character by means of the design of the intervention structure: what moral development could take place in the short time available anyway?

Although we do agree with the point that, compared to whole range and span of a human life, an episodic intervention is a quite limited enterprise, we do not draw the conclusion that paying attention to the moral dimension of the intervention structure is not very relevant.

First, there is an instrumental reason. In the case of an episodic intervention that transforms a high parameter value structure into a low parameter value structure, an organization that *inhibits* the development and application of the work-related moral character of its members is transformed into an organization that *enables* the development and application of moral character. As may be imagined, the new structure that enables the application and development of work-related moral character makes new and different demands on the outlook and interactive behaviour of organization members. In the new structure, organization members need to learn to feel and be responsible for the moral implications of their work-related decisions. For organization members who used to work in a high parameter value structure that inhibited feelings of responsibility, this may require quite a steep learning curve. In order to help organization members to get used to the responsibilities they have *after* the intervention, a participative low parameter value intervention structure that *prefigures* these responsibilities may be a suitable instrument.

Second, there is a more principled reason to pay attention to the virtuous character of an intervention structure. Episodic interventions, particularly those in the structure of an organization, are interventions with a deep impact on the working lives of the parties involved.

For this reason, it is relevant to create conditions enabling affected parties to assess and deal with the moral aspects of this impact.

So, in spite of the 'limited' character of episodic interventions, we still think it is relevant to pay attention to their moral dimension and think about intervention structures that can contribute to developing and applying one's moral character. In order to structure this argument, we first want to say a few words about *moral character*, second we want to specify *conditions* that are needed to apply and develop one's moral character in the work one performs, third we want to argue that participative low parameter value *intervention structures* meet these conditions.

Moral character

To summarize the point made earlier, moral character is the acquired disposition to do what is right for the right reasons in a given situation. In order to apply one's moral character, one should:

1. be able to see a given situation as morally relevant;
2. be aware of the relevant values at stake in that situation;
3. weigh the values involved;
4. develop an intention to act in that situation which does justice to both the situation and the values involved;
5. act accordingly;
6. reflect on the action, its intention, and outcome (and, if required, go back to 1).

Developing a moral character is tightly coupled to applying it. According to virtue ethics, it is impossible to develop a moral character without practising it. Just as it is impossible to develop the skill of good carpentry without actually practising good carpentry, developing a moral character and reflectively applying it in concrete situations are reciprocally related.

Note that in organizations, applying and developing one's (work-related) moral character relates to both *what* organizations do, i.e. to the goals that constitute their meaning, and *how* organizations realize these goals.

To give an example, in a school, the advancement of the emotional and intellectual development of its pupils may be a goal that is at the core of the school's meaningful survival. This goal may be considered 'the right thing to do' (i.e. because it adds to the fulfilled life of its pupils) and it may be pursued 'because it is the right thing to do' (and not, for instance, just because there is money in it). In this school, applying and developing one's moral character in the work one does means assessing the value of the school's goals in terms of their contribution to the fulfilled life of the persons affected by the school, acting on the basis of this assessment, and reflecting on one's actions (including their intention and outcome).

In this school, particular methods may be used. Of course, these methods have an instrumental dimension. They should contribute to the goals they are supposed to realize. However, these methods also have a moral dimension. They too should be selected and applied because they are considered the right thing to do in terms of 'living a fulfilled life'. Here, applying and developing one's moral character in the work one does refers to assessing the value of the selected methods, acting based on this assessment, and reflecting on the value of one's actions.

Finally, the actual work in this school has a moral dimension. Take 'grading' and 'giving feedback'. Under particular circumstances and with respect to a particular pupil, a teacher may decide to spend more time on giving feedback because he or she thinks this is the right thing to do. Here, applying and developing one's moral character in the work one does means assessing what is the right thing to do with respect to this particular pupil in the given situation, acting on this assessment, and reflecting on the action.

Conditions

In order to be able to develop and reflectively apply one's moral character in one's work, we think the structural design of this work needs to meet three conditions: it should provide a teleological, a deliberative, and a social context for moral action.

The *teleological context* refers to a structural design that allows organization members, by means of the tasks they perform, to actually experience and reflect on the realization of the goals that constitute the organization's meaning (e.g. a structural design that allows a teacher to actually experience and reflect on the development of his or her pupils). This teleological context is relevant because, if organization members can experience and reflect on the realization of the goals that constitute the organization's meaning, it becomes easier for them to assess the moral dimension of these goals, the means that are used to realize these goals, and their own work as a contribution to these goals. They are enabled to become aware of the values that are at stake in work situations, to weigh these values, and to reflect on the moral dimension of their work-related actions. In this way, a teleological context is a condition for moral action. In the case of episodic interventions, the teleological context requires that organization members, by means of the intervention tasks they perform, get the opportunity to envision and reflect on both the goal of the intervention and functional and social goals in the intervention.

The *deliberative context* refers to a structural design that provides organization members with the freedom to deliberate and act on morally salient work-related issues. Moreover, a deliberative context enables them to reflect on and learn from their actions. A deliberative context requires that tasks are broad, providing organization members with operational variety. Moreover, it requires that sufficient regulatory variety is built into tasks, allowing organization members to actually take action if work-related moral issues require this (e.g. a teacher having sufficient task-related operational and regulatory variety to act as he or she sees fit in order to further the development of his or her pupils). In the case of episodic interventions, this means that intervention tasks provide organization members with sufficient possibilities to address morally salient issues relating to the intervention.

The *social context* is about a structural design that provides organization members with the opportunity to reflectively discuss the moral dimension of their work, i.e. of work-related issues and the goals that constitute the organization's meaning (e.g. a teacher who, as a part of the job, is enabled to discuss work-related problems with a moral dimension with his or her colleagues). A social context allows organization members to support each other in dealing with day-to-day work-related moral issues. Moreover, it allows them to develop and reflect on what may be called a shared 'work ethos'. Applied to episodic interventions, this means that intervention tasks are structured in a way that allows organization members to discuss with each other moral issues related to the intervention:

> HP_s 13: In order to increase the chances that organization members develop and apply moral character in organizations in general and episodic interventions in particular, three context criteria should be met: the teleological, deliberative, and social context criteria.

Please note that structural designs (of either the organization or the intervention organization) that meet these conditions, of course, cannot *guarantee* that organization members apply and develop their moral character in the work they do. At best, these structures provide organization members with the opportunity, and possibly stimulate them to do so. Equally, structural designs that do not meet these conditions do not necessarily bar organization members from applying and developing their moral characters in their work. However, they make this quite difficult, stifling their efforts to do so.

Virtuous intervention structures

Now, what type of intervention structures can meet the conditions specified previously? To begin answering this question, it can be argued that high-participative intervention structures should be preferred over low-participative ones.

Low-participative intervention structures do not provide organization members working in the organization's primary processes (or clients, or other stakeholders) with the opportunity to be involved in intervention tasks beyond the minimum that is required for any intervention to succeed. In these intervention structures, these organization members (and other stakeholders) only have basic and minimal intervention tasks that do not satisfy the context conditions required for applying and developing moral character in the work one does.

High-participative intervention structures do actively involve organization members (and other stakeholders) in intervention tasks that can satisfy the three context conditions. Of these high-participative intervention structures, ideal typically low parameter value structures should be preferred over ideal typically high parameter value structures. Table 8.5 summarizes and compares the two ideal types with respect to their capacity to meet the teleological, deliberative, and social context condition:

> HP_s 14: In order to fulfil the three context criteria, intervention structures should be (1) participative and (2) have low parameter values.

8.5.3 Linking the design of the intervention structure to the procedure

In Section 8.3.1, we developed our procedure for the goal-driven design of intervention infrastructures. The first three steps of this procedure were about establishing the proximate 'intervention effort' (see Figure 8.1) in terms of the gap between the intervention's current status and new proximate functional and social goals in the intervention. The fourth step consisted of asking 'what', 'how', and 'who' questions with regard to the interactions needed to bridge the gap between the current status of the intervention and its new proximate functional and social goals. Answering 'what' questions helps to specify operational intervention activities needed to close the gap. 'How' questions refer to issues like the required levels of participation or the required pace and type (e.g. convergent or divergent) of interaction. 'Who' questions refer to who should be involved in what operational intervention activities (given the required levels of participation). Based on step 4, the last step, then, was about designing the infrastructure of the intervention organization, i.e. about designing the intervention structure, technology, and human resources.

In Section 8.3.1, we deferred the question of the design of each of these aspects of the intervention infrastructure until their elaboration in this and the forthcoming sections.

TABLE 8.5 High and low parameter intervention structures and the three conditions

	High-participative intervention structures with . . .	
	high parameter values	low parameter values
Teleological context	Because of high functional concentration, specialization (operational and regulatory), and separation, participating organization members (or other parties) have little opportunity to get a clear understanding of and contribute to the development of the goal of the intervention. Moreover, they have little opportunity to be involved in selecting functional or social goals in the intervention.	Functional de-concentration, low specialization, and separation allow organization members to be involved in the formulation of the goal of the intervention and to experience and reflect on the realization and adaptation of functional and social goals in the intervention.
Deliberative context	Because of high specialization and separation, organization members (or other parties) have little operational and regulatory variety in the intervention. Their small intervention tasks do not provide them with the deliberative freedom to reflect on and act with respect to moral issues related to the intervention.	Intervention tasks are broad and comprise the regulatory activities needed to reflect and act with respect to intervention-related moral issues.
Social context	High functional concentration, specialization (operational and regulatory), and separation inhibit communication about morally salient issues related to the intervention.	Broad and coherent intervention tasks of intervention teams allow organization members (and other stakeholders) in these teams to discuss morally salient issues related to their part of the intervention.

So here, at the end of our discussion of the design of intervention structures, we can link the heuristic principles developed in this section to step 5 of the procedure for goal-driven design. In order to do this, we pick up the thread with step 4 (asking 'what', 'how', and 'who' questions). Then we shortly specify: (1) which steps should be taken in order to design the intervention structure and (2) how the heuristic principles figure in these steps.

Step 4: Reflect on what topics should be addressed in what way and by whom in order to close the gap between the current and the desired status of the intervention in terms of functional and social goals

It is relevant to notice that the reflection that is at the heart of step 4 should be guided by the heuristic principles about participation and addition (HP 1–3). Reflecting on what should be done in what way and by whom in order to advance the intervention can benefit from a heuristic principle that:

- emphasizes the value of *participation* (HP 1);
- in the case of 'addition', underlines the possible advantages of *affinities* between activities performed by organization members in the organization and activities performed in the intervention organization (HP 2);
- in the case of addition, points at the danger of *overburdening* organization members by giving them intervention tasks on top of their tasks in the organization (HP 3).

Step 5: Design the infrastructure of an intervention organization that can support the realization and adaptation of (proximate) functional and social goals

Step 5.1: Design an intervention structure

Step 5.1.1: Based on the answers to the 'what', 'how', and 'who' questions, specify operational intervention activities, and group operational intervention activities into tasks that can be performed by human resources involved or participating in the intervention

Step 5.1.1 is about the design of the *operational aspect* of the intervention structure – i.e. about the grouping of operational activities into intervention tasks. As indicated, to this purpose:

- an inventory should be made of the operational intervention activities that are needed to realize proximate functional and social goals;
- the operational intervention activities should be grouped into tasks that can be allocated to human capacities involved or participating in the intervention.

In this step, heuristic principles 1–3 again have a role to play (attention to participation, affinities, and overburdening). In addition, heuristic principles 4 and 5 should be taken into account. Principle 4 underlines that the grouping of operational intervention activities in intervention tasks should further specify and finalize the more general ideas about participation resulting from the 'what', 'how', and 'who' questions. Principle 5 emphasizes that the design should be made in the mode of either simple or programme planning because of the functional dynamics of intervention activities and the experimental nature of episodic interventions. Moreover, principles 6, 7, and 8 should be applied in order to keep the functional concentration of the intervention structure low. Given the desired levels of participation, operational intervention activities should be grouped in such a way that participants in the intervention, as much as possible, both can understand the reasons why and become the co-creators of the flows and teams they will be working in. Finally, principle 9 should be applied in order to keep the specialization of operational intervention tasks low. By applying this principle, coherent and broad intervention tasks are designed, keeping the network of related intervention tasks simple. This reduces the need for coordination between intervention tasks, and thereby the probability of structure-related disturbances.

Step 5.1.2: Given the design of the operational aspect of the intervention structure, allocate regulatory intervention activities to intervention tasks

By means of step 5.1.2, regulatory intervention activities are added to the intervention tasks that were designed in the previous step. The heuristic principles related to the level of separation between operational and regulatory intervention activities in intervention tasks (HP_s 10) and the specialization of regulatory intervention activities (HP_s 11) are relevant in this step. Together, low levels of separation and specialization ensure that (groups of) human resources involved in the intervention have the regulatory capacity to:

- deal with operational problems related to their intervention task (operational regulation);
- make adjustments to 'their' task-related part of the intervention infrastructure, for instance by selecting new intervention techniques that can help them perform their intervention task (design regulation);
- select new proximate functional and social goals in the intervention as the intervention proceeds (strategic regulation).

Please note that organization members working in high parameter value structures may have 'unlearned' to take responsibility for their own work and working conditions. This may imply that, at the start of an episodic intervention, they neither have the knowledge and skills nor the motivation to design 'their' part of the intervention infrastructure or select new proximate goals in the intervention. For this reason, it may be wise to relate the decrease of the levels of separation and specialization to the progress of the intervention. Ideal typically, this means that at the start of the intervention, organization members participating in the intervention have little regulatory autonomy (the level of separation is still high). However, as the intervention proceeds, organization members may acquire experience in performing operational intervention activities, grow more self-confident, and develop feelings of ownership: they may start to feel responsible for the regulation of what they see as 'their' part of the intervention. As a result, they may start to add the regulatory intervention activities they need to the operational intervention activities they already perform. In this way, organization members *themselves* decrease the level of separation and specialization as the intervention progresses, thereby increasing their regulatory autonomy in the intervention. As a bonus, this experience with increased regulatory autonomy prepares organization members for the autonomy they will have in the new low parameter value structure that results from the intervention.

Once operational and regulatory intervention activities have been assigned to intervention tasks, the final workload should be checked and, if required, adjusted.

8.6 Intervention technology

By intervention technology, we understand *tools and techniques that can be selected to support the performance of intervention activities by the human resources that are involved in the intervention.*

8.6.1 Intervention technology: explaining the definition

In order to perform intervention activities, intervention technology may be required. As defined, this technology consists of tools and techniques that can support the performance of intervention activities. Please note that this is quite a broad conception of technology. For instance, 'dialogue' as a discussion technique to unearth deeply held values of organization members is seen as technique that can support the creation of shared vision. Other examples of intervention technology are:

- a technique that can help simulate the processing of an order through a flow (e.g. System Dynamics);
- an intervention accounting system;
- a game that helps organization members to develop a feeling of their future work in the restructured organization;
- a shared conceptual framework, a 'language', that allows different stakeholders involved in an intervention to discuss the intervention's progress;
- an ICT-supported discussion forum allowing intervention teams to share learning experiences.

Given the number and variety of tools and techniques that can be used in episodic interventions, we will not try to classify them using their characteristic features as a basis. Instead, for purposes of classification, it is more useful to take the intervention goals and activities that can be supported by these tools and techniques as a point of departure (see Table 8.6). It then becomes possible to search for tools or techniques that can support one or more activities in for instance 'diagnosis' and 'motivation' or in the operational regulation of the intervention.

TABLE 8.6 Goals and activities that may be served by intervention technology

Intervention activities		
Operational intervention activities		Regulatory intervention activities
Related to functional goals	Related to social goals	
Activities related to:	Activities related to:	Activities related to:
Diagnosis	Motivation	Operational regulation
Design	Adoption	Design regulation
Implementation	Integration	Strategic regulation
Evaluation	Creating/maintaining change relationships	

8.6.2 Intervention technology: design-related issues

It is impossible in this section to provide a separate discussion of each technique or tool that can support episodic interventions in organizational structures (another book would be required). Instead, we want to present some heuristic principles that can support the design of the 'technology' aspect of the intervention's infrastructure. Of course, the basic technology-related heuristic principle (HP_t) is that:

> HP_t 1: intervention tools and techniques should be selected *because* they support the intervention activities needed to realize set functional, social, or regulatory goals in the intervention.

Although HP_t 1 is beyond trivial, we know from experience that, in organizations, techniques or tools are sometimes selected for quite other reasons than the one mentioned in HP_t 1 – for instance, because they are 'available', because they are enforced by top managers or outside consultants, or because some organization members invested a lot of time and energy in learning to apply a particular tool or technique (becoming prone to 'seeing everything as a nail because they learned to use a hammer').

Moreover, although HP_t 1 by itself may be obvious, it is not always easy to argue *why* a particular tool or technique, given its characteristic features, is particularly suited to support the performance of particular intervention activities and to support that argument with relevant evidence. For instance, it may be alleged that *Group Model Building* is a suitable tool for finding causes of work-related stress in organizations. However, it is not so easy to argue why this is so or whether there are other tools (such as *WEBA*; see, for instance, Christis, 1994) that are better matched to this task.

Table 8.6 provides an overview of activities and goals related to the 3-D model that may be served by intervention technology. Given this overview, three different classes of techniques and tools may be distinguished: 'dedicated', 'cross-functional', and 'enabling' techniques and tools. Dedicated technology only serves one particular type of intervention activity or goal (e.g. only 'diagnosis' on the functional dimension). Cross-functional technology has characteristics that allow it to support the performance and realization of different types of interaction activities and goals (e.g. 'diagnosis' on the functional dimension and 'motivation' on the social dimension). Because there may be affinities between realizing functional and social goals in an intervention (e.g. between diagnosis and motivation; for other affinities, see Chapter 7), it is advisable to develop and select cross-functional technology that can help realize such 'related' goals:

> HP_t 2: In order to exploit possible affinities between the realization of functional and social goals, it is advisable to develop or select cross-functional techniques that are geared to these 'related' goals.

Enabling technology provides general conditions that are needed to perform intervention activities. As such, it is not directly, but indirectly related to the performance of particular intervention activities (e.g. to 'motivation' or 'adoption'). An example of an enabling technology is a tool supporting communication in an episodic intervention irrespective of the question whether this communication is related to, for instance, 'diagnosis' or 'motivation'.

Although enabling technology does not directly contribute to the performance of particular intervention activities, it can still have a profound influence on the success of episodic interventions in organizational structures. For instance, by selecting and enforcing mainly ICT-based communication in an intervention, other forms of communication that may be needed in order to perform intervention activities may be neglected.

Often, enabling technology is already part of the infrastructure of the organization in which the intervention is performed (e.g. an organization may already have an ICT infrastructure that can be used for the purpose of the intervention). In this case, it can be 'borrowed' from the organization for the purpose of the intervention.

Because it is hard to foresee what enabling technology will be required for the purpose of the entire episodic intervention, it is advisable to first select technology that is directly related to the realization of functional or social goals. Based on this selection, an inventory can be made of 'missing' enabling technology which can then be added.

Therefore, instead of making a comprehensive and a priori overview of all required enabling techniques and tools, this technology can be added either step-by-step (when the need for it arises, given the selection of technology supporting the realization of functional or social goals) or by trial and error (when problems occur because particular conditions are missing):

HP_t 3: It is advisable to design enabling technology step-by-step or by trial and error given the progress of the intervention.

Selecting intervention technology is not only about gearing available techniques and tools to intervention activities and goals (HP_t 1–3). Intervention technology needs to be used as well. This means that users should be taken into account when selecting tools and techniques. As the level of (desired) participation increases, more and more users may be involved in the intervention. Some of these (intended) users may lack the knowledge, skills, or motivation needed to use a particular technique or tool. For instance, managers involved in an intervention may lack knowledge about organizational structures that is needed to successfully use a tool supporting the structure's redesign, or workers and professionals may be fed up with yet another 'brown paper' session, milking them for ideas that, as they experienced in the past, end up in the drawer of some consultant.

If a gap exists between requirements set by the selected technology and the available knowledge, skills, or motivation of its intended users, it is unadvisable to use the technology anyway or change the selection of parties that should be involved in the intervention. In the former case, functional or social goals that were set will probably not be realized. In the latter case, functional or social goals are changed (other parties than the intended ones are involved in intervention activities), not because this is beneficial to the intervention's progress, but because of requirements set by the selected technology.

Instead of pursuing one of these two 'failing' strategies, it is advisable to stick to selected functional and social goals (according to HP_t 1, these goals are 'in the lead' for the purpose of the selection of supporting technology), search for, adapt, or develop technology that both can support the realization of these goals and fits the competencies of its users, or train intended users in the intervention so that they learn to use the selected intervention technology:

HP$_t$ 4: In the case of a gap between the requirements set by selected intervention technology and the knowledge, skills, or motivation of its intended users, it is advisable to stick to selected functional or social goals and adapt the technology or facilitate or train its intended users.

8.6.3 Linking the design of the intervention technology to the procedure

In order to actually design the intervention technology, 'what', 'how', and 'who' questions (step 4 of the procedure for goal-driven design) and the design of the intervention structures should be taken into account (step 5 of the procedure for goal-driven design).

Step 4 is about asking 'what', 'how', and 'who' questions with respect to functional and social goals that have been set: 'what' topics of interaction are relevant, 'how' should interaction proceed, and 'who' should be involved in interaction in order realize set functional and social goals.

The 'what' question is relevant because it provides information about the function(s) that should be supported by the selected intervention technology (e.g. 'diagnosis', 'integration', etc.). The 'how' question is relevant because it provides information about the type of interaction that should be supported. For instance, in a particular phase of an episodic intervention, interaction may be required that discusses as clearly and sharply as possible the pros and cons of a proposed design. In this case, intervention technology can be selected that aims to support the production of 'divergence' (e.g. by means of a 'devil's advocate' or a 'debate') instead of 'convergence' (e.g. by means of dialogue). The 'who' question provides a first indication of the users of the intervention technology and of the possible gap between their knowledge, skills, and motivation and the requirements set by the available technology.

The information provided by the 'who' question is further specified by the results of step 5.1 of the procedure: the (simple or programme) design of the intervention structure. Given the (desired) level of participation and the intervention tasks of human resources involved in the intervention, the intervention technology can be geared to these tasks and the human resources performing them. As indicated, this means that first dedicated and cross-functional tools are selected (HP$_t$ 1–3) and then condition-providing tools are added (HP$_t$ 4)

8.7 Human resources and measures related to human resources

By human resources, we understand the persons – workers, professionals, managers, staff, consultants, clients, suppliers, etc. – including their knowledge, skills, and motivation, that are involved in intervention tasks, possibly using intervention technology.

8.7.1 Human resources: explaining the definition

Episodic interventions in high parameter value structures are organizational interventions – that is, interventions 'in' and 'by' organizations. As such, these interventions necessarily involve human resources. We already saw that this involvement can – but, in our view, should not – be basic and minimal, for instance only involving organization members in a passive role during the 'implementation' of a 'blue-print' design. It also can – and, in our view, should – reach higher levels of participation, making organization members, clients, etc.

330 Designing interventions

into the co-creators of the organizational structure they work in. In any case, it is important that the human resources that are involved in the intervention either have or acquire the knowledge, skills, and motivation needed to both perform 'their' intervention tasks and use the selected intervention technology. This, however, is easier said than done. As was argued in Section 8.4, high parameter value structures have a tendency to undermine the development of the knowledge, skills, and motivation needed to successfully participate in the episodic interventions that aim to reduce the parameter values of these structures.

In order to ensure that human resources in the intervention have the required knowledge, skills, and motivation, more is needed than a well-designed intervention structure and intervention technology. Although the intervention structure and technology can alleviate problems (see later text), additional measures seem to be required that enable human resources to contribute to the intervention. We will now discuss two human resources-related design issues that are relevant to this support.

8.7.2 Human resources: design-related issues

In this section, we want to discuss two relevant design issues related to the human resources that are involved in episodic interventions. The first issue pertains to the support of human resources (workers, professionals, clients, etc.) that are involved in (primarily) operational intervention activities, i.e. intervention activities that directly aim to realize proximate functional or social goals in the intervention. The second issue relates to the criteria that are used to select the facilitators of these human resources. However, before we start addressing these two issues, we should address why and how the two issues are relevant and how they are related. 'Selection' plays a central role in this argument.

Selection: 'goal-based' and 'job-based'

In human resources literature, selection, in its rudimentary form, is about finding the 'right' person, with the 'right' knowledge, skills, and motivation for a particular organizational job. Here, the knowledge, skills, and motivation needed to do the job provide the criteria for the selection of the 'right' person: selection and its criteria are 'job-based'.

In episodic interventions and their intervention organizations, this basic conception of selection also holds for the selection of, for instance, managers of the intervention or consultants that support it. In their case, the knowledge, skills, and motivation required to do their job in the intervention provide the rationale for the selection of the manager or consultant: in their case, selection and the related criteria are job-based.

However, in the case of episodic interventions, there is also a relevant exception to this basic conception of selection.

Human resources may also be selected to participate in intervention activities, not primarily because they have the knowledge, skills, or motivation to perform these intervention activities, but because their involvement is considered crucial for realizing proximate functional or social goals in the intervention. For instance, suppose that 'diagnosis' and 'motivation' are the proximate functional and social goals for some organizational unit. Moreover, suppose that in order to realize these goals, it is desirable to involve all the members of that unit in diagnostic intervention activities. In this example, the unit's members are not selected *because* they have the knowledge, skills, or motivation that is required to do the diagnostic job that is required of them (it may even be known in advance that some, most, or all of them lack the required knowledge, skills, or motivation). The reason for their selection is that it is considered relevant to involve them in order to realize the selected proximate functional and social goals: their selection is not job-based, but *goal-based*.

Apparently, selection in episodic interventions, can be driven by criteria that are either job-based or goal-based. As a rule, job-based criteria are applied to the selection of human resources that perform regulatory or support tasks in the intervention. Goal-based criteria, again, as a rule, are applied to the selection of human resources that participate in operational intervention activities geared to the realization of functional or social goals in the intervention:

> HP_h 1: Selection (and selection criteria) in episodic interventions can be job- or goal-based. Goal-based selection criteria, as a rule, should be applied to the selection of human resources participating in intervention activities that should contribute to the realization of functional or social goals. Job-based selection criteria, as a rule, should be applied to the selection of human resources involved in regulatory and supporting intervention activities.

It is important not to confuse the two bases for selection, since it would be quite counterproductive not to select organization members who should be involved in intervention activities in order to realize proximate functional or social goals because they do not (yet) have the required knowledge, skills, or motivation to perform these activities. The same holds for selecting only those organization members who are expected to have the 'right' knowledge, skills, and motivation. In both cases, human resources who are needed to realize proximate functional or social goals would be excluded from the intervention activities that realize these goals:

> HP_h 2: In order to prevent the exclusion of human resources who are needed for the realization of functional or social goals in the intervention, goal- and job-based selection should not be confused.

Given the distinction between goal- and job-based selection (HP_h 1) and the warning not to confuse them (HP_h 2), the relevance of the two issues mentioned at the beginning of this section can be easily understood.

The first issue concerns *goal-based* selection. In the case of goal-based selection, human resources are selected to perform intervention activities *because* their involvement in these activities is desirable in order to realize proximate functional or social goals in the intervention. Because, in this case, selection is not job-based, it is probable that gaps exist between the required and actually available knowledge, skills, or motivation of the selected human resources. For instance, organization members participating in diagnostic activities may lack knowledge about the relation between parameters of organizational structures and variables measuring organizational performance. Because such gaps can have a disruptive effect on the progress of episodic interventions, it is fundamental to be aware of them and, if possible, help bridge them:

> HP_h 3: In the case of goal-based selection, it is fundamental to be aware of and bridge gaps between required and actually available knowledge, skills, or motivation of human resources involved in operational (and possibly regulatory) intervention activities that aim to realize functional or social goals in the intervention.

So this is the first issue: how to support human resources (workers, professionals, clients, etc.) who are involved in operational intervention activities that aim for the realization of proximate functional or social goals?

The second issue is linked to *job-based* selection. In episodic interventions, 'facilitators' (whether they be co-workers, consultants, managers, or leaders) can play an important role in bridging the gap between the required and available knowledge, skills, and motivation of human resources involved in the intervention's operational intervention activities. These facilitators are selected *because* they are supposed to have the knowledge, skills, and motivation needed to perform the job they are selected to do. They are selected because they fulfil *job-based* criteria. Here, an important issue is what selection criteria should be applied, given the role that these facilitators have in episodic interventions in high parameter value structures.

First issue: bridging gaps

As argued, goal-based selection can imply that gaps exist between the required and available knowledge, skills, or motivation of human resources who participate in operational intervention activities. If these gaps are not somehow bridged, this can have a negative effect on the realization of proximate functional or social goals in the intervention. Learning and training can help bridge these gaps. However, before we start discussing how they can help, we would like to note that the intervention structure and technology can also contribute to bridging gaps between required and available knowledge, skills, or motivation.

To begin with, the intervention structure can be designed in such a way that human resources can help each other. In this case, structural conditions should enable both inter- and intra-group learning, discussing intervention tasks, and peer assessment and feedback.

Intervention technology can also be designed to bridge gaps between required and available knowledge, skills, and motivation. For instance, an intervention technique can be designed in such a way that, by using the technique, organization members, in a more or less natural way, are introduced to the concepts that underpin it and develop the skills to use it. Moreover, the design of the technique may be so attractive that organization members are motivated to use it:

> HP 4_h: The intervention structure and technology should be designed to help bridge gaps between required and available knowledge, skills, or motivation of human resources involved in the intervention.

Given this preliminary note, we will turn to intervention-related learning and training.

In the case of intervention-related learning, the initiative for learning preferably lies with participants in the intervention. These participants, then, can learn 'for' and 'on' the (intervention) job.

Learning for the job entails that organization members foresee that they do not have the knowledge or skills required to perform upcoming intervention activities. Given this understanding, they themselves attempt to bridge the gap, thus engaging in learning processes that are tightly related to the intervention activities they are supposed to perform. In this way, organization members learn for the job.

Learning on the job refers to more or less implicit processes by means of which organization members, by actually performing intervention activities, acquire the knowledge or skills needed to perform these intervention activities.

Both learning 'for' and 'on' the job can benefit from 'facilitation'. Facilitators can create conditions for learning, for instance by ensuring that sufficient time, means, and intra-organizational support are available, by encouraging ongoing learning processes, by providing examples or pointing at best practices, by protecting organization members if learning processes fail, or by providing sufficient freedom as long as learning does not undermine the realization of overall goals in the intervention:

> HP_h 5: Facilitated learning 'for' and 'on' the job initiated by organization members who were selected on goal-based criteria can help bridge gaps in their intervention-related knowledge and skills.

Facilitated learning can be accelerated and focused by means of training. By 'training', we understand a coherent set of activities that helps trainees to acquire particular task-related knowledge, skills, or attitudes (Salas and Cannon-Bowers, 2001). For instance, in the case of episodic interventions in high parameter value structures, organization members may be trained to understand the relation between high and low parameter value structures and organizational performance: knowledge related to the functional dimension. Another example is that organization members are trained to systematically discuss rivalling opinions: skills related to the social dimension. Training can be initiated by different kinds of parties involved in the intervention (including organization members involved in learning processes). Moreover, because training is focused on the acquisition of particular task-related knowledge or skills, it presupposes that:

- gaps between required and available knowledge and skills are carefully identified in order to specify learning goals;
- the training is carefully designed or selected to realize the specified learning goals;
- the progress of organization members involved in the training process is monitored and assessed;
- the training is evaluated, given its learning goals.

> HP_h 6: Training can be used to accelerate and focus intervention-related learning.

Until now, we concentrated on the acquisition of knowledge and skills. Nothing was said about *motivation*. And, of course, facilitated learning and training may motivate organization members to participate in intervention activities. However, in order to *start* learning or to successfully *engage* in training, organization members need to be motivated in the first place. So bridging the gap between the required and actual motivation of human resources that were selected using goal-based criteria is a separate issue deserving attention.

According to some authors, organization members should be motivated to participate in interventions by means of compensation systems – that is, by means of what we would call 'appraisal and (monetary) rewards'. Wruck (2000), for instance, argues that effective compensation systems: "(1) improve the motivation and productivity of employees, (2) promote productive turnover in personnel, (3) mobilize valuable specific knowledge by allowing effective decentralization, and (4) help overcome organizational inertia and opposition to change" (p. 270). For these reasons, compensation systems should be 'leading' in episodic interventions. By 'leading', Wruck means that the compensation system that will be used *after*

334 Designing interventions

the intervention is introduced, and applied *during* the intervention. In this way, organization members are motivated to:

- start acting during the intervention as is wanted after the intervention (thus realizing social goals in the intervention);
- 'self-select' and quit during the intervention if they cannot comply with the requirements set for their behaviour after the intervention (productive turnover);
- overcome organizational inertia and opposition to change.

In sum, motivation, in this view, heavily depends on appraisal and (monetary) rewards.

Although we agree with Wruck that compensation systems can have a strong influence on the behaviour of organization members, we do not agree that motivation in the case of episodic interventions in organizational structures should be enforced by means of compensation systems, let alone by means of 'leading' compensation systems.

To begin with, there is a practical objection (see also Ledford and Heneman, 2000, p. 322). An episodic intervention in the structure of an organization changes the tasks organization members perform in the organization. Appraising and rewarding these new tasks may require a new compensation system that can only be designed once it is known what these tasks are. This, however, may be quite late in the intervention, making it impossible to use the new compensation system as a 'leading' motivator during the intervention. Therefore, in the case of episodic interventions in organizational structures, 'leading' compensation systems seem to be impractical.

There is also a more fundamental objection to appraisal and rewards as prime and leading motivators in episodic interventions. If organization members choose to change their behaviour *only* because they are financially rewarded for doing so, their behavioural transformation is purely externally motivated. In this case, it is not improbable that, just because they are rewarded to do so, they will go along with changes that, in their hearts and minds, strike them as unwise. However, realizing social goals, such as 'motivation', 'adoption', and 'integration', requires that organization members transform their behaviour not because they are externally motivated, but because they themselves understand and experience that it is a good idea to do so. This means that the transformation itself and its effects on the working lives of the organization members affected by it should be the prime motivating factor. Instead of financial compensation, 'confidence' in the intervention, 'reduction of change-related uncertainty', and 'participation, understanding, and evidence' should be leading.

'Confidence' here means that, at the start of the intervention, top sponsors and trusted leaders should be seen to subscribe to the urgency and vision of the intervention. Moreover, during the intervention, participants should be able to fall back on facilitators they trust and identify with (see also Schein, 1987, on 'identification with a role models'). Finally, participants should be enabled to become owners of the intervention and start seeing the intervention as something positive (see the discussion of participation, understanding, and evidence that follows).

'Change-related uncertainty' can be reduced, for instance by making clear that the episodic intervention in the organization's structure aims to make the organization more effective and efficient by means of restructuring *work* – that is, by changing, *not* by cutting jobs.

'Participation, understanding, and evidence' means that organization members actually participate in and thereby influence the design of their own work. By means of participation organization members also have a first-hand understanding of decisions that are made in the intervention (in most cases, because they made them themselves). Moreover, they can experience the effects of these decisions on their own work and that of their colleagues, and if required, do something about it. Together, participation, understanding, and evidence can support a feeling of 'ownership' of the intervention which, in turn, can increase motivation:

> HP_h 7: Motivation should not be extrinsic and driven by 'leading' compensation systems. It should be intrinsic and driven by 'confidence', 'reduction of change-related uncertainty', 'participation, understanding, and evidence'.

Second issue: facilitators and criteria

The second issue is the job-based selection of facilitators supporting organization members (or other parties) who are selected to participate in the intervention by means of goal-based criteria. As should be clear by now, this job-based selection of facilitators is a 'natural' complement to the goal-based selection of these participating organization members (and other parties). Because of goal-based selection, gaps may exist between the required and available knowledge, skill, or motivation of participants in the intervention. In order to bridge these gaps, facilitators may be needed who support learning or train participants in the intervention. These facilitators should be selected using job-based selection criteria. Therefore, the question arises what these job-based criteria may be.

Before addressing this issue of job-related criteria for the selection of facilitators, three remarks are in order. First, by 'facilitator', we understand a *role* that can be fulfilled by co-workers, managers, staff-members, change leaders, or (internal or external) consultants. This role consists of enabling organization members, clients, or other parties participating in the intervention to perform the operational (and, in some cases, regulatory) intervention activities they are asked to do, thereby realizing functional or social goals in the intervention. Second, the criteria listed below are only minimal criteria that can be derived from the 3-D model, so additional criteria can be added to the list. Third, not all facilitators need to meet all the criteria in the list. Which of the criteria are applicable depends on the particular intervention job a facilitator is supposed to do. This means that the list can be used as a checklist: given a particular intervention job, job-based criteria can be selected from the list and applied to the selection of a facilitator.

In order to list the job-based criteria for facilitators, we once again take Aristotle as an inspiration. In particular, his distinction between 'making' and 'acting' and the related distinction between 'skill' (related to making) and 'moral virtues' and 'practical wisdom' (related to acting) are relevant here (for a more comprehensive treatment of making and acting, see Achterbergh and Vriens, 2010, Chapter 10).

Complicating things a bit, it can be said that 'making', according to Aristotle, is about selecting and applying means in order to realize some goal that is external to the perfection of the actor as a human being. Examples of making are 'building a boat', 'making a chair', or 'treating a patient'. In these examples, the boat, the chair, and someone's health are goals that are external to the perfection of the actor as a human being. Finding and using the means to realize these goals is what 'making' is about. Please note that making, according to Aristotle, always and necessarily involves uncertainty. Making is about individual 'things' (including the maker) that always have unknown properties and histories that can affect the making process in unexpected ways. Making always remains, to some extent, within the domain of the probable and experimental.

Someone is called a 'good' maker if that person is able to effectively and efficiently select and apply the means in order to realize a selected goal with high predictability. In order to become a 'good' maker, one has to develop what Aristotle calls 'skill' (*techne*). In Aristotle's terminology, 'skill' is the *virtue*, i.e. the desirable acquired disposition, related to making. 'Skill' makes a maker into a *habitually* 'good' maker – i.e. a maker who is disposed to make things well.

If we take a closer look at skills, two components can be distinguished: 'knowing that' and 'knowing why' (see also Chapter 4).

In order to explain what 'knowing that' means, imagine a gardener who has tended to an old rose garden for the best part of her life. Based on her *experience*, she knows *that* this particular rose – that was planted in this particular soil and this particular spot in the garden, getting this much sunshine and rain on this particular day – needs to get this much water in order to grow: not too much, not too little, but the exact optimum. And what is more, she does not even have to deliberate in order to touch upon the optimum, she just sees the rose and acts. How do we know that this gardener has this 'knowledge that'? We just need to look at her garden, at how it thrives after all these years.

Probably everyone will agree that the gardener from the example is skilled in gardening. And indeed, 'knowledge that' is part of any skill. However, according to Aristotle, 'knowledge that' is tied to *experience*, and experience is tied to *particulars*. Skill, however, also can and should involve more *general* knowledge of *causes*: it should involve 'knowledge why'. Based on knowledge of causes, the skilled person can reason and deliberate about the means that can be used to realize some end. Moreover, based on knowledge of causes, the skilled person can explain why these, and no other means, are selected in order to realize a particular goal. Thus, alongside 'knowledge that', 'knowledge why' contributes to the skill of the craftsperson.

For instance, someone may know from experience that making a production flow in some organization increases product quality. Because of this experience, this person is not yet a skilled designer of organization structures. Now, suppose that this person is involved in multiple interventions, repeatedly experiencing that making a flow leads to higher product quality. This repeated experience may add to this person's skill as a designer. Finally, suppose that, based on repeated experiences with flow production, this person starts to wonder why the relation between flow production and product quality exists. After some research and reading, she finds out what causes this relation. This, once more, adds to her skill as a designer, allowing her to deliberate about and explain why she acts as she does. In Aristotle's words in *Metaphysics*:

> But yet we think that *knowledge* and *understanding* belong to art rather than to experience and we suppose artists to be wiser than men of experience [. . .]; and this because the former know the cause, but the latter do not. For men of experience know that the thing is so, but do not know why, while the others know the 'why' and the cause. Hence we think that master-workers in each craft are more honourable and know in a truer sense and are wiser than manual workers, because they know the causes of things that are done.
>
> (Aristotle, 1984a, 981^{a}24–981^{b}1)

Please note that 'knowledge that' and 'knowledge why' should come together in a fully developed skill. 'Knowledge why' *without* 'knowledge that' remains 'mere' theory (who wants to be operated on by a doctor who has only 'knowledge why'?). 'Knowledge that' *without* 'knowledge why' remains 'mere' practice (who wants to consult a doctor who only has 'knowledge that'?).

If we take the 3-D model as a template (see Table 8.7 for an overview), it can be argued that facilitators may be required to combine 'knowledge that' and 'knowledge why' (Table 8.7, column 2) with respect to:

1. facilitation itself, since 'facilitation' can be seen as a skill that involves experience with and knowledge about learning processes in organizations – this means that facilitators should have knowledge about both conditions that can be created in order to support organizational learning and the actual support of organizational learning processes (Table 8.7, column 3);
2. operational or regulatory intervention activities they are asked to support (Table 8.7, columns 4–6), for instance:
   - design activities (e.g. by bringing in expert design-related 'knowledge why');
   - the creation of change relationships (e.g. by engaging different parties in a dialogue, using activity- and technology-related 'knowledge how');
   - the selection of new proximate functional and social goals by some intervention team (e.g. by bringing in 'knowledge that' in order to support the team's assessment of its progress);
3. the selection and application of intervention technology that is used to support operational or regulatory intervention activities (Table 8.7, row 5).

It should be underlined once more that, of course, not all facilitators need to be skilled in all of these subjects. Still, in the case of episodic interventions in high parameter value

TABLE 8.7 Job-based criteria for the selection of facilitators

Facilitation: job-related criteria			*Intervention activities*		
			Operational intervention activities		*Regulatory intervention activities*
			Functional dimension	Social dimension	
Skill	Knowledge that about . . .	Conditions for and processes of organizational learning related to the support of . . .	Diagnosis Design Implementation Evaluation	Motivation Adoption Integration Creating/ maintaining change relationships	Strategic regulation Design regulation Operational regulation
	Knowledge why about . . .		The selection and application of activity related technology		
Communication and cooperation between specialized facilitators					

structures, it is vital that sufficient knowledge 'that' and 'why' is present about both the functional and the social dimension of these interventions:

- Deficient knowledge about the functional dimension can lead to the successful social integration of a functionally bad design, i.e. a design that cannot realize the goal of the intervention.
- Deficient knowledge about the social dimension can lead to social integration problems with respect to a functionally well-designed structure, once again, undermining the realization of the goal of the intervention.

If the point that not all facilitators need to be skilled in all subjects is combined with the requirement that sufficiently skilled support should be present with respect to both the functional and social dimensions of the intervention, it is likely that different facilitators, specialized in different subjects, need to *cooperate* in the intervention. This cooperation requires a lot from the communication between these specialized facilitators. For instance, a group of facilitators specialized in 'change' (social dimension) may be required to cooperate with a group of hard-boiled 'design' facilitators (functional dimension). Each of these groups probably brings in its own concepts, theoretical models, experiences, and practices (they may even think differently about what is and is not funny). And what is more, each group may have its own prejudices about the other group, making constructive communication between members of the different groups very hard. Therefore, a final job-related criterion for the selection of facilitators is their ability to communicate and cooperate with 'other' facilitators (Table 8.7, bottom row):

> HP_h 8: Dependent on the content of their facilitating job, facilitators should have 'knowledge that' and/or 'knowledge how' about (1) learning processes in organizations, (2) supporting operational and regulatory intervention activities, (3) the selection and application of activity-related technology, and (4) communication and cooperation.

Reflecting on the job-related selection criteria listed in Table 8.7, it may be noted that they are all 'instrumental' criteria. They are all about how good a 'maker' some facilitator is. However, being a skilled 'maker' is not the only criterion that applies to facilitators in interventions. As argued, episodic interventions also have a moral aspect. This implies that other questions may arise than those about the means that should be selected in order to realize some goal. Questions about what is the right thing to do in a given situation will also present themselves. Facilitators should also be able to deal with these questions – not only because they should be trusted by the persons they facilitate (this would be a mere instrumental reason), but also because facilitators, principally, have a professional responsibility towards themselves, their clients, and the larger society they are a part of.

This is the point where Aristotle's ideas about 'action' come in. Again complicating things a bit, according to Aristotle, action is about the selection of ends that are internal to the perfection of the actor as a human being. Someone is called a 'good' actor if that person is able to select an end 'here and now' that 'makes' that person into a more perfect, more fulfilled, human being (that is why acting is about ends that are *internal* to the perfection of the actor as a human being). Please note that the relation between the selected end and the end of becoming a more fulfilled human being, according to Aristotle, is not a 'means–goal' relation (otherwise acting and making would become the same). In the case of action, the selected end 'here and now' is not a means towards a goal, but an *instantiation* of what it means to live a fulfilled human life here and now. In more simple terms, a 'good' action is about what we called earlier 'doing what is right for the right reasons' in the situation we find ourselves in.

In order to become a 'good' actor, one has to develop what Aristotle calls 'moral virtues' and 'practical wisdom' (*phronesis*). Both moral virtues and practical wisdom are *virtues*, they are desirable acquired dispositions related to acting. Moral virtues and practical wisdom make an actor into a habitually 'good' actor, i.e. an actor who is disposed to act 'well'. Moral virtues and practical wisdom come together in what we called earlier the moral character of the actor:

> HP_h 9: Because facilitators should merit the trust of the persons they facilitate and because facilitators have a professional responsibility towards themselves, their clients, and society, 'moral character' should be a basis for their selection.

In order to get a somewhat richer picture of what 'moral character' means, it will be useful to take a closer look at the moral virtues and practical wisdom that constitute it.

'Moral virtues', according to Aristotle, are related to our emotions and desires. Just like in the example of 'watering roses', a moral virtue is about doing neither too much nor too little. It is about doing exactly what is needed in a given situation. For instance, with respect to emotions of fear and confidence, the morally virtuous person would neither act cowardly (an emotional under-reaction; doing too little) nor act rashly (an emotional over-reaction; doing too much). The virtuous person would act courageously in the given situation, which is the virtuous optimum.

In our lives, we can *develop* our moral virtues. This development is possible, because, in Aristotle's view, our emotions and desires are not purely irrational. As we grow up, our emotions and desires can be cultivated by reason – at first, because we imitate the behaviour of older persons who have already developed moral virtues; later, because we learn to reflect on our emotions, desires, and actions, and thereby, change them. So, according to Aristotle, our emotions and desires are not purely 'irrational'. We call them 'rational' or 'cultivated' or 'morally virtuous' to the extent that they harmonize with what a practically wise person would do.

Because human beings live complex emotional lives with others in communities, Aristotle distinguishes a plurality of emotions. Examples of these emotions are fear and confidence, pleasure and pain, feelings related to getting and spending, honour and dishonour, anger, etc. Each of these emotions is related to possible under- and over-reactions and a possible virtuous optimum related to these under- and over-reactions. That is why there is a plurality of moral virtues. This plurality, however, is not a *mere* plurality. According to Aristotle, the different moral virtues are related in such a way that it is impossible to develop one of them without developing all others. So, although particular moral virtues may be particularly relevant for facilitators (e.g. *courage*, between rashness and cowardice; *truthfulness*, between boastfulness and understatement; *friendliness*, between obsequiousness and cantankerousness), it would be nonsensical to try to isolate these moral virtues and develop them apart from the others.

'Practical wisdom' is the virtue related to our capability for practical reason. It is the acquired disposition of thinking well about particular ends here and now as an instantiation of what it means to live a fulfilled life. As explained earlier, someone who is practically wise can see a situation as morally relevant, be aware of the values that are at stake, weigh these values, select an act that does justice to the situation, act accordingly, and reflect on the moral value of the action.

According to Aristotle in *Nicomacheian Ethics*, moral virtues and practical wisdom come together in the moral character and moral decisions of the actor. Given the moral character of the actor, acting well means doing the right things, choosing them, choosing them for the right reasons, and choosing them from a morally virtuous habitual disposition of character (Aristotle, 1984b, 1105^{a}30–1105^{b}1).

Given Aristotle's ideas on moral character, selecting a facilitator who has developed a moral character is easier said than done. In order to be able to judge someone's moral character, one should know that person quite intimately and over a long period of time. Just as the thriving garden may be sign of the gardener's skill, the life of the morally virtuous person, the way this life was conducted, the obstacles and opportunities that presented themselves, the choices that were made, and the reasons for these choices may be a sign of the moral character of this person. Applied to the selection of facilitators, this means that 'personal acquaintance', 'recommendation' by trusted parties, and 'reputation' seem to be quite important.

8.7.3 Linking human resources in the intervention to the procedure

The last step of the procedure for the goal-driven design of intervention infrastructures specifies that human resources and human resources support measures should be selected (step 5.3). In order to take this final step, it is useful to depart from the design of the intervention structure and the selected intervention technology: the intervention structure and its technology provide the background for the selection of human resources and the design of their support.

As a part of the design of the intervention structure, human resources have already been selected to participate in operational intervention activities in order to realize proximate functional or social goals in the intervention. In order to perform their operational intervention tasks, these human resources may be asked to use intervention technology. Because these human resources were selected using goal-based (and not job-based) criteria, a gap may exist between the available and required knowledge, skills, and motivation. In order to deal with these gaps, two further steps should be taken.

Step 5.3.1: Make an inventory of gaps between required and available knowledge, skill, and motivation of human resources that were selected using goal-based criteria and bridge these gaps by means of facilitated learning, training, and measures increasing intrinsic motivation

In order to enable learning, training, and motivation, facilitators may be needed in order to help human resources that participate in the intervention. These facilitators should be selected based on job-related criteria.

Step 5.3.2: Make an inventory of the required facilitation and select facilitators using: (1) instrumental job-based criteria in order to safeguard the fit between the required and available knowledge and skills of facilitators and (2) criteria related to the facilitator's moral character

8.8 Conclusion: two final checks

In the three previous sections, design issues related to the intervention's structure, technology, and human resources have been discussed. It was the goal of these sections to derive heuristic principles that can support the flexible design of these aspects of intervention infrastructures. Together, the heuristic principles should help human resources involved in an intervention to design an intervention infrastructure that can realize proximate functional and social goals in the intervention. However, before this design is put into practice, two final checks may be relevant: one concerning the *robustness*, the other concerning the *coherence* and *simplicity* of the design. This leads to the first final heuristic principle, HP_f:

> HP_f 1: Proposed designs for intervention infrastructures should be checked for robustness as well as for coherence and simplicity.

8.8.1 Checking for robustness

The robustness check is related to factors that, due to the high parameter value structures of the organizations in which these interventions take place, can affect the progress of that episodic intervention (see Section 8.4 and Table 8.8 for an overview of these factors). The actual presence of such factors may require adjustments to the proposed design of the intervention infrastructure. For instance, at some stage of an intervention, it may be considered highly likely that 'aspectual refraction of problems and solutions' will inhibit the progress of an intervention. In order to counter this probable problem, you should check whether the proposed design of the intervention infrastructure is sufficiently robust to deal with this problem. If this is not the case (or doubtful), it might be useful to pay extra attention to, for instance, the structure of the relevant intervention teams, technology supporting the intervention, or the facilitation of intervention teams. So the first check concerns the robustness of the intervention infrastructure in relation to factors that (without infrastructural counter measures) are likely to affect the intervention's progress. Table 8.8 can be used for this 'robustness' check.

In the first column of Table 8.8, factors are mentioned that may be 'active' in high parameter value structures and can affect the progress of an episodic intervention that attempt to reduce the value of these parameters (these are the factors described in Section 8.4). The second column is a reminder that each of these factors is related to power issues that may need to be taken into account when designing an intervention infrastructure. In the third and fourth columns, 'parties' who may be active in high parameter value structures are mentioned. Because in these structures 'separation between operational and regulatory activities in tasks', by definition, is high, these parties are separated into 'workers', 'professionals', and 'operational managers' on the one side (possibly supplemented by clients and other parties involved in the intervention) and 'strategic and design managers' on the other. The fifth column provides room for the assessment of the robustness of the design of the proposed intervention infrastructure in the face of factors that can affect the progress of the intervention. The sixth column lists adjustments to the proposed design of the intervention infrastructure that should be made in order to counter the effects of these factors.

In order to check for robustness, the following questions should be asked with respect to each of the factors present in Table 8.8:

1. Is this factor 'active' in the organization in which the intervention takes place (column 1)?
    For instance, in some organizations, 'social distance' may be considered an 'active' factor. This means that, due to high separation, workers and managers in that organization have difficulty understanding each other because, due to high separation, they almost inhabit different worlds.

342 Designing interventions

TABLE 8.8 Checking the intervention's infrastructure for robustness

Factors and parties 'active' in the current high parameter value structure	Workers, professionals, operational managers, clients, or other parties involved in the intervention	Strategic and design managers involved in the intervention	Assessment of the proposed design of the intervention infrastructure	Relevant adjustments to the proposed design of the intervention infrastructure
Knowledge related factors:				
– departmental focus				
– social distance	P			
– aspectual refraction	O			
– structure-blindness	W			
– deep metaphors	E			
Skills-related factors:	R			
– Problem solving	I			
– Cooperation	S			
– Skilled incompetence	S			
Motivation-related factors:	U			
– reluctance	E			
– departmental focus	S			
– personal loss				
– rootedness				

2. To what power issues is this factor related (column 2)?

   For instance, social distance is related to the self-definition of both workers and managers. Overcoming social distance therefore means that workers and/or managers start to change this self-definition, relinquishing some of the power that is associated with it.

3. What is the expected impact of this factor and its related power issues on the behaviour of parties involved in the intervention, and is there evidence that this expected behaviour actually occurs (columns 3 and 4)?

   For instance, because of social distance, managers may fail to see or understand problems as experienced by workers, and vice versa, making both parties dismissive of each other.

4. How can the expected behaviours mentioned under 3 affect the progress of the intervention in terms of realizing proximate functional or social goals, are expected effects positive or negative, and is there any evidence supporting the probability of the actual occurrence of these positive or negative effects (column 5)?

   For instance, suppose that 'diagnosis' and 'motivation' are the proximate functional and social goals. Social distance can then hinder constructive communication between workers and managers about problems faced by the organization. This may hinder both the diagnostic process and the motivation of workers and managers to even start an episodic intervention.

5. Are there features in the proposed design of the intervention infrastructure that help to deal with expected negative effects? What are these features, and how do they help? Should additional features be built into the design (column 5)?

For instance, in the proposed design, workers and managers are expected to work together in intervention teams. Given the presence of 'social distance', these mixed intervention teams are both a risk and an opportunity. Social distance can either increase or decrease by working together. Perhaps extra features should be built into the design of the intervention's technology and human resources in order to exploit the opportunities presented by working together.

6. How should the proposed design of the intervention's structure, technology, or human resources be adjusted in order to be able to better cope with expected negative effects of present factors that affect the intervention's progress (column 6)?

For instance, in order to decrease the risk involved in using mixed teams, intervention techniques should be added that allow for the search for shared values. Moreover, extra attention should be paid to facilitation: extra facilitators with experience and knowledge about 'creating change relationships' should be hired.

Reflecting on these questions and answers, it can be argued that they involve a lot of assumptions, suppositions, and conjectures (in spite of the questions asking for 'evidence'). Moreover, a lot of the answers to these questions seem to depend on the engagement, character, experience, and knowledge of the persons asking them. We think this is unavoidable. No one can oversee the complex processes that drive forward the self-production of concrete organizations, there is no all-knowing outside perspective. Episodic interventions remain experiments. Error and one-sided or failing judgement are an unavoidable part of them.

The only thing that can be done about this is to design the intervention infrastructure in such a way that it enables continuous processes of experimentation. Just as in the case of organization structures, this requires both coherence and simplicity: 'coherence' because all the aspects of the intervention infrastructure – intervention structure, technology, and human resources – should be designed to work together and be geared to the realization of proximate functional and social goals; 'simplicity' because the intervention's infrastructure should (1) as little as possible, be itself a source of problems (attenuation) and (2) enable, as much as is needed, the regulation of problems that actually occur (amplification). One final check seems to be required.

8.8.2 Checking for coherence and simplicity

Indeed, one final check *does* seem to be required. Or does it? It could be objected that the *order* of activities proposed in the previous sections already minimizes the probability of incoherent and complex intervention infrastructures.

If 'coherence' is defined as the degree to which all the aspects of the intervention infrastructure (its structure, technology, human resources) are designed to both work together and be geared to the realization of proximate functional and social goals, then it can be argued that a coherent intervention infrastructure is designed by:

1. beginning with the selection of proximate functional and social goals;
2. asking 'what', 'how', and 'who' questions in order to make an inventory of operational intervention activities, their required characteristics, and parties who should be involved in order to realize the selected proximate functional and social goals;

3. grouping operational and regulatory intervention activities in a low parameter value network of intervention tasks that is geared to the realization of proximate functional and social goals (intervention structure);
4. selecting intervention technology that can help human resources to perform the intervention tasks needed to realize proximate functional and social goals (intervention technology);
5. enabling human resources to perform their intervention tasks using the selected intervention technology (human resources).

This particular order systematically links intervention tasks to (proximate) goals in the intervention, intervention technology to intervention tasks, and human resources to both intervention tasks and intervention technology. Additions to the intervention infrastructure in order to increase the robustness of its design, then, can be easily checked for coherence.

If 'simplicity' is defined as both attenuation of the probability of the occurrence of problems caused by the intervention infrastructure and amplification of potentials created by the intervention infrastructure to deal with problems, both the order and principles that support the design of the intervention structures enable simplicity. Both this order and these principles lead to the low parameter value intervention structures that are needed for attenuation and amplification.

Seen in this way, a check for coherence and simplicity seems to be superfluous. Or does it? Perhaps, as a final check, it is useful to *change* the perspective from that of a 'designer' of the intervention infrastructure to that of a 'participant' (please note that, given the 'logic' of the 3-D model, and given the point that 'designer' and 'participant' are roles that may be performed by the same person(s), 'participants' in the intervention infrastructure will often also be its 'designers').

In more concrete terms, this means that 'designers' are asked to step into the shoes of 'participants'. They are asked to imagine what the world looks like from the perspective of the participants who need to work in the intervention organization. So if, according to the design, some intervention team should perform particular intervention activities to realize particular proximate functional and social goals, using particular intervention tools, supported by particular facilitators, it can be asked how coherent and simple the design appears in the eyes of the persons working in that team. Here, the following questions can be useful:

1. Are the proximate functional and social goals understandable and meaningful from the participant's perspective; are participants helped to see the 'bigger picture' the proximate functional and social goals are part of (coherence)?
2. Can participants in the intervention understand how their intervention activities contribute to realizing proximate functional and social goals (coherence)?
3. How dependent are participants on other parties involved in the intervention in order to realize their operational intervention activities (simplicity: attenuation)?
4. Can participants regulate with regard to problems related to their own operational intervention activities (simplicity: attenuation and amplification)?
5. Can participants understand how the selected intervention technology can help them to perform their intervention tasks (coherence; simplicity: attenuation)?

6. Are participants actually helped by this type of facilitator (coherence; simplicity: amplification)?
7. Are participants in the intervention overburdened by their combined intervention and organizational tasks (simplicity)?

Asking these questions can be a final check contributing to the coherence and simplicity of the design of the intervention infrastructure. Further problems and opportunities, that unavoidably will present themselves, should be addressed by the procedure for improvement-driven design regulation (see Section 8.3.2).

REFERENCES

Achterbergh, J., & Vriens, D. (2010). *Organizations: Social Systems Conducting Experiments* (2nd revised edn). New York: Springer.
Anand, N., & Daft, R.L. (2007). What is the right organization design? *Organizational Dynamics*, 36(4), pp. 329–344.
Argyris, C. (1986). Skilled incompetence. *Harvard Business Review*, 64(5), pp. 74–79.
Argyris, C., & Schön, D.A. (1978). *Organizational Learning*. Boston, MA: Addison Wesley.
Aristotle. (1984a). *Metaphysics*. In: J. Barnes (Ed.), *The Complete Works of Aristotle*. Bollingen Series LXXI-2. Princeton, NJ: Princeton University Press.
Aristotle. (1984b). *Nicomacheian Ethics*. In: J. Barnes (Ed.), *The Complete Works of Aristotle*. Bollingen Series LXXI-2. Princeton, NJ: Princeton University Press.
Armenakis, A.A., & Bedeian, A.G. (1999). Organizational change: A review of theory and research in the 1990s. *Journal of Management*, 25(3), pp. 293–315.
Ashby, W.R. (1958). *Introduction to Cybernetics*. London: Chapman & Hall.
Axelrod, D. (1992). Getting everyone involved: How one organization involved its employees, supervisors, and managers in redesigning the organization. *Journal of Applied Behavioral Science*, 28(4), pp. 499–509.
Banks, S. (2004). *Ethics, Accountability and the Social Professions*. Basingstoke, UK: Palgrave Macmillan.
Beer, M., & Nohria, N. (2000). Introduction. In: M. Beer & N. Nohria (Eds), *Breaking the Code of Change*. Boston, MA: Harvard Business School Press, pp. 1–33.
Beer, S. (1979). *The Heart of Enterprise*. Chichester, UK: Wiley.
Bourdieu, P. (1977). *Outline of a Theory of Practice*. Cambridge, UK: Cambridge University Press.
Bourdieu, P. (1990). *The Logic of Practice*. Cambridge, UK: Polity Press.
Breen, K. (2012). Production and productive reason. *New Political Economy*, 17(5), pp. 611–632.
Bunker, B.B., & Alban, B.T. (1992). Editors' introduction: The large group intervention – a new social innovation? *Journal of Applied Behavioral Science*, 28(4), pp. 473–479.
Bunker, B.B., & Alban, B.T. (2005). Introduction to the special issue on large group interventions. *Journal of Applied Behavioral Science*, 41(1), pp. 9–14.
Burnes, B. (2000). *Managing Change: A Strategic Approach to Organizational Dynamics*. Harlow, UK: Financial Times/Prentice Hall.
Burnes, B. (2004). Kurt Lewin and the planned approach to change: A re-appraisal. *Journal of Management Studies*, 41(6), pp. 977–1002.
Burns, T., & Stalker, G.M. (1961). *The Management of Innovation*. Oxford, UK: Oxford University Press.

References

Buurtzorg (2018). The Buurtzorg Model. www.buurtzorg.com/about-us/buurtzorgmodel. Retrieved March 9, 2019.

Coghlan, C., & Jacobs, D. (2005). Sounds from silence: On listening in organizational learning. *Human Relations*, 58(1), pp. 115–138.

Cohen, S.G., & Bailey, D.E. (1997). What makes teams work: Group effectiveness research from the shop floor to the executive suite. *Journal of Management*, 23(3), pp. 239–290.

Christensen, C.M., Grossman, J.H., & Hwang, J. (2010). *The Innovator's Prescription*. New York: McGraw-Hill.

Christis, J. (1994). *Taakbelasting en taakverdeling: een methode voor de aanpak van werkdruk in het onderwijs*. Amsterdam, The Netherlands: Nederlands Instituut voor Arbeidsomstandigheden.

Christis, J. (1998). *Arbeid, organisatie en stress*. Amsterdam, The Netherlands: Het Spinhuis.

Christis, J., Achterbergh, J., & van Laar, H. (2018). Multidimensionaal organiseren: is dat slim? *M&O*, 1, pp. 4–29.

Cummings, S., Bridgman, T., & Brown, K.G. (2016). Unfreezing change as three steps: Rethinking Kurt Lewin's legacy for change management. *Human Relations*, 69(1), pp. 33–60.

Daft, R. (2009). *Organization Theory and Design*. Mason, OH: South-Western Cengage Learning.

de Sitter, L.U. (1994). *Synergetisch produceren*. Assen, The Netherlands: Van Gorcum.

de Sitter, L.U., & den Hertog, J.F. (1997). From complex organizations with simple jobs to simple organizations with complex jobs. *Human Relations*, 50(5), pp. 497–534.

Donaldson, L. (2001). *The Contingency Theory of Organizations*. London: SAGE.

Døving, E. (1996). In the image of Man: Organizational action, competence, and learning. In: D. Grant & C. Oswick (Eds), *Metaphor and Organizations*. London: SAGE, pp. 185–199.

Elrod, P.D., & Tippett, D.D. (2002). The Death Valley of change. *Journal of Organizational Change Management*, 15(3), pp. 273–291.

Emery, F.E. (1976). *Futures We Are In*. Leiden, The Netherlands: Martinus Nijhoff.

Evetts, J. (2013). Professionalism: Value and ideology. *Current Sociology*, 61(5–6), pp. 778–796.

Fagerberg, J., Mowery, D.C., & Nelson, R.R. (Eds) (2005). *The Oxford Handbook of Innovation*. Oxford, UK: Oxford University Press.

Feldman, M. S., Orlikowski, W.J. (2011). Theorizing practice and practicing theory. *Organization Science*, 22, pp. 1240–1253.

Ferreira, A, & Otley, D. (2009). The design and use of performance management systems: An extended framework for analysis. *Management Accounting Research*, 20, pp. 263–282.

Foucault, M. (1977). *Discipline and Punish: The Birth of the Prison*. London: Allen Lane.

Freidson, E. (2001). *Professionalism, the Third Logic*. Chicago, IL: University of Chicago Press.

Fruytier, B. (1994). *Organisatieverandering en het probleem van de Baron von Münchhausen: een systeemtheoretische analyse van de overgang van het Tayloristische Produktie Concept naar het Nieuwe Produktie Concept*. Delft, The Netherlands: Eburon.

Galbraith, J.R. (1973). *Designing Complex Organizations*. Boston, MA: Addison-Wesley.

Galbraith, J.R. (1977). *Organization Design*. Reading, MA: Addison-Wesley.

Galbraith, J.R. (2000). The role of formal structure and process. In: M. Beer & N. Nohria (Eds), *Breaking the Code of Change*. Boston, MA: Harvard University Press, pp. 139–158.

Gherardi, S. (2000). Practice-based theorizing on learning and knowing in organizations. *Organization*, 7(2), pp. 211–223.

Giddens, A. (1979). *Central Problems in Social Theory*. Berkeley, CA: University of California Press.

Ghoshal, S., & Bartlett, C.A. (2000). Rebuilding behavioural context. In: M. Beer & N. Nohria (Eds), *Breaking the Code of Change*. Boston, MA: Harvard University Press, pp. 195–222.

Grant, D., & Oswick, C. (1996). Introduction: Getting the measure of metaphors. In: D. Grant & C. Oswick (Eds), *Metaphor and Organizations*. London: SAGE, pp. 1–20.

Hackman, J.R. (1987). The design of work teams. In: J. Lorsch (Ed.), *Handbook of Organizational Behavior*. Englewood Cliffs, NJ: Prentice Hall, pp. 315–342.

Hackman, J.R. (2002). *Leading Teams: Setting the Stage for Great Performances*. Boston, MA: Harvard Business School Press.

Hatch, M.J. (1997). *Organization Theory: Modern, Symbolic and Postmodern Perspectives.* Oxford, UK: Oxford University Press.

Hirschhorn, L. (2000). Changing the structure is not enough: The moral meaning of organizational design. In: M. Beer & N. Nohria (Eds), *Breaking the Code of Change.* Boston, MA: Harvard University Press, pp. 161–176.

Janis, I.L., & Mann, L. (1977). *Decision Making: A Psychological Analysis of Conflict, Choice, and Commitment.* New York: Free Press.

Jensen, M.C., & Meckling, W.H. (1976). Theory of the firm: Managerial behavior, agency costs and ownership structure. *Journal of Financial Economics,* 3(4), pp. 305–360.

Jos, P.H. (1988). Moral autonomy and the modern organization. *Polity,* 21(2), pp. 321–343.

Kant, I. (2010). *Grundlegung zur Metaphysik der Sitten.* Frankfurt am Main, Germany: Suhrkamp Verlag.

Kanter, R.M., & Stein, B.A. (1982). Building the parallel organization: Creating mechanisms for permanent quality of work life. In R.M. Kanter & B.A. Stein, *Productivity and the Management of Participation.* Cambridge, MA: Goodmeasure.

Kanter, R.M., Stein, B.A., & Jick, T.D. (1992). *The Challenge of Organizational Change.* New York: Free Press.

Kaplan, R.S., & Norton, D.P. (1996). *The Balanced Scorecard.* Cambridge, MA: Harvard Business Review Press.

Karasek, R., (1979). Job demands, job decision latitude and mental strain: Implications for job design. *Administrative Science Quarterly,* 24, pp. 285–307.

Kolb, D.A., & Frohman, A.L. (1970). An organization development approach to consulting. *Sloan Management Review,* 12(1), pp. 51–65.

Kotter, J.P. (1995). Leading change: Why transformation efforts fail. *Harvard Business Review,* 73(2), pp. 59–67.

Kramer, H., & Sprenger, J. (1971). *The Malleus Malleficarium of Heinrich Kramer and James Sprenger* (M. Summers, Ed.). New York: Dover Publications.

Kuipers, H., van Amelsvoort, P., & Kramer, E.H. (2010). *Het nieuwe organiseren.* Leuven, Belgium: Acco.

Lawrence, P.R., & Lorsch, J.W. (1967). *Organization and Environment: Managing Differentiation and Integration.* Boston, MA: Harvard Business School Press.

Ledford, G.E., Jr., & Heneman, R.L. (2000). Compensation: A troublesome lead system in organizational change. In M. Beer & N. Nohria (Eds), *Breaking the Code of Change.* Boston, MA: Harvard Business School Press, pp. 307–322.

Levy, A., & Merry, U. (1986). *Organizational Transformation: Approaches, Strategies, Theories.* New York: Greenwood Publishing.

Lippitt, R., Watson, J., & Westley, B. (1958). *The Dynamics of Planned Change.* New York: Harcourt, Brace and World.

Luhmann, N. (1984). *Soziale Systeme. Grundriss einer allgemeinen Theorie.* Frankfurt am Main, Germany: Suhrkamp Verlag.

Luhmann, N. (2000). *Organisation und Entscheidung.* Wiesbaden, Germany: Westdeutscher Verlag.

MacIntyre, A. (1999). Social structures and their threat to moral agency. *Philosophy,* 3, pp. 311–329.

Marshak, R. (1996). Metaphors, metaphoric fields and organizational change. In: D. Grant & C. Oswick (Eds), *Metaphor and Organizations.* London: SAGE, pp. 147–165.

Mathieu, J., Maynard, M., Rapp, T., & Gilson, L. (2008). Team effectiveness 1997–2007: A review of recent advancements and a glimpse into the future. *Journal of Management,* 34, pp. 410–476.

Merton, R.K. (1957). *Social Theory and Social Structure.* New York: Free Press.

Mintzberg, H. (1983). *Structures in Fives: Designing Effective Organizations.* Englewood Cliffs, NJ: Prentice Hall.

Mohrman, S.A., Cohen, S.G., & Mohrman, A.M., Jr. (1995). *Designing Team-based Organizations: New Forms for Knowledge Work.* San Francisco, CA: Jossey-Bass.

Monsen, K., & de Blok. J. (2013). Buurtzorg Nederland: A nurse-led model of care has revolutionized home care in the Netherlands. *American Journal of Nursing,* 113(8), pp. 55–59.

Moore, G. (2005). Humanizing business: A modern virtue ethics approach. *Business Ethics Quarterly*, 15(2), pp. 237–255.
Morgan, G. (1986). *Images of Organization*. London: SAGE.
Mumford, E. (2006). The story of socio-technical design: Reflections on its successes, failures and potential. *Information Systems Journal*, 16(4), pp. 317–342.
Nadler, D.A., & Tushman, M.L. (1997). *Competing by Design*. Oxford, UK: Oxford University Press.
Nandram, S. (2015a). 'Buurtzorg': A case of being-centredness as example of an organic worldview for corporate peace. In: S. Nandram (Ed.), *Business, Ethics and Practice*. Bingley, UK: Emerald Group Publishing, pp. 333–349.
Nandram, S. (2015b). *Organizational Innovation by Integrating Simplification: Learning from Buurtzorg Nederland*. Heidelberg, Germany: Springer.
Nicolini, D. (2012). *Practice Theory, Work, and Organization*. Oxford, UK: Oxford University Press.
Offereins, A.C., & Fruytier, B.G.M. (2013). *Handreiking sociale innovatie. Samen op reis met de cliënt als kompas*. Bunnik, The Netherlands: Libertas.
O'Neill, O. (2002). *A Question of Trust*. Cambridge, UK: Cambridge University Press.
Perlman, D., & Takacs, G.J. (1990). The 10 stages of change. *Nursing Management*, 21(4), pp. 33–38.
Pierce, J.L., & Delbecq, A.L. (1977). Organization structure, individual attitudes and innovation. *Academy of Management Review*, 2(1), pp. 27–37.
Porter, M.E. (1985). *Competitive Advantage: Creating and Sustaining Superior Performance*. New York: Free Press.
Pugh, D.S., Hickson, D.J., Hinings, C.R., & Turner, C. (1968). Dimensions of organization structure. *Administrative Science Quarterly*, 13(1), pp. 65–105.
Romanelli, E., & Tushman, M.L. (1994). Organizational transformation as punctuated equilibrium: An empirical test. *Academy of Management Journal*, 37(5), pp. 1141–1166.
Romein, J.W., & Roy, O. (2015). Individual and social deliberation: Introduction. *Economics and Philosophy*, 31, pp. 1–2.
Salas, E., & Cannon-Bowers, J.A. (2001). The science of training: A decade of progress. *Annual Review of Psychology*, 52, pp. 471–499.
Schatzki, T.R. (2002). *The Site of the Social*. University Park, PA: Penn State University Press.
Schein, E.H. (1987). *Process Consultation*. Reading, MA: Addison-Wesley.
Schein, E.H. (1992). *Organizational Culture and Leadership*. San Francisco, CA: Jossey-Bass.
Schein, E.H., & Bennis, W.G. (1965). *Personal and Organizational Change through Group Methods: The Laboratory Approach*. New York: Wiley.
Schön, D. (1993). Generative metaphor: A perspective on problem setting in social policy. In: A. Ortony (Ed.), *Metaphor and Thought* (2nd edn). Cambridge, UK: Cambridge University Press, pp. 135–161.
Schwartz, B.E., & Sharpe, K. (2010). *Practical Wisdom: The Right Way to Do Things Right*. New York: Riverhead Books.
Scott, W.R. (2008). *Institutions and Organisations* (3rd edn). Los Angeles, CA: SAGE.
Simon, H.A. (1962). The architecture of complexity. *Proceedings of the American Philosophical Society*, 106(6), pp. 467–482.
Smith, A. (1977). *Wealth of Nations*. Chicago, IL: Chicago University Press.
Standard, C., & Davis, D. (1999). *Running Today's Factory*. Cincinnati, OH: Hanser Gardner.
Suddaby, R., & Viale, T.P. (2011). Professionals and field-level change: Institutional work and the professional project. *Current Sociology*, 59(4), pp. 423–442.
Thompson, J.D. (1967). *Organizations in Action*. New York: McGraw-Hill.
Tichy, N.M., & Devanna, M.A. (1986). The transformational leader. *Training and Development Journal*, 40(7), pp. 27–32.
Tsoukas, H. (1997). The tyranny of light: The temptations and the paradoxes of the information society. *Futures*, 29(9), 827–843.
van Amelsvoort, P. (1998). *Het programmeren en regisseren van veranderingsprocessen*. Vlijmen, The Netherlands: ST-groep.

van Hooft, M. (Ed.) (1996). *Synergetisch produceren in de praktijk*. Assen, The Netherlands: Van Gorcum.

van Laar, H., Achterbergh, J., Christis, J., & Doorewaard, H. (2016). Shared services. Hoe effectief is een regieorganisatie? *M&O*, 4, pp. 76–102.

Vennix, J.A. (1996). *Group Model Building. Facilitating Team Learning Using System Dynamics*. Chichester, UK: John Wiley.

Verloop, W., & Hillen, M. (2014). *Social Enterprise Unraveled: Best Practices from the Netherlands*. Amsterdam, The Netherlands: Warden Press.

Vermeulen, P. (2011). *De verankerde organisatie. Een institutioneel perspectief op veranderen en vernieuwen*. Den Haag, The Netherlands: Boom Lemma Uitgevers.

Vriens, D., & Achterbergh, J. (2011). Cybernetically sound organizational structures I: De Sitter's design theory. *Kybernetes*, 40(3/4), pp. 405–424.

Vriens, D., Achterbergh, J., & Gulpers, L. (2018a). Virtuous structures. *Journal of Business Ethics*, 150(3), pp. 671–690.

Vriens, D., Vosselman, E., & Groß, C. (2018b). Public professional accountability: A conditional approach. *Journal of Business Ethics*, 153(4), pp. 1179–1196.

Weber, M. (1968). *Gesammelte Aufsätze zur Wissenschaftslehre*. Tübingen, Germany: Mohr.

Weick, K.E. (2000). Emergent change as a universal in organizations. In: M. Beer & N. Nohria (Eds), *Breaking the Code of Change*. Boston, MA: Harvard University Press, pp. 223–242.

Weick, K.E., & Quinn, R.E. (1999). Organizational change and development. *Annual Review of Psychology*, 50, pp. 361–386.

Womack, J.P., & Jones, D.T. (1996). *Lean Thinking*. New York: Simon & Schuster.

Womack, J.P., Jones, D.T., & Roos, D. (1990). *The Machine that Changed the World*. New York: Macmillan.

Worley, C.G., Mohrman, S.A., & Nevitt, J.A. (2011). Large group interventions: An empirical field study of their composition, process, and outcomes. *Journal of Applied Behavioral Science*, 47(4), pp. 404–431.

Wruck, K.H. (2000).Compensation, incentives, and organizational change: Ideas and evidence from theory and practice. In: M. Beer & N. Nohria (Eds), *Breaking the Code of Change*. Boston, MA: Harvard University Press, pp. 269–305.

Young, M. (2009). A meta-model of change. *Journal of Organizational Change Management*, 22(5), pp. 524–548.

INDEX

3-D model: description 7–9, 133–135,139–150; functional dimension of 7, 11–12, 120–122, 134, 142–143, 145, 151–208, 221, 226–227, 235–236, 258, 261–263; infrastructural dimension of 8–9, 134, 144–145, 256–345; lay-out 7; logic of use 146–149; relevance 6; social dimension of 7–8, 11–12, 120–122, 134, 143–144, 208, 209–255, 258, 261–263; use of 7, 10

adoption as sub-goal of the social dimension 8, 144,212–213, 221–227; affinity with functional dimension 226–227; invention 222–224; socio-psychological drivers 224–226; testing 222–224

basic assumptions 29, 30–33; 36–37; in HPV structures 81–83; in LPV structures 96–99; structural conditions for reflecting on and changing 83–84, 96; 99–100; types of 81–83, 96–99

cause analysis as part of the diagnosis (functional dimension) 106, 164–181, 221
change 12–14; 116–117
change relationships 144, 215–216
consultants 16, 250; facilitating, directive, combinatory 316–318
continuous interventions 123–126
control structure 51–52, 55, 183–184; design parameters of the 59–61
culture 2, 11, 36–37, 120; and self-inhibiting structures 5,6, 131–133

decomposition of tasks: into aspects 49–51; description 48–51; into parts 48–49
design as a sub-goal of the functional dimension 7, 107, 108, 143, 153, 181–201; design of the control structure at the macro level 196–197; design of the control structure at the meso level 195–196; design of the control structure at the micro level 193–195; design of the production structure at the macro level 184–187; design of the production structure at the meso level 187–191; design of the production structure at the micro level 192–193; parallelisation 183, 184–187; segmentation 183, 187–191; steps and heuristics overview 198
design parameters 48; description 54–61; differentiation of operational tasks 58–59; differentiation of regulatory activities into aspects 60; differentiation of regulatory activities into parts 59; functional concentration 55–58; separation 60–61; specialisation of operational tasks 59; specialisation of regulatory activities 60
design steps and heuristics: overview 198
diagnosis 7, 105–106, 108, 143, 152, 155–181; cause-analysis 106, 155, 164–181; gap-analysis (problem identification) 106, 155, 156–164; solution space 106, 155, 181
diagnostic variables 156–162; actual values 163; norm values 162–163; problematic difference between norm and actual values 163–164
differentiation of operational tasks 58–59
differentiation of regulatory activities into aspects 60
differentiation of regulatory activities into parts 59
dimensions of episodic interventions: functional dimension 7, 11–12, 120–122,134,142–143,145, 151–208, 221, 226–227, 235–236, 258, 261–263; infrastructural dimension 8–9, 134, 144–145, 256–345; social dimension 7–8, 11–12, 120–122, 134, 143–144, 208, 209–255, 258, 261–263

disturbances: probability of 65–66, 67, 68; means to deal with; *see also* regulatory potential

episodic interventions: cybernetic character of 147; deliberative character of 104–105, 115; description 5–6, 126–133, 140; experimental character of 115, 146–149, 239–240; factors affecting the progress of 281–293; goal of 115; intentional character of 104–105, 115; moral aspect of 115, 149–150, 318–322, 338–340; object of 115; power and politics of 115, 149–150, 249–259, 293–295; triggers of 130–131; *see also* dimensions of episodic interventions; functional dimension, infrastructural dimension; social dimension
evaluation 7, 107, 108, 143, 153; process evaluation 107, 204; product evaluation 107, 204; steps 204–208
exercising as sub-goal of integration (social dimension) 229–231
experimental character of organizing 24, 41–43; of intervening 115, 146–149

flow 55–58, 84–89; *see also* parallelisation
flux 12–14, 37, 45, 116–117, 239–240
functional concentration 55–58
functional dimension: description 7, 11–12, 120–122,134, 142–143, 145, 151–208; design 181–201; diagnosis 155–181; evaluation 204–208; implementation 201–204

gap-analysis as part of the diagnosis (functional dimension) 106, 155, 156–164
goal of the intervention 110–112, 115, 140–142
goal-driven design of the intervention organization: description 258–259, 262–263; procedure 264–279
goals: as interaction premise 2–3, 33–36; in the intervention 7–8, 120–122, 142–144; of the organization 1–3, 26

high parameter value structures (HPVS): effect of 71–84, 174–180; of interventions 305–316; of organizations 68–71, 153–155
human resources of the intervention infrastructure: description 329–330; design related issues 330–340; goal- and job-based selection of 330–332
human resources: of organizations 26–28; of the intervention infrastructure 8–10, 329–340

implementation 7, 105, 107, 108, 143, 153, 201–204, 226–227, 235–236
improvement-driven design of the intervention organization: description 258–259; procedure 279–281
infrastructural dimension of interventions, constituents: description 8–9, 134, 144–145;

goal-driven design 258–259, 262–263, 264–279; human resources 8–10, 129, 144–145, 329–340; improvement-driven design 258–259, 279–281; intervention structure 8–10, 129, 144–145, 295–326; intervention technology 8–10, 129, 144–145, 326–329; procedure for design of 147, 258–281; relation with functional and social dimension (what, how and who of interaction) 145–149, 258–262; robustness, coherence, simplicity 340–345
infrastructure: of interventions 8–10, 129, 134, 144–145, 256–345; of organizations 26–29, 33–36
integration as sub-goal of the social dimension 8, 144, 212–213, 227–236; affinity with functional dimension 235–236; exercising 229–231; reinforcing/adjusting 229–231; socio-psychological drivers 231–235
interaction premises: basic assumptions as 30–33; culture and 36–37; description 2–3, 24; formal and informal 33–34; function of 29–37; goals as 33, 34–36; infrastructure as 33, 34–36; relation with episodic interventions 210, 211–220; relation with interactions 2–3, 24, 37–40
interaction 2–3, 24–29; relation with interaction premises 2–3, 24, 37–40
intervention organization: infrastructural dimension of 8–9, 134, 144–145, 256–345
intervention structure: addition and overlap 129, 301–302; description 8, 295–296; design related topics 296–302; moral aspect of 318–322; participation and 297–302; types of 311–316
intervention technology 9, 10, 14, 326–329; description 326; design related issues 327–329
interventions in general: activities 104–105; agonistic/political character of 112, 115, 135; description 103–104; ethical character of 112, 115, 135; experimental character of 104–105, 115, 134–135; goal of 110–112; object of 112–114; practice, recursion, and iteration 108–110; social character of 104–105, 115
invention as sub-goal of adoption (social dimension) 222–226

knowledge related factors affecting the progress of episodic interventions: aspectual refraction 286–287; deep metaphors 288–289; departmental focus 285–286; social distance 286; structure blindness and economies of scale 287–288

low parameter value structures (LPVS): effect of 87–100; of interventions 305–316; of organizations 84–87

meaningful survival 1, 12, 17–18, 40–45, 47, 61, 67, 104
moral aspect of interventions 111–112, 115
motivation as sub-goal of the social dimension 8, 144, 212–213, 214–221; affinity with functional dimension 221; socio-psychological drivers 216–220; urgency 214–216; vision 214–216
motivation related factors affecting the progress of episodic interventions: departmental focus 292; personal loss 292–293; reluctance 292; rootedness 293

operational regulation 25–26; in interventions 147, 243, 259, 279, 296, 325–326
organization 1–3, 23–45; as experiment 3, 41–43; infrastructure of 26–29, 33–36; interactions in 2–3, 24–29; interaction premises of 2–3, 24; as social system 2, 24–40; societal contribution of 1, 12, 17–18, 40–45, 47, 61, 67, 104
organizational development 3–5, 5–7
organizational interventions 118–133; by organizations 119; for organizations 118–119; in organizations 119–120

parallelisation 53, 56–58, 84–89, 183, 184–187; of the intervention structure 306–309; *see also* flow
politics *see* power in episodic interventions
power in episodic interventions 115, 149–150, 249–259, 293–295
primary processes 2, 25
problem inventory *see* gap-analysis
production structure 51, 54, 183–184; design parameters of the 55–59

quality of organization 63–64; effect of HPVS on 77; effect of LPVS on 92–93
quality of work 63–64; effect of HPVS on 78–79, effect of LPVS on 93–95

regulation by design 25, 26–28
regulation: operational regulation 25–26; regulation by design 25, 26–28; strategic regulation 25–26
regulatory potential 66–67, 67, 68
reinforcing/adjusting as sub-goal of integration (social dimension) 229–231

Schein's model of change 213–214; critique of 236–239; learnings from critique of 239–255
segmentation 183, 187–191
self-coordinating task groups 84–86, 93, 192–195; *see also* teams

self-inhibiting character of structures 5, 6, 131–133
separation 60–61
skill related factors affecting the progress of episodic interventions 290–291; cooperation 290; problem solving 290; skilled incompetence 291
social dimension: adoption as sub-goal of 8, 144, 212–213, 221–227; description 7–8, 11–12, 120–122, 134, 143–144, 208, 209–255, 258, 261–263; integration as sub-goal of 8, 144, 212–213, 227–236; motivation as sub-goal of 8, 144, 212–213, 214–221
socio-psychological drivers: of adoption 224–226; cognition-related 216–218; context-centred 216–218; emotion related 216–218; individual-centred 216–218; of integration 231–235; of motivation 216–220
solution space as part of the diagnosis (functional dimension) 106, 155, 181
specialisation: of operational tasks 59; of regulatory tasks 60
strategic regulation 25–26
structural adequacy: form 68–100; requirements 61–68; structure should be able to deal with disturbances 65–67; structure should not be a source of disturbances 65–66
structural parameters *see* design parameters
structure 2, 46–101; contribution of 7, 47–48; description 48–61; formal and informal 33–36; as interaction premise 33–36, 38; of the intervention infrastructure, 295–326; of organizations 26–28, 46–101; parameters 54–61; (problematic) development of 3–5; self-inhibiting nature of 5,6, 131–133; *see also* structural adequacy

teams 84–86, 93, 192–195
technology: as interaction premise 33, 35; as part of the organization infrastructure 11, 26–29
testing as sub-goal of adoption (social dimension) 211–212, 222–224
type of intervention structure 303–305, 311–316; low/high parameter value intervention structure 311; macro-micro (programme design) 311, 315–316; micro-macro (programme design) 311, 313–315; programme design 304–305, 311, 313–316; project design 304, 305, 311; simple design 304–305, 311, 312–313

urgency (sense of) as sub-goal of motivation (social dimension) 214–216, 221, 222

vision as sub-goal of motivation (social dimension) 214–216, 221, 222

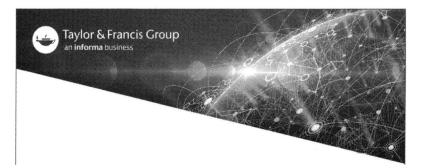

Printed by Amazon Italia Logistica S.r.l.
Torrazza Piemonte (TO), Italy